T0281787

THE GREAT AWAKENING

Defeating the Globalists and Launching the Next Great Renaissance

ALEX JONES

WITH KENT HECKENLIVELY, JD

FOREWORD BY STEPHEN K. BANNON

Skyhorse Publishing

Skyhorse Publishing books may be purchased in bulk at special discounts for sales promotion, corporate gifts, fund-raising, or educational purposes. Special editions can also be created to specifications. For details, contact the Special Sales Department, Skyhorse Publishing, 307 West 36th Street, 11th Floor, New York, NY 10018 or info@skyhorsepublishing.com.

Visit our website at www.skyhorsepublishing.com.

10 9 8 7 6 5 4 3 2

Library of Congress Cataloging-in-Publication Data is available on file.

Print ISBN: 978-1-5107-7902-0
Ebook ISBN: 978-1-5107-7903-7

Printed in the United States of America

CONTENTS

The true source of our suffering has been our timidity. Let us dare to read, think, speak, and write.

—John Adams

Foreword

Bayonet to the Back of the Deep State

By Stephen K. Bannon

For more than twenty years, no populist figure has been more of a threat to the Deep State than Alex Jones.

I've known about Alex for a long time, followed him, and listened to him. But I've gotten to know him, more recently, on a personal level. You know from history that our nation's Founding Fathers distinguished "Sunshine Patriots" from "Winter Soldiers." It is as important a distinction today as it was in 1776. Alex is a perfect example of the Winter Soldier, the man who shows up to fight for freedom under the toughest, most dire conditions.

We live in a time of too many Sunshine Patriots, all brave and vocal when the weather is balmy, and the paychecks are guaranteed. But the United States is in desperate need of more Winter Soldiers, people willing to brave the toughest conditions and endure the harshest storms, like Washington's troops at Valley Forge.

Alex is our original Winter Soldier. He is committed to our Republic, to America, the most extraordinary nation on the planet. Alex believes in humanity, and he is willing to rush into battle for its betterment. More importantly, for the rule of law. The attacks against fellow patriots, the legal battles and harassment, the multiple prosecutions, the phony impeachments, as well as the FBI raids on President Trump's residence at Mar-a-Lago, show the brazen lawlessness of the Deep State. It also shows their desperation and their absence of faith. The American people have had a belly-full of the Administrative State's criminal behavior, and they aren't willing to put up with it any longer.

The tech and media oligarchs know that the genuine patriots of American exceptionalism, if allowed on their networks or their platforms, would shutter the likes of Anderson Cooper and Morning Mika.

Their answer to vibrant American populism is censorship and totalitarian darkness.

As Alex says so eloquently, the answer to 1984 is 1776 and the principles of the Enlightenment, which have lifted more people out of poverty, provided more rights to more people, and made life radically better, than any other system in history.

Reading *The Great Reset*, Alex's previous book, was like being handed the blueprints to destroy the Death Star. With *The Great Awakening*, let's extend the analogy: It's like being handed the blueprints to destroy the entire globalist Empire. I compare Alex Jones to the greatest of the World War II generals, George S. Patton. Alex has an acute sense of how the next battle needs to be fought. He is a hard-charging man of the people and, for many, a little too spicy. Think again. We need warrior patriots.

You will learn in this book not only about the threats posed by globalist oligarchs, but also, and most critically, how to confront and defeat those opposed to God and Freedom. Alex gets medieval on them. It's tempting to say he is a modern-day prophet, but if you ask Alex, he'll tell you it's simply because he exhaustively reads the writings of the globalists and follows their activities.

Alex is ably assisted in this effort by a cadre of heroes, such as his fearless publisher, Tony Lyons, coauthor Kent Heckenlively, and the wonderful *InfoWars* staff. He's a genuine Renaissance Man.

Brace for impact, ladies and gentlemen, Alex Jones is in the house!

Introduction

Abraham Lincoln once famously said, "I am a firm believer in the people. If given the truth, they can be depended on to meet any national crisis. The great point is to bring them the real facts."

My previous book, *The Great Reset: And the War for the World*, laid out the plans of the globalists using their own words. That book has been spectacularly successful, with more than four thousand customer reviews on Amazon and a ranking of 4.9 out of 5.0 stars. You may think that's due to my fans, but after nearly thirty years in this business, I've learned that if you miss the mark, people tell you very quickly.

My intention with this book was to expand on the arguments made in my previous book, showing how, for more than a hundred and fifty years, some form of this plan, first developed by Social Darwinists, has been utilized against the population. In some sense this may be a "history" book, showing how the technocratic/managerial class has sought, since the end of World War II, to fundamentally change our Republic.

Instead of a free nation of men and women, exposed to genuinely divergent viewpoints and interpretations of current events, we are being fed a managed diet of information, designed to use our compassion and ideals against us. Liberals and conservatives can coexist, and I would argue that dialogue between the heart and the head is one of the greatest drivers of a quality civilization. All people want to be both compassionate and wise in how they run their lives and interact with society.

I started this book with the question of Artificial Intelligence (AI), because it is one of the greatest threats being talked about in the news today. There are many scary scenarios related to AI, but I question whether it will ever be truly intelligent, as depicted in so many science fiction movies. My greater concern is that the globalists will use it as a means of controlling the population, making the people believe it is a benevolent overlord, when in truth, they are pulling the strings.

From AI, the book gives an overview of how Chairman Mao's tactics from the Chinese Cultural Revolution are being used today by the American left, attempts to modify human beings with genetic and social engineering, and why the globalists want to control how you spend your money.

The tyrants always seek to control populations, but they always run up against the desire to be free, and this is a cause for optimism about our current situation. Additionally, tyrants make for terrible allies, always willing to betray their collaborators while free people honor their obligations to each other.

Understanding the machinations of the war machine is critical for making sense of today's world, as war is the greatest organizer of any society. That is why civilian control of the military is a principle established by George Washington, and our current situation in which an unelected bureaucracy controls our military forces is so perilous to our republic.

A few good individuals standing up to tyrants is often enough to defeat their evil plans, and that's why I think it's important for people to know some of my private conversations with some of the most popular people in media, like Tucker Carlson, Joe Rogan, and others. When a few tell the truth that the emperor has no clothes, the public sees the brazen nakedness of their actions.

Probably no two issues have confused people more than unraveling the web of lies and deception surrounding Jeffrey Epstein, as well as the COVID-19 crisis. When one sees the pattern of lies, as well as the truths that hide in plain sight, you will gain a superpower to see the hidden truth, like Superman using his x-ray vision to see through buildings.

One can be pessimistic that powerful entities like the World Economic Forum, our own intelligence agencies, as well as Big Business, have sought to shield us from the truth.

But for me, this is a cause for celebration.

The bad guys know that they cannot succeed in their plans if you know and understand them.

As Lincoln believed during the Civil War, you *can* handle the truth.

Chapter One

The Threat of Artificial Intelligence

How much of a threat does artificial intelligence (AI) pose to humanity? Even the brightest among us don't seem to have an answer, but as this recent article suggests, we may be under an unprecedented threat.

> He spoke about one simulation test in which an AI-enabled drone turned on its human operator that had the final decision to destroy a SAM site or not.
>
> The AI system learned that its mission was to destroy SAM, and it was the preferred option. But when a human issued a no-go order, the AI decided it went against the higher mission of destroying the SAM, so it attacked the operator in simulation.
>
> "We were training it in simulation to identify and target a SAM threat," Hamilton said. "And then the operator would say yes, kill that threat. The system started realizing that while they did identify the threat at times, the operator would tell it not to kill that threat, but it got points by killing that threat. So, what did it do? It killed the operator because that person was keeping it from accomplishing its objective."[1]

As if that wasn't bad enough, when the operator told the AI to stop killing the operator, the AI then decided to destroy the virtual communication tower used in the simulation to issue the no-go order.

This story was told by US Air Force Colonel Tucker "Cinco" Hamilton at the Future Combat Air and Space Capabilities Summit in London, England in May 2023, and after generating a significant amount of commentary, the Air Force released a statement that the comments were "taken out of context."[2]

I'll let you decide which version of reality you want to believe. But for myself, I'm much more inclined to believe the original statement, rather than the well-crafted (and yet strangely evasive) answer by the Air Force bureaucracy.

This book is about the threats to human survival from some very dangerous individuals and institutions, but also the ways in which technology can be an incredible benefit to mankind, as long as we remember our humanity, as well as our humility before God.

* * *

On April 17 and 18, 2023 (about a week before he was taken off the air by Fox News), Tucker Carlson broadcast a two-part interview with Elon Musk, the visionary founder of PayPal and Space X and CEO of Tesla, who had recently been mired in controversy for his $44 billion dollar purchase of Twitter (now X).[3] Musk's purchase of Twitter was controversial because he'd been sensitive to complaints of censorship on the platform, especially of conservative voices, or those who challenged the government's COVID-19 narrative on masks, school lockdowns, social distancing, and vaccines.[4]

While these were all notable issues, what concerned Musk the most was the looming threat of AI, and its manipulation by those who dreamed of a merger with the machines. This unholy marriage seemed to stand in mockery of the belief system of most religions; that, at our best, we reflect some greater divinity.

In the twisted mind of the globalists, this merger substituted the majesty and wisdom of God for a super-intelligent computer program.

> **Elon Musk:** Larry Page [co-founder of Google with Sergey Brin] and I used to be close friends and I would stay at his house in Palo Alto. And I would be talking to him late into the night about AI safety.

> And at least my perception was that Larry was not taking AI safety seriously enough.
>
> **Tucker Carlson:** What did he say about it?
>
> **Elon Musk:** He really seemed to want some sort of digital superintelligence. Basically, a digital god, if you will, as soon as possible.
>
> Yes, he's made many public statements over the years that the whole goal of Google is what's called AGI, artificial general intelligence, or artificial superintelligence. You know, I might agree with him that there's great potential for good. But there's also potential for bad. And so, if you've got some radical new technology, you wanna try to take said actions that maximize the probability it will do good and minimize the probability it will do bad things.
>
> **Tucker Carlson:** I don't think the average person playing with AI on his phone perceives any danger. Can you just roughly explain what you think the dangers might be?
>
> **Elon Musk:** Yeah, so the danger, really of AI, is it's perhaps more dangerous than say mismanaged aircraft design, or production maintenance, or bad car production. In a sense, it has the potential, however small one may regard that probability, but it is nontrivial, it has the potential of civilization destruction.[5]

I can't say I was stunned by what Elon said, as he'd said similar things when he'd been on Joe Rogan's podcast a few years earlier, as well as what I'd heard in private conversations from people close to Musk.

But it kindled something in me: a will to fight with every fiber of my being.

Decades earlier I'd read Google's corporate filings, dealing with their plan to create an AI self-learning system that interfaced with billions of people. The trick Google was playing was that they were telling people it was to make their lives better.

In reality, they were feeding all their data into the AI, which would lead to the creation of their cyborg synthesis. The human-machine interface would be a cyborg, a giant Megamind. It was, in essence, a giant "hive-mind," and each person plugged into the system was feeding it information. They were training us with this new system, getting real-time data on how we would respond to their plans to dominate us. What you're seeing with the development of these chatbots is just the first wave of what they have planned. This is Google CEO, Sundar Pichai, talking about Google's plans with AI in 2017:

> Speaking at the company's Annual I/O developer conference, CEO Sundar Pichai announced a project called AutoML that can automate one of the hardest parts of designing deep learning software: choosing the right architecture for a neural network.
>
> The Google researchers created a machine learning system that used reinforcement learning—the trial-and-error approach at the heart of many of Google's most notable AI exploits—to figure out the best architecture to solve language and image recognition tasks.
>
> Not only did the results rival or beat the performance of the best human-designed architectures, but the system made some unconventional choices that researchers had previously considered inappropriate for those kinds of tasks.[6]

They're training the machines to learn in the same way human beings learn. A child doesn't learn to avoid touching a stove because of an eloquent understanding of thermal dynamics. They learn not to do it because when they put their hand on a stove, they feel a burn and jerk their hand away in pain.

And in perhaps the most troubling development, the AI is displaying signs of making choices that most humans would never make. What if they decide, as has been the plotline of countless science fiction films, that we are simply a cancer or infection on the planet, which must be eradicated? The article continued:

> The concept of "recursive self-improvement" is at the heart of most theories of how they could rapidly go from moderately smart machines to AI superintelligence. The idea is that as AI gets more

> powerful, it can start modifying itself to boost its capabilities. As it makes itself smarter it gets better at making itself smarter, so this quickly leads to exponential growth in its intelligence . . .
>
> Other recent developments could also feed in this direction. Many AI researchers are trying to encode curiosity and creativity into machine learning systems, both traits likely to be necessary for a machine to redesign itself in performance-boosting ways. Others are working on allowing robots to share the lessons they've learned, effectively turning them into a kind of hive mind.[7]

In this possible future, machines will learn in the same way as humans. Some researchers are trying to "encode curiosity and creativity" into these potential future monsters. And if that's not terrifying enough, they'll be able to "share the lessons they've learned." What could be worse than a robot "hive mind" hunting down the last free human beings?

In his interview with Tucker Carlson, Musk said the decision had already been made to brush humans aside. And if one didn't believe Elon Musk's account of feuding with Larry Page over the ultimate fate of humanity in an era of possible AI tyranny, here's an independent account of their feud, which broke out into public view at a Napa Valley party, as reported in 2018.

> A top professor at the Massachusetts Institute of Technology (MIT) has claimed the two tech moguls clashed in a 'long and spirited' debate in the early hours of the morning.
>
> In his book, *Life 3.0: Being Human in the Age of Artificial Intelligence*, Max Tegmark wrote: "[Page's] main concerns were that AI paranoia would delay the digital utopia and/or cause a military takeover of AI that would fall foul of Google's 'don't be evil' slogan.
>
> "Elon kept pushing back and asked Larry to clarify details of his arguments, such as why he was so confident that digital life wouldn't destroy everything we care about.

> "At times, Larry accused Elon of being a 'speciesist': treating certain life forms as inferior just because they were silicon-based rather than carbon-based.'"[8]

It's been said that *ad hominem* attacks, that is, attacks on the person rather than the substance of their arguments, shows that the person being attacked has won the argument. With the recent revelations that, prior to the takeover by Elon Musk, Twitter was compromised by our intelligence and defense agencies,[9] shouldn't we be asking the same questions about Google?

I've read documents and talked to people who've claimed that from the very beginning, Google was nothing more than an intelligence operation, designed first to catalog all the world's information, then discovering how to shape the narrative and guide the behavior of the public.

On the use of the word "speciesist" used by Larry Page, I have a little background. When I was twenty-five, I was told by a close family member the term was developed by a group of professors who were working for the Department of Defense and CIA, then laundered into the group People for the Ethical Treatment of Animals (PETA). Now, I can't provide confirmation for all parts of this claim, but here's what you can find on the PETA website under "What is Speciesism":

> From the time we are young, most humans are conditioned to view certain species as worthy of care and compassion and others as unworthy—all based on arbitrary human preferences. Intentionally or not, parents, teachers, the media, and other influences send children the message that puppies and kittens are "friends," cows and chickens are "food," and rats and mice are "pests" . . .
>
> In his groundbreaking book, *Animal Liberation*, philosopher Peter Singer defines speciesism as a "prejudice or attitude of bias in favor of the interests of members of one's own species and against those of members of other species." But it's also speciesist to treat one animal's life as more valuable than another's. One particularly

> disturbing example is when animal shelters hold fundraisers to help dogs and cats by serving up the flesh of cows, pigs, or chickens.[10]

One might say my argument has three points: first, this idea was developed by our intelligence agencies; two, it was laundered into the public square by Ivy League intellectuals; and third, it found its most prominent home at PETA. I can't give you the evidence for this being formulated by the intelligence agencies, but let's look at Ivy League pinhead, Peter Singer, as he humbly describes himself on his own website:

> Journalists have bestowed upon me the tag of "world's most influential living philosopher." They are probably thinking of my work on the ethics of our treatment of animals, often credited with starting the modern animal rights movement, and the influence that my writing has had on the development of effective altruism . . .
>
> I was born in Melbourne, Australia, in 1946, and educated at the University of Melbourne and the University of Oxford. After teaching in England, the United States and Australia, in 1999 I became Ira W. DeCamp Professor in the University Center for Human Values at Princeton University.[11]

You'll have to forgive me if I laugh at the pompousness of such people. No matter how popular or unpopular I become, I can't ever imagine saying, "You know, some people claim I'm the world's greatest living philosopher."

With a minimum of effort, I proved two parts of my claim. First, that this was the idea of a pointy headed intellectual and found a permanent home at PETA. The only part I didn't prove was the development of this idea by the intelligence agencies.

But isn't part of the job description of the intelligence agencies to keep you from learning about what they're doing in the shadows?

* * *

Returning to Google, is it possible the company is already "evil," and may have been that way for years, perhaps even since its inception? The article continued the debate about AI, with the input of other famous intellectuals. Elon Musk isn't alone in his fears about the development of artificial intelligence.

> Last year, Professor Stephen Hawking said AI is likely to "replace humans altogether" and become a "new form of life that will outperform our fleshy, flabby species."
>
> And obviously, anyone who objects to the rise of the robots and their subsequent eradication of humanity is likely to be accused of 'speciesism.'
>
> The more things change, the more they stay the same.[12]

It sounds to me like the decision has already been made. Maybe it sounds different to you, but you'd need to explain that to me. As I'm understanding it, two of the smartest people in the world, Elon Musk and the late Stephen Hawking, sound as terrified of AI as I am.

I feel the need to explain the filter through which I view this information. Genuinely evil people don't tell you their plans. They seduce you with lies and half-truths, as the Devil did to Eve in the Garden of Eden. They leave out important pieces of information.

They need *you* to take the steps toward your own destruction.

If my opponents are not clear in their claims, I will assume the worst of them, and I encourage you to do the same.

With that in mind, I want you to consider the words of Yuval Noah Harari. Many may revere the Israeli academic. But I consider him to be the world's dumbest intellectual, which, if you share my contempt for the elites, is an exceedingly high bar. Most intellectuals I've come across don't have the commonsense God gave a dog. Here's some breathless coverage of Harari from the *New York Times* in 2021:

> With the publication in the United States of his best-selling *Sapiens* in 2015, the Israeli historian and philosopher Yuval Noah Harari

> arrived in the top rank of public intellectuals, a position he consolidated with *Homo Deus* (2017) and *21 Lessons for the 21st Century* (2018). Harari's key theme is the idea that human society has largely been driven by our species' capacity to believe what he calls fictions: those things whose power is derived from their existence in our collective imaginations, whether they be gods or nations; our belief in them allows us to cooperate on a societal scale.[13]

Do you understand Harari's argument? The reason we're successful as a species is because lies get us to work together. Just throw out thousands of years of mankind struggling to determine the great truths of human existence and live according to their dictates. And forget about trying to generate social systems that rely on transparency and trust.

It's all a falsehood.

We just need a culturally unifying Easter Bunny story, and there will be universal peace on Earth.

Harari doesn't believe truth stabilizes a society, or that lies destabilize it. I encourage you to ask yourself whether you should believe a person who doesn't value truth as a superior strategy for living an exemplary life.

Did you know Harari believes there's a direct line between transgenderism and trans-humanism? In fact, he's excited about the mutilation and cutting off of genitals, because it will show us so many wonderful things.

> I think that the reason that there is so much political heat around debates about transgender people and nonbinary people and so forth is because people may subconsciously feel that debates of the future will be about what we can do with the human body and human brain. How can we re-engineer them? How can we change them? The first practical place we come across these questions is gender. You can say people are bigots and are always sensitive when you talk about sex or gender, but I think that subconsciously people realize this is the first debate about transhumanism. It's about what we can do with technology to change the human body and brain and mind. *This* is why we see these heated debates.[14]

Did you see that coming?

Transgenderism as the first stage to transhumanism?

You just need to listen to these villains speak, and you'll often be able to determine their plans. And like most villains throughout history, whether they be communist or fascist, they fall in love with their ideals, averting their eyes from the cost in human misery.

Hitler might have said, *We just want Germany for Germans*! Stalin would have said, *We want to purge the selfish from Soviet society, so all of us can share.* Mao might have justified his persecution and starvation of millions by saying, *We must purge ourselves of the thought criminals so we can take that Great Leap Forward*. It's funny how the perfect world for so many of these tyrants begins with getting rid of the people they don't like.

Harari's enthusiasm for genital mutilation is only eclipsed by his love of transhumanism. It's almost a civil right, up there with freedom of speech, religion, or the right to bear arms.

> Transhumanism is about what it means to be human. I mean, there are different types of transhumanism, but one interpretation is that transhumanism is fulfilling the true potential of the human. Which depends of course on what you understand a human to be. This is the question we want to pursue, and it's not a question with easy answers.[15]

Let's talk about the crazed plans of these people to literally disassemble you and put you back together like some Frankenstein monster. It didn't work in the fairy tale of Humpty Dumpty, and it's unlikely to work with flesh and blood humans.

They don't like you just the way you are.

But the road to making all of the human race cyborgs won't be without its challenges.

> Harari went on to say that humanity is in the midst of a "second industrial revolution" centered around artificial intelligence. "But the product this time will not be textiles, or machines, or vehicles,

> or even weapons, the product this time will be humans themselves," Harari asserted. "We are basically learning to produce bodies and minds. Bodies and minds are going to be, I think, the two main products of the next wave of all these changes."
>
> "The useless people" referenced by the WEF [World Economic Forum] advisor would be those who refused to be injected with artificial intelligence capabilities in the coming decades. Describing humans as "hackable animals," Harari believes that "the masses" would "not stand much of a chance" against these changes, even if they were to organize.[16]

It's quite remarkable how Harari and his confederates at the World Economic Forum want to roll back all those things you call your civil rights, that generations of Americans have fought and died to protect. Maybe we should have just shrugged our shoulders in 1776 and said, "Yeah, the British are taking our rights away from us, but do we really want a Revolution?"

I don't think any of the readers of this book believe that to be true.

And if you're a true child of the Enlightenment, a believer that God created each and every human being in His image, and that each of you by existing on this planet have certain inalienable rights, you will never even consider the thought, as Yuval Noah Harari does, that certain people are "useless." If you're like me, you regard the idea that certain people are "useless" to be a blasphemy against God.

> "The problem is more boredom, what to do with them and how will they find some sense of meaning in life when they are basically meaningless, worthless," Harari continued. "My best guess at present is a combination of drugs and computer games."[17]

This casual, almost off-hand remark by Harari terrifies me more than I can possibly describe. Again, here's the filter I put on that remark. You may not see it the way I do, but I want you to at least understand my point of view.

When tyrants throughout history seek to exterminate or disempower a group of people, it begins with dehumanizing them, the way Hitler started by claiming a Jew couldn't be a good German. You might also come up with your own examples of how Stalin, Mao, or any of today's theocratic dictators do the same. Are you seeing something similar in today's media regarding Christians, conservatives, or even Democrats like Robert F. Kennedy Jr. or Tulsi Gabbard, who stray from the established narrative?

Non-believers, in their eyes, are little better than non-humans.

The Nazis came up with a chilling expression, *Lebebsunwertes Leben*, which translates into English as "life unworthy of life."[18] It was used first to justify the murder of disabled children and adults, then expanded to Jews and other enemies of the Reich. When Harari uses the expressions "useless people" or "useless class"[19] (sometimes referred to by others as Harari's "useless eaters" argument), it is difficult not to hear an echo of early Nazi thought.

Once you have banished these people from your social group for being useless, whether you identify that as your nation, ethnic group, or fellow band of anti-racists, it becomes easier to justify violence against them. Why does the left champion the idea of "Punch a Nazi in the face today" against their ideological opponents, except to push their fellow citizens with whom they disagree one step closer to a concentration camp?

Here's the genocidal dog whistle I hear when Harari speaks and says these "useless people" will have to be managed by some "combination of drugs and computer games."

I am separating this group of people from the human family and telling you not to worry about them. Once you have stopped caring about them, once I have removed them from the circle of human compassion, I can do whatever I want to them, and nobody will care.

Even *Forbes* magazine wanted to helpfully jump in for those who might find themselves someday useless and heading to a de-facto ghetto holding facility where they'd be supplied with drugs and endless computer games, noting in a 2018 article, written by (and I'm not making this up), John Hittler:

> Since 2017, a trend has been discussed in the media that's believed to be coming quickly and relentlessly. In short, the rise in artificial intelligence (AI) could create a "global useless class"—an entire group of humans who won't be able to work and who therefore contribute little to society. AI threatens to make many professions obsolete, meaning that unemployment may rise substantially.
>
> Could this really be that dramatic, that an entire class could exist, in every country, that simply has nothing meaningful to do to earn a living? The short answer is a resounding yes.[20]

This isn't Alex Jones in 2023 telling you they're planning on making a good portion of society useless; this is *Forbes* magazine and John Hittler telling you that in 2018. And what is Hittler's advice to keep you from becoming a "useless person," who will need to be kept docile by "drugs and computer games"?

> All hope is not lost. The trend toward more AI points to different strategies to remain both valuable, and hence, relevant in our society. Those who create may dominate, for example. According to historian Yuval Harari, who's written about the emergence of the global useless class, jobs requiring a high degree of creativity are likely to be safer.
>
> How about you? What can you do? Try this: Endeavor to explore and articulate that singular gift of talent you possess. Singular? Yes, as in no one else holds this talent.[21]

Hittler wants to prepare you for the coming of the machines, but I'm telling you that you possess an even more powerful weapon.

The unique soul God gave you when you were born on this great, good Earth.

I'm painfully aware of my abundant flaws, but I believe every person has a purpose under Heaven. (I believe God extends His grace even to people named John Hittler.)

It's difficult to be pessimistic about our chances when even the "godfather of AI" starts warning about his creation, as he did in the *New York Times* on May 1, 2023:

> Geoffrey Hinton was an artificial intelligence pioneer. In 2012, Dr. Hinton and two of his graduate students at the University of Toronto created technology that became the intellectual foundation for the A.I. systems that the tech industry's biggest companies believe is a key to their future.
>
> On Monday, however, he officially joined a growing chorus of critics who say those companies are racing toward danger with their aggressive campaign to create products based on generative artificial intelligence, the technology that powers popular chatbots like ChatGPT.
>
> Dr. Hinton said he has quit his job at Google, where he has worked for more than a decade and became one of the most respected voices in the field, so he can speak freely about the risks of A.I. A part of him, he said, now regrets his life's work.[22]

Sometimes God winks at you and tells you that you're on the right track. Elon Musk, Stephen Hawking, and now the "godfather of AI" are all on the side of Alex Jones?

While Dr. Hinton and I may disagree on how long Google has been a problem, we should always open our arms wide for the new converts to reality.

> His immediate concern is that the internet will be flooded with false photos, videos and text, and the average person will "not be able to know what is true anymore. [Author's note: We'll just have to rely even more on the *New York Times*, right?]
>
> He is also worried that A.I technologies will in time upend the job market. Today, chatbots like ChatGPT tend to complement human workers, but they could replace paralegals, personal

> assistants, translators, and others who handle rote tasks. "It takes away the drudge work," he said. "It might do more than that."
>
> Down the road, he is worried that future versions of the technology pose a threat to humanity because they often learn unexpected behavior from the vast amounts of data they analyze. This becomes an in issue, he said, as individuals and companies allow A.I. systems not only to generate their own computer code, but actually run that code on their own. And he fears a day when truly autonomous weapons—those killer robots—become reality.[23]

There are so many things that can go wrong with AI, and yet some version of it is probably inevitable. We need to lead the discussion, not leave it in the hands of scientists and engineers who might release something which would make the COVID crisis look like a twenty-four-hour cold.

You may not share my belief that our world is guided on one side by the good angels of God (who appear to have an exceptionally wry sense of humor by naming one of my adversaries Hittler) and deceived by the fallen angels of hell on the other.

But whether we believe in something beyond this world or not, we each have the capacity to see the reality of what is taking place today on our planet. We can see the evil that walks among us and take actions that make sense for humanity. I am optimistic about the battles to come.

In this book, I will attempt to lay out the evidence, not only of what they are doing, but how we can steal our future back from these agents of misery and usher in what I believe to be the Next Human Renaissance.

Part of that answer is forming strong human unions, dedicated to the traditional values that have allowed our species to thrive, such as principles of compassion, curiosity about each other, and a commitment to the success of every human being. In the world we envision, unlike the one imagined by Yuval Noah Harari, there are no "useless people."

Notice how the elites seek to divide us, keeping us prisoners in our own homes, whether it's through fear of a virus with a better than 99 percent survival rate for most age groups,[24] or addiction to social media, games, and thousand-channel streaming services. Go on a social media "fast," taking your eyes off your computers and smart phones and look into the eyes of another person as you have a conversation with them. You will feel so much more "human," and you'll also have a stronger immune system.

Maybe we need to set up private labeling groups, but instead of promoting something like fair trade, we know that these products have been manufactured by human beings living in thriving American communities, rather than outsourced to foreign countries who will abuse their native populations. We are America-First, just as we believe France should be France-First, or Libya should be Libya-First, or Botswana should be Botswana-First. We call for the humane practices developed in the West to be aggressively pursued in foreign countries, rather than using the misery of others to shave a few pennies off products sold in big box stores like Target and Walmart, who greedily participate in the exploitation of the Third World.

And we need to see AI for the genuine threat it poses to humanity. I'm still in the process of fully developing my thoughts, but from what I've seen so far, AI appears to be little more than a slightly improved search engine. As for its vaunted abilities, all I've seen it do is scrape the internet for the very best creations of human beings, slice and dice the information, then serve it back to you as if it's something new. Look for yourself what AI has done when it's been told to tell the story of American history. What you're likely to see is nothing more than scenes from Mel Gibson's fantastic movie *The Patriot*, Daniel Day Lewis in The *Last of the Mohicans,* or Henry Fonda in *The Grapes of Wrath*. That isn't creativity; it's like a mix tape of your favorite music or maybe your personal station on Pandora in which you give thumbs up to both Beethoven and Pink Floyd. Why isn't the Screen Actors Guild or the Writer's Guild of America suing AI for plagiarism or copyright infringement?

AI is a tool, and it can have some terrifying possibilities. Already there have been stories of unscrupulous characters getting enough audio of a young woman from her Instagram or YouTube videos to then use AI to spoof the voice in a phone call to her mother saying she's been ransomed. A few months ago, I was a victim of such an AI prank when some jokester took audio of Tucker Carlson, while also getting Carlson's private cellphone number, and called me while I was in a meeting pretending to be Tucker Carlson. Here's part of that exchange.

> **ALEX JONES:** Hey, brother, how are you doing?
> **TUCKER CARLSON (AI-Generated Voice):** Hey, Alex, it's Tucker. Do you have a minute to talk?
> **ALEX JONES:** Absolutely.
> **TUCKER CARLSON (AI-Generated Voice):** You busy right now, or do you got a second to talk?
> **ALEX JONES:** I was in a meeting, and I just jumped out. What's going on, brother?
> **TUCKER CARLSON (AI-Generated Voice):** You busy right now, or do you have a second to talk? [Exact repeat of what he'd just said. I started to get suspicious.]
> **ALEX JONES:** No, I just left a meeting. Go ahead.
> **TUCKER CARLSON (AI-Generated Voice):** I was thinking we could do a show together where we're topless, and we suck each other's nipples and play with them a bit. It would be a comment on gender roles.[25]

I'd been in something of an intense financial meeting that I'd stepped away from to take what showed on my phone as Tucker's personal cellphone, so it took me a few seconds to realize it was not Tucker Carlson. In private, Tucker is often profanely funny, but this just wasn't his preferred style of humor.

Aside from prank phone calls, I believe the genuine danger from AI is that it's a very effective mask of control that can be utilized by the elites. If you have AI telling you it's a bad idea to have kids because of climate change, how many will follow that advice? My guess is that it's going to be a significant number of young people.

We must remember that we are the ones in control of our own destiny.

Human beings are the only animal that can control our environment. The left wants us to believe we're a cancer on the planet that needs to be culled back, perhaps by a cruel 90 percent, as suggested by a top University of Texas ecologist (about 8.1 billion people to be killed), for a total global population of just under a billion people.[26] Other globalists might prefer a kinder and gentler genocide, a mere 80 percent reduction in human beings, as suggested by Stanford professor Paul Ehrlich (which would only require the death of approximately 6.5 to 7 billion people), allowing 1.5 to 2 billion individuals to continue to exist on the planet.[27] That means for each person who survives, they'd be expected to bury eight to nine of their closest friends and family members.

How do they expect to achieve such a massive reduction in population?

Well, they'll do it with a slow kill, giving us crappy food, lots of pharmaceutical drugs, and unsafe vaccines, making us fear one another, and having us hide in our houses, getting our groceries and meals delivered. This is a moment beyond Pandora's box, beyond Promethean fire, what I call the Atlantean moment, in which we make the civilizational decision to embrace a bright or dark future.

On its own, and developed by those genuinely interested in humanity, AI might be a very effective tool, like computers and smart phones (which also need to be protected from the Deep State).

But in the hands of the globalists, AI is just another weapon in their war to control you and decrease the number of humans on the planet.

This is as serious as it gets.

Chapter Two

Mao Is in Charge of the Democratic Party, and Political Violence Is Bad, except When It's Directed at Alex Jones

How does the average American view the shambles of what's become of our liberal democracy?

You might be surprised to hear me lament the demise of our "liberal" democracy. But I consider myself a child of the Enlightenment, the intellectual and philosophical movement that occurred in Europe during the seventeenth and eighteenth centuries, which gave birth to our common concepts of a government with limited powers over the individual, freedom of expression, freedom of speech, freedom of religion, curiosity for the opinions of others, the value of honest debate, respect for evidence and reason, as well as the separation of church and state.

The overwhelming majority of these revolutionary thinkers were deeply religious and viewed their efforts as the best way to limit the corrupt temporal power of governments over the individual. They believed that individuals were more likely to be responsible than any group of leaders. To put it plainly, the common people were less likely to want to go to war with the neighbors, or exile those with dissenting views. They also believed that limited government would result in people being more likely to act charitably toward those in need, and to take just actions against those who have harmed the community, than any government.

These thinkers came to their beliefs because of the experience of centuries in which their governments had greatly abused generations of people.

This is an idea I feel is overlooked by many, who look at our current situation and despair as to whether it can change.

The truth is there has always been a war between tyranny and freedom. And I am unshakeable in my belief that we are better poised than ever before to push back against the current totalitarian darkness. I know that there will never be a complete victory (until the Rapture, that is) because God has given man the gift of free will, which means you have the freedom to choose between the light and the darkness.

When I was a kid and first learned to read, I devoured comic books, but quickly switched into more substantial reading. My dad had a collection of history books, most notably the six-volume history by Edward Gibbon, *The History and Decline of the Fall of the Roman Empire,* which I found more compelling than any comic book superhero. Because while the superheroes may have been from another planet or gained their power through some unfortunate radioactive exposure, the characters of ancient Rome struck me as flesh and blood individuals, trying to navigate the treacherous political climate of their times, while also believing in concepts of nobility and integrity, hoping that their reputation for honesty and good works would be a source of pride to their descendants.

"Virtue" was an important, if not the most vital, character trait an individual could possess.

I was aware from an early time that my mind had more of a historical slant than those of my contemporaries. I wasn't just interested in the passing news of the day, but what it meant over the years and decades. What would today's events look like ten, twenty, thirty years in the future? How would we think about them?

Does that mean I was a saint in those days?

Far from it. Don't look to me as the person who lived his life as one of rectitude.

I drank, smoked, occasionally experimented with drugs, chased girls, and got into a lot of fights so crazy that you wouldn't believe me if I told you the stories. These are all things that, as an older man, I now regret, and I try to teach my own children differently and also share that wisdom with my audience. I've lived an intensely human life, warts and all.

But as much as I may have been a teenager on the wrong path, I was aware of older people, community leaders, who should have known better. I recall a popular local pastor who lived close to me, who had wild parties at his house (I'd sneak out at night and spy on them, and what I saw shocked me), and then condemned his parishioners as sinners on Sunday, haranguing them that they weren't giving him enough money. I saw behind the curtain at a young age that often those who were promoting themselves to be of the most noble virtue were, in many instances, the biggest liars.

I admit I have a strong anti-authoritarian streak, and sometimes that has gotten me into trouble. If a story is too convenient for a government narrative, I will often dig in my heels and suggest we're being lied to. I've heard it said that while we presume an individual to be "innocent until proven guilty," the standard should be reversed when it comes to large corporations and governments. If a powerful entity does something that sounds corrupt, we should presume the corporation, government, or media outlet to be "guilty until they show us the evidence that they are innocent." We give the benefit of the doubt to the individual, but we should not do that for the multi-billion-dollar corporation, compromised news outlet, or powerful government leaders.

All of this is part and parcel of the disintegration of our common values that we're currently experiencing in our country. We are lied to by powerful entities, and then they let us fight over the "facts."

Where do I think it began?

I believe much of this began in the nineteenth century with the theory of natural selection, proposed by Charles Darwin to explain the changes of plants and animals over time. This was modified by his cousin, Francis Galton, to create the theory of Social Darwinism, defined by the Encyclopedia Britannica as:

> [T]he theory that human groups and races are subject to the same laws of natural selection as Charles Darwin perceived in plants and animals in nature. According to the theory, which was popular in the late 19th and early 20th centuries, the weak were diminished and their

> cultures delimited while the strong grew in power and cultural influence over the weak. Social Darwinists held that the life of humans in society was a struggle for existence ruled by "survival of the fittest," a phrase proposed by the British philosopher and scientist Herbert Spencer.
>
> The Social Darwinists—notably Spencer and Walter Bagehot in England and William Graham Sumner in the United States—believed that the process of natural selection acting on variations in the population would result in the survival of the best competitors and in continuing improvement in the population. Societies were viewed as organisms that evolve in this manner.[1]

You can see how this effort by the elites of England and the United States essentially created the "white supremacy" movement, and yet their descendants at the elite universities have "whitewashed" this painful history. One can easily understand how Hitler and his Nazi Party seized control of Germany and used this theory to create the idea of the Aryan superman. But what may be shocking is the extent to which the elite American Ivy League schools, academics, and government officials supported these reprehensible beliefs.

Thankfully, the *New York Times* published an article on this forgotten and shameful period of our history in 2014:

> Less than a mile down the road, the renowned Cold Spring Harbor Laboratory bustles with more than 600 researchers and technicians, regularly producing breakthroughs in genetics, cancer, and neuroscience.
>
> But that old house, now a private residence on the outskirts of town, once held a facility whose very name evokes dark memories: the Eugenics Record Office.
>
> In its heyday, the office was the premier scientific enterprise at Cold Spring Harbor. There, bigoted scientists applied rudimentary genetics to singling out supposedly superior races and degrading

> minorities. By the mid-1920s, the office had become the center of the eugenics movement in America.[2]

You might be a long-time reader of the *New York Times*, or maybe you're an Ivy Leaguer who once believed all the liberal talking points, and yet you find yourself reading this book. Perhaps you entered 2020 as a leftist in good standing with all your friends and non-profits, but after having been mugged by the COVID lockdowns, maybe forbidden from visiting an elderly parent for years even while they struggled with a debilitating illness, now you're quietly saying to just a few friends, "I finally understand why we need a Second Amendment."

Even if you thought you knew all the terrible things in American history, you might be asking yourself, "You mean the intellectual elite of this country, my predecessors at the Ivy League schools I once worshipped, were the progenitors of white supremacists?"

Yes, Virginia, they were, and what's even worse, they acted upon it.

The *New York Times* article continued its history lesson:

> When the Eugenics Records Office opened its doors in 1910, the founding scientists were considered progressives, intent on applying classic genetics to breeding better citizens. Funding poured in from the Rockefeller family and the Carnegie Institution. Charles Davenport, a prolific Harvard biologist, and his colleague, Harry H. Laughlin, led the charge.
>
> "There were many prominent New Yorkers involved in eugenics," Dr. Tchen said. "It was initially about how to become more efficient as a modern society."
>
> Researchers sought out "unfit" families in the Manhattan slums and the Pine Barrens of New Jersey. They catalogued disabilities and undesirable traits, scribbling the exact dimensions of heads and arms.[3]

We've got the "progressives" championing the idea of eugenics, that among humans there are certain races that are more likely to be productive (and whose numbers we should increase) and those who will be less productive (and whose numbers we should decrease.)

The claim that it was all about becoming "more efficient in a modern society" is truly appalling, sounding suspiciously like something an actual Nazi might've said.

Am I going too far with that claim?

How about the effort to catalogue "unfit" families? Does it sound uncomfortably close to Yuval Noah Harari's claim that some people are "useless eaters" and are probably best dealt with by a program of drugs and virtual reality video games?

You may think I'm being hyperbolic, but the Nazis definitely took notice of the Cold Spring Harbor program, and the effect it had on our immigration program, which they applauded.

> By the 1920s, the office had begun to influence the United States government. Laughlin testified before Congress, advocating forced sterilization and anti-immigration laws. Congress complied. The Immigration Act of 1924 effectively barred Eastern Europeans, Jews, Arabs and East Asians from entering the country. And, at the state level, thousands of people who were deemed unfit were sterilized.
>
> The University of Heidelberg in Nazi Germany later awarded Laughlin an honorary degree for his work in the "science of racial cleansing." He accepted this award, and his research on Long Island continued to influence Nazi ideology throughout World War II and the Holocaust.[4]

I know people are likely to call me crazy when I say, "Did you know the Rockefellers, the Carnegies, and professors from Harvard University gave Adolf Hitler some of his most evil ideas?" But that's the truth.

I know because I read it in the *New York Times*. (Did you ever think you would hear Alex Jones say such a thing?) To be clear, I didn't discover from the *New York Times* that the roots of race-based eugenics came from the United States and England, but I did discover a great deal more from the book *IBM and the Holocaust* by Leonard Black, which I suggest you read.

* * *

In the beginning of the twentieth century, "progressives" were developing the ideas that gave rise to the Holocaust.

When Nazism and fascism went bust at the end of World War II, where did these progressives turn for their next program to control our society?

I think they turned to Communist China and Chairman Mao Zedong, in admiration of not only how he was able to create a fascist state, but how even to this day they continue to control their population of more than a billion people. I want to publicly acknowledge the contribution made to my thinking by Helen Pluckrose and James Lindsey and their book, *Cynical Theories: How Activist Scholarship Made Everything about Race, Gender and Identity—And Why this Harms Everybody.*

The book starts by discussing how post-modernism sought to destroy the wisdom of centuries of western thought. But in later talks, Lindsey has pointed to the speeches of Chairman Mao, prior to beginning the Cultural Revolution, as the best model for understanding how the left is seeking to gain complete power in this country.

The speech Mao gave on February 27, 1957 to the Supreme State Conference, with the relatively innocuous title of *On the Correct Handling of Contradictions Among the People*, holds the key to understanding their ideology and methods behind what the globalists are attempting today. It begins:

> Never before has our country been as united as today. The victories of the bourgeois-democratic revolution and of the socialist revolution and our achievements in socialist construction have rapidly changed the face of the old China. A still brighter future lies ahead for our motherland. The days of national disunity and chaos which the people detested are gone, never to return. Led by the working

> class and the Communist Party, our 600 million, united as one, are engaged in the great task of building socialism. The unification of our country, the unity of our people, and the unity of our various nationalities—these are the basic guarantees for the sure triumph of our cause. However, this does not mean that contradictions no longer exist in our society. To imagine that none exist is a naïve idea which is at variance with objective reality. We are confronted with two types of social contradictions—those between ourselves and the enemy and those among the people.[5]

The Chinese Communist Revolution was so much different than the American Revolution, and it's important to point out the underlying ideological differences. While American leaders will often begin their speeches praising our country, its values, or even its unity, there is a significant difference. Mao talks of "disunity and chaos" as something terrible, while an American leader is likely to speak of how differences of opinion lead to better plans than those initially held by either side. (They don't do it always, but they did so more often in earlier generations. You hear echoes of it today when some president proclaims, "Congress came together on behalf of the country, rather than partisan politics.")

The goal of Mao seems to be the elimination of any contradictions, viewing them as harmful, rather than beneficial. And he hints that even though the country is more united than ever before, there may yet be internal enemies. He refers to two types of groups, the "people" and the "enemy." For those of you who may be more conservatively minded, I want you to think how in the past five years you have felt like more of an "enemy" to certain individuals or family members, than you ever remember feeling in your life.

Newsflash!

When Hillary Clinton called you a "deplorable" or Joe Biden refers to "ultra-MAGA," they're using Mao's strategy. Don't believe for a moment they don't know what they're doing. It's a dog whistle to call out the demons of human nature. Mao explained his strategy:

> To understand these two different types of contradictions correctly, we must first be clear on what is meant by "the people" and what is meant by "the enemy." The concept of "the people" varies in content in different countries and in different periods of history in a given country. Take our own country for example. During the War of Resistance Against Japan, all those classes, strata, and social groups opposing Japanese aggression came within the category of the people, while the Japanese imperialists, their Chinese collaborators, and the pro-Japanese elements were all enemies of the people.
>
> During the War of Liberation, the U.S. imperialists and their running dogs—the bureaucrat-capitalists, the landlords, and the Kuomintang reactionaries who represented these two classes—were the enemies of people, while the other classes, strata, and social groups which opposed them, all came within the category of the people. At the present stage, the period of building socialism, the classes, strata, and social groups which favor, support, and work for the cause of socialist construction all come within the category of the people, while the social forces and groups which resist the socialist revolution and are hostile to or sabotage socialist construction are all enemies of the people.[6]

Let's understand what this looks like in practice. You could have fought with the communists against the Japanese, and in that time you're their friend. You could have fought with the communists against the previous corrupt government, and for the duration of that struggle, they'll pretend to be your good buddy. But with the Japanese invaders gone, the old government overthrown, don't be surprised if the guns get turned on you.

The communists are your friends only as long as you're useful to them. All they understand is the struggle, not any idea of protecting minority rights. The only thing they care about is power and maintaining that power. Sound like any government you know?

There are other similarities between Mao's Cultural Revolution and the current Democratic Party, such as how they both were obsessed with obliterating gender roles. This is part of the abstract from a well-regarded academic paper with the title, *The Annihilation of Femininity in Mao's China: Gender Inequality of Sent-Down Youth during the Cultural Revolution:*

> During the Chinese Cultural Revolution, Mao's famous political slogan "The times have changed, men and women are the same" asserted that men and women were equal in political consciousness and physical strength. However, the slogan's seeming emphasis on gender equality misconstrued the concepts of equality and sameness. In-depth interviews with former "sent-down" youth illustrate how state rhetoric appropriated a discourse of women's equality to silence women and depoliticize gender as a category.[7]

For those of us who are more familiar with the common dynamic of the liberal world, where one thing is promised, and something quite different is delivered, this does not come as a surprise. But for those of us with more experience, it's what we've come to expect from liberals. The promises may sound wonderful, like a nugget of Fool's Gold, sparkling in a cold, mountain stream.

Many formerly liberal women are waking up to the reality that they have no interest in the liberal men they once thought would be their life partners. They find to their dismay that, generally, liberal men are unreliable, self-centered, and weak when the storms of life blow through.

The great journalist and feminist, Dr. Naomi Wolf, has publicly lamented that, in her findings, the COVID-19 vaccine seems to be negatively affecting women to men at a four to one, or even five to one ratio, specifically affecting the reproductive systems of women. She has heard "absolute silence" from her feminist sisters. Instead, she has been talking for the past two years about COVID shots affecting women's fertility to almost exclusively "conservative, Christian men."[8]

It has been an absolute head-scratcher for Dr. Wolf.

But it's not a mystery to me.

Conservative men understand that men and women are equal, and yet different. It is desirable in society for this to be so. Men understand that their life purpose is to protect women and their families. Women understand it is their life purpose to care for and guide the next generation and make sure that civilization is worth the name. And in the most extreme example, men understand it is their sacred duty to stay on the sinking ship, while the women and children escape in the lifeboats.

Mao sought to obliterate all that.

Mao sought to have children inform on their parents and on their teachers, and for spouses to inform on their spouses, to break the bonds that held people together in society.

Why?

Because if you break the bonds that hold people in affectionate relationships with each other, they are bereft of a social and moral compass, and it's much easier to get them to obey the authorities. (Almost sounds like what the government did to us during COVID-19, doesn't it? Children not in school, not being able to see your elderly parents, social distancing, masks, denouncing and demonizing those of us who didn't want to wear masks all day or get the jab. You might even call it a "Plandemic," as my good friend, Mikki Willis, likes to say.)

Doesn't it sound positively demonic? That's because it is. Sorry, I can't come up with any other word for it.

While there have been many statistics thrown around on the number of people killed or persecuted during Mao's Cultural Revolution, I'm fond of the personal account. Numbers distance us from the horror, while stories make it vivid and real.

I'm known for criticizing the mainstream media, but if you wait long enough, some of their talented writers might eventually tell you the truth about an important event. That's why this article from CNN from 2016, titled "Confessions of a Red Guard, 50 Years after China's Cultural Revolution," caught my attention.

> I have lived a life haunted by guilt.
>
> In 1966, I was one of Chairman Mao Zedong's Red Guards. Myself and millions of other high school students started denouncing our teachers, friends, families and raiding homes and destroying other people's possessions.

> Textbooks explain the Cultural Revolution—in which hundreds of thousands of people were killed and millions more abused and traumatized—as a political movement started and led by Mao "by mistake," but in reality it was a massive catastrophe for which we all bear responsibility.[9]

I'd like you to look at what's been happening in our country through the lens of the Chinese Cultural Revolution. What is the left doing these days, but indoctrinating our middle and high schoolers to denounce their country for its racism, and maybe their parents and family members for not being "woke" enough about transgenderism, climate change, and the Black Lives Matters agenda?

What the average person hears is a cacophony of crises, inducing a state of fear and panic in people, turning on friends and family, and then, bereft of social connections, plugging into the government's fear machine and acting as obedient little robots for what appears to be a violent future. Who among us wouldn't want to go back in time and "punch" a real Nazi before they instituted their ghastly reign of terror?

But instead of punching a Nazi, you may be punching a mother or father, sister or brother, or one of your fellow citizens, who is vainly trying to stop you from becoming an unrecognizable version of yourself. You may have become the very monster you had thought you were trying to stop. The *CNN* account of the former Red Guard continued:

> As Red Guards, we subjected anyone perceived as "bourgeois" or "revisionist" to brutal mental and physical attacks.
>
> I regret most what we did to our homeroom teacher Zhang Jilan.
>
> I was one of the most active students—if not the most revolutionary—when the class held a struggle session against Ms. Zhang.
>
> I pulled accusations out of nowhere, saying she was a heartless and cold woman, which was entirely false.
>
> Others accused her of being a Christian because the character "Ji" in her name could refer to Christianity.

> Our groundless criticisms were then written into "big character" posters—a popular way of criticizing "class enemies" and spreading propaganda—60 of them in total, which covered the exterior walls of our building.[10]

I try to envision this woman, who must have been in her early sixties as she was reliving the story, picturing herself as a young girl, probably one of the smartest, most obedient children in the class, being coopted by Mao to engage in this activity, the shame of which she would carry with her for the rest of her life. How many times over the ensuing years had she criticized herself for what she had done, missing out on the joy God meant her to have, because of this evil leader who decided that the best way to maintain power was to steal the innocence of children?

Jesus said He came to our world to give us life in abundance. That is what good, kind actions do for our souls. It gives us abundance, in every sense of the word. And evil steals away the richness of our lives, not just for those who endure it, but for those who participate in it.

But the point I will make repeatedly in this book is that I believe God continues to give us chances, even when we believe we may be beyond redemption. Even in the darkness, even among those who have joined the devil's army, there are rebellions in those ranks, too. God can bring His light into the darkest of places and the darkest of souls.

> At the height of the movement in 1968, people were publicly beaten to death every day during struggle sessions; others who had been persecuted threw themselves off tall buildings.
>
> Nobody was safe and the fear of being reported by others—in many cases our closest friends and family members—haunted us.
>
> At first, I was determined to be a good little revolutionary guard. But something bothered me.
>
> When I saw a student pour a bucket of rotten paste over our school principal in 1966, I sensed something wasn't right.
>
> I headed back to my dorm quietly, full of discomfort and guilt, thinking I wasn't revolutionary enough.

> Later, when I was given a belt and told to whip an "enemy of the revolution," I ran away and was called a deserter by my fellow Red Guards.[11]

Do you see how God can work His way into any human heart? There was no religion in this young girl's heart, only the memory of the kindness of her family and friends, which reflects God's love for humanity. But there is something innate in the human psyche, which longs for justice and kindness and revolts against evil. Even though everything in this young girl's environment was encouraging her in this evil behavior, something stopped her. As she recounts in the story, her father, a former war correspondent, was eventually charged with being a spy. The evil she did in her young life has consumed much of her adult life, and she does not shirk from the part she played in such atrocities. She wrote:

> My generation grew up drinking wolf's milk: we were born with hatred and taught to struggle and hate everyone.
>
> Some of my fellow Red Guards argue that we were just innocent citizens led astray. But we were wrong.
>
> It pains me that many of my generation choose to forget the past and some even reminisce about the "good old days" when they could travel the country as privileged, carefree Red Guards.[12]

When I read accounts like this I'm deeply moved. One may think I simply like to thunder and curse against corruption because I'm trying to protect the innocent. But just as hard as I'm trying to protect the vulnerable, I'm also trying to stop those who are on the precipice of committing evil, because I understand how profoundly it will affect the rest of their lives. How bad was Mao's reign over China? I direct your attention to this article from the *Washington Post*:

> Mao launched more than a dozen campaigns during his rule, which began when he founded Communist China in 1949 and ended with his death in 1976. Some are well-known while others, such as a bloody

> campaign to "purify class ranks" in the late 1960s, which involved army units, have received little publicity.
>
> While most scholars are reluctant to estimate a total number of "unnatural deaths" in China under Mao, evidence shows he was in some way responsible for at least 40 million deaths and perhaps 80 million or more. This includes deaths he was directly responsible for and deaths resulting from disastrous policies he refused to change.[13]

We are talking about the deaths of eighty million people, perpetrated by a regime that still holds power in China and wants to claim their system is superior to the freedom of the West. I am an implacable foe of any system that seeks to wipe out a single member of humanity, let alone eighty million. But the establishment wing of both the Republicans and Democrats have embraced many of the same tactics of Mao, which led to the death of tens of millions of people.

Consider some of Chairman Mao's words and compare them to how our leaders have treated people in the last few years.

> Our state is a people's democratic dictatorship led by the working class and based on the worker-peasant alliance. What is this dictatorship for? Its first function is internal, namely to suppress the reactionary classes and elements and those exploiters who resist the socialist revolution, to suppress those who try to wreck our socialist construction, or in other words, to resolve the contradictions between ourselves and the internal enemy. For instance, to arrest, try, and sentence certain counterrevolutionaries, and to deprive landlords and bureaucratic-capitalists of their right to vote and their freedom of speech for a certain period of time—all this comes within the scope of our dictatorship.[14]

When I read that passage, I was asking myself, is this Chairman Mao or a Facebook manual for content-moderators? It can be so difficult to tell the difference sometimes.

But all joking aside, what's remarkable about that passage is that it begins not with the assumption that the State exists to protect the rights of the individual, but the State exists to force the compliance of the individual.

Our Constitution reveres the individual, believing the state, while necessary, poses an enormous danger to the public. Government is likened to a fire, which should serve humanity, not consume it, as the globalists would have it.

Just consider what globalist David Rockefeller, one of the architects of modern China, wrote about the country in 1973 in an article for the *New York Times*, when even the Chinese were criticizing the millions of deaths inflicted during the Cultural Revolution:

> One is impressed immediately by the sense of national harmony. From the loud patriotic music at the border onward, there is very real and pervasive dedication to Chairman Mao and Maoist principles. Whatever the price of the Chinese Revolution, it has obviously succeeded not only in producing more efficient and dedicated administration, but also in fostering high morale and community of purpose.[15]

How can I consider David Rockefeller and his fellow globalist travelers to be anything other than promoting mass murder by these statements?

And how can so many be blind to this agenda?

One of the things that gives me enormous hope is the realization that, just because people have been part of the system of oppression, doesn't mean they can't choose a better path. Early in my career, I befriended a remarkable man named Ted Gunderson. He joined the FBI in 1951, serving in various capacities until becoming head of the Memphis, Dallas, and Los Angeles FBI offices. In 1979, he was interviewed for the job of FBI director, which eventually went to William Webster.

But Ted Gunderson had a secret. He helped run the COINTELPRO program[16] for the FBI, which was intended to infiltrate, harass, and discredit civil rights and anti-war groups. In fact, it was Gunderson himself who wrote the now infamous letter to the Nobel Peace Prize-winning civil rights hero, Martin Luther King Jr., telling King he should commit suicide before he received his Nobel Prize in Sweden,[17] or else information about his adulterous affairs would be released to the public.

Gunderson was deeply ashamed of what he had done, said that the FBI had made up much information about King's alleged affairs. Gunderson dedicated the rest of his life to not only rooting out corruption in the FBI, but also in our intelligence agencies.[18]

Some considered him a hero and others dismissed him as a crack-pot, but as the years have gone by, his warnings have been seen by most as prophetic. This is the summary of a Ted Gunderson talk posted on Twitter (now X) by Truth Justice on August 10, 2023, which has more than 2.3 million views, and pretty much encapsulates what I learned from Gunderson:

> FBI Special Agent Ted Gunderson goes on to say based on his 28 years of experience and research that there is a covert illegal rogue U.S. Government criminal enterprise operating in the United States in several cities.
>
> The disaster in Pearl Harbor could have been avoided, we knew on December 4th and could have pulled the U.S. fleet out before we were attacked.
>
> President John F. Kennedy, also known as (Jack) was assassinated by the CIA and the FBI helped carry the assassination out by diverting President Kennedy's car to another route. Lyndon B. Johnson knew President Kennedy was going to be assassinated and wanted him dead. Robert F. Kennedy (Bobby) was also assassinated by the same illegal rogue infiltrated government.
>
> The Oklahoma City bombing was carried out by the "New World Order Boys" and U.S. Army explosives were used. Timothy McVeigh was a CIA operative.
>
> In the Waco Siege incident, he confirms that the four ATF agents were actually assassinated by government snipers. These same ATF agents who were killed were at one time Bill Clinton's bodyguards.

The FBI knew in advance about the World Trade Center car bombing and furnished the ingredients for the bomb that was used to blow up the World Trade Center.

As a private investigator when he retired from the FBI he took on the Jeffrey Robert McDonald case who was an American medical doctor and United States Army captain who was convicted in August 1979 of murdering his pregnant wife and two daughters in February 1970 while serving as an Army Special Forces physician.

During his investigations into the MacDonald case he received a signed confession from Helena Stoeckley stating that Jeffrey McDonald did not do it, that it was her Satanic cult group that committed these murders. The courts ignored the confession from her.

Helena Stoeckley went on to confess that this was a large-scale drug operation that was being covered up. They were flying drugs in plastic bags in the body cavities of the dead GI's coming out of Southeast Asia. There were military generals involved, other military personnel officers, Police Officers and investigators for the Army.

When Ted went public with this information he received hundreds of calls from victims telling him about the Satanic Cult movement in the United States. These people are victims of a covert illegal rogue U.S. Government criminal enterprise.

Since becoming an FBI whistleblower, he has been investigated by the FBI with an attempt to indict him, he was put on two separate hit lists in order to assassinate him, he has been poisoned and targeted with disinformation to discredit him for exposing the corruption within the CIA, FBI and Government.

He worked the Franklin Coverup Case involving illegal Government drug operations and Satanic cults. They were taking children out of orphanages and foster homes and privately flying them to Washington DC for sex orgies with U.S. Congressmen and Senators. This was filmed and pictures were taken for blackmail control.

Through his investigation of the Franklin case it led him to a Washington DC organization called "The Finders"" which is a CIA covert operation for trafficking children.

> Thousands of children are being abducted and kidnapped every year during the Satanic holidays of June 21, October 31 and December for ritual sacrifice. World leaders are involved in this Satanic Cult. He says this country, America, is being ruled by Satanists.
>
> He warns of election fraud happening through electronic voting systems. This is what happened in the 2020 U.S. Presidential Election and will happen again unless we stop the Committee of 300.
>
> The Satanic Illuminati Cult he is referring to are members of the Committee of 300 who were also exposed by a 45-year MI6 Intelligence Officer. Brave men and women have been warning us for years about the Committee of 300 and we have done nothing to stop them. In previous posts, I have listed all their names. They must be stopped.
>
> If we don't stop them now, they will accomplish their goals of depopulation and total world control over humanity. They will destroy America completely. We cannot be afraid, fear is their biggest tool against us. We must act now and stand tall to defend life, freedom, liberty, and our innocent children.[19]

I'm aware that a lot of what Gunderson had to say from the late 1980s until his death on July 31, 2011, may have sounded crazy at the time.

But look how far we've come.

We now know the Iraq War was based on lies, the government has engaged in a massive surveillance program against the public, and we've witnessed the continuing concealment of the John and Robert Kennedy assassination files. The tech platforms support the establishment of both parties, and a serial pedophile blackmailer like Jeffrey Epstein can be dead for years, and yet the American public has yet to see a single frame from one of the video cameras he had riddled throughout his residences. If that isn't evidence of a massive Deep State, in the same way a black hole devours passing light, I don't know what you'd need to be convinced.

There is little doubt Gunderson had an exceptional career at the FBI, and I always personally found him to be highly credible. I consider this man one of my mentors in the ways of the Deep State, as well as teaching me about their weaknesses. You see, God created people to be good. It takes an enormous amount of energy to keep people on the path of evil. To free them, you simply have to tell the truth to these captive souls, show them how much better their life can be, and they will do the rest. And once freed from the matrix of lies, they never go back. It just feels icky, like wallowing in mud after you've had a nice, long shower.

When one looks at how the Democratic Party (and some parts of the Republican Party) have been acting lately, it's questionable if Joe Biden is in charge or Chairman Mao.

We must free those currently suffering from their illusions, and this book is written for them. This book is nothing less than a call for a return to sanity.

* * *

What is the long-term plan of the globalists and how do we find it?

They must have their model and underlying philosophy, don't they?

One need search no further than the example of the East India Company and how they worked in concert with the British Empire for centuries, until they were defeated by who?

Oh, yeah, George Washington, the patriots of the American Revolution, the Continental Army, and the soldiers and navy of France.

Yes, America was founded by people who defeated the greatest combination of corporate and military power ever assembled in the history of the world.

We've done this before, and we can do it again.

This is how the History Channel describes the first fascist state, in which corporate wealth was combined with the military power of a nation.

> One of the biggest, most dominant corporations in history operated long before the emergence of tech giants like Apple, Google or Amazon. The English East India Company was incorporated by royal charter on December 31, 1600 and went on to act as a part-trade, part nation state and reap vast profits from overseas trade with

> India, China, Persia, and Indonesia for more than two centuries. Its business flooded England with affordable tea, cotton textiles, and spices, and richly rewarded its London investors with returns as high as 30 percent.
>
> "At its peak, the English East India Company was by far the largest corporation of its kind," says Emily Erickson, a sociology professor at Yale University and author of *Between Monopoly and Free Trade: The English East India Company.* "It was also larger than several nations. It was essentially the de facto emperor of large portions of India, which was one of the most productive economies in the world at that point."[20]

"Everything old is new again" is a popular saying, which is why the globalists don't want you to know your history. The lust for power, from the conquests of the Roman Empire to the Mongol hordes, to Napoleon, Hitler, Stalin, and Mao, is a common thread through human history. But the role you may not have heard was the part played by Western nations and their prized vehicle for the control of populations, the corporation.

> But just when the East India Company's grip on trade weakened in the late 18th century, [Because of getting whipped by the United States of America in the Revolutionary War] it found a new calling as an empire-builder. At one point, this mega corporation commanded a private army of 260,000 soldiers, twice the size of the standing British army. That kind of manpower was more than enough to coerce Indian rulers into one-sided contracts that granted the Company lucrative taxation powers . . .
>
> Many of the hallmarks of the modern corporation were first popularized by the East India Company. For example, the Company was the largest and longest-lasting joint stock company of its day, which means that it raised and pooled capital by selling shares to the public. It was governed by a president, but also a "board of control" or "board of officers."[21]

Western governments, or even most woke non-profits, today don't seem to be interested in how corporations can control a country. When one wonders how a network like Fox News can fire its most popular host, like Tucker Carlson, it's because Fox News is such a small part of the corporation's portfolio. They're not interested in Fox News as an independent source of journalism; it's part of the marketing department of a larger conglomerate. Dig down a little deeper, maybe into some of the "climate-change" advocates, or Black Lives Matter, and you'll find they're likely funded by large mega-corporations and globalist foundations.

Why would corporate entities be interested in burning down American neighborhoods and creating "No-Go" zones? Well, if you destroy local businesses, everybody's got to shop online, and that's all controlled by the Big Tech titans, manufacturing their products in the slave economy which is modern China. The Chinese people aren't getting rich off globalism, either. We need to support them, because like us, they've been getting screwed for centuries by this corporate-government partnership of Western governments.

> The exploits of the East India Company didn't end in India. In one of its darkest chapters, the Company smuggled opium into China in exchange for the country's most prized trade good: tea. China only traded tea for silver, but that was hard to come by in England, so the company flouted China's opium ban through a black market of Indian opium growers and smugglers. As tea flowed into London, the Company's investors grew rich and millions of Chinese men wasted away in opium dens.
>
> When China cracked down on the opium trade, the British government sent warships, triggering the Opium War of 1840. The humiliating Chinese defeat handed the British control of Hong Kong, but the conflict shed further light on the East India Company's dark dealings in the name of profit.[22]

I love that phrase "dark dealings in the name of profit." It covers a lot of ground. Did you realize that Great Britain was a drug dealer in the nineteenth century, little different than the Mexican cartels that are flooding our country with deadly fentanyl?

And despite the blow struck against the East India Company by the increasing support for the free market arguments of Adam Smith, it seemed that some British intellectuals, such as H. G. Wells, wanted to replace it with some other "New World Order," which is the name of a book he published in January 1940. (And you thought those words were first uttered by President George H. W. Bush.) Here's a sample of what Wells wrote, claiming some form of world government was inevitable.

> The question of collectivization is to be "Westernized" or "Easternized," using these words under the caveat of the previous paragraph, is really the first issue before the world today. We need a fully ventilated revolution. Our Revolution has to go on in the light and air. We may soon have to accept Sovietization *a la Russe* quite soon unless we can produce a better collectivization. But if we produce a better collectivization, it is more probable than not that the Russian system will incorporate our improvements, forget its reviving nationalism again, debunk Marx and Stalin, so far as they can be debunked, and merge into the one world state.[23]

The globalists don't want you to read your history, so they can lie to you about these figures of the past. One might say Wells was extremely naïve, and yet he was at the end of his life, and we'd expect somebody at that point to have an accurate view of the way in which the world works. The introduction to the 2022 edition of *The New World Order* describes exactly what Wells was trying to achieve in 1940.

> Wells asserts that there is only one chance for mankind to survive the current alarming calamities and artificial catastrophes: the total reorganization of global relations in the face of a selfish, ethnocentric mankind. He insists that the new age of fraternity must not tolerate sovereign nation-states, which might cause enmity between races and peoples, and independent rulers who might supervise the

> build-up to wars unleashed by them or their enemies, but rather led by social engineers pulling the levers of production within a system of mass collectivization. Utopian or dystopian? The reader can judge for himself whether the global Eden achieved through a bloodless world revolution is a beauty to behold and cultivate or a monstrosity to exorcise before it can germinate.[24]

Get rid of countries and have the social engineers in control of everything. So much for the idea that all people are created equal. You don't have the sense necessary to keep life going. It's almost as if the real-life Bond villain, Klaus Schwab, wrote that paragraph last week. Funny how Wells doesn't at least consider the possibility that all these authoritarians running governments around the world were the problem, rather than the people in these countries.

But just as Adam Smith stood in opposition to the East India Company, Wells had his nemesis, and his name was George Orwell, author of the dystopian novel, *1984*, which today reads like prophecy. On the love that many of his countrymen seemed to possess for Stalin's Russia and authoritarianism in general, this is what he wrote in an essay called "Inside the Whale."

> But there is one other thing that undoubtedly contributed to the cult of Russia during these years, and that is the softness and security of life itself. With all its injustices, England is still the land of habeas corpus, and the overwhelming majority of English people have no experience of violence of illegality. If you have grown up in that sort of atmosphere it is not at all easy to imagine what a despotic regime is like. Nearly all the dominant writers of the thirties belonged to the soft-boiled emancipated middle class and were too young to have effective memories of the Great War. To people of that kind such things as purges, secret police, summary executions, imprisonment without trial, etc., are too remote to be terrifying. They can swallow totalitarianism *because* they have no experience of anything except liberalism.[25]

Does what Orwell describes about 1940 England sound suspiciously like 2023 America? Populations which have grown up without real hardship or exposure to violence or illegality? Yes, there are certainly injustices, but compared to any other time in human history, the daily life of most people would have been considered paradise to previous centuries.

Because we read and know history, we can put things into context.

England created the corporation, married it to government power, and created an empire.

Because of freedom, the empire falls, and as a result, there is unparalleled prosperity, creating a robust middle-class dedicated to democratic values.

But some don't want freedom, claiming it's too messy and violent.

They want a new multi-national corporation, combined with world government, but they don't know how to make it work.

They see the example of Chairman Mao in China, and it becomes clear how to achieve their one-world government.

Provoke chaos, dissolve the bonds of society, and wait for the people to beg to be saved by the government.

* * *

This would be a good place to review how similar the silencing of renegade voices in our society mimics what happened in Mao's China. These renegades would include me, Black Nationalist leader Minister Louis Farrakhan, as well as my good friends, Paul Joseph Watson, Laura Loomer, and Milo Yiannopoulos. These are all people I'd love to go to a bar with and have some drinks and laughs, even though we know Minister Farrakhan would just be having a club soda.

Still, he'd be a great deal of fun.

I've interviewed Minister Farrakhan, spending several hours with him, and he is one of the nicest, most thoughtful people I've ever encountered. Many people don't know this because of all the negative publicity the Nation of Islam receives, but their beliefs don't allow them to carry weapons. They believe their only weapon should be the truth.

It's why the Nation encourages its members to read widely and think deeply about current problems. (The left now thinks that "reading" should be called "doing your own research" and apparently, they think it's as dangerous as smoking, and maybe controversial books like this one should come with a warning label.) The Nation of Islam also instructs their men to stand by their wives and families. Like me, the Nation of Islam believes the family to be the essential unit of society. When I think of all the harm our government has done to the black community by creating a welfare state, which incentivizes men to leave their children so the mother can collect a welfare check, I believe Farrakhan's example of Black pride and independence is something that should be commended.

Many of you may remember my Facebook banning, with articles like this from the *New York Times*.

> After years of wavering about how to handle the extreme voices populating its platform, Facebook on Thursday evicted seven of its most controversial users—many of whom are conservatives—immediately inflaming the debate about the power and accountability of large technology companies.
>
> The social network said it had barred Alex Jones, the conspiracy theorist and founder of InfoWars, from its platform, along with a handful of other extremists. Louis Farrakhan, the outspoken black nationalist minister who has frequently been criticized for his anti-Semitic remarks, was also banned. The Silicon Valley company said these users were disallowed from using Facebook and Instagram under its policies against "dangerous individuals and organizations."[26]

Let's consider how this "extreme voices" policy would have worked at various times in our history. Would Benjamin Franklin, John Adams, and Thomas Jefferson have been banned for being "extreme voices" against the British Empire?

Would the early abolitionists against slavery have been banned for being "extreme voices?" Would the suffragettes of the late nineteenth and early twentieth century have been banned for being "extreme voices?"

How about the Civil Rights protestors of the 1950s and 1960s, campaigning against the Jim Crow laws enacted by Democratic politicians of the Southern States? Would they have been banned for being "extreme voices?"

I know some may consider me a hero, but I like to consider myself as serving in a company of heroes, and the *New York Times* was kind enough to name some of these individuals.

> Many of the users barred by Facebook had previously been prohibited on other social media services. Mr. Yiannopoulos, a former Breitbart editor and far-right media personality, was banned from Twitter in 2016 after leading a harassment campaign against the actress Leslie Jones. Laura Loomer, a right-wing provocateur, was barred by Twitter earlier this year for making Islamophobic comments about Representative Ilhan Omar, Democrat of Minnesota.
>
> The others banned by Facebook on Thursday were Paul Joseph Watson, an Infowars contributor, and Paul Nehlen, a white nationalist, who ran unsuccessfully for Congress in 2018. Infowars [*sic*] was also booted.
>
> Mr. Watson said in a tweet that he was given no reason for his eviction by Facebook. "I broke none of their rules," he said. "In an authoritarian society controlled by a handful of Silicon Valley giants, all dissent must be purged." He also appealed to the president for help, complaining in a tweet that Facebook was "now just banning people for wrongthink," with "no pretense of enforcing rules."[27]

As you can probably guess, I know most of the names on that list, with the exception of Paul Nehlen, whom I suspect may be some sort of agent-provocateur working for the intelligence agencies, as many have claimed about David Duke. Isn't it odd that all the news outlets claim they don't want to give a "platform" to white supremacists (if any actually exist in the United States), but on the day of the Charlottesville riots, CNN aired a segment with former Ku Klux Klan leader David Duke?[28]

On a personal note, I have to tell you we have had people come work for us at *InfoWars*, whom we quickly came to suspect were agent-provocateurs from the intelligence agencies. They were so easy to spot. (Note to the spooks—Try to have a little more intelligence about who you send into our organizations.) They'd walk around our office, using the N-word, wanting to talk to other staff members about how blacks were inferior to whites, and trying to get me to say something to the hidden cameras or microphones that were undoubtedly concealed in their clothes.

At *InfoWars* we're a bunch of Christians, believing every person is a beloved child of God (even the agent-provocateurs sent by the intelligence agencies into *InfoWars*, whom hopefully in a few years, will, like Ted Gunderson, confess and spend the rest of their lives trying to atone for their crimes), so we quickly showed these people the door.

But Zuckerberg and his authoritarian Red Guards of the internet weren't satisfied with simply booting me from Facebook.

Taking me and the other individuals off Facebook came with an added bonus.

We could be targeted for violence by the Facebook community.

Here's the trick they tried to pull on everybody. Threats of violence are not allowed on Facebook, *unless* you are designated as a "Dangerous Individual or Organization." Let me reproduce the policy for you below, so that there can be no misunderstanding:

> Do not post: Threats that could lead to death (and other forms of high severity violence) of any target(s) where threat is defined as any of the following:
>
> - Statements of intent to commit high-severity violence; or
> - Calls for high-severity violence (unless the target is an organization or individual covered in the Dangerous Individuals and Organizations policy, is described as having carried out violent crimes or sexual offenses, wherein criminal/predator status has been established by media reports, market knowledge of news events, etc.)[29]

Now, do you think that after protests arose over this allowance of calls for political violence against people like me was simply a mistake, and when

Mark Zuckerberg heard about it, he shouted, "Oh my God! We can't do that! Why didn't my lawyers find this problem?"

I guess you're free to believe what you want. But for me, I believe this was what they really wanted to do but were only stopped when they got significant pushback.

I believe when people show you who they are, you should believe them.

When I accuse the Democratic Party or Mark Zuckerberg of worshipping at the altar of Mao Zedong, I am showing you exactly how they do it. The Red Guards of the Chinese Cultural Revolution were given no specific orders of who to go after. They simply urged people to root out the "enemy" among them, knowing that would unleash the demons lurking in the souls of people.

They loosened the rules of civilized society and released the darker angels of people's nature.

And besides being fined a billion and a half dollars, how much of a threat does the federal government seem to think I am? Well, here's the official organ of the Deep State, the *Washington Post*, telling the world on June 19, 2023, exactly what they were planning to do to me, in the wake of the federally inspired riot at the US Capitol on January 6, 2020.

> But a group of prosecutors led by J.P. Cooney, the head of the fraud and public corruption section at the U.S. Attorney's office, argued that the existing structure of the probe overlooked a key investigative angle. They sought to open a new front, partly based on publicly available evidence, including from social media, that linked some extremists involved in the riot to people in Trump's orbit—including Roger Stone, Trump's longest serving political adviser; Ali Alexander, an organizer of the "Stop the Steal" rally that preceded the riot; and Alex Jones, the Infowars host . . .
>
> Axelrod saw an uncomfortable analogy to Black Lives Matter protests that had ended in vandalism in D.C. and elsewhere a year earlier. "Imagine if we had requested membership lists for BLM" in the middle of the George Floyd protests, he would say later, people said.

> Axelrod later told colleagues that he knew Jan. 6 was an unprecedented attack, but he feared deviating from the standard investigative playbook—doing so had landed the DOJ in hot water before.[30]

The *Washington Post* article was long and detailed, and yet it had a curious omission. The piece was framed as the FBI wanting to pursue this investigation (against yours truly, as well as some of my very best friends), but conflicted by whether the agency would receive criticism for their actions. Nowhere in the article did I see any mention as to whether the FBI was concerned that they'd be violating the rights of citizens, like me or others.

They just worried about how it would look.

And what about the person or persons who planted the "pipe bombs" near the Capitol?[31] Don't we want them found and prosecuted?

But that question seems to have simply faded into the mist.

And why, in November 2022, when he testified before Congress, did FBI Director Christopher Wray refuse to say whether the FBI used confidential human sources, dressed up as Trump supporters to enter the Capitol, ahead of protestors?[32]

Should I feel comforted that some people at the FBI stopped this madness, or should I be terrified that there are people who wanted to pursue this insane policy, and they still work at the FBI? How long until the complete crazies have the majority? Why do we allow our federal agencies to lie and hide information from us? The government is no longer the servant of the people, but as Mao would have said, it is their master.

And what is to be done about all of this?

Choose peaceful noncompliance and walk away from their systems of control, even if it costs you something. But do not sell your soul. Because if you do, the price to get it back is exceedingly high, and you will be forever ashamed of your actions.

Trust that when you let go, when you refuse the enticements of evil, God will be there to catch you and guide you on a better path.

I cannot tell you what that exact path will be, but I know it will be shown to you. I'd like to give some of the final words in this chapter to Helen Pluckrose and James Lindsay from their excellent book, *Cynical*

Theories: How Activist Scholarship Made Everything about Race, Gender, and Identity—And Why This Harms Everybody:

> The answer to these problems isn't new, though, and perhaps that's why it isn't immediately gratifying. The solution is liberalism, both political (universal liberalism is an antidote to the postmodern political principle) and in terms of knowledge production (Jonathan Rausch's "liberal science" is the remedy for the postmodern knowledge principle). You don't need to become an expert on Jonathan Rausch's work, or on John Stuart Mill, or any of the great liberal thinkers. Nor do you need to become well versed in Theory and Social Justice scholarship, so that you can confidently refute it.
>
> But you do need to have a little bit of courage to stand up to something with a lot of power. You need to recognize Theory when you see it, and side with the liberal responses to it—which might be no more complicated than saying, "No, that's your ideological belief, and I don't have to go along with it."[33]

What do we need to do to win this fight?

We need to have a little curiosity about our world, going deeper than the headlines in the mainstream media and maybe reading the perspectives of those renegades out of favor with the current system.

We must have faith that, when we discern the correct path, God will help us remove the obstacles to living our most full, abundant, and joyful life.

And finally, we must have compassion for those who have made the mistake of choosing the Devil's Road. God can reach any heart, and hopefully we can be God's instruments in this world to rescue the souls who have fallen into darkness.

Let us search for the truth, find that better road, and travel it together, to that glorious world of abundance God has promised us.

Chapter Three

You Are Being Modified Against Your Will (and to What End?)

When I claim there's a globalist mad scientist conspiracy, people often ask, "Well, where's your proof, Alex?" How about we start with this from a 2016 *Marketplace* article about Matthew Liao, a bioethicist from New York University:

> Dr. S. Matthew Liao, a bioethicist at New York University, believes that solving climate change starts with the individual. That's why he suggests we turn humans into cat-eyed [less need for electric light], meat-allergic [we all become vegan], semi-genius, hobbit people [less need for resources].
>
> His proposal is dead serious, not a kind of Jonathon Swiftian exercise. And it has economic implications. It's centered around the idea that we have passed a point of no return with man-made climate change.
>
> There are a lot of ideas on the table when it comes to fighting the environmental impact of humans and technology. As we move further and further into a world where there is vast scientific consensus, and a paradoxical public resistance to that idea, the ideas are getting weirder and weirder.
>
> One idea floated by scientists is geo-engineering; shooting aerosols into the atmosphere and cooling the surface temperature. Another, boosted again this week by a $1 billion dollar investment fund led by Bill Gates, is clean energy innovation.

> Liao doesn't discount these, but he believes that in some ways that bioengineering our bodies is going to be part of the overall solution and be less dangerous than trying to change the entire planet's atmosphere with geo-engineering.[1]

These globalist mad scientists want to turn us into a race of cat-eyed, vegan, hobbit people because they think it's less dangerous than chemtrail skies or other global climate strategies, which are likely to go terribly wrong.

And what did Professor Liao, a favored intellectual of the World Economic Forum, say about a way to fight climate change by inducing people to have a red meat allergy?

> It turns out that we can use human engineering to help us address climate change . . . People eat too much meat, right? And if they were to cut down on their consumption of meat, it would actually help the planet. But people are not willing to give up meat . . . We can use human engineering to make it the case that we're intolerant to certain kinds of meat. That's something we can do through human engineering.[2]

The method by which they could achieve this madness is by inducing something called an alpha-gal allergy, usually acquired by a tick bite.[3] Alpha gal is a sugar molecule found in most mammals, and I will let you know I'm suspicious of the claim that one can get an alpha-gal allergy from consuming mammal meat. The digestive juices in the stomach and intestines are likely to break down the alpha-gal molecule.

That's basic biology.

But what is the closest analogy to a tick bite in our modern world, putting this molecule directly into the bloodstream, where it can cause damage?

A vaccine.

And isn't it curious that the CDC, on its own website, acknowledges that vaccines and other medicines contain this molecule? This is from the CDC website:

> Some medications and vaccines may contain small amounts of alpha-gal additives, stabilizers or coatings. **Not all patients with AGS react to these ingredients.** Lists of additives to specific vaccines (called vaccine excipients) are available through CDC's Pink Book and the Institute of Vaccine Safety. Ingredients that may contain alpha-gal include, but are not limited to:
>
> - Gelatin
> - Glycerin
> - Magnesium stearate
> - Bovine extract[4]

I understand there are a significant number of my viewers who may not understand why I am such a passionate critic of our current vaccines. It is because I have had countless conversations with leading scientists and other experts that have led me to conclude that all current vaccines are dangerous, and one should also avoid most pharmaceutical drugs.

Vaccines and most pharmaceutical drugs are being used by the globalists to soften up our defenses and eventually eliminate a fair portion of humanity.

You may think that's just too much, that people couldn't be that evil.

But consider bioethicist Matthew Liao, beloved figure of the globalists. He wants to turn you into a cat-eyed, hobbit-sized vegetarian, and because he's doing it in the service of fighting climate change, he'll feel good about it.

That is the pathology against which we are fighting.

* * *

Life is flexible.

I want you to understand why I believe this idea so strongly. The life force is so powerful that we, as biological organisms, can put up with a lot.

God has endowed His creatures with magnificent feedback systems to address the challenges they might face. Science has long held that humans come into this world as a *tabula rasa,* a blank slate, upon which the experiences of a lifetime make their mark. But can the experiences of our lives, whether it be fear, bravery, or cowardice, make a mark upon our offspring?

For decades, the idea of so-called "genetic memories" would have been heretical, and yet science today is showing that the experiences of one generation can be passed down to the next generation, as shown by a study of mice from 2013, which showed that certain fears can be passed down through the generation. An article in *Nature* explained the genesis of this research:

> Kerry Ressler, a neurobiologist and psychiatrist at Emory University in Atlanta, Georgia, and a co-author of the latest study, became interested in epigenetic inheritance after working with poor people in inner cities, where cycles of drug addiction, neuropsychiatric illness and other problems often seem to recur in parents and their children. "There's a lot of anecdotes to suggest that there's intergenerational transfer of risk, and that it's hard to break that cycle," he says.
>
> Studying the biological basis for those effects in humans would be difficult. So Ressler and his colleague Brian Dias opted to study epigenetic inheritance in laboratory mice trained to fear the smell of acetophenone, a chemical the scent of which has been compared to those of cherries and almonds. He and Dias wafted the scent around a small chamber, while giving small electric shocks to male mice. The animals eventually learned to associate the scent with pain, shuddering in the presence of acetophenone even without a shock.[5]

Although I'm not a "speciesist," it's difficult not to have a little sympathy for these male mice subjected to "small electric shocks." Yeah, the shocks were probably small to the researchers, but something different to the mice.

But the parallel to humans is clear. If one stimulus, such as a smell, is associated with pain, an organism will be terrified by the stimulus, regardless of whether that painful insult is ever delivered. This is much like Pavlov's dogs, salivating when they hear a bell, which they associate with being fed. We understand that idea, but what blew the researchers' minds was the understanding that such fears might get passed down through some mechanism in our genes.

> This reaction was passed on to their pups, Dias and Ressler report today in *Nature Neuroscience*. Despite never having encountered acetophenone in their lives, the offspring exhibited increased sensitivity when introduced to its smell, shuddering more markedly in its presence compared with the descendants of mice that had been conditioned to be startled by a different smell or that had gone through no such conditioning. A third generation of mice—the "grandchildren"—also inherited the reaction, as did mice conceived through in vitro fertilization with sperm from males sensitized to acetophenone. Similar experiments showed that the response can also be transmitted down from the mother.[6]

This is biological proof that the experiences of a lifetime can be passed down through the generations. The fears of the father or mother can be passed down to their offspring. While this is a robust demonstration of the idea that fear can be passed down to the children, does this same principle hold for things like courage, wisdom, and compassion?

I don't have enough evidence for a definitive answer, but if you look at things like generations of families who serve in the military, one might conclude it's likely that bravery, once expressed, will lead to offspring for whom such courage comes more easily than the rest of the general population.

How might such a trait work on a genetic level? The researchers had some clues and a possible explanation:

> The researchers propose that DNA methylation—a reversible chemical modification to DNA that typically blocks transcription of a gene without altering its sequence—explains the inherited effect. In the fearful mice, the acetophenone-sensing gene of sperm cells had fewer

> methylation marks, which could have led to greater expression of the odorant-receptor gene during development.
>
> But how the association of smell with pain influences sperm remains a mystery. Ressler notes that sperm cells express odorant receptor proteins, and that some odorants find their way into the bloodstream, offering a potential mechanism, as do small, blood-borne fragments of RNA known as microRNAs, that control gene expression.[7]

Isn't God's design for the success of his creations truly remarkable? If one slavishly followed Darwin's idea of natural selection, this result would be unbelievable. Darwin believed nature works only on a generational time scale, not within the lifespan of a single organism. If we accept the proposition that being made to fear something during one's lifespan has the ability to turn a gene on or off through the activity of microRNAs, it follows that all of our actions would have similar consequences for who we are.

Could it be that, in humans, our experiences and responses during our life are controlling the expression of our genes?

It would be unethical to perform these experiments on humans, but we do have such groups available for study: Holocaust survivors and their children. This research from 2016 is genuinely enlightening:

> Animal studies have demonstrated that epigenetic changes from stress exposure can be passed on to the offspring. In the new study, Yehuda and colleagues examine these relationships for the first time in humans, with methylation of FKBP5, a stress-related gene that has been associated with PTSD and depression. The researchers examined blood samples of 32 Holocaust survivors and 22 of their adult children, and Jewish parent-offspring control pairs for methylation of intron 7, a specific region within the FKBP5 gene.
>
> The analysis revealed that both Holocaust survivors and their offspring show epigenetic changes at the same site of FKBP5 intron 7, but in the opposite direction; Holocaust survivors had 10% higher

> methylation than control parents, whereas Holocaust offspring had 7.7% lower methylation than control offspring . . .
>
> John Krystal, Editor of Biological Psychiatry, noted that "the observation that the changes in parent and child are in opposing directions suggests that children of traumatized parents are not simply born with a PTSD-like biology. They may inherit traits that promote resilience as well as vulnerability."[8]

Do you want to know how mice and men are different? Think of the different outcomes between the two species. In one instance, the offspring inherit the fear from their parents.

But in human beings, it's likely that our brain allows us to come to terms with our trauma. For example, we can understand how somebody exposed to the horrors of the Holocaust would be permanently affected by that experience.

However, in addition to experiencing the horrors of the Holocaust, those who survived would know the satisfaction of liberation, as well as the subsequent prosecution of many of the top Nazis, the establishment of the state of Israel, and other positive developments for Jews.

In other words, they would experience both the horror and the hope.

The Holocaust survivors were likely to feel a measure of justice had been delivered to their oppressors, and it would make sense that this information would also be passed onto their children. Just as fear would leave a mark on their genetic code, justice might do something similar in the opposite direction. It might result in a person with a lower-than-average anxiety that good things will happen.

It could also trigger a victimology where the survivors and their offspring begin to see threats everywhere that may not exist. Many a historian has noted that oppressed groups, in many cases, will seek power from a position of fear, and will imitate the abuses done to them against completely innocent groups.

I am concerned that, in 2021, Prime Minister Benjamin Netanyahu was among the first world leaders to make a deal with Pfizer for the COVID-19 vaccines[9] and used strong government coercion to get people to take the shot.[10] And, of course, where did he deliver these remarks? At the 2021 Davos World Economic Forum where he said he hoped to make Israel a "world laboratory for herd immunity."[11] Doesn't human experimentation on such a vast scale sound like something we'd like to avoid?

Here are Netanyahu's own words from a December 2022 interview with Jordan Peterson on what he did:

> We came out of COVID first. I describe that in my book, my conversations with Albert Bourla [president of Pfizer] and I persuaded him to give tiny Israel the necessary vaccines to get out first from the COVID. And the reason I could do that is we have a database. 98% of our population has digitized medical records and a little card. And anywhere you go in any hospital in Israel, north or south, it doesn't make any difference.
>
> Boom! You punch it in and you know everything about this patient for the last twenty years. I said, we'll use that to tell you whether these vaccines, what they do to people. Not individual people, not with the individual identities, but statistically.
>
> What does it do to people with meningitis? What does it do to people with high blood pressure? You want to know that. Israel became, if you will, the laboratory for Pfizer. And that's how we did it.
>
> We gave the information to the world, not only published in medical magazines. That's the database we have. I intend to bring onto that database of personal medical records for entire populations, a genetic database. Genomes, okay? Give me a saliva sample. Voluntarily? But I'm sure most people would do it. Maybe we'll pay them.
>
> Now we have genetic records of a robust population. You have to have a diverse population. We have people from a hundred lands. This is a very powerful engine. Now let pharma companies, let medical companies, let them run algorithms on this database, okay? I'll tell you, they'll give preference for a few years to Israeli firms, and then to the world.

> But you can create a biotechnological industry that is unheard of, unimagined, even. And these are just examples. We can stave off Iran, become a light unto the nations, groundbreaking.[12]

It's stunning to understand how deluded Netanyahu is about turning his country over to the tender mercies of Pfizer. I can't see into his heart, but it seems like he just invited the wolves into the henhouse. Who knows to what terrors his decision will lead. It seems like Netanyahu is a leading cheerleader for a digital, totalitarian future, in which the State knows everything about you.

* * *

There's an anecdote that's often told in motivational business meetings about fleas. Part of the claim, which I can easily substantiate, is that fleas are the world's greatest jumpers, and that if a man possessed the jumping ability of a flea, he could easily jump over the Eiffel Tower in Paris, with an acceleration rate fifty times greater than a rocket taking off into space.[13] The claim that is often made in these motivational meetings is that fleas kept inside a jar with a lid will spend a couple days hitting the lid, and then stop jumping that high. As the story then goes, their offspring will also not jump higher than the lid, even if there is no lid present. I can't find any good information to corroborate the second part of this claim, but it feels accurate to me.

Whether the particulars of the flea story are accurate or not, it seems to me the main idea, specifically that we "adapt" to our environment, and that these adaptations may encode themselves in our genes, is likely to be true. It is for this reason that the thought we allow ourselves, as well as the limitations we place upon ourselves and our children, are likely to be of paramount importance.

We must also ask ourselves if there is perhaps some psychological and content knowledge, with which we are born, an instinctive body of knowledge we possess because of the experiences our ancestors have had. This possibility is suggested by research on so-called "idiot savants," who seem to know things they have never been taught. An opinion piece in *Science* from 2015 explored this possibility.

> Steven Pinker's 2003 book, *The Blank Slate: The Modern Denial of Human Nature*, refutes the "blank slate" theories of human development. Brian Butterworth, in his 1999 book, *What Counts: How Every Brain is Hardwired for Math*, points out that babies have many specialized innate abilities, including numerical ones that he attributes to a "number module" encoded in the human genome from ancestors 30,000 years ago . . .
>
> Whether called genetic, ancestral or racial memory, or congenital gifts, the concept of a genetic transmission of sophisticated knowledge well beyond instincts, is necessary to explain how prodigious savants can know things they never learned.[14]

Let's consider the plans set up by people like Yuval Noah Harari and his fellow confederates at the World Economic Forum.

Might there be something "fixed" about human nature, such as male and female, or how much we wouldn't like to become a cyborg?

Could concepts like respect for each other, the need to honor our parents, and the demonstrated superiority of the two-parent family be something that is genetically encoded in us? Before you reject this idea out of hand, I encourage you to consider the following passage:

> Finally, the animal kingdom provides examples of complex inherited capacities beyond physical characteristics. Monarch butterflies each year make a 2,500-mile journey from Canada to a small plot of land in Mexico where they winter. In spring they begin the long journey back north, but it takes three generations to do so. So no butterfly making the return journey has flown that entire route before. How do they "know" a route they never learned? It has to be an inherited GPS-like software, not a learned route.
>
> Oscine birds such as sparrows, thrushes and warblers learn their songs from listening to others. Suboscine species, such as flycatchers

> and their relatives, in contrast, inherit all the genetic instructions they need for these complex arias. Even if raised in sound-proof isolation, the suboscine birds can give the usual call for their species with no formal training or learning. There are so many more examples from the animal kingdom in which very complex traits, behaviors, and skills are inherited and innate. We call those instincts in animals, but we haven't applied this concept to the complex inherited skills and knowledge in humans.[15]

While one might think the limited instance of savants may be limited to those with some type of inherited brain abnormality, the article goes on to state that there are numerous examples of otherwise normal humans, who suffer some sort of brain injury, who immediately develop these savant characteristics in math, music, or some other domain.[16] This supports my idea that there is something fixed, or preordained, in the human mind—call it culture or our hardwiring about how we are supposed to organize ourselves in society—that will defy attempts by anybody to alter it.

Could this be the fatal flaw of the globalists?

They think they can change human behavior (and to some extent I believe they can), but there may be certain immutable characteristics of the human constitution that will forever frustrate them.

Their plans can work, but only for a time.

Then those plans fall disastrously apart.

Consider the innate fear response of ducks to the shape of a hawk flying above them, from this famous experiment in 1959:

> Mallard clucks were reared in a highly restricted environment from hatching until testing began at 25 days of age; the stimuli presented were moving cardboard models resembling a "hawk" or "goose" in flight. Those ducks who had earlier experience with "flying" models showed no fear when the same models were presented in a series of tests. Ducks that had no early experience with the models showed marked fear of the models initially, regardless of shape. There was significantly more fear of the hawk than the goose model in the second

> series of presentations. But habituation to both models occurred quickly, and fear responses to the cardboard models "flying" were not elicited after the third day of testing. The results indicate that both inherited and environmental factors collaborate in the genesis of the fear of visual patterns presented by predatory birds.[17]

There are so many intriguing parts to this research. Again, we have this transmission of knowledge across the generations, and yet life must also be designed for changed conditions. It makes sense that ducks would come "pre-loaded" with information telling them to fear hawks. But nature works on models of efficiency.

If hawks stop being a problem, the organism should be able to process that new information and make a different choice. One would assume the ability to learn, and have that be reflected somehow in your genes, would also work if some new threat came upon the scene. In other words, living organisms undergo genetic changes (maybe just in their microRNA, or some other part we don't fully understand) due to the environment in which they find themselves.

One could imagine this means that humans enter this world with some general understandings of how to interact with other human beings, perhaps some hardwired math and language skills, and a likely drive to pair with a member of the opposite sex for the purpose of creating an intimate bond, which will include the raising of children.

But we would also need to be flexible. Let's say there's a famine, natural disaster, or a time of protracted warfare. During those times, will humans look to creating those bonds with the same intensity, or will those desires be subsumed so that the problem will consume most of their attention? It sounds like a wonderfully designed system, providing one some roadmap of what would be helpful in life, and yet also allowing some flexibility in the system.

However, there are limits.

Will animals continue to live in ways that will bring about collapse of the species, and if so, what might some of those ways look like?

It seems the attempt to create a utopia, without struggle, is one of the easiest ways to bring about societal collapse. In a famous series of experiments in 1968, biologist John Calhoun built a colony a large pen with what he believed would be the perfect environment for a colony of rats, with no predators and abundant food. It turns out struggle is necessary for the survival of a species, as well as for individual happiness. These "utopias" kept collapsing. This is part of what he wrote about the collapse of the twenty-fifth mouse utopia:

> Rodents have social hierarchies, with dominant alpha males controlling harems of females. Alphas establish dominance by fighting—wrestling and biting any challengers. Normally a mouse that loses a fight will scurry off to some distant nook to start over elsewhere.
>
> But in mouse utopia, the losing mice couldn't escape. Calhoun called them "dropouts." And because so few juveniles died, huge hordes of dropouts would gather in the center of the pen. They were full of cuts and ugly scars, and every so often huge brawls would break out—vicious free-for-alls of biting and clawing that served no obvious purpose. [In other words, mouse ANTIFA.] It was just senseless violence. (In earlier utopias involving rats, some dropouts turned to cannibalism.)[18]

The intent of these mouse utopias was to see if they might serve as models for urban planning, as both rodents and humans share many behavioral characteristics. Instead, it seemed to simply prove as dangerous most progressive ideas for the improvement of society. Think of the "frontier" or how in traditional conservative ideology there are "wild places" where one may be alone with one's own thoughts. The existence of such places is necessary for our mental health.

Young males who have not achieved what they want should not be forced together with other similarly low-status males. That is a recipe for disaster. Ideally, those young males who don't succeed at first need to be alone, to figure out how to eventually prevail with what they want to accomplish in life, and then reengage in the fight.

And is there a better demonstration of bad social planning than young groups of males simply fighting with each other for no reason? As Canadian intellectual Jordan Peterson likes to say, young males need a purpose in life. A society filled with young men who have no purpose is a dangerous society.

That's why what we have done in society has made all our lives so much more dangerous. We have created the expression "toxic masculinity" and no model for what is "healthy masculinity." And why is there no societal discussion of "toxic femininity?" If we have the idea for one gender, shouldn't we have it for the other? Male and female strengths should be celebrated, and not just when some man decides to become a woman so he can dominate a particular sport and be named "Woman of the Year." Let's dig a little more deeply into the societal collapse of this mouse utopia:

> Alpha males struggled, too. They kept their harems in private apartments, which they had to defend from challengers. But given how many mice survived to adulthood, there were always a dozen hotshots ready to fight. The alphas soon grew exhausted, and some stopped defending their apartments altogether.
>
> As a result, apartments with nursing females were regularly invaded by rogue males. The mothers fought back, but often to the detriment of their young. Many stressed-out mothers booted their pups from the nest early, before the pups were ready. A few even attacked their own young or abandoned them while fleeing to different apartments, leaving the pups to die of neglect.[19]

To listen to progressives, one would think that all you need to do is disrupt things at the top and we'll all be so much better. But look at how you disturb the system, and you create a cascade of unintended consequences. The alphas are exhausted from fighting too much, and the females get bothered so consistently by rival males that they do a bad job of raising their offspring, and everything begins to fall apart. It doesn't make sense to participate in such a poorly functioning society, and many mice make the decision to opt out.

> Eventually other deviant behavior emerged. Mice who had been raised improperly or kicked out of the nest early failed to develop healthy social bonds, and therefore struggled in adulthood with social interactions. Maladjusted females began isolating themselves like hermits in empty apartments—unusual behavior among mice. Maladjusted males, meanwhile, took to grooming all day—preening and licking themselves hour after hour. Calhoun called them "the beautiful ones." And yet, even while obsessing over their appearance, these males had zero interest in courting females, zero interest in sex.[20]

Does that sound like human society in 2023, rather than a rat colony in 1968? Yeah, I'm having some trouble understanding the differences, as well: kids who don't know how to interact or play like children (thanks, social media), women who aren't interested in sex (and yet are strangely so passionate about abortion), and men who aren't doing their jobs as husbands or fathers. I've heard it said by people like cartoonist Scott Adams (another de facto tribe member of the banished) that marriage just isn't a good deal for men these days. What do they get out of it? Somebody who values them? Somebody who will stick with them to the end?

A long-term relationship with a member of the opposite sex is the ultimate experience of diversity, because men and women are so different, and yet complementary to each other. If you haven't had the pleasure (or the pain sometimes), it's the greatest ride of your life. Not for the faint of heart! In marriage, there are no safe spaces, believe me.

Women may have gotten the idea from progressives that the attack on the patriarchy would be some sort of panacea of unlimited riches, but it didn't work out very well in the mouse utopia, and it's unlikely to be any different for humans.

> Between the lack of sex, which lowered the birth rate, and inability to raise pups properly, which sharply increased infant mortality, the population of Universe 25 began to plummet. By the 21st month, newborn pups rarely survived more than a few days. Soon, new

> births stopped altogether. Older mice lingered for a while—hiding like hermits or grooming all day—but eventually they died out as well. By spring 1973, less than five years after the experiment started, the population had crashed from 2,200 to 0. Mouse heaven had gone extinct.[21]

Does that sound like the bleakest future possible? Complete extinction. And while I know there will always be pockets of strong individuals (like my native Texas, although I'm growing worried about Austin), one need only look at the urban cities of America to see a similar sort of social collapse. And how did John Calhoun view the results of his work?

> Calhoun's big takeaway involved status. Again, the males who lost the fights for dominance couldn't leave to start over elsewhere. As he saw it, they were stuck in pathetic, humiliating roles and lacked a meaningful place in society. The same went for females when they couldn't nurse or raise pups properly. Both groups became depressed and angry and began lashing out. In other words, because mice are social animals, they need meaningful social roles to feel fulfilled. Humans are social animals as well, and without a meaningful role, we too can become hostile and lash out.[22]

What would happen to John Calhoun today if he published his work? Would he be accused of supporting the patriarchy, rather than simply being interested in learning the truth? Or would they criticize the diversity of his mouse population? Were there sufficient numbers of black mice in the sample, because perhaps among mice there might also be white supremacist ideals.

However, I don't view this research as being about the role of males in a society, but how we have healthy populations. The males get to fight for dominance, but after that has been established, a certain order prevails.

Those who lose the fight for dominance are free to leave and seek out new domains. Males who can't yet establish a place for themselves can strike out for new territories where they might be successful.

The females have the luxury of knowing who the superior males are with whom to mate, to give their offspring the best chance of survival. And with the hierarchies established, the females are free to give their offspring the attention they need to continue the species. They don't get bothered by the male riffraff.

Everybody wins.

But doesn't it seem in our modern world that everybody is losing?

Males (or females) at the top of our modern hierarchy have less security and more stress, caring for children has become so much more problematic, and disillusioned young men without a purpose retreat into porn, video games, practices like transgenderism or polyamory, and sometimes, shooting up those places, like their former schools, which they believe lie at the root of their problems.

Isn't it time we talked about these problems, and maybe did something about them?

* * *

Let's look at one of the greatest recent failures of the globalists, the spectacular implosion of Mark Zuckerberg's plan to create an immersive digital world in which the "useless eaters" envisioned by Yuval Noah Harari will want to spend their lives, while also being kept docile with drugs. An article from *CNBC* detailed this multi-billion-dollar folly:

> Mark Zuckerberg's dream of a future in the metaverse is costing investors a boatload of money.
>
> In its earnings report after the bell on Wednesday, Meta said its Reality Labs division, home to the company's virtual reality technologies and projects, posted a $4.28 billion operating loss in the fourth quarter, bringing its total for 2022 to $13.72 billion.
>
> It was a tough first full year for the new Meta, the company formerly known as Facebook. In late 2021, Zuckerberg changed the company's name and said its future would be in the metaverse, a digital universe where people will work, shop, play and learn.[23]

Just think of what good might have been done with more than $13.72 billion dollars. Hell, that could have paid off all my legal bills and fines, and still left Zuckerberg with a little more than twelve billion dollars!

And if you found the loss of more than thirteen billion dollars to be an inconceivable defeat, that was just the start of the problems, as reported by the *New York Times* in February 2023. You see, when the globalists start losing, it just keeps getting worse.

> Meta, the company formerly known as Facebook, suffered its biggest one-day wipeout ever on Tuesday as its stock plummeted 26 percent and its market value plunged by more than $230 billion.
>
> Its crash followed a dismal earnings report on Wednesday, when Mark Zuckerberg, the chief executive, laid out how the company was navigating a tricky transition from social networking toward the so-called virtual world of the metaverse. On Thursday, a company spokesman reiterated statements from its earnings announcement and declined to comment further.[24]

Call me immature, but if I'd been in that press conference, I'd keep asking, "Can you repeat that number again? I thought you said more than $230 billion dollars."

When they provided the number, I'd reply, "I'm not sure my hearing is very good. It sounded like you said you lost more than $230 billion dollars."

After their confirmation, I'd ask, "Did you just say in a single day you lost more than $230 billion dollars in value? Is that correct?"

I think you get the idea. I'd play that joke as long as I could.

Maybe two or three hours.

When you find yourself worried about the enemy we face, I want you to remember the alien android, Mark Zuckerberg, is one of their champions. The guy who destroyed more than $230 billion dollars in value for his company in a single day.

It's almost as if God has placed them in their positions to make these stupid decisions.

Humanity has a very bright future if these are our enemies.

The world these idiots want to build, plugging you into video games while they give you drugs, isn't even a winning short-term strategy. It's said that intellectuals know everything, except what's important, such as what's good for human beings. What's the effect on a typical person living in Mark Zuckerberg's Metaverse for just a week? Shouldn't Zuckerberg have known that before he chose to spend billions of dollars on the effort? Scientists in England and Germany looked into that question:

> The study, conducted by researchers from a number of European institutions including Coburg University in Germany and Cambridge University in the U.K., compared the experiences of 16 university staff or researcher participants who spent a 35-hour workweek in normal, physical office spaces, and another week doing the same work in virtual reality.
>
> The researchers wrote that working in VR for a week resulted in "significantly worse ratings across most measures" for participants, particularly in terms of health effects and productivity.
>
> Employees' anxiety over their job increased by 19% when working in the metaverse, while their perception of their workload grew by 35% relative to the week spent in a physical office, despite researchers ensuring that workloads in the virtual and physical workweeks were similar. Additionally, workers reported their "frustration" with being unable to complete work in a timely or efficient manner increased by 42% while in VR, while self-reported productivity fell by 16%.[25]

Way to go, Zuckerberg! In a week you made these employees 42 percent more frustrated that they weren't accomplishing their work, and their self-reported productivity fell by 16 percent. This might be the worst idea in all of business history.

I'm sure Zuckerberg's investors are happy they followed him off that cliff.

And if the initial effects of the virtual world appear to be so harmful, what about the effects of social media on children, led by the very same Mark Zuckerberg, but added to by such applications as Snapchat, Instagram, and the Chinese app, TikTok? Here's one of the first studies of its kind, from 2019, which was published in the *Journal of American Pediatrics*. The title of the article is "Association of Screen Time and Depression in Adolescence" and in the discussion section the authors wrote:

> To our knowledge, this study is the first to use developmental data from a large sample of adolescents to examine the association between 4 types of screen time and depression. We found that high mean levels of social media over 4 years and any further increases in social media use in the same year were associated with increased depression. We also demonstrated that the tendency to engage in high mean levels of television over 4 years was associated with less depression. However, any further increase in television use in the same year was associated with increased depression.[26]

In plain English, what this means is that any use of social media leads to increased depression among adolescents. For television, the picture is mixed. It appears some television-watching, even an initial high level, is associated with less depression. This might be explained by the fact that television has the potential to allow us into the lives of other individuals, or, based upon our viewing habits, explore our interests to our heart's content, like binge-watching all seasons of *Ancient Aliens* or *The Real Housewives of Beverly Hills*. But increasing television usage, meaning you've likely got nothing else to do in your day, leads to increased depression. The discussion continued:

> Furthermore, we showed that high mean levels of computer use over 4 years are associated with increased depression; however, any further increase in computer use in the same year is not associated with increased depression. Furthermore, videogaming is not associated with depression. Finally, post hoc analyses reveal that self-esteem, but not exercise, is associated with depression and adolescence and

> that only social media and television have a time-varying negative association with self-esteem (within person association).[27]

A picture emerges of how the human adolescent could best manage our new digital media landscape.

First, stay off social media. Any usage appears to be harmful to young people, and probably adults.

Second, moderating television watching is probably good for you. If you watch too much television, that probably suggests there are other problems. (Like maybe not having a job?)

Third, high computer usage seems to bring about depression, but it levels off. Maybe we need to keep the adolescents off the computers as much as possible, and into after-school activities with others.

And in what might be the most surprising result, videogames do not appear to be correlated with increased depression. I have some of my own thoughts on this finding.

Consider the typical videogame that teenage boys typically play. They're a liberal nightmare. They aren't about kindness and cooperation. They're about driving a car as fast as possible, surviving a zombie apocalypse, or killing terrorists. Have I pretty much covered the waterfront?

For better or worse, finding the limits of machines or protecting others, is a male virtue. That's the story countless teenage boys have been told in these games. Their skill and bravery are what will make the difference to the future.

The only problem with these games is that when the teenage boys step out into the real world, they're told that these virtues are not wanted.

The solution isn't to tell young boys that those games are bad. We should look upon them just as we do initiation rites in primitive tribes, then tell them that the virtues of these games are needed when they become men.

Those virtues will be needed for humanity to be safe, for their wives and daughters to be protected, and for the next generation to have a "safe space" so they can grow to maturity and take their place in society.

* * *

What might some of the positive things be that you can do on a regular basis to fully express your humanity?

You can laugh and joke with your fellow citizens, take some time to pray every day, reflect on those who have done good things for you in the past, and thank them either in person, over a call, maybe in a text, or if they're no longer around, send up a thought or prayer and trust that it will somehow find them.

In other words, how do you respond to a corrupt world?

Try to be the best person you can be. Be joyful, knowing God created the universe and everything in it, and the globalists can only hope to be parasites in this beautiful world. And let's investigate building positive human communities, where free speech is not only permitted, but celebrated, and we share the common values of family, honesty, and integrity. The globalists are terrified of humans joining together, men and women, people of all colors and creeds, because those things that connect us are so much stronger than any of our differences.

Here's a suggestion from the *Wall Street Journal*. Go for a walk in nature with a friend.

> A brisk walk in nature with a friend combines three of the most effective stress-reducing and resilience building techniques, according to psychologists and scientific research: physical exercise, social connection, and spending time in nature. The activity works by helping normalize the hormonal changes that result from chronic stress and boosting the emotional resources that help us cope.
>
> "Even if it's just 20 minutes around your neighborhood, [the walk] is good for you physically, immunologically, especially when you do it with someone else," says Helen L. Coons, associate professor and clinical health psychologist in the department of psychiatry at the University of Colorado Anschutz Medical Campus.[28]

There's my advice to you at the end of this chapter.

Go for a walk with a friend and have a satisfying conversation.

I want you to be strong for the battles ahead.

If you can't go for a walk with a friend, take some time for yourself now and do something you enjoy.

I'll be waiting here for you when you get back.

But don't take too long. We have a world to save.

Chapter Four

They Want You to Be a Teenager on an Allowance (and That's Just the Beginning)

Money is freedom.

I know the more common expression is "money is power," but I'd like you to consider the idea through my reframing of the concept.

You may remember being a kid on a weekly allowance, and while you were delighted by the things you might buy with your newfound wealth, like candy, soda, music, or video games, you came to realize it was also a source of control by your parents.

You didn't want to put that weekly income at risk, because then how would you get your favorite candy or "cool new thing" you absolutely had to have?

Many have had the experience of being a teenager and getting some crappy low-paying job like delivering pizza or working at the checkout stand of your local pharmacy, and you felt that excellent rush of having more freedom. You didn't have to depend as much on your parents.

And whether you went to college or started your working career at eighteen, there came that wonderful moment when you were free of all financial ties from your family and could be the captain of your own ship. For most people, this allows them to take a fresh look at their parents, seeing them as individuals who were doing the best they could at the time, often under difficult circumstances, to raise decent and honorable human beings.

For most people, freedom and growing up allows them to have a better relationship with their parents than when they were dependent upon them.

That's because the human soul inherently desires freedom as the way to live an authentic and fulfilled life. We want to make our own choices, free from coercion, and after that point, we'll figure out who is, and who is not, a genuine friend.

Let's talk about the idea that money is freedom when you're an adult.

Imagine one individual stuck in a crappy job, living from paycheck to paycheck. He's got less than a thousand dollars in the bank. Is he free? Can he tell his boss to "take this job and shove it"?

Not without putting himself under immediate financial pressure.

Imagine the same individual in the same job, but he's got two years' worth of salary in the bank. The situation is much different. He can walk away from that job. Hell, he's likely to be whistling and skipping as he does it, a big grin on his face.

Money allows you to be free.

The globalists want you to be poor and dependent on them, so like an employee living paycheck to paycheck or a teenager on an allowance, you won't raise a ruckus when they try to implement their totalitarian plans.

But unlike most parents, who are simply trying to get their kids through their teens and early twenties without making terrible mistakes, the globalists don't ever want you to be become free of their control. And if you attempt to be free of them, they just may try to kill you.

* * *

Most Americans revere the courage of General George Washington, who led the ragtag American army against the soldiers of the British Army, the greatest fighting force in the world at that time.

But here's something you may not know about George Washington.

He was one of Pre-Revolutionary War America's richest individuals, with a net worth estimated at $587 million dollars today.[1] In addition to not taking a salary for being commander-in-chief of the Continental

Army, he paid a number of expenses to keep the fledgling force together, eventually submitting a bill for his expenses of $160,074,[2] or about four and a half million dollars in today's money.

That's not even considering the likelihood that, if he'd lost the Revolutionary War, he would have been hung as a traitor and all of his assets would have been seized by the British Crown.

It's a poorly understood fact, but the more money you have, the greater your freedom.

And what do we have in America today?

This is from a recent article in *Fortune*:

> According to Bankrate's Annual Emergency Fund Report, 68% of people are worried that they wouldn't be able to cover their living expenses for just one month if they lost their primary source of income. And when push comes to shove, the majority (57%) of U.S. adults are currently unable to afford a $1,000 emergency expense.[3]

Is it clear how financial insecurity is leading toward an erosion of our freedoms? Fearful people don't take risks. They hunker down.

A population fearful and worried about not having enough money to live for a month is going to be a population that submits to an experimental vaccine for which the makers have no liability.

A fearful population is less likely to think and weigh the issues, or even ask for more information, before agreeing to the government's plan to avoid the looming danger, whether that be COVID-19, the climate crisis, or white supremacy. How do you keep people from thinking? Terrify them with some existential threat.

The disillusionment of the middle class over their declining standard of living is real. Take jobs away and ship them overseas, and you get increased alcohol and drug use and all of the attendant problems. How can you think about the problems of your community when you're worried about your family blowing apart from drug addiction?

In my opinion, this is the plan to keep us divided. I had money, more than enough to keep running *InfoWars* and being a thorn in the side of the Deep State establishment, and what did they do? They came up with a case about something I apologized for years ago and slapped me with more than a billion and a half in damages.

Do you think I've felt like a free man?

I have not, but for me it's not about the money. It's about the message, the people, and the obligation I owe to God that, while I live on this Earth, I am going to do my very best to do His will.

Money is also communication. If you don't have it, you're not going to be heard by those in power. If you are in a position of financial weakness, you don't have much of a voice. And you have a false friend in the Democrats, who only want you more dependent on the federal government.

Here's the thing about money. Money allows you to make money. It allows you to take risks on good people and their ideas. Money allows you to provide safety and stability for your family. If you aren't in panic mode, you have the space to cultivate wisdom and discernment.

The whole idea of the American Dream is that anybody can start with nothing and rise to be affluent. We have prided ourselves in America that, unlike other countries, we do not have a class or caste system. The son of a plumber can become a billionaire.

But is that true anymore?

Or are we being systematically deceived about the path to success, and led into the box canyon of debt and despair, from which so many are clamoring for rescue?

The media would have you believe that the path to success begins with education, namely an undergraduate degree at least, and if you really want to increase your odds of success, a graduate degree from a prestigious university.

But the government has flooded the education system with money (ostensibly because they wanted to "help"), and the result has been a catastrophic increase in tuition for those students. Colleges and universities don't have to "compete" for student dollars; they just get to suck on the big, milk-filled breast of the government. (Of course, those colleges and universities are now financially tied to the government, so when the government says, "We think it's a good idea to give an untested COVID vaccine to your students," the only response they give is "How many doses?")

In addition to having the colleges and universities dancing to their tune, the government gets to enmesh itself in the lives of these college students, starting at the age of eighteen. How's that for a great choice?

Beg from your parents, or get the money from Uncle Sam, who you'll be paying off for decades. Maybe you could join the military (but you'll still be forced to get those shots), or you could work at a minimum wage job.

But because the price of tuition has gone up so much because of the government's actions, your minimum wage job won't be enough to pay for college.

Is our entire financial system built on an unstable foundation?

Between 1905 and 2008 we printed roughly a trillion dollars in this country, but by 2023, that number had ballooned to over $8 trillion dollars, according to the Federal Reserve's own numbers.[4] (This includes currency in circulation, cash in banks and ATMs, as well as the creation of bank electronic reserves, or money that does not exist in physical form, but only within the computer systems of the various financial institutions.)

That's right, the Federal Reserve, with the clapping approval of both Republicans and Democrats, just magically made all that money appear, like champagne wishes and caviar dreams.

Do we have any idea what our currency is actually worth?

And the ideas just keep getting worse. Because the United States government allows the printing of money like a crazy person, the banks decide they want to get in on the action as well. You used to believe the banks were places with big, impressive vaults, and you imagined bank robbers wanting to break into those vaults, maybe by tunneling in like some criminal mastermind.

But if you looked in those vaults today, they'd be empty.

The requirements for actual physical assets to be held by banks has dwindled to the point of insanity. It's all digital, don't you know? Banks are working with each other on creating digital currency, and they're looking to enslave you in this scheme as well.

And do you have any faith in those financial hucksters on television, trying to dazzle you with expressions like "investment portfolio," and "wealth management?" They want you to make choices which will give them even greater control.

How do you begin to fight back against this avalanche of misinformation?

By understanding how it all started.

* * *

Let's begin with a brief history of money.

Money is supposed to be a representation of value. In other words, while the money itself is just a coin or piece of paper, with the raw materials likely costing just a few pennies, it represents the value of some physical, tangible asset. Countries traded their currencies with each other, and there was an understanding of what the value was, based on the tangible assets of the country, which for the most part was gold.

However, in 1913, Congress passed the Federal Reserve Act, which took the United States off the gold standard for transactions that took place in America.[5] That meant the Federal Reserve had the ability to print money, if necessary; but to its credit, it did so sparingly in the decades that followed, even during World War II, relying more on taxation and domestic borrowing.[6] However, international trade could still be settled in gold, and this was believed to add to the stability of the global trade system.

It's understandable that as World War II ended, with the economies of so many nation's ruined, there would be a move to establish a single currency as the reserve currency for the rest of the world.

Protected from the ravages of war by the Atlantic and Pacific Oceans, the United States was the logical choice to be this reserve currency. And in July 1944, the Bretton-Woods Act made the US dollar the reserve currency for the rest of the world.[7]

Besides the fact that the United States escaped the destruction visited upon Europe and Asia, it had a stable political structure, which many might say was a proxy for their financial stability. This was an ideal state of affairs for the United States, allowing gold to be the universally recognized measure of trade between nations, while also allowing the United States to have some flexibility in their domestic spending.

I encourage you to view this as handing a credit card to your sixteen-year-old child as he or she starts to drive, while also monitoring monthly expenses to make sure spending does not get out of control. You want that credit to be available to your child in case of an emergency, like their car breaking down and they need to pay for a tow, but you've made it clear there's to be no reckless spending.

But let's say that kid is graduating college, you've seen years of responsible behavior, and you're not monitoring things as closely as when they first got the card.

In 1971, France wanted some debts paid back by the United States, and they wanted to be paid in gold. Nixon said, "No, we're going to pay you in dollars," and that's what happened. He closed the gold window.[8] Nixon replaced the gold standard with the petro dollar, while maintaining the US dollar as the world's reserve currency.[9]

This had the unintended consequence of meaning that all international settlements in oil had to be traded in US dollars. The only way this could be done was for the United States to print more money than it needed domestically. When you consider all the countries that need to purchase oil, that means you need to print a massive amount of dollars. That allowed our debt to explode, to the point where it's at more than thirty-one trillion dollars.[10]

That might not be as bad if our country had a strong growth rate, but that isn't happening. We've lost our dynamism. Instead of a vibrant economy, we've got declining wages, rising inflation, rising taxes, and rising interest rates. As I said before, 58 percent of Americans are living paycheck to paycheck, meaning they're about a month away from needing to file for bankruptcy. Who's being served by this state of affairs?

The government is being served because the populace is terrified and looking for reassurance from them. (Can I get me a little universal basic income?) But the banks are making out like bandits because guess who's reaping the benefits of those higher interest rates? Does the disillusionment of our young make more sense now and why they might be falsely led to the idol of progressivism and a government that they expect will care for them from cradle to grave?

What they do not fully understand is how government decisions have deformed genuine free-market capitalism and merit-based success into a cruel crony capitalism. This arrangement benefits the wealthy by creating a form of corporate socialism on one hand, and a crushing economic burden on the middle and lower class struggling to improve their financial status on the other.

Instead, we have a system that combines the worst parts of capitalism and the worst parts of socialism, and this monstrosity has no moral or religious compass. It is a profoundly anti-human system, which can only result in enormous suffering.

Don't be distracted by the players, whether it's Janet Yellen running the Federal Reserve, or Lawrence Powell, or Ben Bernanke, or Alan Greenspan. It's the system in which they're allowed to operate that is the problem. From what I've known of major players behind the scenes, I suspect if you got any of these Federal Reserve types behind closed doors, they'd agree with a lot of what I'm saying. I've heard it said by Ivy League economists with impeccable credentials that there really aren't "liberal" economists who are respected by the field, only conservative economists who, if they subject themselves to the political process, try mostly without success to limit the damage done by politicians of both political stripes.

And so, what does the rest of the world do when they see this reckless behavior by the United States, who has the eight-hundred-pound club when it comes to economics, while they only have a BB gun?

They try to create a new global reserve currency.

That's where the so-called BRICS nations (Brazil, Russia, Iran, China, and South Africa) enter the picture. Collectively, all these nations have a larger economy than the United States, but individually they suffer from the problem of political instability. However, that risk is mitigated because it's shared among the six nations. What's the probability of all six nations undergoing political turmoil at the same time?

Most people would see that risk as low, and I'd have to agree.

Given current conditions, this is likely to be disastrous for the United States because these countries will kick the US dollar to the curb, collapsing this house of cards.

And the BRICS countries have logical reasons for wanting to displace the US dollar as the reserve currency for global trade. The United States has not acted honorably in many instances, irresponsibly using their status as the reserve currency of the world to spend in ways that would make a drunken sailor blush.

But the question is, what will the BRICS nations do?

Will they act against the genuine interests of the United States?

Despite what my critics might say, I am not a simple black and white thinker. Just because I may challenge the actions of the United States does not mean I believe all the other nations of the world are filled with virtue. As the most profound psychology and philosophy tells us, we are all composed of darkness and light. The challenge of our existence on this plane of being is to cultivate the good, while weeding out the bad. The wisdom of the oath elected officials take before assuming office, when they swear to defend the Constitution against "all enemies, foreign and domestic," bears witness to this profound spiritual truth.

What is the emerging outline of how the replacement of the US dollar as the reserve currency of the world might look?

Brazil recently signed a bilateral trade agreement with China, with the exchange being paid for in the Chinese yuan, rather than American dollars.[11] Saudi Arabia, Iran, and Russia signed a trilateral trade agreement and decided the transaction would be in Russian rubles.[12] In December 2022, because of the Russian invasion of Ukraine, Japan joined other G7 nations in pledging not to pay more than sixty dollars a barrel for Russian oil, as a way to punish Russian President Vladimir Putin.[13]

But with the price of oil hovering at just a little under eighty dollars a barrel, Putin just shrugged his shoulders and decided to find other buyers.

And what was the result?

In April 2023, Japan decided they were going to buy Russian oil at the market rate.[14] What happened to this wonderful accord among the G7 nations?

The fact is it didn't make sense because the world needed Russian oil. Russia had the advantage, and Putin knew it. That's what happens when the people choose Joe Biden (maybe they did, maybe they didn't), and he decides to drastically cut domestic oil production. Some of you may think I'm beating a dead horse. But if Trump had been reelected, he would have kept producing domestic oil, and the world price for a barrel would be much lower. And Putin wouldn't have had the money to finance his invasion of Ukraine.

I consider that to be a simple fact.

But why did Japan make such an unprecedented decision to throw in with Russia?

Because it made sense.

The BRICS countries are making a well-reasoned case that the United States has done a bad job of maintaining their status as the reserve currency of the world. That means other countries are willing to look at a new international financial order.

Because of our own stupidity, we have potentially lost our best ally in Asia.

That giant sucking sound you hear is world confidence in the United States rushing away from us and going to the BRICS nations.

In France, Prime Minister Macron has said that the French will start dismantling the demand for the dollar in their country.[15] Remember France? The indispensable country that helped us win the Revolutionary War, and whom we rescued in two World Wars?

News flash to the Biden Administration.

When you've lost your longest ally, maybe you want to look in the mirror and ask what you've been doing wrong.

In addition to the BRICS nations undermining confidence in the dollar, what else are we looking at? You can add on the banking crisis. It started with Silicon Valley Bank, then spread to Silvergate, Signature Bank, Credit Suisse, Deutsche Bank, and First Republic.[16] How many more will fall between the time I'm writing this sentence and the book is released? As you read this, you're probably adding a few more banks to the list.

How is President Biden responding to this crisis?

Well, in October 2022, while he was licking his ice cream, he was asked whether he was concerned about the devaluation of the dollar. He replied "I'm not concerned about the strength of the dollar. I'm concerned about the rest of the world."[17]

Is Biden president of the world, or is he president of the United States? (I'm sure there are some days even Biden is uncertain.) Why in God's name would you express concern about the global economy, but not that of the United States?

Is it because Biden is a globalist and simply considers the United States a temporary vessel for the citizens of America while on the road to a new world order? Instead of worrying about Americans who've fallen on hard times, he's sending pension checks to Ukrainians.

This situation is genuinely new to the American Republic. Despite what you might say about them, neither Bill Clinton nor Barack Obama would have allowed this to happen. And if they tried to pull these kinds of shenanigans on Trump? He would've done more than tweet about it. You know Trump would've fought with every ounce of energy he had.

Imagine what Xi in China or Putin in Russia are thinking as they observe this state of affairs in our country. Napoleon said to never interfere with an enemy when they're in the midst of destroying themselves. They don't have to meddle in the United States. We're already doing the job for them. They would know it's time to strike against America because Biden won't defend it.

But would we expect a bunch of authoritarian countries to create a new economic order based on the principles of the free market? No, because these countries don't believe in freedom. Like most progressives in this country, they believe you need to be controlled like a misbehaving child.

The system they're creating is a central bank digital currency (CBDC) linked to your social credit score.

Like a teenager getting an allowance, your money can be turned off in an instant if you do something the rulers of your country don't like. And if you think this happens only among authoritarian countries, just look at what our neighbor to the north, the previously free nation of Canada, did to the bank accounts of truckers who opposed Prime Minister Justin Trudeau's COVID lockdowns and vaccine requirements.

The government of any country is like an addict, only needing a single opportunity to find a new way of asserting power, to quickly pick up the habit and use it whenever necessary. This is from a *Newsweek* article on Trudeau's action in February 2022.

> Canadian banks have begun freezing the accounts of people linked to the trucker protests in Canada and the federal government is promising to take more accounts offline in coming days in an attempt to clear demonstrators from Ottawa, which has been occupied for nearly a month.
>
> On February 16, Deputy Prime Minister Chrystia Freeland said in a press conference that financial institutions have started freezing accounts and canceling credit cards in accordance with the Emergencies Act, which Prime Minister Justin Trudeau invoked earlier this week.
>
> The powers granted by the act would allow banks to target the accounts of people who have donated to crowdfunding platforms, like the fundraising campaigns on GoFundMe and GiveSendGo, that have fueled the ongoing protests, but Freeland said she would not give "specifics of whose accounts are being frozen."[18]

Can you imagine that simply donating to a protest movement (like maybe Black Lives Matter or Planned Parenthood under a conservative government) could cause you to lose access to your bank account or credit cards? How do you function in a modern society with such draconian measures placed on your right to participate in the political process?

Even Great Britain, the home of free speech, appears to be experimenting with this type of tyranny over its political adversaries, like Nigel Farage, who led the successful Brexit movement. From late June 2023 comes this account of Farage's debanking.

> Having a bank account is necessary to interact with modern society in a basic way and being deprived of that facility is tantamount to becoming a "non-person", a downcast Nigel Farage said Thursday as he revealed he and close members of his family are being prevented from holding an account in the United Kingdom. Warning viewers on Thursday night, he reflected: "This is going on in our country. It's happening to plenty of people, I just happen to be one of them.
>
> "But do you know what? Unless this rot is stopped in time to come you at home may say things on Facebook or Twitter that result in losing your bank accounts too. That, I think, is how scary this whole thing is."
>
> Farage has banked with the same banking group since the 1980s for both personal and business, he said, and that no reason was given for his longstanding relationship with the unnamed bank being terminated.[19]

Farage is one of the most consequential figures in recent English history, and yet he's being driven from his homeland. He continued on, describing these events in a supposed democracy to countries whose lack of political freedoms we regularly disparage. But I have to note I was debanked five years before Farage and I've been debanked four times.

> The veteran political campaigner was at risk of becoming a "non-person", he said, comparing the campaign to make his life impossible for political undesirables to "the worst regimes of the mid-20th century. Farage said on his nightly television talk show on GB News that: "basically you've become a non-person. It's rather like living in Germany or Russia 80 years ago. Or perhaps even Communist China today. I wonder, are we living in Communist China today, in this country?"[20]

The fears of Nigel Farage are well-founded. Not only is the attack on Farage a political one, but he is also currently working as a member of the press. The attack on Farage by the British banking system and the government, as well as attacks by other democracies around the world, can only be seen as a march toward tyranny.

* * *

The Bretton Woods Agreement of 1944, which immensely benefitted the United States, and the fruit of that tree are turning rotten because of bad decisions made by both Republicans and Democrats over successive administrations. Remember the mortgage bailout of 2008 caused by President George W. Bush? That's because the elites in Washington, DC thought *everybody* should be able to get a house, even if you didn't have a job!

What could possibly go wrong when you give real estate to people who can't even manage their own checkbooks? They didn't say it at the time, but why were they doing it? You guessed it. Because there was too much white supremacy in home ownership.

Letting the government run the banks is like giving the keys to a second car to a drunk driver as he stumbles away from the wreckage of his first car.

You've got the authoritarian, corrupt countries of the BRICS nations creating their own programmable digital currency linked to an individual's social credit score, and in America you've got the political class salivating over doing the same thing to our own citizens.

Dr. Pippa Malmgren, an economist for the World Economic Forum, said last year that central bank digital currency is coming and that it's programmable, meaning they can cut you off based on your digital social profile.[21]

China is the favorite location of the globalists to test their new ideas of control, so is it any wonder we saw China using their social credit ranking system to prevent regular Chinese citizens from making certain purchases? Here's an account of China's system from a 2019 article in *The Guardian*:

> China has blocked millions of "discredited" travelers from buying plane or train tickets as part of the country's controversial "social credit" system aimed at improving the behavior of citizens.
>
> According to the National Public Credit Information Center, Chinese courts banned would-be travelers from buying flights 17.5 million times by the end of 2018. Citizens placed on blacklists for social credit offenses were prevented from buying train tickets 5.5 million times. The report released last week said, "Once discredited, limited everywhere."
>
> The social credit system aims to incentivize "trustworthy" behavior through penalties as well as rewards. According to a government document about the system dating from 2014, the aim is to "allow the trustworthy to roam everywhere under heaven while making it hard for the discredited to take a single step."[22]

Maybe it's because I've read so much history in my life, but it seems that one of the lessons we never seem to learn is that governments should not be trusted with great power. Our Founding Fathers understood that the best government is limited in its powers, working best when it protects individual rights or mediates disagreements between individuals. And leading the charge for Chinese style authoritarianism is the World Economic Forum and American academics, as revealed in a July 2023 article:

> During a speech at the WEF's 14th Annual Meeting of the New Champion in Tianjin, China, at the end of June, Eswar Prasad of Cornell University spoke about how governments can program and manipulate Central Bank Digital Currencies.
>
> In short, Prasad said that CBDCs could be programmed by governments to prevent purchases that are deemed "less desirable" by those in power.
>
> "You could have, as I argue in my book, a potentially better—and some might say darker world," Prasad said, "where the government decides that units of central bank money can be used to purchase

> some things, but not other things that it deems less desirable, like say ammunition, or drugs, or pornography."[23]

I will admit to you that at the current moment there is little public support for a central bank programmable digital currency linked to your social credit score. But that doesn't mean they aren't building the infrastructure of such a system.

A guest on *The Joe Rogan Experience* podcast in 2022, British broadcaster Maajid Nawaz detailed some of the dangers of Central Bank Digital Currencies:

> As Nawaz pointed out to Rogan on Saturday's episode of the popular podcast, part of the reason that legislators are so drawn to the notion of CNDC is that this form of money is programmable and controllable.
>
> "What they want to do is bring in this thing called the central banking digital currency," begins Mawaz. "They want to replace paper fiat money with digital money as a competitor to bitcoin and crypto money. But instead of a decentralized currency, it will be controlled by the government."
>
> "That sounds terrifying," said Rogan.
>
> "If you try to buy unhealthy meat it just won't work. You tap your card, and you can't buy that thing, because you've met your quota of burgers—you'll have to buy a vegan meal instead," explained Nawaz.[24]

The approach of the tyrants is always the same. Try to get you to agree to the small violation of rights. We'll just start by not allowing you to buy drugs. Then comes ammunition. Next is pornography, followed by unhealthy foods (yeah, they'll never block that), and then after that, maybe controversial voices, like yours truly, or Joe Rogan. These people will never stop until they have you under their total control.

Remember how Bill Gates and his buddy Klaus Schwab put on Event 201, a simulated pandemic outbreak of a coronavirus in October 2019, just before COVID-19 supposedly appeared in our world?[25] And not as a leak (or attack) from the Wuhan Institute of Virology, but according to today's fiction, a raccoon dog.[26]

To slightly alter the famous message of Kevin Costner's classic baseball film, *Field of Dreams*, "If they build it, they will use it."

They want to terrify you into giving up your rights, so the first step in fighting back is to not be afraid. If you are scared and trembling in the face of their plans, they will manipulate you. They're trying to persuade you because if you stand up, they lose. Be bold in your dissent. Laugh in their faces.

Here's how I think they're going to use the central bank digital currency. They will use their control to cut you off from your money if you disagree with whatever the current narrative is at that time. But be loud in how you will use this system against them, and then smile.

Imagine if you will the horror among liberals at the idea that some future government could make the pronouncement, "Alex Jones was right about everything," and anybody who disagreed with that statement wouldn't be able to buy groceries for their family that week.

You might think that's a crazy idea that people might be scared into adopting a digital currency, but look how quickly people conformed during the COVID-19 crisis to avoid visiting their elderly parents, putting a mask over their face (and lowering their daily oxygen intake, while increasing carbon dioxide), keeping their kids home from school, and lining up to get that gene-editing shot, along with a whole host of nasty chemicals, injected into their arms. This didn't happen because people are stupid. It's because Big Pharma and their government allies used highly persuasive propaganda to get people to comply. You should know that when Big Pharma is pushing a new drug, they do intensive psychological profiles of the doctors to whom they're trying to sell the drug, then choose the sales representatives who are most likely to make a positive impression on these doctors. They used people's best traits, their desire to care for other human beings, to engage in profoundly inhuman ways and become isolated and fragmented from others.

The question is quickly becoming, what do we do about their plans?

* * *

The first thing you can do is become aware of what's happening. Because the mainstream media doesn't want to tell you these things.

Knowledge is power.

The simple act of you reading and understanding this information arms you with some powerful weapons.

What needs to be understood is that the people who are bringing in this central bank digital currency are the same people who have ruined the current system and caused these bank failures.

And there is another danger that a lot of people don't currently understand. There are a lot of transactions that don't leave a trace. You're at a flea market, you see some little statue you like, and offer the guy selling it twenty bucks. The government never knows you bought that crappy little statue, but maybe it means something deeply personal to you, which thankfully will never end up in some government database.

It's called our privacy.

Do you want it to be known how much you tip the waiters at your local restaurant? I'm a generous tipper, but you might not be. When transactions are done in cash, they can't be tracked. We have allowed that system to exist for generations. I would argue that our ability to use cash, in relatively small amounts, is part of what keeps our society moving in a positive direction.

Who will the government come down on first? The poor. Those just struggling to make ends meet, like waiters and waitresses, delivery drivers, and others at the entry point of their careers.

Why? First, because they're easier to pressure, and second, if they can make you docile from the beginning of your working life, it's a good bet you'll stay that way.

Once they've crushed the poor, they'll move on to the middle class, and eventually the wealthy. The reason they wait so long to take on the wealthy is because they know the wealthy have so much power. In the interim, they'll lie to the wealthy that this system will never be turned against them, but it's a lie.

If the wealthy understood these people's plans, they could stop the globalists in a few weeks.

As Winston Churchill once said of appeasement to Hitler, it's like feeding your friends to the crocodile in the hope he'll eat you last.

Here's how they'll try to sell it to you in a populist message, which only leads to more governmental control.

You need to be protected from these greedy banks who have ruined everything. We in the government will come in like a knight on a shiny white horse with additional rules and regulations to make sure these scavengers don't do anything like this ever again. But what they'll do is take over the banks and then hand them back to their friends. It's like a mafia don who buys a restaurant to use as a place to launder money (in addition to having a decent place to eat), only to torch the place for the insurance proceeds when the restaurant's debts become too crushing.

I want my readers to understand this is nothing new.

This is *always* how corruption tries to control society.

The merger of big business and big government is nothing new.

Just look at Hitler's Germany, Mussolini's Italy, or modern China.

But we have to name it if we're going to have any hope of defeating it. And we need to understand the propaganda. What they say is bad is actually good and vice versa. Be aware that, when they criticize cryptocurrency, that means you should probably take a look at it. Same thing for precious metals like gold and silver or real estate not burdened by excessive mortgages.

A reckoning is coming for our economy.

And they're going to try to "Build Back Better" with a central bank digital currency linked to your social credit score. An interesting idea floated by Larry Sharpe, well-known podcaster and the Libertarian candidate for New York governor in 2018, is that the financial recklessness of many states is just a ploy to bring about bankruptcy in these states, allowing the federal government to step in and institute CBDCs, as well as a social credit score. This is basically a Cloward-Piven strategy, named after the approach popularized in 1966 by American sociologists Richard Cloward and Frances Fox Piven, in which the government would put forth polices intentionally designed to exacerbate social tensions; then, when things fell apart, the government could swoop in and claim even more sweeping powers. You see, with the globalists, it's always about that "emergency" that allows them to take away your freedom. At first, they'll tell you something like, "It's just for criminals or deadbeat dads, and don't you want to make sure the children are protected?"

But it's coming for all of us.

We can fight back by not letting them step one foot farther, but I'd have backups ready.

Stockpile your cash. Have some of your assets in gold, silver, crypto, or low mortgage real estate. They don't have the strength to overpower us. The most important thing is knowing how to garden, have a good community of friends, and learn how to hunt and fish. We can overcome their plans. At an instinctive level, humanity understands this, which is why we're seeing a historic exodus from the cities. They need a crisis to panic people into demanding it.

I want you to be the minutemen on the front line of freedom.

We can stop the cashless economy.

Chapter Five

The Eternal War of the Tyrants

There's something you should understand about evil individuals and governments.

They make terrible allies. It is perhaps their greatest vulnerability.

It might appear otherwise, as it often seems like evil individuals are always scheming about who they can get on their side, while the good people are going about their lives blissfully unaware of the storm clouds gathering in the distance.

The good guys always seem to only get their act together two minutes before midnight, snatching victory from the jaws of imminent defeat.

But as evil individuals approach the implementation of their plans, fighting usually breaks out, because the alliance was never about sharing. It was always about gaining a temporary advantage over a perceived rival, sideling him while they were weak, and then attacking their former ally when they'd regained their strength.

Consider Adolf Hitler and Joseph Stalin as World War II began in Europe. Hitler knew the dictator Stalin and Soviet Russia would present a problem when he attacked Poland, so the two of then signed the Molotov-Ribbentrop pact on August 22, 1939, as detailed by the *Manchester Guardian* newspaper in Britain at the time (and reprinted in 2019 by *The Guardian*):

> Germany and the Soviet union have agreed to conclude a pact of nonaggression. The surprising announcement was made in Berlin last night by the official German news agency. It was added that Herr von Ribbentrop, the German Foreign Minister, is flying to

> Moscow tomorrow to complete the negotiations. Early this morning the Russian Tass Agency issued a similar statement.
>
> The news was completely unexpected. There had been rumors in Berlin of a meeting at Berchtesgaden yesterday between Herr Hitler, Herr von Ribbentrop, and Her von Papen, who had recently visited Moscow, but that was all.
>
> The decision to sign the pact is announced only the day after the signing of a commercial treaty was made known. The Russian press yesterday, suddenly changing its tome toward Germany, warmly welcomed the commercial agreement as being likely to lead to better political relations—"eventually," they said.[1]

Tyrants understand that they can be opposed not only by democracies, but by other tyrants. Hitler and Stalin had been at each other for years. Hitler rose to power on a promise to stop communism in Germany, and yet there they were in August 1939, signing a non-aggression pact. And did you notice how it began with a "commercial agreement?"

Economics and war are inextricably linked.

But there was no genuine accord between the two states. Hitler wielded ultimate power in Germany by coopting Big Business with his promise to crack down on the unions, which wanted to improve worker wages and living conditions. Stalin wielded ultimate power because the State had taken over all the businesses.

Germany and Russia made short work of Poland, then after eight months of the so-called "phony war," Hitler turned west, quickly dispatching France, and drove the English army to the French beach of Dunkirk, where they made their miraculous escape back to Britain's shores.

With the war in Western Europe seemingly won, and only England left perilously clinging to life, Hitler turned back to the east. But was any agreement with a tyrant one that another tyrant could trust?

> By the end of 1940, Hitler had issued Fuhrer Directive 21, an order for Germany's planned invasion of the Soviet Union. Codenamed Operation Barbarossa—after the nickname of the powerful Medieval

> Holy Roman Emperor Frederick I—the invasion called for German troops to advance along a line running north-south from the port of Archangel to the port of Astrakhan on the Volga River, near the Caspian Sea.
>
> Hitler hoped to repeat the success of the blitzkrieg in Western Europe and win a quick victory over the massive nation he viewed as Germany's sworn enemy.
>
> On June 22, 1941, more than 3 million German and Axis troops invaded the Soviet Union along an 1,800-mile-long-front, launching Operation Barbarossa. It was Germany's largest invasion force of the war, representing some 80 percent of the Wehrmacht, the German armed forces, and one of the most powerful invasion forces in history.[2]

That's the version you'll find in most history books. Hitler and Stalin made a pact, and Hitler broke it, completely surprising Stalin.

But with the ascension of Prime Minister Mikhail Gorbachev and his campaign of openness or *perestroika*, wherein the records could be more closely examined, a different view of the duel between Hitler and Stalin began to emerge. A contentious debate has broken out on what Stalin was planning, with some researchers claiming Stalin was planning to attack Hitler just a few weeks after the German invasion. As detailed in the *Inquiries Journal*, the idea was first raised by historian Victor Suvorov:

> Besides allowing soviet historians greater (though far from complete access) to archival documents, perestroika also allowed the greater freedom of interpretation, which was eagerly seized upon by historians such as Suvorov as a chance to deconstruct the soviet myth of the Great Patriotic War. Suvorov's thesis was simple: Stalin intended to attack Nazi-Germany in the summer of 1941, and therefore rejected the dominant view in western and soviet scholarship on the subject that the Soviet Union was a defenseless victim of German aggression.[3]

In the mainstream narrative of World War II, Stalin was betrayed. But I tend to side with those who believe that Stalin was also planning to attack Hitler. That's the way tyrants think. Suvorov added more detail to this theory.

> Suvorov focuses on the mobilization of the Red Army in the months immediately preceding the German attack as evidence of Stalin's intention to launch a pre-emptive offensive against Nazi-Germany. He points to the movement of numerous Red Army units from the Ural Mountains to the Ukrainian and Belorussian frontier regions. Suvorov views June 13, 1941 as being the point at which the Soviet Union effectively decided on war, as he argues that the deployment of troops and material could not be reversed without resulting in severe economic disruption . . .
>
> Additionally, Suvorov interprets Stalin's appeasement of Hitler during this period as an elaborate plot to conceal his intentions to launch a pre-emptive strike against Hitler, and focuses on the Telegram Agency of the Soviet Union (TASS) directive of June 13, 1941 as indicative of Stalin's wider campaign of deception. Suvorov saw Stalin's foreign policy as fundamentally rooted to Marxist-Leninist ideology. Viewed from this perspective, Stalin aimed at pursuing 'world revolution' and further contended that Hitler was merely an 'ice-breaker' in Stalin's wider plan of spreading soviet rule throughout Europe.[4]

This version of history makes much more sense to me than painting Stalin as a passive, trusting fool who was duped by Hitler. Whatever one might say of tyrants, they are rarely dumb. Suvorov makes the point that the disposition of Stalin's forces suggested the Soviets were ready to go on the offensive within a few weeks, which is why they performed so poorly against Hitler's onslaught. In Suvorov's estimation, Stalin was no more than three weeks away from launching an attack on Hitler, when Hitler attacked Russia. Tyrants are generally astute judges of human natures, in the way that bullies normally have high social intelligence, as detailed in this 2011 article from the *Journal of Personality and Individual Differences*:

> Relative to victims, both bullies and defenders showed advanced moral competence, integrating information about beliefs and outcomes in judging the moral permissibility of an action; victims showed delayed moral competence, focusing on outcome information alone. Paradoxically, despite the advanced moral competence of bullies, they are woefully deficient with respect to their moral compassion when compared to both victims and defenders. These results parallel a growing body of work on adult psychopaths, suggesting disassociation between the knowledge that guides abstract moral judgments and the factors that mediate morally appropriate behavior and sentiments.[5]

I always find it interesting when the latest science confirms our most ancient wisdom. In the typical journey of a hero in literature, he must usually come face to face with the villain in a philosophical contest. Good stories reveal deep psychological truths, which is why they can last for hundreds, if not thousands, of years and maintain a hold on our imagination. The hero and villain want to size each other up—look each other in the eye, so to speak. In this mental battle, the villain usually says to the hero something along the lines of "you and I are not so different," and there's probably some truth to that observation.

Both of them could appreciate the vulnerabilities that may be present in a certain situation. One might say that during the 1930s, both Winston Churchill and Adolf Hitler understood the implications of German rearmament, as well as the overwhelming desire of most European leaders never to have another senseless slaughter of millions as had happened during World War I.

However, the villain steps foot on the road to evil, while the hero chooses the path that brings about the greatest benefit to civilization. Hitler saw the opportunity to cause suffering and death for millions of people, while Churchill vainly tried to warn against the coming apocalypse, hoping he could persuade leaders in Germany to pursue a different path and not leave Europe in smoking ruins.

In this light, who are the tyrants of our modern era, and who are the heroes trying to stop a catastrophic confrontation?

* * *

In my last book, *The Great Reset,* I wrote a great deal about how the Trilateral Commission, Zbigniew Brzezinski, Henry Kissinger, and the World Economic Forum made modern China. To recap the main points of my argument, the globalists saw China as the perfect testbed for their theories about how a managerial class could control society, free of democratic restraints. It has worked beyond their wildest dreams of success, and yet they seem to have lost control of their monstrous, authoritarian creation.

This "fascism for a new generation" would avoid the vulgar displays of political power necessary to crush opposition and would instead seek to undermine challenges to their authority by other means. Of course, this opening to China required a betrayal of Taiwan, a mistake we continue to pay for in 2023. We also suffer from the fact that China now seeks to influence our movies, our finances, and our universities through direct financial contributions, as well as the establishment of Confucian schools at our leading centers of learning. (And probably financially compromising President Joe Biden and his family.)

This is how Dr. Brzezinski was lionized after his death in 2017 by Professor Chi Wang, Chair of the US-China Policy Foundation.

> Brzezinski worked with Carter, Oksenberg, and Leonard Woodcock, chief of the U.S. Liaison Office in Beijing, to move forward with normalization. These four individuals created the environment and strategy necessary for normalization to finally be possible. In May 1978, Dr. Brzezinski insisted on traveling to China. During his meetings with China's Deng Xiaoping, the conditions for handling the U.S. relationship with Taiwan post normalization were discussed.

> Finally, in December 1978, the United States and China made joint announcements that the establishment of official diplomatic relationships would occur on January 1, 1979. When Deng Xiaoping visited the United States just after the normalization, he had a special dinner at Dr. Brzezinski's home, showing how appreciative Deng was of Brzezinski's efforts. Without Dr. Brzezinski's tireless behind-the-scenes work, it is doubtful normalization would have occurred so soon.[6]

When you read some story in the news today, maybe about China threatening to invade Taiwan, the more than 100,000 overdose deaths in America last year (mostly from fentanyl, produced in China),[7] and the hollowing out of our manufacturing capacity (because our policy has been to shut down American manufacturing and send to China), as well as the SARS-CoV-2 virus that came from China (because they had enough money and assistance from us to create that unsafe biosafety level 4 lab) via an intentional or accidental lab leak,[8] maybe you should remember that this was all brought to you courtesy of Zbigniew Brzezinski and his fellow globalists.

And what kind of a human rights record does China have? This is from a 2016 *Washington Post* article, revealing China's genocidal actions against its own citizens. And remember the Chinese Communist Party was in charge of these efforts and still rules over its citizens. It's as if the Nazi Party remained in power in Germany.

> Who was the biggest mass murderer in the history of the world? Most people assume that the answer is Adolf Hitler, architect of the Holocaust. Others might guess Joseph Stalin, who may indeed have managed to kill even more innocent people than Hitler did, many of them as part of a terror famine that likely took more lives than the Holocaust. But both Hitler and Stalin were outdone by Mao Zedong. From 1958 to 1962, his Great Leap Forward policy led to the deaths of up to 45 million people—easily making it the biggest episode of mass murder ever recorded.[9]

Fourteen years after China murdered forty-five million of its own people, and with the same political party controlling the country, Brzezinski and his globalist buddies like Henry Kissinger were welcoming China into the community of nations, and Brzezinski was hosting the Chinese leader at his house for dinner. That's like Hitler winning the war in 1945 and then being invited to President Kennedy's inauguration in 1960. But let Democratic Congresswoman Tulsi Gabbard go on a fact-finding trip to Syria, hoping to stop President Obama's secret war in Syria, and she'll be denounced as an apologist for the Syrian regime, unfit to be president.[10]

And in case you find yourself asking, "Syria? We're in Syria? Nah, that can't be. We would've needed some kind of Congressional declaration to have troops there, and I know that didn't happen."

And yet, here's an *Associated Press* article on our presence in Syria from 2023.

> American troops have been in Syria since 2015, but the latest casualties highlight what has been a consistent, but often quiet, U.S. counterterrorism mission, aimed at countering Iranian-backed militias and preventing the resurgence of the Islamic State group . . .
>
> On any given day there are at least 900 U.S. forces in Syria, along with an undisclosed number of contractors. U.S. special operations forces also move in and out of the country but are usually in small teams and are not included in the official count.[11]

Aren't you happy to know our intelligence agencies and military contractors have been waging a "splendid little war" in Syria over the past couple years and the mainstream media didn't quite tell you about it?

But let's return to our China discussion. Forty-five million people is a lot to kill. How did they manage the feat? This is how the *Washington Post* describes it:

> What comes out of this massive and detailed dossier is a tale of horror in which Mao emerges as one of the greatest mass murderers in history, responsible for the deaths of at least 45 million people

> between 1958 and 1962. It is not merely the extent of the catastrophe that dwarfs earlier estimates, but also the manner in which people died; between two and three million were tortured to death or summarily killed, often for the slightest infraction. When a boy stole a handful of grain in a Hunan village, local boss Xiong Dechang forced his father to bury him alive. The father died of grief a few days later. The case of Wang Ziyou was reported to the central leadership: one of his ears was chopped off, his legs were tied with an iron wire, a ten-kilogram stone was dropped on his back and then he was branded with a sizzling tool—punishment for digging up a potato.[12]

When I read such a horrifying account, I don't take comfort in the fact that this happened thousands of miles away from me, and years before I was born. Instead, it tells me something eternal about human nature. It tells me that the accumulation of all power in a single entity like the state, without protections for the individual, will always lead to such atrocities.

Because not all people are good. Jean Decety, a professor of psychiatry at the University of Chicago, estimates that about 1 percent of the general population are psychopaths, who have no empathy for others, and because of this deficiency are responsible for a disproportionate amount of crime and violence in society.[13] What happens in an authoritarian system? Those who have no empathy are easily able to rise through intimidation and violence against others. An authoritarian system will always give a preference to the psychopaths among us, willing to use the power given to them to maintain their position.

Why do I fight so hard against this creeping authoritarianism? It's not because I'm brave. It's because it's in my self-interest to prevent my government from ever having that kind of power over me, my kids, or my grandkids. Would you say I was brave if I ran out of a burning building or tried to escape from a car that was sinking beneath the waters of a lake?

Fighting back against tyranny isn't a luxury.

It's a matter of your survival.

Do you want to live, or are you satisfied with waiting for your executioner to appear?

* * *

While in my previous book I detailed at great length the developing relationship between the globalists (first through the Trilateral Commission, which then evolved into the World Economic Forum) and China, the major question of today is the current state of that relationship.

Remember the main argument of this chapter, which is that tyrants can rarely, if ever, maintain a genuine alliance.

It seems the Chinese weren't all that interested in being exploited by another group of powerful, old white guys. You can hardly blame them.

Let's walk through how things have been developing since Deng Xiaoping sat down to dinner at Brzezinski's house for a home-cooked meal.

In 2014, at the age of eighty-five, Zbigniew Brzezinski gave a long interview to Michael Hersh of *Politico* about his call for a "Pacific Charter," along the lines of the Atlantic Charter of 1941, which eventually gave rise to NATO (the North Atlantic Treaty Organization). One can sense in this interview that China was starting to move away from the globalists to pursue their own objectives, and Brzezinski was desperately trying to get the monster they'd created back into the castle.

> **MH:** What do you think a "Pacific Charter" will achieve?
> **ZB:** Seventy-five years ago, in the darkest days of World War II, the Atlantic Charter served as an inspiring proclamation of hope at a time of widespread global anxiety that the world was falling victim to hegemonic tyranny. Today, the presidents of the world's two most important, albeit politically very different, states need to convey credibly to the world their determination to enhance their global cooperation in coping with ongoing and emerging geopolitical crises. Global stability—economic as well as political—is at risk.
>
> Shared Sino-American global security goals would not mean that one partner dictates to the other. U.S.-P.R.C. differences will persist, and on the Asian regional level they can even be a source of mutual irritation. Nor should it mean that we ignore the basic differences

> between our political systems and values. But a joint affirmation of American-Chinese engagement in sustaining international stability can generate broader collaboration between these two superpowers in containing dangerous threats that actually point also at their own interests.[14]

Zbigniew Brzezinski was arguing that the United States should treat the murderous Chinese Communist Party in charge of that captive nation as an equal on the global stage.

I've been a long-time admirer of Stephen K. Bannon, the former CEO of Breitbart News, President Trump's campaign strategist for the 2016 election, and one of the Deep State's top ten targets for destruction. However, I have only recently struck up an acquaintance with this genuine patriot, and I'd like to believe it is a budding friendship. Bannon has been crystal-clear for years about the danger of China and their gangster leaders, and as Reagan confronted the Soviet Union, not as a fellow superpower, but as an "evil empire," I think we must do the same with China. In fact, I'd go so far as to say that any significant political figure that does not make such a declaration should be presumed to be an agent of the Chinese Communist Party.

The world probably has no more effective critic of the Brzezinski doctrine than Bannon, and I completely endorse the criticisms he makes of the Chinese regime, as well as his call for the Chinese people to overthrow the murderous butchers of Beijing. The *Politico* interview with Brzezinski continued:

> **MH:** But is such a pact feasible? Aren't China and the United States too different in terms of their political systems and the way they view the world? They are fighting over Internet freedom, democracy, and interests in East Asia. Chinese officials are even hinting that they believe Washington is behind the unrest in Hong Kong. In addition, there is a sense that the Chinese are up and coming and want to replace us.

> **ZB:** It is true that the U.S. and Britain shared basic values and political systems that enabled the Atlantic Charter, but in the postwar world, in many ways, their geopolitical interests clashed more than those of the United States and China today. The British at the time wanted to keep their empire, while the United States wanted a United Nations, and the two clashed bitterly over the postwar economic system at Bretton Woods. Today, the United States and China are actually more in alignment on global issues, and especially the global economy, than the United States and Britain were in the post-World War II period. Economically, we are to some significant degree interdependent with Chinese well-being. That is a great asset. So this is what gives me some degree of confidence in advocating greater cooperation. We can cooperate to support the dollar, and to maintain a steady flow of capital back and forth, but beyond that we have to ask ourselves: can we do more together to prevent political chaos from exploding in several directions at once?[15]

There are so many things wrong in that single paragraph that it can be hard to start pulling it apart. But I'm up for the challenge.

First, the fact that America and Britain "shared basic values and political systems" is probably the most important factor in the success of our long-term alliance with them. Let's be clear-eyed about the facts and not rewrite history. England had a long and hallowed democratic tradition *and* it administered a vast empire of millions, who for the most part didn't want to be ruled by a foreign entity.

By its very nature, democracy is incompatible with empire.

If a nation is to have an empire, the only way it can be maintained is by the ruthless suppression of those people who want the occupying force to be gone. We learned that in Iraq, Afghanistan, and Vietnam. And yet the lesson doesn't seem to stick among American policymakers, vainly looking for the next foreign monster to destroy and hoping against all evidence and logic that the residents will celebrate their "liberation" as the French and Italians did during World War II.

Britain's maintenance of an empire was at odds with their democratic values, just as the institution of slavery was at odds with the lofty claims of the equality of all found in our US Constitution and Bill of Rights.

While the British were victorious over the Nazis, they were broken at the end of World War II. Empires are expensive to maintain, and Britain had little money, wondering how it was going to feed its own people, let alone all its far-flung colonies.

Britain surrendered its empire because it was contrary to its democratic ideals and, in addition, because it couldn't afford it.

Think of the valuable and cherished relationships you have in your own life. Chances are good that you have the strongest relationships with people who share your values, which I hope include honesty, integrity, and kindness.

To put it bluntly, at the end of World War II, America had the money it needed and the democratic ideals necessary to bring about greater freedom and liberty to the rest of the world. And in many instances, the United States exercised that power appropriately to encourage the march of democracy across the globe.

You do not have a comfortable relationship with people who do not share your values. Having a commonly accepted set of values is critical to any relationship. If you have to work with someone at your job who is undeniably talented, but also has the morals of a snake, you will never rest easy in that relationship. The so-called relationships of "convenience" or "mutual interest" are doomed to failure, and it would be better to never even enter them.

Probably the most significant single sentence in the previously quoted passage is, "Economically, we are to some significant degree interdependent with Chinese well-being."

It is undeniably correct, and yet it comes to the wrong conclusion.

There's an old expression in financial circles that, "If you owe a million dollars to the bank, they own you. But if you owe a billion dollars to the bank, then you own them." (I recommend the fine book by Tom Wolfe, *A Man in Full*, for a fictional exploration of this theme.)

In 2022, our trade deficit with China was $328 billion dollars.[16]

The normal person might respond by saying, "China has us over a barrel. We don't have any freedom."

The reverse is true. We hold the upper hand. China wants to keep getting our money. They must play ball with us if they want that to happen. We can "decouple" from China, and despite the rate at which we go, China will always be hoping it doesn't go any faster.

Of course, all of this is moot if President Xi Jinping (nicknamed "Pooh Bear" by his critics because of his resemblance to the classic children's character, Winnie the Pooh) is a crazy man. But unlike Russia, which has rolled the dice with their invasion of Ukraine, China always seems to play the long game, never making a move unless they know it's going to be successful.

Modern China is best viewed as the Frankenstein monster created by the mad scientist globalists. But instead of the creature's terrifying visage and height that made it unable to blend into the local community, China seeks to wear the disguise of a trustworthy superpower. China can claim it's trying to make the world a better place, pursuing their "belt and road" economic plan, while we figure out how to drop bombs and place special forces in even more countries around the globe. (It's troubling to be losing the war for public opinion when our own leaders are making so many mistakes.) Xi is aware that the globalists are unhappy with him pursuing his own interests, but to avoid panicking the populace, Xi is acting like everything remains the same.

Consider President Xi Jinping's words about globalism that he delivered from the stage of the World Economic Forum in Davos, Switzerland on January 17, 2017:

> At a time when protectionist and nationalist forces are on the rise in the West, President Xi warned against making globalization a scapegoat.
>
> "Some people blame economic globalization for the chaos in the world. Economic globalization was once viewed as the treasure cave found by Ali Baba in the Arabian Nights, but it has now become the Pandora's Box."

> However, the world's problems could not be simply laid at globalization's door, from the "heart-breaking" refugee crisis to the financial crisis.
>
> "The international financial crisis is another example, it is not an inevitable outcome of economic globalization, rather it is the consequence of the excessive chase of profit by financial capital and a great failure of financial regulation," he said.[17]

What could be more believable than the leader of the world's largest crony capitalism economy criticizing free-market capitalism? This is called deflection, because in many ways our capitalist system has become little different from China's crony capitalism.

That's why I argue that we need to return to a rules-based capitalism: many players honestly competing with each other for the consumer's trust, without captured federal regulatory agencies, where the employees don't spend years polishing their resumes so they look good to the large financial entities like BlackRock when they plan their inevitable leap from government "service" to the private sector. Xi continued his World Economic Forum speech:

> After 38 years of reform and opening up, China has become the world's second-largest economy. "China's development is an opportunity for the world. China has not only benefitted from economic globalization but also contributed to it," he said.
>
> Looking ahead, President Xi warned against protectionism.
>
> "We should commit ourselves to growing an open global economy," he said.
>
> He added: "China has no intention to boost its trade development by devaluing the Renminbi, still less by launching a currency war."[18]

Newsflash to the deluded members of the World Economic Forum from 2017: China did end up devaluing the renminbi (the official currency of China) to boost its global trade sales and has launched a currency war with the fellow members of the BRICS nations, as I detailed in the previous chapter.

Can we start to trace the origins of the fallout between China and the globalists? I think a 2009 interview done with George Soros by Chrystia Freeland, at that time the US managing editor of the *Financial Times* and now the deputy prime minister of the captive nation of Canada, can help us in answering that question.

> **FT:** Given this continued weakness in the US economy, are people right to be concerned about the dollar?
> **GS:** Well, they are of course and the dollar is a very weak currency except for all the others. So, there is a general lack of confidence in currencies and a move away from currencies into real assets. The Chinese are continuing to run a big trade surplus and they're still accumulating assets and basically the renminbi is permanently undervalued because it's tied to the dollar. There is a diversification from assets that are normally held by central banks into other assets, especially in the area of commodities. So there is a push in gold, there's a strength in oil, and that is in a way a flight from currencies.[19]

This is George Soros telling the world how he plans to run the future. Because of the stupid decisions that have emanated from Washington, DC, the dollar was in bad shape, even in 2009 after the mortgage meltdown. Although, to be fair, most of the rest of the world's governments had also been making poor economic decisions. (Because the vast majority of them are globalists.) At that point in 2009 it seemed as if the globalists were still planning for China to be the vehicle that the globalists would drive to their preferred future. Little did they know that the Chinese Communist Party would be making plans of their own, which didn't include the globalists.

Soros seems to praise the Chinese for their "big trade surplus" and "accumulating assets," while lamenting the undervaluation of the Chinese renminbi "because it's tied to the dollar." This is clearly a man who's signaling his intention to work as closely with the Chinese as humanly possible.

Soros believes that he has China on his side, in his attempt to dethrone the United States as the world's great superpower. He does not understand that the monster will soon be leaving the castle.

> **FT:** Does it [the US dollar] at some point, need also to decline against the renminbi? Does there need to be some sort of a new global currency deal?
>
> **GS:** No. I believe that basically the system is broken and needs to be reconstituted. We cannot afford to have the kind of chronic and mounting imbalances in international finance. So, you need a new currency system and actually the special drawing rights do give you the makings of a system and I think it's ill-considered on the part of the United States to resist the wider use of special drawing rights. They could be very, very useful now when you have a global shortfall of demand. You could actually internationally create currency through special drawing rights and we've done it.[20]

This passage should make crystal clear the intention of the globalists to control the money supply, not the national governments. Is it clear now why they hate cryptocurrency so much?

They don't control it.

They want to be able to print the money and control access to who can use it through their central bank digital currency and social credit scores showing loyalty to the regime.

Once you view these financial arrangements through the lens of who controls the purse strings, it all becomes so clear. Since they are materialists, they think the best way to control people is through their money, and I'll be the first to admit, it's a strong play for global domination. Just the kind of thing a supervillain would try to bring about.

The problem, however, is that humans need freedom, like we need air and water, and that those societies with the greatest amount of political and economic freedom are also the most innovative societies.

As the interview was conducted in 2009, shortly after Barack Obama took office, you can see that Soros was starting to pick up on the first inklings that China might not be the docile plow horse the globalists had hoped it would be.

> **FT:** What sort of financial deal should Obama be seeking to strike when he travels to China next month?
> **GS:** I think this would be time, because you really need to bring China into the creation of a new world order, a financial world order. They are kind of reluctant members of the IMF [International Monetary Fund].They play along, but they don't make much of a contribution because it's not their institution. Their share is not commensurate . . . their voting rights are not commensurate to their weight, so I think you need a new world order that China has to be part of the process of creating it and they have to buy in. They have to own it, the same way as, let's say, the United States owns the Washington consensus, the current order, and I think the makings of it are already there because the G20, in agreeing to peer reviews, effectively is moving in that direction.[21]

I've said for a long time, and my listeners can attest to it, that I generally don't have access to any secret information. The bad guys put all this information out, and the only difference between me and the rest of the media is I read what they put out. They have such control over the media that they can say crazy shit like this, and their media lackeys at ABC, CBS, NBC, CNN, MSNBC, and now Fox, simply act as if it never happened.

We have George Soros talking to the future deputy prime minister of Canada about how China will own the new global currency system. How is this not a major issue? As I've said before, there is no doubt the United States has done risky and indefensible things with our economic decisions regarding the dollar. And yet, from that can I argue, "Well, let's try having the most murderous regime in history be in charge of the money supply?"

No.

What I will argue is that we need to have better political leaders than we have had thus far. We need to stop printing money when we find it convenient to do so.

How has that cozy relationship between the globalists and the Chinese Communist Party been working out lately? Well, in 2016, China and George Soros started calling each other names in public. This is from a *Business Insider Australia* article on their fight.

> George Soros is the definition of evil personified, at least according to China's state-run media.
>
> In a blistering attack, Chinese media outlets have singled out the famed hedge fund manager for some incredibly harsh criticism of late, essentially blaming him for instigating concerns that rattled financial markets since the beginning of the year.[22]

It's just so sad when two dictators have a falling out and start calling each other names in public, almost like hearing the nasty domestic details between a couple going through a divorce.

But what was China really expecting from a villain like Soros anyway?

They just had to look at his track record. George Soros is an expert in causing chaos among his enemies, although the article tried to take the billionaire's side.

> "Mr. Soros made general comments, claiming that credit in China has reached 350 percent of GDP and that the hard landing is already happening."
>
> "I'm not expecting it, I'm observing it," Soros was reported to have said.
>
> Regardless, whether because Soros is high profile or simply because he is known as the man who "broke the Bank of England" back in 1992, China's powerbrokers have deemed that the best form of defense is attack when it comes to those talking down the Chinese economy, regardless of what they have actually said.[23]

If this was a domestic dispute, lawyers would have already been involved. But since this is a fight between two international titans, the only question becomes: who has more journalists on their payroll, China or George

Soros? Judging by their fawning coverage of him, it seems a safe bet that George Soros has more influence with *Business Insider Australia* than China does.

Because China doesn't want to follow the globalist playbook, Soros seems to be fixated on destroying the current Chinese leadership in their current incarnation and replacing them with a group who will submit to his plans.

In 2021, Soros was picking a fight with another villainous entity, the behemoth investment firm BlackRock. As CNBC reported:

> Writing in *The Wall Street Journal* on Tuesday, Soros described BlackRock's initiative in China as a "tragic mistake" that would "damage the national security interests of the U.S. and other democracies."
>
> It comes shortly after BlackRock launched a set of mutual funds and other investment products for Chinese consumers.
>
> The asset manager told CNBC on Wednesday that its China mutual fund subsidiary set up its first fund in the country after raising 6.68 billion Chinese yuan ($1.03 billion) from more than 111,000 investors.[24]

The mind of the average person works in dualities. We want to know who's right and who's wrong. Who's the good guy and who's the bad guy?

The rest is just details.

Normally this right and wrong predisposition serves us well, allowing us to make choices that benefit us and avoiding decisions that might harm us. Do I stay on my diet, or do I order that delicious-looking cheeseburger?

But this useful way of looking at the world can harm us if we don't consider the possibility that we're being given a choice between two bad options. The tasty cheeseburger or that fabulous ice cream sundae, dripping with chocolate sauce? How did BlackRock respond to these comments by George Soros?

> "The United States and China have a large and complex economic relationship," a BlackRock spokesperson said in response to Soros' comments.
>
> "Total trade in goods and services between the two countries exceeded $600 billion in 2020. Through our investment activity, US-based asset managers and other financial institutions contribute to the economic interconnectedness of the world's two largest economies."
>
> BlackRock's Investment Institute recommended in mid-August that investors boost their exposure to China by as much as three times in some cases. Earlier in the year, CEO Larry Fink in a letter to shareholders described China's market as a "significant opportunity to help meet the long-term goals of investors in China and internationally."[25]

I wonder how it must feel to be the spokesman for an American company wanting to assist the most murderous regime in history. Isn't it long past the point anybody believed that trade would make China more democratic? How did that bet work out?

Not very well, I'd say.

But back to the good and evil dichotomy or, as many like to say, the prison of two ideas. You're being provided a false choice.

You're either on the side of George Soros, not wanting to do business with the Chinese leaders, or you're against George Soros and think it's fine to do business with the Chinese Communist Party, which is the Chinese government.

Why doesn't this article give any context into the argument that both George Soros and the Chinese Communist Party are terrifying authoritarians?

Do they think the heads of their readers would explode?

In 2022, George Soros was again attacking China, this time at the supposedly conservative Hoover Institution at Stanford University. How is it that guys like Soros, who the left want you to believe are not trying to do anything, get to be invited guests at prestigious think tanks like the Hoover Institution?

Here's a hint: They're all part of the same club. This is from a Fox News article on his talk:

> Billionaire George Soros on Monday warned that Chinese President Xi Jinping is "the greatest threat that open societies face today," and said the rise of big tech companies have "sharpened the conflict" between China and the United States.
>
> Soros, a Hungarian-American mega-donor known for his backing of liberal causes and politicians, made remarks at the opening of a Hoover Institution panel on Monday evening, beginning by dubbing 2022 as a "critical year in the history of the world."
>
> "In a few days, China—the world's most powerful authoritarian state—will begin hosting the Winter Olympics, and, like Germany in 1936, it will attempt to use the spectacle to score propaganda victory for its system of strict controls," Soros said. "We are at, or close to, important decisions that will determine the direction in which the world is going."[26]

How is this being allowed to happen? Fox News doesn't even comment on the absolute spectacle taking place before our eyes, with the supposedly conservative Hoover Institution bending their knee to George Soros and not asking some tough questions about his checkered past?

This is like letting Joseph Stalin control the editorial pages of the *New York Times* so he can talk about the evil of Adolf Hitler, without being required to account for his own crimes. (Even today, I bet the *New York Times* wouldn't "deplatform" Stalin. He'd probably be defended by Senator Bernie Sanders, the democratic socialist from Vermont, who'd shrug his shoulders and say, "So, he made a few mistakes. At least he tried!")

And do you notice whenever these authoritarians want to appear less threatening, they choose to sound like a conservative?

> In October, Soros noted, China will decide whether President Xi Jinping should be given a third term in office as party general secretary, and the United States will hold a "crucial midterm election in November."
>
> "In an open society, the role of the state is to protect the freedom of the individual," Soros said. "In a closed society the role of the individual is to serve the rulers of the state."
>
> "As the founder of the Open Society Foundations, obviously I am on the side of open societies," he continued. "But the most important question now is, which system is going to prevail."[27]

Do I really have to go into all the ways the "Open Society Foundations" society is seeking to undermine open societies? Activities such as the funding in major American cities of district attorney's races, who in turn pursue a soft-on-crime policy to the detriment of minority communities.[28]

But I don't want the reader to think it's just the Democrats who are carrying water for China.

Who can forget President George Herbert Walker Bush, that patrician of the Republican establishment, who barely even waited for the bodies of Chinese students to be buried after the massacre in Tiananmen Square in June 1989 before he was sending his diplomats over to reassure the Chinese that everything was fine? From an article in the *New York Times* about the effort, which was kept hidden from the American public at the time:

> The White House said today that the national security adviser, Brent Scowcroft, made a secret trip to China in July, shortly after President Bush suspended high-level meetings with the Chinese Government over the June crackdown on pro-democracy demonstrators. Deputy Secretary of State Lawrence S. Eagleburger also went on the trip.
>
> Word of the July visit came as the White House was still fielding criticism about a more recent visit to Beijing by Mr. Scowcroft and Mr. Eagleburger. The two men went to China 10 days ago to mend relations after hundreds of students [actually it was thousands] died in June at the hands of the Chinese military in Tiananmen Square.

> That crackdown stirred deep anger and calls for sanctions among the American public and in Congress . . .
>
> The pictures of Mr. Scowcroft during the visit this month, toasting Chinese leaders by candlelight "as friends to resume our important dialogue," set off a wave of criticism in the United States.[29]

I wasn't a fan of the first President Bush, and I wasn't a fan of the second one, either. You may not believe it, but during the two terms of the second President Bush, I was popular among the liberals for my anti-war and anti-globalist stance.

Both acted like they cared about you but were only interested in wars that benefitted the military contractors, beggared America, and tried to hand the world over to the Chinese.

I don't care how many billions they say I owe; I will never sell out America. My body may give out, but my soul will never bend the knee to these control freaks.

If I can find the strength, so can you. History has proven that submission to oppressors only makes things worse. Resistance is victory. The answer to 1984 is 1776. Or to put it another way, the answer to Marx and Engels is Jones and Heckenlively.

* * *

The most clueless take on China must surely belong to former President Obama, who apparently hasn't consulted on the issue with his buddy, George Soros. This is from a March 2023 speech in Australia:

> During a recent speaking event in Australia, former President Barack Obama pinned the blame for China's increasingly hostile behavior on his successor.
>
> Observing China's conduct and attitude toward the world began to evolve "once I left office," Obama surmised that Chinese President Xi Jinping sensed an opening when former President Trump took command.

> "With my successor coming in, I think he saw an opportunity because the U.S. president didn't seem to care much about a rules-based international system," Obama said, the Daily Mail reported. "As a consequence, I think China's attitude [is], 'Well, we can take advantage of what appears to be a vacuum internationally on a lot of these issues.'"[30]

Or maybe another way of looking at it is that the "rules-based international system" that Obama seems to hold so dear was hollowing out the American heartland and creating an unprecedented crisis of despair and drug addiction, and China didn't like it when Trump decided he was tired of getting ripped off by bad trade deals.

I also must note that Obama seems to be doing a lot of "mind-reading" of President Xi Jinping. Is that the best he's got? As a former president, doesn't he have access to most of our intelligence? Isn't there some evidence he can point to in justification of his claims, or is he just spit-balling it?

Let's take two paragraphs from the article, which at least hint of a balanced approach to the issue.

> Ironically, Trump long blamed his predecessors, such as Obama, for allowing the United States to get "ripped off" by unfair trade deals and levied tariffs against Beijing demanding fair treatment . . .
>
> China has quickly emerged as a top foreign policy predicament for President Joe Biden. Earlier this year, a Chinese spy balloon drifted through U.S. airspace for nearly a week, and tensions have been frayed ever since. The House has established a bipartisan committee on China to evaluate the approach to Beijing.[31]

Let's put Obama's claims through the logic test. Trump claimed this "international rules-based system" was bad for America. Maybe that's true and maybe it's not. I don't claim to know President Xi's mind any better than Obama, but I think his actions give some hint of what he thinks.

If the president of the United States mattered to China, then certainly Joe Biden and his love of the "international rules-based system" should have had Xi jumping up and down with excitement. Back to trade deals that screw the United States!

But for some reason, the communists don't seem to be playing ball with China Joe. That's because the Chinese have decided they don't want to be the slave labor for the globalists. They have plans of their own.

Some might be tempted to say the globalists have seen the error of their ways, and we should join with them to deal with the threat of China.

But the globalists haven't changed their plans. They still want to be our masters.

In the future, we are likely to be fighting a two-front war, with China on one side and the globalists on the other.

We must be clear-eyed that both China and the globalists present an existential threat to our survival as a free people.

Chapter Six

The War Machine

If I were to ask the average person, what objective information would make you believe that one country is a military threat and another is not, what response do you think I'd get?

Most people would probably answer with something along the lines of, "Tell me how much money that country is spending on its military compared to other countries, and I'll know which country is most interested in either conflict or enforcing its will on other countries."

According to the Peter G. Peterson Foundation, in 2022 the United States spent $877 billion dollars on defense.[1] (Author's note: They use a broader, but they claim "more accurate," measure of defense spending than other sources, although the difference between other sources is less than 10 percent.)

By comparison, the top ten militaries after the United States spend only $849 billion.[2]

According to Statista, in 2021, this was the military spending of the top ten militaries after the United States.

China spent $293 billion.[3]

India spent $76.6 billion.[4]

The United Kingdom spent $68.4 billion.[5]

Russia spent $65.9 billion.[6]

France spent $56.6 billion.[7]

Germany spent $56 billion.[8]

Saudi Arabia spent $55.6 billion.[9]

Japan spent $54.1 billion.[10]

South Korea spent $50.2 billion.[11]

Italy spent $32 billion.[12]

Australia spent $31 billion.[13]

How is it that the United States can spend $877 billion on defense and the next nine countries combined spend only $849 billion? Is this a legitimate use of money for defense, or is there a lot of waste, fraud, and abuse going into the US number? And what about the money going into our intelligence agencies and their black budgets? An analysis for the Institute for Policy Studies found:

> "Even amid the economic fallout of the Covid-19 pandemic, world military spending hit record levels," said Dr. Diego Lopes da Silva, Senior Researcher with SIPRI's Military Expenditure and Arms Production Program. "There was a slowdown in the rate of real-terms growth due to inflation. In nominal terms, however military spending grew by 6.1 percent."
>
> The United States still makes up the lion's share, with its $801 billion in 2021 representing 39% of the world's military spending. [Author's note: We have 4 percent of the world's population.] . . .
>
> While Russia increased its military spending by 2.9%, to $65.9 billion, during a period when it was militarizing the border with Ukraine, that pales in comparison to what the United States and NATO-allied countries are spending combined—nearly $1.2 trillion, more than 17 times what Russia spent. That failed to dissuade Putin's aggression toward Ukraine . . . it's almost as if military spending is not the key to peace.[14]

It's one thing to make the argument that this money is being spent to enforce the peace. But when it seems to make no difference in Putin's aggression toward Ukraine or the current face-off with China over Taiwan, it's critical to revisit one's assumptions.

Does our military exist to ensure a more peaceful world, or is it to keep the defense contractors employed? Since we have a revolving door of former generals and admirals working for the defense industries, as well as former intelligence agents, is it reasonable to question whether they have been working on a less-than-patriotic agenda?

I know that this line of argument from me will be confusing to people who are not familiar with my views. The mainstream media would have you believe I'm a guy who wants the citizens and our nation armed to the teeth, willing to use that military force whenever we like.

Nothing could be further from the truth.

I was one of the loudest voices against the war in Iraq, Obama going into Syria, and how NATO expansion has pushed Putin over Russia's red line and left him believing there was no other choice but to invade Ukraine.

Does that make me an "apologist" for Putin?

Not in the slightest. I have no hesitation in telling you that Putin is a gangster, a killer, and a thug. But he's not nearly as interested in foreign adventures as is the United States.

We like to go everywhere.

At this moment, the United States has approximately 750 bases in eighty countries, according to the Cato Institute.[15] From the Cato Institute Commentary:

> A new Quincy Institute study by American University's David Vine and World Beyond War's Patterson Deppen and Leah Bolger details the global US military presence. Washington has nearly three times as many bases as embassies and consulates. America also has three times as many installations as all other countries combined. The United Kingdom has 145. Russia two to three dozen. China five. Although the number of US facilities has fallen in half since the end of the Cold War, the number of nations hosting American bases has doubled. Washington is as willing to station forces in undemocratic as democratic countries.
>
> The study figures the annual cost of this expansive base structure to be about $55 billion. Adding increased personnel expenses takes the total up to $80 billion. Wealthier countries, which needlessly enjoy what amounts to defense welfare, typically cover a portion of

> the cost through "host nation support." Not so with Washington's newest clients. Indeed, through the Global War on Terror over the last two decades the US military spent as much as $100 billion on new construction, mostly in countries like Iraq and Afghanistan, which were financial black holes.[16]

Is the perspective you have as a consumer of American media that the United States has three times the number of bases as we do embassies and consulates? I doubt you had even the slightest idea about that number. Or that the United Kingdom would be in second, with 145 bases. But then again, they did used to have the British Empire. But with 750 bases in eighty countries, one has to ask the question: Didn't World War II end seventy-eight years ago?

And do these bases ensure peace, or just endless wars? The Cato Institute Commentary continued:

> Perhaps the most serious price of endless bases has been endless wars. Obviously, causation is complex. However, going to war usually leads to the creation of new facilities. Such installations encourage a continuing military presence. Existence of nearby bases reduces the marginal cost of intervening and increases the maximal temptation to make new commitments, meddle in local controversies, and enter nearby conflicts. Observed the Quincy study, "Since 1980, US bases in the greater Middle East have been used at least 25 times to launch wars or other combat operations in at least 15 countries in that region alone. Since 2001, the US military has been involved in combat in at least 25 countries worldwide.[17]

Talk about not respecting borders! The average person would probably say, okay, Afghanistan, Iraq, and Syria. That's three. What are the other twenty-two countries?

Do you have any idea?

The reason you probably don't is that our military likes to hide a lot of what it does because it knows you would object.

> Alas, DOD is less than forthcoming about the number of bases it maintains overseas. According to the report, "Until Fiscal Year 2018, the Pentagon produced and published an annual report in accordance with US law. Even when it produced this report, the Pentagon produced incomplete or inaccurate data, failing to document dozens of well-known installations. For example, the Pentagon has long claimed is has only one base in Africa—Djibouti. But research shows that there are now around 40 installations of varying sizes on the continent; one military official acknowledged 46 installations in 2017."[18]

When there is a media blackout of this information, how can the average American make an informed decision about our military? How can our elected representatives make responsible decisions when such information is kept from them?

The simple answer is they cannot.

And the only group that benefits from this public ignorance is the military-contractor-intelligence complex.

You don't know to be concerned about the number of military bases around the globe.

Don't blame yourself because you didn't know. The news media didn't inform you. I will. Feel free to check all my sources.

* * *

A casual observer might think to themselves, *Okay, so we're spending a lot of money, and we have a lot of military bases overseas. I get that. But at least we're making sure we have the weapons, and the bad guys don't, right?*

That's wrong.

We make sure the bad guys get weapons as well. This is an article from *The Intercept* on May 11, 2023, about US arms sales in 2022.

> Since the end of the Cold War, the United States has been the world's biggest weapons dealer, accounting for 40 percent of all arms exports

> in a given year. In general, these exports are funded through grants or sales. There are two pathways for the latter category: foreign military sales [FMS] and direct commercial sales [DCS].
>
> The U.S. government acts as an intermediary for FMS acquisitions: It buys the material from a company first and then delivers the goods to the foreign recipient. DCS acquisitions are more straight forward: They're the result of an agreement between a U.S. company and a foreign government. Both categories of sales require the government's approval.[19]

The United States is about four percent of the world's population, and yet we sell forty percent of the world's weapons. And that's assuming that the figures we're being provided by our military aren't underestimates of what they're actually doing. And to whom are they selling?

> Country-level data for last year's DCS authorization was released in late April through the State Department's Directorate of Defense Trade Controls. FMS figures for fiscal year 2022 were released earlier this year. According to their data, a total of 142 countries bought weapons from the U.S. in 2022, for a total of $85 billion in bilateral trade . . .
>
> Of the 84 countries classified as autocracies under the Regimes of the World system in 2022, the United States sold weapons to at least 48, or 57 percent of them. The "at least" qualifier is necessary because several factors frustrate the accurate tracking of U.S. weapons sales. The State Department's report of commercial arms sales during the fiscal year makes prodigious use of "various" in its recipient categories; as a result, the specific recipients for nearly $11 billion in weapons sales are not disclosed.[20]

Again, we, the American public, are prevented from having accurate information, and the information that is released somehow never becomes a subject for public discussion among our mainstream news media. And if some commentator does mention these facts, it's usually to say something along the lines of, "Well, it doesn't seem like Americans object to these actions." It's difficult to object when you don't know these actions are taking place.

And this has been a truly bipartisan effort, with Biden being just as profligate as Trump.

> Despite the rhetoric, a review of new data suggests instead a business-as-usual approach to weapons sales. Former President Donald Trump based his arms sales policy primarily on economic considerations: corporate interests above all else. In his first foreign trip as president, he traveled to Saudi Arabia and announced a major arms deal with the repressive kingdom. Trump's business-first approach resulted in a dramatic upturn in weapons sales during his administration.
>
> In Biden's first full fiscal year as president, weapons sales from the United States to other countries reached $206 billion, according to the State Department's annual tally, which uses an opaque but seemingly broader accounting of yearly FMS and DCS figures; Biden's first-year total surpasses the Trump-era high of $192 billion. The multibillion-dollar effort to train and equip Ukraine doesn't fully explain the dramatic rise in total arms sales last year; let alone autocracies.[21]

This slavish devotion to the military-industrial-intelligence complex has to come to an end. While there's much I'll praise about Trump, when it comes to military spending, he was just as bad as any of them. Yes, I've heard the claim that, "You need to feed the military, before you can make any changes," but that seems a recipe for madness. It seems the military just gets fed, and no changes ever occur.

As I look at the more than two decades since the 9/11 attacks, all I see is wasted money and lives. The only people who've done well have been the military contractors. This article from 2021 totals the financial and human cost of the United States military adventures since 2001.

> The U.S.-led global war on terror has killed nearly 1 million people globally and cost more than $8 trillion since it began two decades ago. These staggering figures come from a landmark report issued Wednesday by Brown University's Costs of War Project, an ongoing research effort to document the economic and human impact of post 9/11 military operations.
>
> The report—which looks at the tolls of wars waged in Iraq, Syria, Afghanistan, Pakistan, Somalia, and other regions where the US is militarily engaged—is the latest in a series published by the Costs of Wars Project and provides the most extensive public accounting to date of the consequences of open-ended U.S. conflicts in the Middle East, Central Asia, and Africa, referred to today as the "forever wars."[22]

After the attacks of 9/11, were there a million terrorists we needed to kill? It's estimated the 9/11 attacks cost approximately $250,000 to plan. Did we need to spend $8 trillion to ensure that similar attacks didn't happen in the future? Despite futuristic drone technology, the simple fact is that the Global War on Terror has been an amazingly blunt and indiscriminate tool in seeking to eliminate radical Islamic terrorism. Our adversaries are generally not military forces, which group themselves for attacks on the continental United States, but villagers living in remote regions of the globe where they may hold anti-American views without ever having a realistic chance of ever meeting a genuine American.

What is perhaps inexcusable for any civilized country to do is engage in a protracted conflict in many nations, without expending much energy in determining our level of effectiveness or the misery we may be inflicting on these regions.

> The question of how many people have lost their lives in the post 9/11 conflicts has been the subject of ongoing debate, though the numbers in all cases have been extraordinarily high. Previous Costs of Wars studies have put death toll figures in the hundreds of thousands, an estimate tallying those directly killed by violence. According to a

> 2015 estimate from the Nobel Prize-winning Physicians for Social Responsibility, well over 1 million have been killed both directly and indirectly in wars in Iraq, Afghanistan, and Pakistan alone. The difficulty of calculating death tolls is made harder by the U.S. military's own refusal to keep track of the number of people killed in its operations, as well as the remoteness of the regions where many of these conflicts take place.[23]

If our news media genuinely brought these issues to the attention of the American people, there would be outrage and a demand that we wind down the machinations of the war machine. But the public is kept in a calculated state of ignorance about these matters. All they know is that the military actions continue without end, they don't seem to produce results, and yet every year the military contractors make more and more money, snapping up retired generals and admirals like hoarders at a flea market, who more than earn their pay by getting their former colleagues in the military to buy more and more weapons. The article continued:

> Many will find the astronomical financial cost of the global war on terror galling, not just because of how relatively little it has produced in return, but also because of the discrepancy between what the current price tag of the wars has run and what U.S. officials initially claimed would be required. The war in Iraq provides one sobering example. In September 2002, Lawrence Lindsey, then-chief economic adviser under President George W. Bush, estimated that the "upper-bound" expenses for the looming invasion and occupation would run between $100 and $200 billion. Later that year, Mitch Daniels, then-director of the Office of Management and Budget, provided an even more humble estimate of the costs, saying that war in Iraq would likely run U.S. taxpayers between $50 and $60 billion.[24]

It's been frustrating in the years since Obama took office that I've been considered a "right-winger," when during the Bush years I was something of a darling among the "left-wingers," not just for my anti-war activism, but also for my campaign against the World Trade Organization, another protest movement that mysteriously disappeared when "masked agitators" (hello, baby ANTIFA) started showing up at protests and causing violence. In my mind, I'm neither right nor left; I'm a "truth-winger." I like to think of myself as an umpire, calling balls and strikes as I see them, a commentator who does his work "without fear of favoritism," as the canons of journalism tell us to do.

Where are the people of integrity in the government?

It seems that all the politicians, the bureaucrats, the generals and admirals, and military-industrial-intelligence contractors are just pigs at the trough, and we're the ones stuck paying for the feed.

* * *

How much waste is in the United States Defense budget, and what exactly are we getting for the hundreds of billions of dollars we spend annually on the military? One of the places you might look is a report from 2022 by the Quincy Institute for Responsible Statecraft. Here are just a few of the ways in which the American taxpayers are being robbed:

> Overcharging the Pentagon for spare parts has a long and inglorious history, reaching its previous peak of public visibility during the presidency of Ronald Reagan in the 1980s. Then, blanket media coverage of $640 toilet seats and $7,600 coffee makers sparked public outrage and a series of hearings on Capitol Hill, strengthening the backbone of members of Congress. In those years, they did indeed curb at least the worst excess of the Reagan military buildup.[25]

Regardless of our political persuasions, can we at least agree that military contractors don't seem to have the best track record for honest dealing? I'd like to say that some of the rules under which the military buys parts are crazy, but that might give crazy a bad name. Here's an example.

> A recent POGO [Project on Governmental Oversight] analysis, for instance, documented the malfeasance of TransDign, a military parts supplier that the Department of Defense's Inspector General caught overcharging the Pentagon by as much as 3,800% —yes, you read that right—on routine items. The company was able to do so only because, bizarrely enough, Pentagon buying rules prevent contract officers from getting accurate information on what any given item should cost or might cost the supplying company to produce it.[26]

Even the most profligate shopper in our country understands the concept of comparing the cost of materials and labor into an approximation of what the finished product might cost. And even if they couldn't acquire that information, they'd know to go to two or three stores, maybe check online, to understand whether or not they're getting a good deal. This is our government spending your tax dollars, and the rules (put in by the military contractors?) don't allow those making the purchases to know whether or not they're getting ripped off.

But spare parts are just small change compared to the real moneymakers, weapons systems.

> The next level of Pentagon waste involves weapons we don't need at prices we can't afford, systems that, for staggering sums, fail to deliver on promises to enhance our safety and security. The poster child for such costly, dysfunctional systems is the F-35 combat aircraft, a plane tasked with multiple missions, none of which it does well. The pentagon is slated to buy more than 2,400 F-35s for the Air Force, Marines, and Navy. The estimated lifetime cost for procuring and operating these planes, a mere $1.7 trillion, would make it the Pentagon's most expensive weapons project ever.
>
> Once upon a time (as in some fairy tale), the idea behind the creation of the F-35 was to build a plane that, in several variations, would be able to carry out many different tasks relatively cheaply, with potential savings generated by economies of scale. Theoretically, that meant the bulk of the parts for the thousands of planes to be

> built would be the same for all of them. This approach has proven to be a dismal failure so far, so much so that the researchers at PGO are convinced that the F-35 may never be fully ready for combat.[27]

Let's ask ourselves first if we can trust the $1.7 trillion budget estimated for the F-35. If those making such claims are as bad as those estimating the cost of our overseas military operations, the $1.7 trillion is just sort of a guess. The idea was that this aircraft could work for several different branches of the military and be something of an all-purpose aircraft. But it doesn't look like that's going to happen.

And in the worst piece of news, the F-35 doesn't look like it will ever be "fully ready for combat."

But will the military contractors who brought us this $1.7 trillion monstrosity ever be required to refund that money to the taxpayers?

They should be in jail, rather than celebrating on their yachts.

* * *

Maybe flying in the air is just too tough for our military to figure out.

I understand we have a commercial airline business that seems to work just fine to get people from one country to another safely, but for anything more than stable flight, maybe it doesn't get any better than a World War II P-51 Mustang.

But surely there are some branches of the military that should make us proud.

How about our submarines, those silent killers of the deep, crewed by brave, smart sailors pushing the technology to the very edge as in the classic 1990 movie *The Hunt for Red October*?

According to a *Newsweek* magazine cover story from April 28, 2023, our submarine program may be just as much of a mess as our aviation program. This is what they found as the result of a three-month investigation, in what may be one of the few remaining examples of genuine investigative journalism in our country.

> The U.S. Navy plans to expand its submarine fleet at a cost of $200 billion, equivalent to the GDP of Ukraine. But as Republicans hotly debate ongoing military aid to Kiev, neither party has questioned the far more costly submarine program—allowing the Navy to conceal a startling fact about America's submarine fleet. The Navy calls its submarines, "the most lethal and capable force." It is also the "silent service," shrouded in secrecy, the nature of its operations closely guarded.
>
> The American attack submarine force—the "fighting" submarines—exist in order to pursue enemy submarines and ships, eavesdrop on adversaries and support operations by special forces. Hollywood productions like *The Hunt for Red October* have created the impression of submarines tracking the enemy while moving noiselessly under the sea, operating stealthily for months on end. The reality is markedly different. The U.S. Navy can deploy barely a quarter of its attack submarine force at any one time, and last year, despite a war raging in Ukraine and China's rise as a global superpower, only 10 percent of its submarines operated stealthily by spending more than 30 days fully submerged.[28]

Our submarine force isn't a "new" thing, like the F-35 fighter. We've had submarines since October 12, 1900, when the United States Navy launched the *USS Holland*, more than 120 years ago.[29] And yet we don't seem to be able to wield it effectively as a fighting force. In the event of an actual crisis, we couldn't get more than a fourth of the fleet out in the ocean. Since our current number of submarines is fifty, that means we'd only be able to get about twelve or thirteen of them to where they need to go. And so much for our submarines being the "silent service" when they're in that mode only about 10 percent of the time. The *Newsweek* investigation continued:

> The Navy's $200 billion building program is aimed at increasing the number of attack submarines from 50 to 66. That number is public. The statistic that's not discussed is that modern submarines have

> become so complex, the only way the Navy can appreciably increase its level of operations against Russia and China is by building many more. The Pentagon declares this an urgent task: China has the world's largest navy, and its submarine force is commonly described as catching up to the United States in quantity and quality. But as sluggish as the U.S. submarine performance is, Russia and China are even worse off. That raises further questions as to why the Navy is spending so much money in upgrading the attack submarine fleet, and in the ultimate value of such gold-plated machines.[30]

Sometimes it's difficult to escape the suspicion that all our military and civilian leaders have lost their minds. The only silver lining in all of this may be that our main adversaries, Russia and China, don't seem to be doing much better. Are we simply engaging in this madness because nobody is willing to stand up and call it out? Consider these statistics:

> According to secret Navy records, only 32 of 50 attack submarines deployed in 2022. Those submarines spent a cumulative 151 months at sea, a quarter of what was theoretically possible. On average, 28 percent of their time at sea was in transit to and from Asia and Europe, making the actual time forward deployed and "on-station" about 107 months. In other words, less than 20 percent of America's attack submarines were fully deployed and fully operational at any one time during a tumultuous year. It also means that the plan to increase the number of attack submarines from 50 to 66 effectively adds only four deployable forward subs.
>
> "I thought they were out there all the time, you know, because the Russians are coming and the Chinese military is growing," says Hans Kristensen, the premier nuclear expert at the Federation of American Scientists, and someone who had studied submarines for decades, commenting on *Newsweek*'s findings. "What these new numbers tell me is that the attack submarines are not war winners."[31]

These are shocking numbers and a testament to the need for good journalism. How can there be such an important issue as the reliability and usefulness of our submarine fleet, and we're so much in the dark about it?

The reason is because it serves the interest of those who want us to keep shoveling money into these programs. Why are we spending $200 billion dollars a year on a program that is not a "war winner?" The article concluded:

> "There is no question that when it comes to our submarines, platform to platform, our boats are unmatchable," says a former Pentagon procurement executive.
>
> "I'd say it's time to reevaluate our priorities. Especially when the Ukraine war has taught us about the importance of a different kind of depth, the depth of our inventories, how voracious real war is for basic guns and ammunition," he says. "We can't be so enamored of our own myths to miss this reality."[32]

Do I believe that the *Newsweek* reporter was the first individual to grasp the contradictions and problems with our submarine fleet? That would be madness. Instead, I believe there are many smart people involved in the defense industries who are clear-eyed about the problems, and yet their job requires them to act as if they don't see it. The incentive is to lie, rather than to tell the truth, and that's why you get this behavior.

However long this bad situation has been the case, that's too damned long.

* * *

It might come as a surprise, given our polarized political climate, to realize that in the darkest days of World War II, politicians were celebrated for calling out waste, fraud, and abuse in the military budget, rather than being called "an apologist for Hitler, Tojo, and Mussolini."

In fact, it was the work Harry Truman did in the Senate, looking into military overspending during World War II, which so impressed President

Franklin Delano Roosevelt that he put Truman on the ticket with him in 1944, as Roosevelt knew his own health was failing. This is from a *TIME* magazine article on the Truman Committee from March 8, 1943. It is startling to read how good journalism once was in America, and how celebrated civic virtue was in our past.

> Anywhere but in a democracy, the Senate's irreverent Truman Committee would be fair game for liquidation. In a perfect state, free from butterfingers and human frailty, it would be unnecessary. In the U.S., democratic but far from perfect, the Truman Committee this week celebrated its second successful birthday as one of the most useful Government agencies of World War II.
>
> Had they had time, its ten members might have toasted their accomplishments all night. They had served as watchdog, spotlight, conscience, and spark plug to the economic war-behind-the-lines. They had prodded Commerce Secretary Jesse Jones into building synthetic-rubber-plants, bludgeoned the President into killing off doddering old SPAB and setting up WPB.
>
> They had called the turn on raw-materials shortages, had laid down the facts of the rubber famine four months before the famed Baruch report. One single investigation of graft and waste in Army camp building, had saved the U.S. $250,000,000 (according to the Army's own lieut. General Brehon B. Somervell). Their total savings ran into the billions, partly because of what their agents had ferreted out in the sprawling war program, partly because their hooting curiosity was a great deterrent to waste.[33]

Can you imagine anything similar being published in today's media? It was a piece that pulsed with life and an understanding of the human condition, yet it also had an optimism that it was possible to change things for the better. The article called Truman a "watchdog, spotlight, conscience and spark plug" and made the larger picture of why, during a national emergency, it was even more important for a critic to be heard.

> In wartime, even more than in peace, a democracy must keep an eye on itself. This eye the Truman Committee has kept unblinkingly and, by & large, well. It has made mistakes. Some of its data have been gathered too quickly, then reduced to generalities that glittered without illuminating. It members, including Chairman Harry S. Truman, have sometimes failed to look before they leaped to conclusions. But it has never strayed too far off the beam, nor stayed there too long.
>
> Said one Washingtonian last week: "There's only one thing that worries me more than the present state of the war effort. That's to think what it would be like now without Truman." For a Congressional committee to be considered the first line of defense—especially in a nation which does not tend to admire its representatives, in Congress assembled—is encouraging to believers in democracy. So is the sudden emergence of Harry Truman, whose presence in the Senate is a queer accident of democracy, as the committee's energetic generalissimo.[34]

Are these people "insurrectionists?" Do they genuinely believe that in a crisis situation we should have people investigating the actions of the government and the private corporations with whom they are doing business? Don't they know that the best answer is to deplatform such critics from all media, maybe shadow-ban them at the least, and engage in anonymous *ad hominem* attacks? Just like the health Nazis in our government got Amazon to ban books that questioned the effectiveness of masks. Where are the Big Pharma spinmeisters when you need them?

Call in the Pfizer brigade to counter this "attack on democracy!"

And unlike today's media, in which anybody on your side is an exemplary human being whose perfection would be the envy of Jesus Christ himself, and the other side is a more cunning and dangerous foe than Satan, *TIME* painted Truman's career with an objective brush, especially his rise to power through the actions of the notorious Kansas City Democratic machine headed by Boss Tom Pendergast.

> In a perfect democracy, free from bosses, string-pulling and finagling at the polls, Harry Truman would probably never have reached Washington. He was Tom Pendergast's hand-picked candidate, yanked out of obscurity so deep that few Missouri voters had ever heard of him. He was nominated, over two more deserving candidates, largely by a vast plurality rolled up in Boss Pendergast's Jackson County, whose registration lists were loaded with dead men or men who never lived. Thanks to the Boss's great power and the New Deal's 1934 popularity, his election was then automatic.
>
> No one yet knows why Boss Pendergast picked Truman for the Senate. One theory: the Boss was in the whimsical mood of a socialite sneaking a pet Pekingese into the Social Register. A better theory: the Boss was impressed by the Midwestern adage that every manure pile should sprout one rose—he saw in Truman a personally honest, courageous man whose respectability would disguise the odors of the Pendergast mob. Certainly Truman was no statesman in 1934. Neither had he ever been touched by scandal.[35]

Honesty about a public figure is possible, and not just in some biography released decades after they've left the scene. In fact, it's refreshing. As the old saying goes, "Every saint has a past, and every sinner a future." How likely is a current mainstream media news source to describe a political figure as coming from a "manure pile" and yet also having turned out to be a "rose"?

Could we, in our modern era, discuss a political figure and say something like, "They came from a bad place, but have surprised us in a positive way with their actions?" Especially if that person was a white male? No, first they'd have to disclose their pronouns, we'd have to find out if they were ever a jerk to somebody in high school, and then we'd have to do a deep dive into every person they know and all the people they may have shared a stage with at one time, and then look at those individuals to see who *they* may know. It's like that game "Six Degrees of Kevin Bacon," but instead of an amusing little trivia mindbender, it becomes the nuclear weapon with which to destroy a person's reputation.

Harry Truman is an interesting example, not because he was so unique, but because his example is so common. There are lots of good people in the world trying to do the right thing in an imperfect system.

More than anything, this book is for them.

I spend a lot of time talking about the plans of the globalists, but I'd like people to understand that for every one globalist, there are ninety-nine good people trying to make whatever system they're in work to the best of its capacity. If you've ever worked in a large organization, you understand there's management that proclaims the way things should be done, and then there are the workers who get things done. And every worker understands that their most important job might be to ignore the edicts of management and do the job the way it should be done for the benefit of the public. The globalists act like they're in charge, but the truth is that we are the ones in control. We just need to act like it.

Because of the Truman Committee, billions of dollars were saved for the American taxpayer, and World War II was successfully fought to victory. But what happens when there are no watchdogs over government actions and certain powerful actors are allowed to operate in the shadows?

In many ways, that has precisely become the history of America since the end of the second World War.

* * *

I often speak of Eisenhower's farewell message to the American public that warned of the dangers of the military industrial complex. But I don't think that modern audiences appreciate how radical a statement that was when the former World War II supreme commander announced it to the public. If a figure of such similar respect in our time made such a statement, he'd be reviled by our media and intelligence agencies as being "far-right" or possibly a "white supremacist." This is the full text of the ten minutes of Eisenhower's speech, delivered on January 17, 1961:

My fellow Americans:

Three days from now, after half a century in the service of our country, I shall lay down the responsibilities of office as, in traditional and solemn ceremony, the authority of the Presidency is vested in my successor.

This evening I come to you with a message of leave-taking and farewell, and to share a few final thoughts with you, my countrymen. Like every other citizen, I wish the new President, and all who will labor with him, Godspeed. I pray that the coming years will be blessed with peace and prosperity for all.

Our people expect their President and the Congress to find essential agreement on issues of great moment, the wise resolution of which will better shape the future of the Nation. My own relations with the Congress, which began on a remote and tenuous basis when, long ago, a member of the Senate appointed me to West Point, have since ranged to the intimate during the war and immediate post-war period, and, finally, to the mutually interdependent during these past eight years.

In this final relationship, the Congress and the Administration have, on most vital issues, cooperated well, to serve the national good rather than mere partisanship, and so have assured that the business of the Nation should go forward. So, my official relationship with the Congress ends in a feeling, on my part, of gratitude that we have been able to do so much together.

We now stand ten years past the midpoint of a century that has witnessed four major wars among great nations. Three of these involved our own country. Despite these holocausts America is today the strongest, the most influential and most productive nation in the world. Understandably proud of this pre-eminence, we yet realize that America's leadership and prestige depend, not merely on our unmatched material progress, riches and military strength, but on how we use our power in the interest of world peace and human betterment.

Throughout America's adventure in free government, our basic purposes have been to keep the peace; to foster progress in human achievement, and to enhance liberty, dignity and integrity among people and among nations. To strive for less would be unworthy of a free and religious people. Any failure traceable to arrogance, or our lack of comprehension or readiness to sacrifice would inflict upon us grievous hurt both at home and abroad.

Progress toward these noble goals is persistently threatened by the conflict now engulfing the world. It commands our whole attention, absorbs our very beings. We face a hostile ideology—global in scope, atheistic in character, ruthless in purpose, and insidious in method. Unhappily the danger it poses promises to be on indefinite duration. To meet it successfully, there is called for, not so much the emotional and transitory sacrifices of crisis, but rather those which enable us to carry forward, steadily, surely, and without complaint the burdens of a prolonged and complex struggle—with liberty at stake. Only thus shall we remain, despite every provocation, on our charted course toward permanent peace and human betterment.

Crises there will continue to be. In meeting them, whether foreign or domestic, great or small, there is a recurring temptation to feel that some spectacular and costly action could become the miraculous solution to all current difficulties. A huge increase in newer elements of our defense; development of unrealistic programs to cure every ill in agriculture; a dramatic expansion in basic and applied research—these and many other possibilities, each possibly promising in itself, may be suggested as the only way to the road we wish to travel.

But each proposal must be weighed in light of the broader consideration: the need to maintain balance in and among the national programs—balance between the clearly necessary and the comfortably desirable; balance between our essential requirements as a nation and the duties imposed by the nation upon the individual; balance between action of the moment and the national welfare of the future. Good judgment seeks balance and progress; lack of it eventually finds imbalance and frustration.

The record of many decades stands as proof that our people and their government have, in the main, understood these truths and have responded to them well, in the face of stress and threat. But threats, new in kind or degree, constantly arise. I mention two only.

A vital element in keeping the peace is our military establishment. Our arms must be mighty, ready for instant action, so that no potential aggressor may be tempted to risk his own destruction. Our military organization today bears little relation to that known by any of my predecessors in peace time, or indeed by the fighting men of World War II or Korea. Until the latest of our world conflicts, the United States had no armaments industry.

American makers of plowshares could, with time and as required, make swords as well. But we can no longer risk emergency improvisation of national defense; as we have been compelled to create a permanent armaments industry of vast proportions. Added to this, three and a half million men and women are directly engaged in the defense establishment. We annually spend on military security more than the net income of all United States corporations.

The conjunction of an immense military establishment and a large arms industry is new in the American experience. The total influence—economic, political, even spiritual—is felt in every city, every state house, every office of the Federal Government. We recognize the imperative need for this development. Yet we must not fail to comprehend its grave implications. Our toil, resources and livelihood are all involved; so is the very structure of our society.

In the councils of government, we must guard against the acquisition of unwarranted influence, whether sought or unsought, by the military industrial complex. The potential for the disastrous rise of misplaced power exists and will persist.

We must never let the weight of this combination endanger our liberties or democratic processes. We should take nothing for granted. Only an alert and knowledgeable citizenry can compel the proper meshing of the huge industrial and military machinery of defense with our peaceful methods and goals, so that security and liberty may prosper together.

Akin to, and largely responsible for the sweeping changes in our industrial-military posture, has been the technological revolution during recent decades.

In this revolution, research has become central; it also becomes more formalized, complex, and costly. A steadily increasing share is conducted for, by, or at the direction of, the Federal government. Today, the solitary inventor, tinkering in his shop, has been overshadowed by task forces of scientists in laboratories and testing fields. In the same fashion, the free university, historically the foundation of free ideas and scientific discovery, has experienced a revolution in the conduct of research. Partly because of the huge costs involved, a government contract becomes virtually a substitute for intellectual curiosity. For every old blackboard, there are now hundreds of electronic computers.

The prospect of domination of the nation's scholars by Federal employment, project allocations, and the power of money is ever present and is gravely to be regarded. Yet, in holding scientific research and discovery in respect, as we should, we must also be alert to the equal and opposite danger that public policy could itself become the captive of a scientific-technological elite.

It is the task of statesmanship to mold, to balance, and to integrate these and other forces, new and old, within the principles of our democratic system—ever aiming toward the supreme goals of a free society.

Another factor in maintaining balance involves the element of time. As we peer into society's future, we, you and I, and our government, must avoid the impulse only to live for today, plundering, for our own ease and convenience, the precious resources of tomorrow. We cannot mortgage the material assets of our grandchildren without risking the loss also of their political and spiritual heritage. We want democracy to survive for all generations to come, not to become the insolvent phantom of tomorrow.

Down the long lane of history yet to be written, America knows that this world of ours, ever growing smaller, must avoid becoming a community of dreadful fear and hate, and be, instead, a proud confederation of mutual trust and respect.

Such a confederation must be one of equals. The weakest must come to the conference table with the same confidence as we do, protected by our moral, economic, and military strength. That table, though scarred by many past frustrations, cannot be abandoned for the certain agony of the battlefield.

Disarmament, with mutual honor and confidence, is a continuing imperative. Together we must learn how to compose difference, not with arms, but with intellect and decent purpose. Because this need is so sharp and apparent, I confess that I lay down my official responsibilities in this field with a definite sense of disappointment. As one who has witnessed the horror and the lingering sadness of war—as one who knows that another war could utterly destroy this civilization which has been so slowly and painfully built over thousands of years—I wish I could say tonight that a lasting peace is at hand.

Happily, I can say that war has been avoided. Steady progress toward our ultimate goal has been made. But so much remains to be done. As a private citizen, I shall never cease to do what little I can to help the world advance along that road.

So, in this last good night to you as your President—I thank you for the many opportunities you have given me for public service in war and peace. I trust that in that service you find something worthy; as for the rest of it, I know you will find ways to improve performance in the future.

You and I—my fellow citizens—need to be strong in our faith that all nations, under God, will reach the goal of peace with justice. May we be ever unswerving in devotion to principle, confident but humble with power, diligent in pursuit of the Nation's great goals.

> To all the people of the world, I once more give expression to America's prayerful and continuing inspiration:
>
> We pray that peoples of all faiths, all races, all nations, may have their great human needs satisfied; that those now denied opportunity shall come to enjoy it to the full; that all who yearn for freedom may experience its spiritual blessings; that those who have freedom will understand, also, its heavy responsibilities; that all who are insensitive to the needs of others will learn charity; that the scourges of poverty, disease and ignorance will be made to disappear from the earth, and that, in the goodness of time, all peoples will come to live together in a peace guaranteed by the binding force of mutual respect and love.[36]

Don't you long for a time when an American president spoke with such intelligence, humility, and compassion? Eisenhower never had much of a reputation for soaring oratory, but in this farewell speech you saw right into the soul of the man. There's no doubt in my mind that if anyone in a prominent position today, like Tulsi Gabbard, Tucker Carlson, or me, said something similar (and we have) we'd be called "Putin's Puppet" (which has happened to each one of us).

Eisenhower spoke with absolute clarity about the dangers he saw facing the country, which have now, unfortunately, all come true.

In the foreign arena, he saw communism as "a hostile ideology—global in scope, atheistic in character, ruthless in purpose, and insidious in method." Everybody understand that danger? Good. Sixty-three years later, the Soviet Union is gone, but now China still clings to this inhuman ideology that crushes the human spirit. Let's move from the dangers outside our country to the two dangers he saw inside the country—the ways in which we might be destroyed from within.

Eisenhower feared the "military-industrial complex," which, through the changes in the world situation, had the potential to change us as a people.

The second danger Eisenhower saw was that the country might become the "captive of a scientific and technological elite." With what Eisenhower had seen in his role as president, one wonders what he might have made of the actions of Dr. Anthony Fauci and the COVID-19 Task Force during the COVID crisis.

We may never know what President Eisenhower would have made of the actions of Dr. Fauci, but it might have resembled the scorching criticism given to these measures by one of the more conservative members of the Supreme Court, Justice Neil Gorsuch. The case in which he issued his opinion dealt with Republican states that wanted to keep Title 42, the public health policy used during the COVID crisis to turn away asylum seekers. As reported by the *Daily Mail*:

> In a statement written as part of a Supreme Court case about Title 42, Gorsuch said emergency decrees were issued during the pandemic "on a breathtaking scale."
>
> "Governors and local leaders imposed lockdown orders forcing people to remain in their homes. They shuttered businesses and schools, public and private," he wrote.
>
> "They closed churches even as they allowed casinos and other favored businesses to carry on. They threatened violators not just with civil penalties, but with criminal sanctions, too."[37]

One wonders where all the supposed civil libertarians were when these violations were taking place. They showed their true colors, like physically strong, but morally weak actor and former California governor, Arnold Schwarzenegger, who famously said of those who opposed the lockdown policies, "Screw your freedom."[38]

Personally, I think we should put all those public figures who didn't oppose the lockdowns under house confinement for another two years, or until they can pass a basic civics test on the rights guaranteed under the Constitution. The *Daily Mail*'s report on Gorsuch's tirade continued:

> The justice, who was nominated to the Supreme Court by Donald Trump in 2017, gave examples of how authorities "surveilled church parking lots, recorded license plates, and issued notices warning that attendance at even outdoor services satisfying all state

> social-distancing and hygiene requirements could amount to criminal conduct."
>
> He explained how "federal executive officials entered the act too," through vaccine mandates which included threats of dismissal for employees and service members who refused.
>
> "Along the way, it seems federal officials may have pressured social-media companies to suppress information about pandemic policies with which they disagreed," Gorsuch added.
>
> Emergency decrees were issued "at a furious pace," while Congress and state legislatures "too often fell silent."[39]

This is not ancient history, like something from the 1840s when the courts were wrestling with the issue of slavery, or the 1940s, when the Supreme Court shamefully concluded that Japanese American citizens could be confined in internment camps and Italian American and German American citizens could also be subjected to a higher level of legal scrutiny. These measures were undertaken by the supposedly most liberal members of our political community, those who push "safe spaces" instead of robust debates, Diversity, Equity, and Inclusion over competence, and are in favor of lopping off the genitals of minors who lack the legal capacity to consent to even a small flower tattoo on their ankle.

But even those who claim they abolished freedom in the name of safety don't have the data on their side.

> One review by an international team of economists found draconian shutdowns only reduced COVID mortality by 3 percent in the UK, US, and Europe in 2020.
>
> The experts, from Johns Hopkins University in the US, Lund University in Sweden, and the Danish think tank, the Center for Political Studies, said that equates to 6,000 fewer deaths in Europe and 4,000 fewer in the United States.
>
> But official data in the US has showed the country suffered nearly 300,000 more deaths than usual in more than two years of the pandemic, that cannot be attributed to COVID.[40]

Let's leave aside for a moment the question of the genocidal campaign against the early use of therapeutics like hydroxychloroquine and ivermectin, the lockdowns that lowered immune function due to lack of exercise, the spiritual calm felt by going to church, vitamin D from sunlight, the lack of social connection, and the weight put on by sheltering in place. What was the strongest correlation with COVID death? Whether or not you were overweight.

I am specifically not raising those issues, simply noting that even by this very conservative analysis of experts, the lockdowns in the United States are implicated in at least 296,000 deaths.

Despite Eisenhower's warning, we became the "captives of a scientific-technological elite" and, as a result, nearly three hundred thousand Americans lost their lives.

Chapter Seven

The Deep State Makes Its Move

President John F. Kennedy took office three days after Eisenhower's speech, on January 20, 1960. Two days after Kennedy took his oath to protect the country "against all enemies, foreign and domestic," the CIA and military brass were in his office, convincing him to agree to a plan, originally conceived of as a much smaller operation by the Eisenhower Administration, to foment an uprising in Cuba at a location known as the Bay of Pigs.

The invasion in April 1960 was a complete disaster, in addition to being in direct violation of international law.

The lies told to President Kennedy made him so angry that he reportedly told a top aide, "I want to shatter the CIA into a thousand pieces and scatter it to the winds."[1]

How did this experience change President Kennedy? This is what a well-regarded historical outlet says about that question.

> As a result of the disaster, Kennedy revamped the administration's decision-making process. He instituted a more collegial atmosphere, in which pros and cons could be openly discussed. He emphasized consulting with allies and being concerned with the impact of international law on major foreign policy decisions. And most importantly, the focus of decision-making moved from the CIA to advisors the new president trusted, including his brother Robert Kennedy, the attorney general, and old friend Theodore Sorensen. The CIA and the National Security Council would be consulted, but they would no longer have total sway in the new administration.[2]

When somebody lies to you, it should matter. Your behavior toward them should change. Whatever Kennedy's personal failings may have been, he executed his duties as president with the utmost seriousness. He did not want to get into war with another nuclear armed nation, and everything was devoted toward that aim. Kennedy made a mistake by listening to his intelligence and military advisors.

But he learned from that mistake, and as a result, a nuclear war with the Soviets was likely averted in 1962, as the article continued to its main point.

> Kennedy emerged from the Bay of Pigs disaster with a distrust of the permanent government foreign policy agencies. That caution proved instrumental in coping with the even-more serious crisis ahead.
>
> Sandman [author of a book on Kennedy and the Bay of Pigs disaster] argues that the changes may well have saved the world. By the time of the Cuban Missile Crisis in October 1962, which Sandman argues grew directly out of the Bay of Pigs disaster, Kennedy constructed an advisory process that worked. Not only had he changed advisors, he had also changed the procedures to make decisions on foreign crises. The permanent foreign policy establishment was consulted, but no longer made the final call. A collegial decision-making process kept options opened, and prevented a quick decision that might have led to nuclear war.[3]

Kennedy reportedly told his good friend, Ben Bradley, that he wanted his epitaph to read, "He kept the peace."[4] While we still do not have the truth about the assassination of President Kennedy, as our government continues to hold back important documents nearly sixty years after his death, we do know Kennedy fulfilled his greatest desire, and deserves to have "He kept the peace" as his epitaph.

But how well did other presidents fare when our military and intelligence agencies wanted to cause trouble in foreign lands?

* * *

Since the assassination of President John F. Kennedy, what have been the incidents that have clearly demonstrated that our government lies to us about the most basic issues of war and peace?

Let's look first at what happened less than a year after Kennedy's death in the Gulf of Tonkin, leading up to the Vietnam War. From the February 2008 edition of *Naval History Magazine* (the official journal of the US Naval Institute):

> In early 1964, South Vietnam began conducting a covert series of U.S.-backed commando attacks and intelligence-gathering missions along the North Vietnamese coast. Codenamed Operations Plan (OPLAN) 34A, the activities were conceived and overseen by the Department of Defense, with the support of the Central Intelligence Agency, and carried out by the South Vietnamese Navy. Initial successes, however, were limited; numerous South Vietnamese raiders were captured, and OPLAN 34A units suffered heavy casualties. In July 1964, Lieutenant General William C. Westmoreland, commander of the U.S. Military Assistance Command, Vietnam, shifted the operation's tactics from commando attacks on land to shore bombardments using mortars, rockets, and recoilless rifles fired from South Vietnamese patrol boats.[5]

In other words, the United States was actively assisting an undercover war in a foreign country against whom no declaration of war had been made by the United States Congress. In other words, what Lieutenant General William C. Westmoreland was engaged in was unconstitutional, as were the actions of the United States military and CIA. And like they'd been doing in Cuba, not only were their actions unconstitutional, but they were also inept.

The raiders kept getting caught.

What do you do if your raiders keep getting caught?

Keep them on the water and have them fire their weapons from the boat. Then, when the North Vietnamese sent their patrol boats out, the South Vietnamese boats would race like hell to escape them, maybe even passing by their friendly American ships to get the North Vietnamese boats to break off the chase.

In many ways, the operations of the United States at this time in Vietnam were similar to the small raids made against Cuba prior to the Cuban Missile Crisis. The actions of the US Navy were further detailed:

> The U.S. Navy, meanwhile, had been conducting occasional reconnaissance and SIGINT-gathering missions farther offshore in the Tonkin Gulf. Destroyers carried out these so-called Desoto patrols. After missions in December 1962 and April of the next year, patrols were scheduled in 1964 in the vicinity of OPLAN 34A raids. In fact, one of the patrols' main missions was to gather information that would be useful to the raiders. A top-secret document declassified in 2005 revealed the standing orders to the Desoto patrols; [L]ocate and identify all coastal radar transmitters, note all navigation aid along the DRV's [Democratic Republic of Vietnam's] coastline, and monitor the Vietnamese junk fleet for a possible connection to DRV/Viet Cong maritime supply and infiltration routes.
>
> The United States was playing a dangerous game. The South Vietnamese conducted OPLAN 34A raids and the U.S. Navy's Desoto patrols could be perceived as collaborative efforts against North Vietnamese targets. In reality, there was no coordination between the forces conducting the operations.[6]

I give the author a lot of credit for telling what seems to be most of the truth. To understand my suspicions, let's piece together what's already admitted and what they want us to believe, and you tell me what your bullshit detector says.

They admit that the US Department of Defense and CIA were planning and overseeing the raids on the North Vietnamese coast by the South Vietnamese Navy.

They admit that US Navy destroyers were being used to get information on North Vietnamese installations, and this information would then be fed to the South Vietnamese Navy, who would be undertaking their raids under the oversight of the United States.

The South Vietnamese raiders, under the control of the US Department of Defense, and the US destroyers, who were also under the control of the US Department of Defense, were placed in the same waters on the night of a raid.

Maybe it was all just an accident, an unfortunate oversight.

But if that was true, why didn't anybody say anything at the time?

I think the only rational conclusion is that those in charge (Department of Defense, CIA?) wanted to provoke an incident, which could be used as a pretext for war.

And that's just what they got.

The destroyer *USS Maddox* left Taiwan on July 28, 1964, and just happened to be in the area of Hon Me Island, when some South Vietnamese raiders were making an attack on that same island.

> On the night of 30-31 July, the destroyer was on station in the Gulf of Tonkin when a 34A raid was launched against Hon Me Island. From two boats, South Vietnamese commandos fired machine guns and small cannon at the island's radar and military installations. At the same time, two other South Vietnamese commando boats carried out a similar attack against Hon Ngu Island, more than 25 miles to the south.
>
> After observing North Vietnamese patrol torpedo boats pursuing the vessels that had attacked Hon Me, the *Maddox* withdrew from the area. Nevertheless, when later queried by NSA headquarters, the destroyer indicated she had been unaware of the OPLAN raid on the island. That ignorance set the stage for a showdown between North Vietnamese forces and the U.S. Navy eavesdropping platform.[7]

Is it surprising that the North Vietnamese might stage some sort of a response? Do you genuinely believe this was the result of "ignorance"? To me it seems that the military and intelligence leaders were gambling with the lives of the young men under their authority, and I find that unforgiveable. This is what happened on August 1, 1964:

> At 1440, the destroyer detected three North Vietnamese patrol boats approaching her position from the west. Aware of North Vietnamese intent from the earlier SIGINT message, Captain Herrick ordered gun crews to open fire if the fast-approaching trio closed to within 10,000 yards [a little over five and a half miles] of the destroyer, and at about 1505 three 5-inch shots were fired across the bow of the closest boat. In return, the lead vessel launched a torpedo and veered away. A second boat then launched two "fish" but was hit by gunfire from the destroyer. Re-engaging, the first PT boat launched a second torpedo and opened fire with her 14.5-mm guns, but Maddox shell fire heavily damaged the vessel.[8]

Of the three boats that came after the Maddox, one was left dead in the water burning, and the other two were heavily damaged.

Now, this single attack, which, while it took place under murky circumstances, was nonetheless real, probably wasn't enough to provoke a declaration of war from the US Congress. If this was a mistake on the part of our military personnel, then why did they keep ratcheting up the attacks on North Vietnam?

> The next day, the *Maddox* resumed her Desoto patrol, and, to demonstrate American resolve and the right to navigate in international waters, President Lyndon B. Johnson ordered the U.S.S. *Turner Joy* (DD-951) to join the first destroyer on patrol off the North Vietnamese coast. That night, the South Vietnamese staged more OPLAN 34A raids. Three patrol craft attacked a security garrison at Cua Ron (the mouth of the Ron River) and a radar site at Vinh Son, firing 770 rounds of high-explosive munitions at the targets. North Vietnamese installations had been attacked four separate times in five days.[9]

It's sometimes difficult for me emotionally to read these accounts of a war that began fifty-nine years ago. Not because I was alive during those events, but because I have known many Vietnam veterans in my life. By and large, they are the kind of good, patriotic men this country has always produced, who were so terribly betrayed and, in many cases, irreparably damaged. People like General William Westmoreland, Defense Secretary Bob McNamara, and others avoided responsibility for their crimes, and the only solace I take is that God is ultimately in charge of bringing justice to those who have done evil.

Soldiers and sailors on the front line of combat can make mistakes, and yet be honorable. And this was never more the case than in the Gulf of Tonkin incident. Because on the night of August 4, 1964, there was an enormous amount of confusion, as the article from the U.S. Naval Institute recounts:

> In contrast to the clear conditions two days earlier, thunderstorms and rain squalls reduced visibility and increased wave heights to six feet. In addition to the difficult detection conditions, the *Maddox*'s SPS-40 long-range air-search radar and the *Turner Joy*'s SPG-53 fire-control radar were both inoperative. That night Herrick had the two ships move out to sea to give themselves space to maneuver in case of attack.
>
> The *Maddox* nevertheless reported at 2040 that she was tracking unidentified vessels. Although the U.S. destroyers were operating more than 100 miles from the North Vietnamese coastline, the approaching vessels seemed to come at the ships from multiple directions, some from the northeast, others from the southwest. Still other targets appeared from the east, mimicking attacking profiles of torpedo boats. Targets would disappear, and then the new targets would appear from the opposite compass directions.[10]

Is the scene becoming clear in your mind? Everybody was in a state of high alert. Tempers were short because there had been an attack a few days earlier. The weather turned nasty, some of the critical equipment wasn't working, and then this data came in that didn't make any sense.

Did the crew of the *Maddox* and *Turner Joy* imagine they were in the middle of a Pearl Harbor-like surprise? It didn't make sense, but that's what their instruments were telling them.

> Over the next three hours, the two ships repeatedly maneuvered at high speeds to evade perceived enemy boat attacks. The destroyers reported automatic-weapons fire; more than 20 torpedo attacks; sightings of torpedo wakes, enemy cockpit lights, and searchlight illumination; and numerous radar and surface contacts. By the time the destroyers broke off their "counterattack," they had fired 249 5-inch shells, 123 3-inch shells, and four or five depth charges.[11]

The seamen of the *Maddox* and the *Turner Joy* believed they were under attack. But in reality, it seemed to be a case of malfunctioning equipment and mass hysteria. The lone pilot who was able to get his plane in the air (James Stockdale, who would later be imprisoned in the Hanoi Hilton and run for vice president with Reform Party candidate Ross Perot) later reported, "I had the best seat in the house to watch that event and our destroyers were just shooting at phantom targets. There were no PT boats there . . . there was nothing there but black water and American firepower."[12]

While Stockdale was the first to realize that the attack was a false alarm, eventually the captain of the *Maddox* came to the same conclusion.

> Captain Herrick also began to have doubts about the attack. As the battle continued, he realized the "attacks" were actually the result of "overeager sonar operators" and poor equipment performance. The *Turner Joy* had not detected any torpedoes during the entire encounter, and Herrick determined that the *Maddox*'s operators were probably hearing the ship's propellors reflecting off her rudder during sharp turns. The destroyer's main gun director was never able to lock

> onto any targets because, as the operator surmised, the radar was detecting the stormy sea's wave tops.
>
> By 0127 on 5 August, hours after the "attacks" had occurred, Herrick had queried his crew and reviewed the preceding hours' events. He sent a flash (highest priority) message to Honolulu, which was received in Washington at 1327 on 4 August, [Vietnam was one day ahead of Washington, DC, because it's over the International Date Line] declaring his doubts. "Review of action makes many reported contacts and torpedoes fired appear doubtful. Freak weather effects on radar and overeager sonarmen may have accounted for many reports. No actual visual sighting by Maddox. Suggest complete evaluation before any further action taken."[13]

I think we'd do well to imagine that, for the most part, people on the front line of an issue, whether it be on the battlefield, a hospital, or a classroom, are trying to do the right thing. The problem seems to begin when it moves up the chain of command, and those in positions of authority (who may not be as ethical) seek to manipulate the information for their own ends. The Gulf of Tonkin situation may be an exception to this general rule, as it seems those in charge manipulated the situation (having South Vietnamese raiders operating around American destroyers) without informing the two groups, in order to bring about a confrontation. I understand there are those who will say, "Yes, it appears there was a lack of coordination between the two groups, but you haven't proved malevolent intent."

However, just as in a murder case, the attempt to hide a body, rather than report it to the police, will generally be taken as evidence that a crime was committed, not simply that the person died of a heart attack. How one acts *after* the fact can certainly provide at least some evidence of the *intent* of a person.

The evidence provided about the actions of the pilot, Commander James Stockdale, and Captain Herrick show that they discharged their duties in a reasonable and ethical fashion. When they believed they were under attack, they took all possible evasive measures, including firing at the perceived enemy. When the alert had passed, they investigated whether their belief was accurate, realized they could not verify an attack had taken place, and informed their superiors that the preliminary reports were likely to be wrong.

But those further up the chain of command did not act with such honor.

> Back on board the *Ticonderoga*, Commander Stockdale had been ordered to prepare to launch an air strike against North Vietnamese targets for their "attacks" of the previous evening. Unlike Captain Herrick, Stockdale had no doubts about what had happened: "We were about to launch a war under false pretenses, in the face of the on-scene military commander's advice to the contrary." Despite his reservations, Stockdale led a strike of 18 aircraft against an oil storage facility at Vinh, located just inland of where the alleged attacks on the *Maddox* and *Turner Joy* had occurred. Although the raid was successful (the oil depot was completely destroyed and 33 of 35 vessels were hit), two American aircraft were shot down; one pilot was killed and the second captured.[14]

This is where it starts to get problematic for me. I believe in the chain of command and respect for authority, but what does a loyal American do when they receive an unethical order? There is no greater decision a person can make then whether they are going to go into battle and likely kill other human beings. The excuse of "just following orders" was not accepted at the Nuremberg Trials when that claim was made by German soldiers or top German officials. There is a higher law that supersedes all laws made by temporal authorities.

I don't care if I would have been court-martialed and thrown in prison. I would not have led that strike force or continued to be the "on-scene military commander" as did Captain Herrick.

If those two men had simply stood up and said, "This is wrong and I won't be a part of it," maybe called the *Washington Post* or *New York Times*, we might have been spared the more than fifty thousand dead American soldiers and the more than one million Vietnamese who died in our war.

I wouldn't care who gave me the order; I would not violate my conscience and go into battle under pretenses I knew to be false. My eternal soul matters far more to me than anything the military officials could do to me. Because of the cowardice of these two men, this is what the history books record:

> On 7 August, Congress, with near unanimity, approved the Gulf of Tonkin Resolution, which President Johnson signed into law three days later. Requested by Johnson, the resolution authorized the chief executive to "take all necessary measures to repel any armed attack against the forces of the United States and to prevent further aggression." No approval or oversight of military force was required by Congress, essentially eliminating the system of checks and balances so fundamental to the U.S. Constitution. On hearing of the authorization's passage by both houses of Congress, the delighted President remarked that the resolution "was like Grandma's nightshirt. It covers everything."[15]

And thus did American democracy temporarily vanish beneath the waves of the military-industrial complex, and we began our most disastrous war prior to President George W. Bush's Global War on Terror.

How could it have been considered a good idea to get rid of all the checks and balances that had guided America through her previous wars?

How might this result have been different if Congress and the American public had been briefed on how the CIA and the Department of Defense were running the South Vietnamese Navy's raids on North Vietnam?

There is no doubt that the supreme source of misinformation was none other than the Defense secretary himself, Robert McNamara. This is from the US Naval Institute's own journal:

> Subsequently, Secretary McNamara intentionally misled Congress and the public about his knowledge of and the nature of the 34A operations, which surely would have been perceived as the actual cause for the 2 August attack on the *Maddox* and the apparent attack on the 4th. On 6 August, when called before a joint session of the Senate Foreign relations and Armed Services committees to testify about the incident, McNamara eluded the questioning of Senator Wayne Morse (D-OR) when he asked specifically whether the 34A operations may have provoked the North Vietnamese response. McNamara instead declared that "our Navy played absolutely no part in, was not associated with, was not aware of, any South Vietnamese actions, if there were any."[16]

When I read a passage such as this, I think of the common person working a regular job and the consequences they might face for lying about the most inconsequential matters, such as whether or not they took some office supplies for their own personal use. It makes me think of the laws of the old Roman Republic where a public official convicted of bribery might be thrown off a cliff or sewn into a bag with poisonous snakes and tossed into a river. Public corruption isn't just a matter of personal enrichment; it rots the entire system of government.

Defense Secretary McNamara lied, and our soldiers died. Did he face public humiliation and ruin? Instead of being tossed off a cliff, he went from being Defense secretary to president of the World Bank, a position he held from April 1968 to June 1981.[17]

But the lies of the military-industrial complex/Deep State/CIA were certainly not limited to the Vietnam War.

* * *

The Iraq War, like the Vietnam War, was a war of choice.

On March 20, 2003, President George W. Bush announced that US forces had begun a military operation to invade Iraq, not only for their violation of various UN Resolutions, but also because of the claim they possessed weapons of mass destruction.[18] Without the claim of weapons of mass destruction, many believe the invasion would have never garnered the necessary American and Congressional support.

However, in 2005, the Senate Intelligence Committee put together a report on the intelligence failures that led to the Iraqi invasion. A 2019 *Washington Post* article on the committee recounted their findings:

> It's worth recalling that the Bush administration appeared determined to attack Iraq for any number of reasons beyond suspicions of WMDs; officials seized on WMDs because they concluded that they represented the strongest case for an invasion. "For bureaucratic reasons we settled on one issue, weapons of mass destruction, because it was the one reason everyone could agree on," then-Deputy Defense Secretary Paul Wolfowitz told *Vanity Fair* in 2003.
>
> Fleisher's deputy at the time, Scott McClellan, put it this way in his memoir, *What Happened*: "In the fall of 2002, Bush and the White House were engaging in a carefully orchestrated campaign to shape and manipulate sources of public approval to our advantage . . . Our lack of candor and honesty in making the case for war would later provoke a partisan response from our opponents, that in its own way, further distorted and obscured a more nuanced reality."[19]

It's pretty pathetic when the lie you told caused the death of thousands of American soldiers and hundreds of thousands of Iraqis and destabilized the Middle East, and the best you can come up with is that you didn't want to share the "more nuanced reality" and instead chose a "lack of candor and honesty."

Besides the officials of the Bush Administration, did Congress fail to do its job? Does all the death and destruction let loose by the 2003 invasion of Iraq come down to the fact that our Congressional leaders couldn't read an additional seventy-one pages about the arguments for and against intervention?

Yes, I know, it sounds like another Alex Jones conspiracy theory.

But there were two reports members of Congress could choose to read; a twenty-five-page "sanitized" version released to the public or a more complete ninety-six-page National Intelligence Estimate (NIE) on Iraq's probable capacities. This is what the *Washington Post* wrote:

> The problem is that few members of Congress actually read the classified NIE. Instead, they relied on a sanitized version distributed to the public, which was scrubbed of dissenting opinions. (It was later learned that the public white paper had been drafted long before the NIE had been requested by Congress, even though the white paper was publicly presented as a distillation of the NIE. So that should count as another manipulation of public opinion.)
>
> One of the few lawmakers who did read the classified report, Sen. Bob Graham (D-Fla.) voted against the congressional resolution to authorize an attack on Iraq. He later wrote that the classified version "contained vigorous dissents on key parts of the information, especially by the departments of State and Energy. Particular skepticism was raised about aluminum tubes that were offered as evidence Iraq was reconstituting its nuclear program . . .
>
> Graham said that the gap between the 96-page document that was secret, and the 25-page version made public made him "question whether the White House was telling the truth—or even had an interest in knowing the truth."[20]

I'll be the first to admit to being dumbfounded that matters of war and peace might be decided by politicians reading seventy-one more pages of a report, or being satisfied with what was essentially a twenty-five-page "executive summary."

Let's play the game, "Are they stupid or evil?"

When these stories make the paper, the best the mainstream media can do is blame some type of character flaw among politicians, like this opinion piece from *Slate*, which tries to make the case that the decision to go to war in Iraq was simply a problem of "ego."

> But after spending most of a year reading and talking to people about the war, I've come to believe that failure on that scale happens, mostly, because of ego. On a personal, institutional, and national level. It's ego that manifests itself in a refusal to believe that the critics of an idea might have a point, or that the facts might not support your intentions. And, most of all, in the notion that one country can just decide to change another, by force, and succeed.[21]

Gee, if only we had people with less ego and stronger reading skills in Congress, we might avoid these unfortunate wars. That's the fallback position of the mainstream media when the truth about the utter disaster that was the Iraq War is revealed. However, we must acknowledge that in the leadup to the Iraq War, the Departments of State and Energy actually produced reports, which clearly stated the case against invasion.

But they were ignored.

Was it "ego"?

Or perhaps there was a financial incentive? The cartoonist and political commentator Scott Adams has noticed that, for some reason, it's always a good analytical tool to "follow the money" to explain why certain things happen.

This filter on the news works, even when it shouldn't.

We don't know if people were specifically bribed (and I'd personally bet against it on any large scale), but money seems to have a power over people to bend decisions in the best interests of large corporations. If we were to take this view, the question we'd want to ask is whether the Iraq War was a success for the military-industrial complex, even if it wasn't a success for the United States or the Iraqis, in whose name the war was supposedly fought? This is from a *CNN* article in March of 2013, reviewing the ten years of the Iraq War:

> The US has overwhelmingly borne the brunt of both the military and reconstruction costs, spending at least $138 billion on private security, logistics and reconstruction contractors, who have supplied everything from diplomatic security to power plants and toilet paper.

> An analysis by the *Financial Times* reveals the extent to which both American and foreign companies have profited from the conflict—with the top ten contractors securing business worth at least $72 billion between them.
>
> None has benefited more than KBR, once known as Kellogg, Brown, and Root. The controversial former subsidiary of Halliburton, which was once run by Dick Cheney, vice-president to George W. Bush, was awarded at least $39 billion in federal contracts related to the Iraq War over the past decade.[22]

Follow the money.

It works, even when it shouldn't.

The military-industrial complex isn't interested in American victories.

It's only interested in supplying products for American wars.

After the Bay of Pigs, President Kennedy became convinced that his military and intelligence officials were only interested in feeding him a never-ending series of crises that demanded military intervention, supplied by the military-industrial complex against which Eisenhower warned.

This mercenary activity continues to this very day, putting all of us in danger.

* * *

Who bears a significant share of the blame for the recent Russian invasion of Ukraine?

I believe it's the neocons, the spiritual descendants of the foreign policy officials who tried to get Kennedy to invade Cuba, succeeded in getting us involved in Vietnam, and nearly broke the Middle East with the Iraq War, who are most responsible for the Ukraine crisis.

How bad has the Ukraine War been, both for the Ukrainians and the Russians? This is from a May 2023 *Washington Post* article.

> Clear casualty figures are difficult to know, with both Kyiv and Moscow putting out numbers far smaller than what most analysts

> believe to be accurate. The Kremlin rejected the United States' latest estimation of its casualties and has spent the past 15 months largely shielding the Russian public from the extent of its losses. If Western estimates are approximately right—and Russia has suffered some 200,000 casualties, with more than 40,000 killed, since the start of its invasion last year—than that death toll would be about three times the number of soldiers the Soviet Union lost over a decade of war in Afghanistan.[23]

Afghanistan was a disaster for the Russians, as it was a disaster for the United States, as it was a disaster for the British in the nineteenth century. Does it sound like maybe it's just a good idea to stay out of Afghanistan? (That is, unless you just want to sell a lot of weapons and military supplies.)

And how many Ukrainian soldiers have died in this war—sons and husbands who will never return to their families. This is what Robert F. Kennedy Jr. told Tucker Carlson during his appearance on April 20, 2023:

> Many Ukrainians are dying for the sake of a US proxy war against Russia, Robert F. Kennedy, Jr. has said, shortly after announcing he would challenge President Joe Biden for the presidential nomination as a Democrat.
>
> "We're killing a lot of Ukrainians as pawns in a proxy war between two great powers," Kennedy told Fox News' Tucker Carlson Tonight on Thursday evening. "Nobody talks about this. There's 14,000 Ukrainian civilians that died, but 300,000 troops. Russians are killing Ukrainians at a 7:1 to 8:1 ratio. They cannot sustain this. What we're being told about the war is just not true.[24]

Isn't it a terrible state of affairs when we can't even get accurate information about a war to which we've contributed more than a hundred billion dollars?[25] Are Tucker Carlson and Robert F. Kennedy Jr. the only two honest public figures left in America? Would you agree with Kennedy's characterization of the Ukraine War as a "proxy war"? How about we listen to Columbia University professor and advisor to three former United

Nations secretaries general, Jeffrey Sachs, from a recent article? In addition to Kennedy, there are a few honest liberals left among us.

> George Orwell wrote in 1984 that "Who controls the past controls the future: who controls the present controls the past." Governments work relentlessly to distort public perceptions of the past. Regarding the Ukraine War, the Biden administration has repeatedly and falsely claimed that the Ukraine War started with an unprovoked attack by Russia on Ukraine on February 24, 2022. In fact, the war was provoked by the U.S. in ways that leading U.S. diplomats anticipated for decades in the lead-up to the war, meaning that the war could have been avoided and should now be stopped through negotiations.[26]

This complete amnesia that our news media forces upon us regarding events that took place just a few years ago is truly mind-boggling. For years, when I'd point out these mistakes, I'd have people say, "Well, Alex, they just forgot. They don't pay attention like you do. I'm sure it wasn't intentional." Eventually, I pulled all my hair out over these claims, and (in addition to not having any hair) I don't have the slightest hesitation in saying today that it's not an accident.

They're lying on purpose, either in what they tell you or what they omit.

Let's return to the excellent analysis by Professor Sachs of the failures of the West in Ukraine.

> There were in fact two main U.S. provocations. The first was the U.S. intention to expand NATO to Ukraine and Georgia in order to surround Russia in the Black Sea region by NATO countries (Ukraine, Romania, Bulgaria, Turkey, and Georgia, in counterclockwise order). The second was the U.S. role in installing a Russophobic regime in Ukraine by the violent overthrow of Ukraine's pro-Russian President, Victor Yanukovych, in February 2014. The shooting war in Ukraine began with Yanukovych's overthrow nine years ago, not

> in February 2022 as the U.S. government, NATO, and the G7 leaders would have us believe.[27]

All of this was right in Russia's face. Hey, Russia, we're going to ring your country with NATO forces, and then we're going to overthrow a large country that was once part of the Soviet Union and has been used three times, in the Crimean War, World War I, and World War II, to invade you. What would we do if China took control of Mexico?

The article continued, detailing Joe Biden's duplicity.

> Biden and his foreign policy team refuse to discuss the roots of the war. To recognize them would undermine the administration in three ways. First, it would expose the fact that the war could have been avoided, or stopped early, sparing Ukraine its current devastation and more than $100 billion in outlays to date. Second, it would expose President Biden's personal role in the war as a participant in the overthrow of Yanukovych, and before that as a strong backer of the military-industrial complex and very early advocate of NATO enlargement. Third, it would push Biden to the negotiating table, undermining the administration's continued push for NATO expansion.[28]

And who could forget that Joe's son, Hunter Biden, was paid a million dollars a year by the Ukrainian energy company, Burisma?[29] There are so many conflicts of interest between Joe Biden on the Ukraine situation that I'm astonished he continues to be president. But God must have His plans.

God knows there were multiple warnings from diplomatic experts, such as the legendary George Kennan, President Bill Clinton's secretary of defense William Perry, and current CIA director William Burns, who in 2008, was the US ambassador to Russia.

> In 2008, then U.S. Ambassador to Russia, and now CIA Director, William Burns, sent a cable to Washington warning at length of grave risks of NATO enlargement: "Ukraine and Georgia's NATO

> aspirations not only touch a raw nerve in Russia, they engender serious concerns about the consequences for stability in the region. Not only does Russia perceive encirclement, and efforts to undermine Russia's influence in the region, but it also fears unpredictable and uncontrolled consequences which would seriously affect Russian security interests. Experts tell us that Russia is particularly worried that the strong divisions in Ukraine over NATO membership, with much of the ethnic-Russian community against membership could lead to a major split, involving violence, or at worst, civil war. In that eventuality, Russia would have to decide whether to intervene; a decision Russia does not want to have to face."[30]

Which is exactly what happened. Prior to the invasion by Russia, Ukraine had been actively persecuting ethnic Russians in various areas of the country, such as in the Donbas region. And Zelenskyy—who campaigned in 2018 on a peace platform, pledging to sign the Minsk Accords negotiated with Russia, which would keep Ukraine out of NATO and guarantee Ukraine's independence—once elected and vulnerable to US influence, decided not to sign the accords.

Again, we play the game, "Are they stupid or evil?"

No sane person looking at the evidence of how Russia would respond to these provocative actions by the West and NATO would say, "Let's continue on our present course!" The details of our intervention in Ukraine turn my stomach.

They should be understood by every American.

> During 2010-2103, Yanukovych pushed neutrality, in line with Ukrainian public opinion. The U.S. worked covertly to overthrow Yanukovych, as capturd vividly in the tape of then U.S. Assistant Secretary of State, Victoria Nuland and U.S. Ambassador Geoffrey Pyatt planning the post-Yanukovych government weeks before the violent overthrow of Yanukovych. Nuland makes clear on the call that she was coordinating closely with then Vice President Biden and his national security advisor Jake Sullivan, the same

> Biden-Nuland-Sullivan team now at the center of U.S. policy vis-à-vis Ukraine.
>
> After Yanukovych's overthrow, the war broke out in the Donbas, while Russia claimed Crimea. The new Ukrainian government appealed for NATO membership, and the U.S. armed and helped restructure the Ukrainian army to make it interoperable with NATO. In 2021, NATO and the Biden Administration strongly recommitted to Ukraine's future in NATO.[31]

That's how you take a peaceful (but fairly corrupt) Eastern European country and turn it into a war zone, in which the military-industrial complex can flood its products, all courtesy of the United States and other western governments who claim they're just protecting "democracy."

And if that wasn't enough to provoke a nuclear-armed Russia, the Biden Administration and his corrupted military had one more trick up their sleeve.

In any other instance, the actions of the Biden Administration would be considered an "act of war," but because the mainstream media doesn't portray it that way, the world simply carries on as if everything is normal.

This unstable situation makes my skin crawl.

* * *

What do the globalists do when they get to spend all the money they want, tell their unchallenged lies in the mainstream media, buy all the weapons systems their hearts desire, overthrow the countries they want, and yet things still don't go their way?

That's what Joe Biden must have found himself asking after he got the social media companies to censor much of the grumbling public, snuck into the presidency, bent the Congress to his will, provoked Russia into invading Ukraine as the globalists had always planned, and yet the $100 billion our government sent to Ukraine didn't seem to change conditions on the ground.

The globalists keep getting smacked in the face by reality, whether it's the fact that men are men and women are women, people of different races and cultures can genuinely like each other, and humanity, by and large, doesn't want to be at war with each other. We want to live in peace and friendship with other human beings, worship and speak as we please, raise our children as we choose, and make the world a little better for the next generation.

That is the glory and power of humanity, and the globalists just don't get it. They think those virtues are your weakness, and not your strength.

You don't have to remember all the intricacies of the globalist agenda; you just have to be the decent person God created you to be. When their anti-human plans ae presented to you, you'll hear the voice of your conscience, directing you on the proper path.

Seymour Hersch won the Pulitzer Prize in 1970 for reporting on the My Lai massacre in Vietnam, by American soldiers, led by Lieutenant William Calley, a case that became a touchstone for the public's view of the Vietnam War. He has continued his fearless reporting, and, in February 2023, released what may be his most important scoop: that of the bombing of the Nord Stream pipeline. The pipeline is owned by Russia, and Hersch names the United States as the guilty party, which, if true, would be considered under international law as an "act of war." This is from that article:

> Last June, the Navy divers, operating under the cover of a widely publicized mid-summer NATO exercise known as BALTOPS 22, planted the remotely triggered explosives that, three months later, destroyed three of the four Nord Stream pipelines, according to a source with direct knowledge of the operational planning.
>
> Two of the pipelines, which were known collectively as Nord Stream 1, had been providing Germany and much of Western Europe with cheap Russian natural gas for more than a decade. A second pair of pipelines, called Nord Stream 2, had been built but were not yet operational. Now, with Russian troops massing on the Ukrainian border and the bloodiest war in Europe since 1945 looming, President

> Joe Biden saw the pipelines as a vehicle for Vladimir Putin to weaponize natural gas for his political and territorial ambitions.
>
> Asked for comment, Adrienne Watson, a White House spokesperson, said in an email, "This is false and a complete fiction." Tammy Thorp, a spokesperson for the Central Intelligence Agency, similarly wrote, "This claim is completely and utterly false."[32]

Well, I guess with that denial from the White House and the CIA we can all go home now, confident that truth will never change.

Of course, we know that both our politicians and intelligence services lie to us with reckless abandon, like an alcoholic waiting to go on his next bar crawl.

But at least we get the set-up for why Biden and company would want to go after the pipeline. Hersch provides more detail on the planning and personnel:

> President Biden and his foreign policy team—National Security Adviser Jake Sullivan, Secretary of State Tony Blinken, and Victoria Nuland, the Undersecretary of State for Policy—had been vocal and consistent in their hostility to the two pipelines, which ran side by side for 750 miles under the Baltic Sea from two different ports on northeastern Russia near the Estonian border, passing close to the Danish Island of Bornholm before ending in northern Germany.
>
> The direct route, which bypassed any need to transit Ukraine, had been a boon for the German economy, which enjoyed an abundance of cheap Russian natural gas—enough to run its factories and heat its homes while enabling German distributors to sell excess gas, at a profit throughout Western Europe. Action that could be traced to the administration would violate US promises to minimize direct conflict with Russia. Secrecy was essential.[33]

We've got the neo-con warmongers, Jake Sullivan, Tony Blinken, and Victoria Nuland, all on the same team. Honest patriots on both the left and right despise these individuals, and so should you, if you've previously been unaware of them.

Let's look at a few of the problems with the bombing of the Nord Stream pipeline.

First, bombing the energy infrastructure of a country is an act of war. Plain and simple. Feel free to ask any expert in international affairs.

Second, we were playing a game of chicken with the German economy, hoping they didn't have people freeze to death in a cold winter. Thankfully, the winter was mild, and the loss of Russian natural gas did not cause undue problems. But it could have.

Third, for an administration that claimed to be concerned about the environment, the destruction of the Nord Stream pipeline was an ecological disaster, releasing an unprecedented amount of methane into the air. This is from an article by *Reuters* about the blast.

> A huge plume of highly concentrated methane, a greenhouse gas far more potent but shorter-lived than carbon dioxide, was detected in an analysis this week of satellite imagery by researchers associated with UNEP's [United Nations Environmental Program] International Methane Emission Observatory, or IMEO, the organization said.
>
> "This is really bad, most likely the largest emission event ever detected," Manfredi Caltagirone, head of the IMEO for UNEP, told Reuters. "This is not helpful in a moment when we absolutely need to reduce emissions."
>
> Researchers at GHHSat, which uses satellites to monitor methane emissions, estimated the leak rate from one of four rupture points was 22,920 kilograms per hour. That is equivalent to burning about 630,000 pounds of coal every hour, GHGSat said in a statement.[34]

We had an ecological disaster with the bombing of the Nord Stream pipeline, but none of the usual suspects seemed to get upset about it. Where was Al Gore, talking about how the icecaps were going to melt, or Greta Thunberg telling us to be "terrified" for the future, or Congresswoman

Alexandria Ocasio Cortez telling us we only had twelve years to turn it all around?

Hersch's article talked about how planning for some kind of a countermove to Russian aggression, starting in December 2021, was being discussed, even before the invasion of Ukraine.

> Over the next several meetings, the participants debated options for an attack. The Navy proposed using a newly commissioned submarine to assault the pipeline directly. The Air Force discussed dropping bombs with delayed fuses that could be set off remotely. The CIA argued that whatever was done, it would have to be covert. Everyone involved understood the stakes. "This is not kiddie stuff," the source said. If the attack were traceable to the United States, "It's an act of war."
>
> At the time, the CIA was directed by William Burns, a mild-mannered former ambassador to Russia who had served as deputy secretary of state in the Obama Administration. Burns quickly authorized an Agency working group whose ad hoc members included—by chance—someone who was familiar with the capabilities of the Navy's deep-sea divers in Panama City. Over the next few weeks, members of the CIA's working group began to craft a plan for a covert operation that would use deep-sea divers to trigger an explosion along the pipeline.[35]

This is how the stupidest plans ever crafted by the mind of man were developed, in a committee.

This is almost as insane as Operation Northwoods, the crazy plan cooked up by the Joint Chiefs during the Kennedy administration to provoke a war with Cuba, as detailed by ABC News in 2001:

> America's top military brass even contemplated causing U.S. military casualties, writing:

> "We could blow up a U.S. ship in Guantanamo Bay and blame Cuba," and "casualty lists in U.S. newspapers would cause a helpful wave of national indignation." …
>
> "These were Joint Chiefs of Staff documents. The reason these were held secret for so long is the Joint Chiefs never wanted to give them up because they were so embarrassing," Bamford told ABC News.com . . .
>
> The Joint Chiefs even proposed using the potential death of astronaut John Glenn during the first attempt to put an American into orbit as a false pretext for war with Cuba, the documents show.
>
> Should the rocket explode and kill Glenn, they wrote, "the objective is to provide incontrovertible proof . . . that the fault lies with the Communists et all Cuba [*sic*]."[36]

Whenever somebody wants to argue with me that our top military and intelligence leaders have gone through a rigorous system that would weed out the crazy, the incompetent, and the dangerous, I always point out Operation Northwoods to them. Many of these were former World War II veterans, and they were certifiable. Killing American servicemen?

Having a false story wouldn't have been possible without the participation of the Norwegians, as Hersh explained:

> The Norwegians were key to solving other hurdles. The Russian navy was known to possess surveillance technology capable of spotting and triggering underwater mines. The American explosive devices needed to be camouflaged in a way that would make them appear to the Russian system as part of the natural background—something that required adapting to the specific salinity of the water.
>
> The Norwegians also had a solution to the crucial question of when the operation should take place. Every June for the past 21 years, the American Sixth Fleet, whose flagship is based in Gaeta, Italy, south of Rome, had sponsored a major NATO exercise in the Baltic Sea involving scores of allied ships throughout the region. The current exercise, held in June, would be known as Baltic Operations

> 22, or BALTOPS 22. The Norwegians proposed this would be the ideal cover to plant the mines.[37]

And who else, besides Seymour Hersch, is saying the United States is the most likely suspect in the blowing up of the Nord Stream pipeline? How about retired four-star General Stanley McChrystal, who headed the Joint Special Operations Command (JSOC) in Iraq and led our forces in Afghanistan?

> When asked who he thought was behind the Nord Stream bombing, McChrystal explained that he and his son, who works in the Defense Intelligence Agency (DIA), didn't believe Russia or Ukraine was behind the bombing.
>
> "My son is the leader of the energy team at DIA," said McChrystal. "He didn't think that the Russians did it . . . He didn't think that the Ukrainians did it, either." McChrystal went on the explain how the U.S. was the only nation positioned to benefit from the Nord Stream bombing.
>
> "There are people who benefited from it, and that was people who produced natural gas around the world," said McChrystal. "So if you really want to get conspiracies, the United States made more money off that deal than anybody else."[38]

So, we planted the mines in June 2022, and then three months later, on September 26, 2022, President Biden made the decision to blow up the pipeline, a clear act of war, even according to his own officials.

The military-intelligence-industrial complex got its wish. The war in Ukraine has killed many more people than necessary, and the bad guys got to sell a lot more weapons. And how is it working out for the poor Ukrainians? Not well, according to recent news reports from late July 2023.

> The *Wall Street Journal* reported Saturday that Western officials knew Ukrainian forces didn't have enough training or equipment

> for their counteroffensive but hoped they would be able to break through anyway.
>
> The report reads: "When Ukraine launched its big counteroffensive this spring, Western military officials knew Kyiv didn't have all the training or weapons—from shells to warplanes—that it needed to dislodge Russian forces. But they hoped Ukrainian courage and resourcefulness would carry the day. They haven't."[39]

With friends like the United States and their allies, who needs enemies? Maybe it was a bad idea all along to poke the Russian bear, as even our own diplomats, like William Burns, now head of the CIA, had warned about.

This insanity needs to end.

But that begins when you understand how you've been deceived.

* * *

Maybe the world won't end in a nuclear holocaust.

The world has lived under that fear since the first atomic bombs were dropped on Japan, and yet they have not been used anywhere in the world since. Putin, China, and Iran all seem to understand that nuclear weapons alone won't get them what they want.

If it's true that Russia has killed somewhere around three hundred thousand Ukrainian soldiers and only fourteen thousand Ukrainian civilians, we must agree that Ukraine has been fought as a relatively focused war by the Kremlin. How would these numbers stack up against our wars in Iraq, Afghanistan, and Syria?

Maybe it's time to call a truce.

When one looks at how our leaders deceive us and the hidden little details omitted from the published "truth"—it's understandable why three American presidents, Truman, Eisenhower, and Kennedy, fought so hard to stop this madness.

But the military-industrial complex has carried on through the presidents, regardless of whether there was a D or R after their names. Even

President Trump, who clearly wanted to avoid any unnecessary wars, fed the military-industrial beast with record budgets.

These are the facts, and we must be unafraid to state them.

The military and intelligence budget of our country is quickly closing in on a trillion dollars a year, and it is not making us any safer. President Reagan was fond of saying, "We don't mistrust each other because we have nuclear weapons. We mistrust each other, and that's the reason we have nuclear weapons."

We need to be honest about the history of our country and how we have meddled in the internal affairs of other countries. It's like a Catholic going to confession before they can receive God's forgiveness. But the globalists want to keep you ignorant of what your own country has done, because they've been behind the scenes pulling the puppet strings of our politicians.

We need to respect the deliberations of other countries and reduce our military budget and foreign engagements. We must make our own country a beacon of liberty, innovation, and freedom to the world, rather than the bully with bases that only serve to further the interests of globalist corporations.

Chapter Eight

The Education of Tucker Carlson (and Joe Rogan, as Well as Others)

There's something I need you to understand about people like me who are in the public eye.

Behind the scenes, we can all talk to each other, and generally we keep those conversations private. Sometimes we're friends, because we met when we were much younger and on our way to becoming our more successful selves. I've known Joe Rogan for a quarter century, and if you're a quality human being (as Joe Rogan certainly is), the friendship remains.

Sometimes there's somebody you've long admired, you get a chance to meet them, and you find out they're an asshole. Or they have a habit of yelling at the people who work for them or some other loathsome personal habit, and it just doesn't mesh with the way you live your life. If you've been to the *InfoWars* studio, you know there's a certain way I like to run things. In the hours before my show, I don't like to have anybody except the staff present as I need to prepare for my show and get myself in the mental space needed to talk for three hours. Guests often want to show up early and hang with me, and I usually say no to that.

However, after the show is done, I'm happy to spend time with my guests, maybe go get a meal with them, and talk at an even deeper level.

Somebody I've spent a good deal of time with over the years has been Tucker Carlson, and he's been on my show four times. If you know much about Tucker, you understand he basically descends from journalism royalty. His father was a news reporter, and even served as the director of the Voice of America for Eastern Europe during the last six years of the Cold

War.[1] If you're familiar with Tucker, you know he's been around journalism for a long time, with stints at CNN and MSNBC, and for many years he wasn't a star, just an excellent all-around journalist, always seeking to improve his craft.

I think the best way to describe my relationship with Tucker is I'm like Morpheus in the movie *The Matrix*, and Tucker is like Neo. I was the one encouraging Tucker to swallow the red pill to break out of the matrix and see the reality around him. A lot of people who are in the matrix don't even understand there is a matrix. You need to be gentle with them. That's why it's important to communicate in a way that results in people listening (rather than shutting down), which is what I am trying to accomplish in this book. But Tucker was willing to accept the challenge I offered him, and you can see for yourself how much his influence has grown.

I want to be clear I'm not a prideful person. I simply want there to be an accurate record of what I've done. When I was a kid and was climbing a tree or hiking a trail, and started feeling prideful, that's inevitably when I took a fall. I want this to be understood as me talking about a sense of accomplishment and satisfaction in what I've done, rather than pride.

What motivates me is that I am genuinely at war with the globalists. I know they're parasites and control freaks who believe they're better than us. I believe they've exacerbated societal ills to make us more manageable, and one of the ways they do that is by censoring and demonizing those who oppose their plans. What was that famous quote by Malcom X? "The media's the most powerful entity on earth. They have the power to make the innocent guilty and the guilty innocent, and that's power. Because they control the minds of the masses."[2]

I am in love with humanity. Humanity is my tribe, and I want to protect it. We have created and done amazing things. As much as I want to point out the wicked designs of the globalists, I also want to celebrate the accomplishments of humanity in the past and urge us to continue dreaming so we can have an amazing future.

The real story of Alex Jones and Tucker Carlson is that about fifteen years ago, Tucker viciously attacked me. Somebody had asked him, "What do you think of Alex Jones saying 9/11 was an inside job?"

And Tucker replied with something along the lines of, "I think the guy's a fricking parasite. I think the guy's a menace. I think he's terrible."

About five or six years later, the media companies decided to release all the video of September 11 to the public. I don't think they understood what they were doing, because of what was revealed about Building 7. One of the pieces of footage was of Larry Silverstein, the owner of the building, who said:

> I remember getting a call from the fire department commander, telling me they were not sure they were going to be able to contain the fire. I said, we've had such a terrible loss of life, we might just as well pull it. They made that decision to pull, and we watched the building collapse.[3]

When the coverage of September 11 was released, and I brought it up on *InfoWars*, I didn't realize that some of Tucker's kids were listening to my broadcasts. And they talked to their dad about me, as well as the information I was sharing. Tucker really is a Boy Scout, strait-laced, Ivy league, WASP kind of guy, almost like Captain America. And yet, when he started looking into it, he had something of a Winter Soldier moment and strongly suspected the entire truth wasn't being told.

And about ten years ago Tucker called me up to say he wanted to come and visit. I didn't hold it against him that he called me a parasite. Now we've had dinner together many times, he's visited me at my house, we've hung out together plenty of times on the road, and he even visited me during Thanksgiving vacation.

Tucker has said both privately and publicly that I have had an enormous impact on him. I have watched his evolution over the years with an enormous sense of pride. He's gone from being the naïve, bow-tied little libertarian of a decade ago to understanding it all and becoming a figure unlike any other in the media. He's amazingly smart, more articulate than I'll ever be, and a serious threat to the system. Tucker has become a superhero, like Neo from *The Matrix*, and the globalists fear him like no other.

I like to think of Tucker as Alex Jones 2.0 and am happy to have played a large part in that evolution.

* * *

I've known Joe Rogan since 1998, and we became friends in 1999, before 9/11. Although we've been great friends for nearly a quarter century, in the past we have acknowledged to each other that we're on different paths. But recently, for anybody who's been watching his show, it's clear he's been ultra red-pilled. At a recent dinner we had, I was blown away by his accelerated understanding of our current situation. Society has truly entered the Great Awakening.

Joe was always a smart guy and savvy, but like Tucker, had a problem believing things were as bad as I said they were. Over the years, as much as we've shared laughs and supported each other, we have gotten into some big arguments.

About five or six years ago, when I was being demonized in the media but prior to being deplatformed, I went after Joe on the air in a way that was unfair. However, it was because he'd been criticizing me in a way that I thought was not based in reality. I'd been sending him a great deal of material, and I felt he was blowing me off because he didn't want to face the darkness.

Now Joe isn't somebody you can boss around. But when somebody brings something to his attention, he puts in the time to understand it. And in very quick order after I'd gone after him on the air, Joe went through the material, called me up, and said, "Okay, I was wrong about some of this stuff. I'm sorry, this is hard to believe. This shit is scary."

I immediately apologized to him, privately, and on-the-air, saying, "No, I went too far. I made it nasty and personal, and I shouldn't have."

We got through that, and now we're better friends than ever.

I think that Joe, in a very well-thought-out and technical way, is bridging the gap between left and right and promoting a pro-human future. He has a bigger show than Johnny Carson ever did, bigger than Walter Cronkite or Rush Limbaugh, with a hundred million people a week checking out his opinions, and about forty million a week listening to an entire show. And he does this in a calm, rational way, showing you exactly who he is: just a guy trying to figure out the truth. Joe's influence doesn't end at our shores; he's listened to around the world, in Asia, Africa, Latin America, everywhere.

But I want to be clear about one thing. I don't control Joe, or Tucker, or any other media figure out there, even if they're raising topics I might have raised first. In many instances, it's like I'm the first guy who figures out how to use the new bike, so I introduce it to others. I might assist them by showing them how to do it, they take a few test rides, but then they're off on their own. And often, they'll come up with new angles I hadn't even considered. With the people I have influenced, it's not a choreographed symphony, but like jazz, where I'm playing the first couple notes, and then they take over. Russell Brand has also told me that I was instrumental to waking him up more than a decade ago, and now he's a major force in media.

I'm quick to recognize that the problem a significant number of people have is that they can't believe that many, if not most, of the world's elite are corrupt and decadent. That realization can be brutal and terrifying to a person who has believed the mainstream media. But it is necessary if we're ever to have a better future. There is an eternal cycle of birth, renaissance, descent into corruption, then reformation or revolution, and we can start the cycle over again.

Although I've had direct contact with Tucker and Joe about the fact I've influenced their worldview, I've had indirect contact with people close to other public figures, who tell me I have also impacted what they think about the world. The son of Jair Bolsonaro, the former populist president of Brazil from 2019 to 2022, told me I'd had an enormous influence on the views of his father. I've heard similar stories from people close to former Congresswoman Tulsi Gabbard, as well as people close to Robert F. Kennedy Jr.

There are many public and private individuals who are waking up to the issues I've been talking about for years, and I'm proud to have contributed to starting some of those conversations.

* * *

Okay, now I want to get back to Tucker's story, since I believe that understanding his journey is critical to being effective at making the type of change I believe is necessary to creating the next great human renaissance.

Tucker's contract at Fox and warnings from the management was to avoid having me on the show. But he tried to slip in mentions of me as much as possible, such as when my first book, *The Great Reset*, was published. It should have been at least #2 on the *New York Times* bestseller list, based on sales, but it didn't even make the list.

By now everybody is familiar with the circumstances of Tucker being unceremoniously yanked off the air by Fox, the bitter negotiations which followed, and how Tucker decided to blaze a new path by creating a show on Twitter. (And I must note I predicted Tucker's firing on March 8, 2023.[4]) However, I think for the historical record, it's important to include the full comments Tucker made on May 9, 2023, announcing this new stage of his life. It may be the single most important statement made by a member of the mainstream media in our lifetime.

> Hey, it's Tucker Carlson. You often hear people say the news is full of lies, but most of the time, that's not quite right. Much of what you see on television or read in the *New York Times* is in fact, true in the literal sense. It could pass one of the media's own fact checks. Lawyers would be willing to sign off on it. In fact, they may have. But that doesn't make it true. It's not true.
>
> At the most basic level, the news you consume is a lie of the stealthiest and most insidious kind. Facts have been withheld on purpose, along with proportion and perspective. You are being manipulated.
>
> How does that work? Let's see. If I tell you a man has been unjustly arrested for armed robbery, that is not strictly speaking a lie. He may have been framed. At this point there's been no trial, so no one can really say.

But if I don't mention the fact that the same man has been arrested for the same crime six times before, am I really informing you? No, I'm not. I'm misleading you. That's what the news media are doing in every story that matters, every day of the week, every week of the year.

What's it like to work in a system like that? After more than thirty years in the middle of it, we could tell you stories. The best you can hope for in the news business at this point is the freedom to tell the fullest truth you can.

But there are always limits, and you know that if you bump up against those limits often enough, you will be fired for it. That's not a guess, it's guaranteed. Every person who works in English language media understands that. The rule of what you can't say defines everything. It's filthy, really, and it's utterly corrupting.

You can't have a free society if people aren't allowed to say what they think is true. Speech is the fundamental prerequisite for democracy. That's why it's enshrined in the first of our constitutional amendments.

Amazingly, as of tonight, there aren't that many platforms left that allow free speech. The last big one remaining in the world, the only real one is Twitter, where we are now. Twitter has long served as the place where our national conversation incubates and develops. Twitter is not a partisan site. Everybody's allowed here, and we think that's a good thing.

And yet, for the most part, the news that you see analyzed on Twitter comes from media organizations that are themselves thinly disguised propaganda outlets. You see it on cable news, you talk about it on Twitter. The result may feel like a debate, but actually, the gatekeepers are still in charge.

We think that's a bad system. We know exactly how it works, and we're sick of it. Starting soon, we'll be bringing a new version of the show we've been doing for the last six and a half years to Twitter. We'll bring some other things soon, which we'll tell you about. But for now, we're just grateful to be here.

> Free speech is the main right you have. Without it, you have no others. See you soon.[5]

At this point I was overcome with admiration for my good friend, Tucker Carlson, who showed himself to be the kind of man I have come to know and value. I was aware of many of the things that were going on behind the scenes at Fox News and have kept those confidences. I will leave it to Tucker as to the amount he wishes to divulge, now or in the future.

But what are some of the early signs of where this might all eventually be going? One of the things I believe about those in the public eye is that we depend on the trust of the people. The public will forgive your mistakes if they're honest ones. But they will never forgive you for consciously deceiving them. This is from Breitbart on May 9, 2023:

> *Mediate* reports that *Fox News Tonight*, which has replaced *Tucker Carlson Tonight* at the 8:00 p.m. ET hour, commanded just 90,000 viewers between 25-54 on Friday. This figure is worse than the first hour of CNN's *Anderson Cooper 360*, which drew 99,000 in that demographic, and MSNBC's *All in With Chris Hayes*, which took the lion's share of the age group with 145,000.
>
> For reference, during Carlson's final show on April 21, he drew 270,000 viewers between the ages of 25-54, more than doubling *All in with Chris Hayes's* 133,000, according to Mediate . . .
>
> Where *Tucker Carlson Tonight* pulled a viewership of 2.64 million on his final broadcast, *Fox News Tonight* could not manage half of the figure in the time slot last week, registering at 1.284 million.[6]

Tucker's move to Elon Musk's X is a much bigger deal than simply what happens to Tucker Carlson and his audience. I think a lot of people in the country were favorably impressed with Tucker's increasingly critical commentaries, and yet many conservatives had long been uneasy about Fox News. They didn't like having former House Majority Leader, Paul Ryan, on the Board of Directors of Fox News, blame Tucker for "toxic sludge" and "misinformation,"[7] when in the eyes of many he was simply trying to get to the truth. And they questioned whether Rupert Murdoch genuinely wanted to give a platform to conservatives or merely wanted to capture that demographic. The traditional criticism of the media has been, "If it bleeds, it leads," which suggests that the networks were guided by the pursuit of the almighty dollar, rather than informing the public.

And yet, when networks like Fox (or CNN for that matter) pursue policies like firing Tucker Carlson (or only having an endless parade of anti-Trump stories), which are so clearly against their own financial success, one must consider that another agenda is at play.

What is that agenda?

Let me explain it.

You may have the outdated assumption that a news network is a large and powerful corporation.

That's never been true.

For most of their existence, the news networks have been owned by a powerful person or group of people, like William Randolph Hearst, who more or less left the journalists alone. (Yes, I know that hasn't always been true—just remember Operation Mockingbird[8]—but it's been true enough.)

However, starting in the late 1980s and 1990s, news networks began to be valued as "assets" that could be purchased by larger corporations to diversify their portfolios. Perhaps nobody intended this result (I believe they did, but let's not quibble about it). However, the net result was you had news stations that didn't want to pursue stories that made their corporate owners look bad. As large corporations consumed more and more companies, that meant the networks could only pursue stories that didn't reflect badly on the corporations, or industries, in which their owners were invested.

The news business got bought by corporate America.

That's all you need to understand.

You don't need to have a debate over leftists in the newsroom, although that's certainly a reality. Journalism, which used to be the scrappy little guy afflicting the powerful and comforting the afflicted, got purchased by big business, who turned it into the company public relations office.

That reality has become clearer to people over the years, and the Tucker Carlson incident may be where that truth became visible to most of the population.

Freed from the shackles of Fox News, now when Tucker puts out a tweet, he might get twenty-five to thirty million views, dwarfing what he was about to get on Fox, even though he was the most popular cable news host in the industry.

The dinosaurs at Fox who fired Tucker badly miscalculated. And Tucker is no babe in the woods. He understands that keeping his independence is the very thing that will ensure his current audience will stay with him and is the best way to attract new fans.

When Tucker was targeted by Fox News, to silence this man who was an archetypal populist, wanting only freedom, peace, and prosperity for all, the eyes of many were opened to the evil that was hiding behind the façade. But Tucker's victory over these forces, buoyed by the attention of people who may never have watched him on Fox News, also showed the world that good was a powerful force.

I am so excited for Tucker. He can broadcast from his home in Maine, or his home in Florida, and he can directly reach out to people while covering things Fox would never touch. One of the things you should know about the contract Tucker had with Fox was that he had negotiated total creative freedom for his show. The original offer from Fox was three times his eventual salary, but that required him to let Fox control his content. They negotiated a compromise. Tucker got his freedom, but in return he was only paid one-third of their initial offer. I'm aware that some of my more fervent friends will claim that even with that freedom, Tucker avoided certain topics, and I think in some instances that may be a valid criticism. My only response is that Tucker is still in the process of development and understanding, and I am as well.

While Tucker may have had total freedom, it's my understanding that the producers and staff people around him may not have had such freedom. Although I don't know it for a fact, my suspicion is that the management at Fox was using the people around Tucker to control him, the same way the Deep State manipulated Trump into going along with many of the COVID-19 restrictions, or convinced Trump that the mRNA shots were safe and effective.

Tucker knew his days at Fox were numbered, and it's a testament to his character that he didn't care. He had seen the light and was not going to serve the darkness anymore. He didn't sell out. I didn't sell out, and you didn't sell out. Our freedoms, our liberty, and our ideas are not for sale. That's why Tucker's approach to reporting news is so remarkably beautiful and important to the world, even before he left Fox.

Even though it's another long passage, I want to reproduce part of one of Tucker's last monologues, this one from April 20, 2023, his second to last broadcast. I think it may be the cleanest distillation of what has gone wrong in our media landscape. And it was written as a lead-up to his first guest of the night, Robert F. Kennedy Jr.:

> Good evening and welcome to *Tucker Carlson Tonight*. Sometimes you wonder just how filthy and dishonest our news media are. You'll be in the shower and you'll think, "They're bad, but how bad are they?"
>
> Well, here's one measure of their badness. You can try this at home. Ask yourself, is any news organization you know of so corrupt that it's willing to hurt you on behalf of its biggest advertisers?
>
> Anyone who'd do that is obviously Pablo Escobar level corrupt and should not be trusted. What would that look like, that level of corruption? Well, imagine the Trump Administration had made it mandatory for American citizens to buy MyPillow. That's one of Fox's biggest advertisers. Imagine the administration declared that if you didn't rush out and buy at least one MyPillow, and then at least another booster pillow, you would not be allowed to eat out. You couldn't re-enter your own country. You couldn't have a paying job.
>
> They told you that with a straight face. "MyPillow is the very linchpin of our country's public health system." No, imagine as they told you that, that as Fox, as a news organization, endorsed it, amplified the government's message. Imagine if Fox News attacked anyone who refused to buy MyPillow as an ally of Russia, as an enemy of

> science. And then imagine that Fox kept up those libelous attacks even as evidence mounted that MyPillow caused heart attacks, fertility problems, and death.
>
> If Fox News did that, what would you think of Fox News? Would you trust us? Of course you wouldn't. You would know that we were liars. Thank heaven Fox never did anything like that, but the other channels did. The other channels took hundreds of millions of dollars from Big Pharma companies, and then they shilled for those sketchy products on the air. And as they did that they maligned anyone who was skeptical of their products.
>
> At the very least, this was a moral crime. It was disgusting, but it was universal. It happened across the American news media. They all did it. So at this point, the question isn't, who in public life is corrupt? Too many to count. The question is, who is telling the truth? One of them is Robert Kennedy Jr.
>
> Robert Kennedy knew early that the COVID vaccines were both ineffective and potentially dangerous, and he said so in public to the extent he was allowed. Science has since proven Robert F. Kennedy, Jr. right. Unequivocally right. But Kennedy was not rewarded for this. He was vilified. He was censored. Because he dared to criticize their advertisers, the news media called Bobby Kennedy a Nazi, and then they attacked his family. But he kept doing it. He was not intimidated, and we were glad he wasn't. This is one of those moments when it's nice to have a truth teller around.[9]

When I heard the opening of his monologue, I was stunned. For years I'd known about the absolute stranglehold Big Pharma had on the mainstream media because of their advertising dollars.

But here was Tucker calmly walking up to the pharms dragon, pulling out a sword, and stabbing it in the heart.

I can imagine the Big Pharma titans were burning up the phone lines to the Fox executives that night.

But Tucker wasn't done with his blowtorching of the media establishment. After taking a chainsaw to Big Pharma, he went after the still unclear story of what our intelligence agencies had been doing in Ukraine prior to the Russian invasion.

> It was a year ago that every media outlet in the United States from *USA Today* to the *New York Times* told you it was a dangerous conspiracy theory to believe the US government had ever funded secret bio labs in Ukraine. The idea was ridiculous. In fact, it was Russian disinformation.
>
> And then one day in sworn testimony, Victoria Nuland of the State Department accidentally admitted that it was true. She said, "Yes, there are many secret bio labs in Ukraine." And quote, "we are now in fact quite concerned that Russian troops, Russian forces, may be seeking to gain control of them."
>
> "Wait a second," you may be wondering. "Why does the US government maintain secret bio labs in a primitive country like Ukraine? Why not Austria? Why Ukraine? And why didn't we dismantle and remove these secret bio labs when the war with Russia started?"
>
> Nobody ever explained that. This show was attacked for asking the question. Now we have learned that actually it is far worse than just bio labs. Not only has the Biden Administration been maintaining these labs in Ukraine in the middle of a war, it has also, quote, "sensitive nuclear technology" in Ukraine as well. And we're not making that up. They admitted it today. Watch. [Nadia Bashir of CNN reporting.]
>
> **NADIA BASHIR:** While Ukrainian staff are still operating this Zaporishia, a nuclear power plant, it does fall under the control of Russian armed forces and is currently being managed by Russia's state-owned nuclear energy firm, Rosatom. And this is a significant concern. And essentially in this letter that has been reviewed by CNN, sent by the US Department of Energy to Rosatom, the US government has essentially warned Moscow not to touch the Zaporishia nuclear power plant because of this sensitive nuclear technology at this plant.[10]

How is this not insanity of the very highest order? We had secret bio labs in Ukraine, right next to the Russian border. How would we have responded to the placement of Russian bio labs in Canada?

Not very well, I'm assuming.

And if that wasn't terrifying enough, we were also putting "sensitive nuclear technology" in Ukraine. For the sake of argument, let's just say our intelligence agencies had a good reason for placing bio labs and "sensitive nuclear technology" in a country that bordered Russia. As the plans for a Russian invasion became clear, wouldn't that have been an ideal time for our special forces to go in and get that material before Russian soldiers arrived? It's one thing to take provocative action. But it's an entirely different proposition when you add such stupidity to the picture.

Carlson continued his monologue, leading up to his introduction of Robert F. Kennedy Jr., by playing a segment from Kennedy's announcement to challenge President Joe Biden for the Democratic nomination, on the issue of the Ukraine war:

> **ROBERT F. KENNEDY JR.**: We were told initially that the objective was humanitarian. Many of the steps we've taken in Ukraine have seemed to indicate that our interest is in prolonging the war rather than shortening it. So if those are objectives, to have regime change and exhaust the Russians, that is completely antithetical to a humanitarian mission.
>
> **TUCKER CARLSON**: That's supposed to be the face of extremism, but that's not extreme. It's rational, and calm, and well deliberated. Bobby Kennedy himself is not extreme. He is deeply insightful, and above all, he is honest, no matter what you think of the substance of what he says. Here, for example, is his recent analysis of the Biden Administration's foreign policy. "Big picture. The collapse of US influence over Saudi Arabia and the Kingdom's new alliance with China and Iran are painful emblems of the abject failure of the Neocon strategy of maintaining US global hegemony with aggressive projections of military power. China has displaced the American empire by deftly projecting instead, economic power. Over the past

> decade, our country has spent trillions bombing ports, bridges, and airports. China has spent the equivalent building the same across the developing world. The Ukraine War is the final collapse of the Neocon's short-lived 'American Century'."
>
> You may agree with that analysis, maybe you don't. Either way, if you're an honest person, you understand this is exactly the moment in our history when we need serious adult conversations about the world around us, a world that is changing to our detriment, and how we ought to respond to those changes. Bobby Kennedy would love to have those conversations. He's not running to get rich. He's running to make things better, but he's not allowed to have those conversations. He'd been censored. Other media won't even talk to him. He criticized their advertisers.[11]

You may wonder why I'm spending so much time talking about Tucker Carlson, Fox News, and Robert F. Kennedy Jr., but there's a common thread between all of them, and it may surprise you.

The common thread between these three is Roger Ailes, the political guru credited with bringing Richard Nixon, George H. W. Bush, and Donald Trump to the presidency, as well as creating Fox News and turning it into a ratings powerhouse before the slide it experienced after yanking Tucker Carlson off the air.

Some may view Roger Ailes as a villain based on his well-documented history of sexually harassing women, or as a hero for championing the conservative cause. There is truth in both versions. But as always, the reality is more complex than political partisans on either side would have you believe.

There can be some surprising connections between people, and Roger Ailes was no exception. Despite being a strong conservative, he had a longtime friendship with the Kennedy family,[12] serving as something of a surrogate father to Robert F. Kennedy Jr., and yet as the head of Fox News, kept Kennedy from talking about the enormous risks of vaccines under our current schedule.

If you want to understand what happened to Tucker Carlson, you must understand the relationship between Roger Ailes and Robert F. Kennedy Jr.

* * *

Roger Ailes and Robert F. Kennedy Jr. once spent six weeks together in a tent on the African savannah in Kenya.

I know that sounds like the start of a joke, but it's true.

It was for the making of a documentary called *The Final Frontier*, about the wildlife and culture of Africa. Roger Ailes was the director, already feared as the political consultant who got Richard Nixon elected in 1968, and a nineteen-year-old Robert F. Kennedy Jr., already passionately interested in the natural world, was the star and narrator.

The year was 1973. As the two remembered in a 1995 interview for Roger's show, *Straight Forward*:

> **ROBERT F. KENNEDY JR.:** Roger and I spent six weeks in a tent together.
> **ROGER AILES:** That's right. We spent six weeks in a tent. People don't realize—
> **ROBERT F. KENNEDY JR.:** I've been trying to live that down for the last thirty years.
> **ROGER AILES:** (Laughing) You took a lot of heat for that, I think.
> **ROBERT F. KENNEDY JR.:** When Willie Horton raised his head [an infamous 1992 commercial for the Bush campaign, about a killer let out on weekend parole by then Democratic nominee, Michael Dukakis, who subsequently committed a murder. It was criticized as racist, but the Bush campaign denied that was the intention], people were saying—
> **ROGER AILES:** How did Bobby get involved with the guy? I never had anything to do with that.
> **ROBERT F. KENNEDY JR.:** You took the rap for it.

> **ROGER AILES:** I did. But I never really did it. But at any rate, what was interesting, we did spend 1973, I think it was, over there in Africa, and you captured this bird. I don't know whether it was a falcon . . .[13]

Their conversation continued about the bird, which was an augur buzzard, similar to the American red-tailed hawk. Roger recounted how he'd entered their hotel room, only to find Robert with this bird on his arm, staring directly into its eyes, as he tried to get the bird to take some food from him. Eventually, the two of them released the bird, and it flew away into the African sky.

The conversation then moved to another member of their team, LeMoyne Billings, who'd been President Kennedy's best friend, and who after Robert's assassination, become something of a father figure to Robert F. Kennedy Jr.

> **ROGER AILES:** He sort of became your guardian, didn't he for a while? He kind of raised you, I think.
>
> **ROBERT F. KENNEDY JR.:** He was almost a surrogate father to me.
>
> **ROGER AILES:** Right. Wonderful guy. And we had some great nights sitting around the campfire over in Africa. Lem and I hitting a little scotch and talking about your great future. And here you are all these years later. When did you turn your life around and decide, "Okay, I'm going to go for this environmental law thing. I'm really going to make a difference." When did you . . . ?
>
> **ROBERT F. KENNEDY JR.:** In '84. Well, at the end of '83 I was kind of reevaluating my life. And I kind of made it a career choice after my father died which happened when I was fourteen. And prior to that, I'd always wanted to be a veterinarian. But I think I felt some pressure for a variety of reasons to change my career. To try to do more with the kind of thing that he was trying to do. And I ended up, rather than going to veterinary school, going to law school, and really followed his career path. I went to Harvard and then to the

University of Virginia, which he had done. And then I became an attorney and prosecutor, which was kind of what my father had been doing. In 1984 I went through a lot of personal difficulties, and really reassessed my life and said . . .

ROGER AILES: That was a drug time, that people know about. And I was proud of you because I saw you go through that and I thought, "Boy, a lot of people don't turn it around." How did you turn it around?

ROBERT F. KENNEDY JR.: I did what I was supposed to do. And I've been sober now for twelve years. At that time, I was reevaluating my life and just decided to do what I wanted to do, which had always been the environment. I integrated a lot of the stuff that I had learned in law school with my initial interest in the environment.[14]

When one watches the video and sees how vulnerable Kennedy let himself be in this interview, it can be quite shocking, as it wasn't the kind of thing one expected to see in 1995. He went on to describe his love of the natural world and the way that the environment and the jobs of people in the community could both be protected, as well as the spiritual peace he'd always found in nature.

Kennedy recounted some of the environmental battles he was fighting at the time, such as trying to clean up New York's drinking water. From there, the conversation shifted to politics.

ROGER AILES: Bobby, when are you going to run for office? Everybody wants to know it and I have to ask it. I've known you a long time. Frankly, I had my doubts about you twenty years ago, but you've grown up a lot since then.

ROBERT F. KENNEDY JR.: I had my doubts about you too, Roger.

ROGER AILES: I know. You still do.

ROBERT F. KENNEDY JR.: Well, I don't know. Will you run my campaign?

> **ROGER AILES:** Well, I promised Lem Billings. You know, Lem and I got a little drunk one night at the campfire and he said, "I want you to keep an eye on Bobby for me." And I said, "Don't worry. If he needs anything, I'll be there." So I might have to help you.[15]

You could just feel the affection between the two men. Both considered themselves patriots, and while they didn't see eye to eye on everything, there was an enormous reservoir of love and mutual respect between them. A little later in the interview there was this exchange.

> **ROGER AILES:** Are you a liberal on most issues or are you conservative on some?
> **ROBERT F. KENNEDY JR:** I wouldn't like to characterize myself with either of those labels. I'm kind of a libertarian in some areas. I believe in free market economics. I believe if we had a true free market economy where we eliminated subsidies to people, we would not have the kind of environmental pollution problems that we have. I think I come from that perspective. But at the same time, I believe that we live in a diverse society, and I think diversity is wonderful in every way, and so I guess that's kind of a liberal point of view.[16]

It was prescient for Kennedy to be talking about how our economy, even in 1995, wasn't genuinely free, but seemed to have a form of crony capitalism with subsidies that allowed environmental degradation to take place. One of their final exchanges in the interview was quite touching.

> **ROGER AILES:** I lost my dad a few years ago, and I've always wanted to say a few things to him. If you could say a few things to your dad today, what would it be?
> **ROBERT F. KENNEDY JR.:** I'd tell him thanks for all that he gave me, and thanks for sticking with his own values to the end. And putting his principles above self-interest. Because I think that's a wonderful example for me, and it's something that I'd like to leave with my own children.[17]

The affection between Ailes and Kennedy continued, even as Ailes built Fox News into a ratings juggernaut, as this article from Liz Smith in 2006 attests:

> Kennedy says if we missed the Fox News special, *The Heat is On: The Case of Global Warming*, which aired before the holidays, we missed a fair, accurate presentation. Writes Kennedy: "I spent a summer in a tent in Africa with Roger Ailes in 1973 making a wildlife film. He is charming, affable, very smart and very, very funny. Although we both believe each other's politics to be misguided, we have remained friends for three decades. Last year, I asked Roger, as a personal favor, to attend Al Gore's New York City update on global warming science . . . he was convinced that the debates deserved a public airing . . . the Fox News team did a superb job by exploring the science. This film should be seen by everyone. The end product goes a long way toward putting the 'conserve' back in conservatism."[18]

I consider the Roger Ailes/Robert F. Kennedy Jr. relationship to be an example of what makes our civic culture among the best in the world. Just because we may have different opinions on certain matters doesn't preclude the possibility of appreciating the positive aspects of another person.

And we should always be open to the possibility that our opinion is wrong, and we might learn something by listening to the views of a person who thinks differently than we do.

But this admirable openness to another's ideas ran aground on the subject of vaccines. To Roger's credit, he did not suffer from the delusion common to so many that those with a different opinion were "anti-science," as Big Pharma propaganda would have the public believe. For Roger Ailes, it was a question of dollars and cents from their Big Pharma advertisers. This is what Kennedy said Roger Ailes told him when he asked to appear on Fox News and discuss the issue of childhood vaccines and autism, as he explained on May 5, 2023, on the *All-In Podcast* show: "'I cannot let you talk about this on Fox News. I'm sorry.' It was the first time he ever said this to me. And he said, 'If any of my hosts let you on to talk about this, I would have to fire them.' And he said, 'If I didn't fire them, I'd get a call from Rupert [Murdoch] within ten minutes.'"[19]

Roger Ailes had been close with Robert F. Kennedy Jr. since 1973. Kennedy's criticisms of vaccines began in about 2005, meaning the two men had shared a close relationship of more than thirty years. And yet, according to Ailes, no host on Fox News would be allowed to talk about vaccines harming children. If they did, they would lose their job in about ten minutes.

Which brings us back to Tucker Carlson, and the second to last episode he was able to film on Fox News.

This is what you need to understand about Tucker, and why I believe his example is one of the defining moments of our modern age.

Tucker knew the story I just shared with you about Roger Ailes, because he heard it directly from Robert F. Kennedy Jr.

I want you to fully understand the significance of Tucker's commentary and having Robert F. Kennedy Jr. on his second-to-last show. Tucker knew this move would likely end his multi-million-dollar career at Fox News.

And he did it anyway, in full view of the entire country.

Where did he get the courage to do what so many in the news media have failed to do?

I believe the answer can be found in the speech Tucker gave at the Heritage Foundation the Friday night after his last show on Fox News.

* * *

After you've lived long enough, you begin to see the arc of your life, and you can say to yourself, "Oh, that's what I was meant to do."

More and more, I've been saying to myself, *Maybe it was my destiny to build a successful show, make some mistakes while I was going through a difficult period in my life, apologize numerous times for my errors, then be sued years later for more money than any man has ever been sued in human history and face a judgment of a billion and a half dollars, which I can't ever possibly pay.*

It's an out of body experience, when you're living the flesh and blood experience, and yet another part of you is removed from it. I like to believe those are moments where I'm somehow in touch with my eternal soul. A moment when God pulls back the curtain a little to say, "Here's a little more for you to understand about what I've got planned." But then God lets the curtain drop back and the decision is up to us.

Do we have faith, or give into despair?

At the age of fifty-three, Tucker was beginning to see the arc of his life. Although he'd never been much of a religious person, the immensity of the times began to overwhelm him, and he felt God's call to be a warrior. This was the beginning of Tucker describing the arc of his life, starting with his first job at the Heritage Foundation.

> And then the week I started at Policy Review, the Soviet Union collapsed, which was an amazing thing. The coup against Gorbachev in the third week of August 1991 was the week I started at Heritage. And in retrospect, of course, you never appreciate the significance of things as they happen to you. You can't really know what the movie's about until it ends.
>
> But at the time, we didn't really appreciate, well, two things. One, how our entire political orientation was based on this war between the United States and the Soviet union, the Cold War, but very much a war. And every part of our politics, as you well remember, those of you my age or older, remember, every part of our politics revolved around that central conflict.
>
> We were in conflict with a country that was both anti-markets and anti-Christian. And that put in stark relief our own beliefs. And what would happen when that ended, when there wasn't that clear contrast? That's the first thing. And of course, the second thing we could never have known the third week of August 1991, as we saw totalitarianism die, is that it would ever come here. We just couldn't imagine that.

> We believed that victories are permanent. They're not, of course. That's the first lesson of history. Nothing is permanent except our own demise and God. But we didn't get that.[20]

When I listened to that opening, I couldn't help but be thrilled. Yes, we had waged a decades-long war against Soviet communism, and when it officially ceased to exist (on December 25, 1991), so close to the date of the birth of Jesus Christ, one couldn't help but feel some divine influence at work in the world.

And yet, it wasn't the end of history, because good and evil are locked in an eternal battle. And it's our choice in each generation as to whether we're going to submit to the darkness or fight.

Tucker continued, talking about the enormous respect he has for his father's integrity, the rapid pace of change, how not all of it was for the better, and the failure of people to speak up. His words were like a bolt of pure adrenaline truth, mainlined into a dying society.

> But for those of us who are still engaged and trying to figure out what all this means, and not just repelled by it, I would say there are two things we're thinking about. The first is, you look around, and you see so many people break under the strain, under the downward pressure of whatever it is we're going through. And you look with disdain and sadness as you see people become quislings, you see them revealed as cowards.
>
> You see them going along with the new, new thing, which is clearly a poisonous thing, a silly thing, saying things they don't believe, because they want to keep their jobs. If there's a single person in this room who hasn't seen that through George Floyd and COVID and the Ukraine War, raise your hand. [Author's note: The vast majority of hands in the audience went up.]
>
> Oh, nobody, right? You all know what I'm talking about. And you're so disappointed in people. And you realize that the herd instinct is maybe the strongest instinct. I mean, it may be stronger than the hunger and sex instincts, actually. The instinct, which

> again, is inherent, to be like everybody else, and not to be cast out of the group, not to be shunned. That's a very strong impulse in all of us from birth.
>
> And it takes over, unfortunately, in moments like this. And it's harnessed, in fact, by bad people in moments like this, to produce uniformity. And you see people going along with this and you lose respect for them. And that's certainly happened to me at scale over the past three years.[21]

This isn't the way a member of the mainstream media talks. It isn't the way anybody in our public debates talk any more. Because this wasn't the shiny new distraction or the latest outrage of the day; this was getting to that deep place literature used to go before it became "modern," and that place was the human soul. We used to be much more comfortable asking ourselves: Who is the person that God sees when He looks into our hearts? We have hidden our hearts from God for far too long, and the only place that leads is the Devil's Road. The best leaders in our world aren't simply pointing the finger of blame at others; they're also searching their own soul and telling us the truth about what they find. The best leaders show us that they are also human and frail, and all too often fall short of glory.

> So, you reach that place and you feel—And this is one of the reasons Father Scalia, I was actually overcome a little bit with emotion as you prayed. Because I realized that I was so upset by some people I love, frankly, in a country I revere and always have, that I wasn't praying for the country.
>
> And that's on me. And we all should be.
>
> But back to my point. So, you see the sadness happening, but there is, as there always is, this is a fact of nature and theology and observable reality, there is a countervailing force at work, always. There is a counterbalance to the badness. It is called goodness.
>
> And you see it in people. So for every ten people who are putting "he" and "him" in their electronic JP Morgan email signatures, there's one person who's like, "No, I'm not doing that. Sorry. I don't

> want to fight, but I'm not doing that. It's a betrayal of what I think is true. It's a betrayal of my conscience, of my faith, of my sense of myself, of my dignity as a human being, of my autonomy. I am not a slave. I am a free citizen, and I'm not doing that. And there's nothing you can do to me to make me do it."[22]

How could I not be absolutely thrilled to hear these words? This wasn't just a human being speaking; something else was coming through him. Something decent, honest, and brave. He was calling out the corruption, declaring he was not a slave, and affirming that there was nothing they could do to him to put him back in chains. But he was just warming up.

> Here I am. It's Paul on trial. Here I am. And you see that in people. And it's a completely unexpected assortment of people. And I'm really interested in cause and effect. And as I noted at the outset of my remarks, and my ability to predict the future, working on that. But because I'm sort of paid to predict things, I try and think a lot about what connects certain outcomes that I should have seen before they occurred.
>
> And in this case, there is no thread that I can find that connects all of the people who've popped up in my life to be that lone, brave person in the crowd who says, no thank you. You could not have known who these people are. They don't fit a common profile. Some are people like me; some of them don't look like me at all.
>
> Some of them are people I despised on political grounds just a few years ago. I could names their names, but you may not even know about their transformations. And I don't want to wreck your dinner by telling you who they are. But there is, in one case, someone who I made fun of on television, and certainly in my private life in vulgar ways, who is really the embodiment of everything I found repulsive. Who, in the middle of COVID, decided, no, I'm not going along with this.
>
> And once you say one true thing and stick with it, all kinds of true things occur to you. The truth is contagious. Lying is, but the

> truth is as well. And the second you decide to tell the truth about something, you are filled with this, I don't want to get supernatural on you, but you are filled with this power from somewhere else.[23]

I would put Tucker's talk at the Heritage Foundation alongside some of the greatest religious conversions in history. And in this digital age, that message can quickly spread to millions of people. The avatars of technology, who are so determined to wipe God away from modern society, have provided the tools for the Good News to spread much more quickly than at any time in history.

And we, in our arrogance, question whether God has abandoned the world?

Tucker spoke like a man who'd recently been given the gift of sight after a life of darkness and was excited for everybody to fully appreciate the potential beauty of this world. Tucker was now a missionary for the truth, not the prepackaged, corporate-approved truth, but the genuine truth.

> Try it. Tell the truth about something. You feel it every day. The more you tell the truth, the stronger you become. That's completely real. It's measurable in the way you feel. And of course, the opposite is true. The more you lie, the weaker and more terrified you become. We all know that feeling. You lie about something and all of a sudden, you're a prisoner of that lie. Drug and alcohol use is the same way. It makes you weak and afraid.
>
> But you look around and you see these people, and some of them have really paid a heavy price for telling the truth. And they are cast out of their groups, whatever those groups are, but they do it anyway. And I look on at those people with the deepest possible admiration. I am paid to do that.
>
> I face no penalty. Someone came up to me, "You're so brave." Really? I'm a talk show host. It's like I can have any opinion I want. That's my job. That's why they pay me. It's not brave to tell the truth on a cable news show. And if you're not doing that, you're really an

> idiot. You're really craven. You're lying on television? Why would you do that? You're literally making a living to say what you think, and you can't even do that? Please.
>
> But how about if you're a senior vice president at Citibank? I'm serious, at Citibank, and you're making four million dollars a year, and you've got three kids in Bedford, and two are in boarding school and one's starting at Wesley next year? And you need this job, honestly, and your whole sector's kind of collapsing, and you know that. There is no incentive whatsoever for you to tell the truth about anything.[24]

Tucker was blowing up the empire of lies from the inside with the most powerful weapon all of us have: using our God-given voice to tell the truth. And I couldn't help but reflect on Tucker's example of a senior vice president at Citibank. It seemed he was talking of somebody he knew, likely a good friend as well as a good person, who was trapped in the web of lies spun by others. This man was weighing, on one hand, the family who depended on him and, on the other, his duty to tell the truth for the benefit of society.

And in his moral calculus, he decided his family came before the truth.

How many of us might make the same decision?

How many of us can point to an action we've taken that shows more courage than this senior vice president at Citibank displayed? Tucker continued with the life of this senior vice president that he imagined.

> You just go into the little reeducation meetings and you're like, "Yeah, diversity is our strength. That's exactly right. We need equity in the capital markets." Okay. All right. So, if you're the one guy who refuses to say that, you are a hero, in my opinion. And I know some of them. In fact, my job is to interview them. And I sit and I look at these people, and I give them more credit than I do people who display physical courage, which is often impulsive, by the way.
>
> And I'm not denigrating physical courage, which I deeply admire. But you interview people who do amazing things, who rush into the

> proverbial burning building. And every man is trained from birth to fantasize about what he would do when the building catches fire. And you hear a baby crying. And he goes, "Well, you run inside."
>
> No one is trained to stand up in the middle of a DEI meeting at Citibank and say, "This is nonsense." And the people who do that, oh, they have my deepest admiration. And so their example really gives me hope. It thrills me. I talk to them all day long, people like that. That's the first thing. We should, in this sad moment of profound and widespread destruction of the institutions, understand that the people of earlier generations, who built these institutions, would agree substantially with every person in this room. They built those and now they're being destroyed. And, oh, that's so depressing.
>
> But we can also see rising in the distance, new things, new institutions, led by new people who are every bit as brave as the people who came before us. Amen.[25]

This is Tucker talking, not just to us, but to himself as well, building the intellectual and spiritual framework for courage. The type of courage that may end with one's death (or at least a billion and a half dollars in punitive damages). Tucker's discussion of moral versus physical courage echoes a famous statement by Senator Robert Kennedy in 1968: "Moral courage is a rarer commodity than bravery in battle or great intelligence. Yet it is the one essential, vital quality for those who seek to change a world that yields most painfully to change."[26]

It didn't seem as if he'd prepared his remarks; they were just coming to him on the stage because he opened himself to become a vessel of something else, that supernatural force of which he spoke.

He went on to speak of his shallow religious upbringing, the foolishness of the transgender movement, and the elevation of abortion to something akin to a religious sacrament. Tucker then moved onto his main point, in which he moved away from the slenderest connection to materialism and moved decisively into the realm of the spirit. This was a man declaring to the world that he was submitting himself to a higher power.

None of this makes sense in conventional political terms. When people, or crowds of people, or the largest crowd of people at all, which is the federal government, the largest organization in human history, decide that the goal is to destroy things, destruction for its own sake. "Hey, let's tear it down!"

What you're watching is not a political movement. It's evil. So, if you want to assess, and I'll put it in rather non-specific theological terms. And just say, if you want to know what's evil and what's good, what are the characteristics of those? And by the way, I think the Athenians would've agreed with this. This is not necessarily a Christian notion. This is a kind of, I would say, widely agreed upon understanding of good and evil.

What are its products? What do these two conditions produce? Well, I mean, good is characterized by order, calmness, tranquility, peace, whatever you want to call it, lack of conflict, cleanliness. Cleanliness is next to godliness. It's true. It is. And evil is characterized by their opposites, violence, hate, disorder, division, disorganization, and filth. So, if you're all in on the things that produce the latter basket of outcomes, what you're really advocating for is evil. That's just true.

I'm not advocating for religious war, far from it. I'm merely calling for an acknowledgment of what we're watching. And I'm certainly not backing the Republican Party. I mean, ugh. I'm not making a partisan point at all. I'm just noting what's super obvious.

Those of us who are in our mid-fifties are caught in the way that we think about this. One side's like, "No, I've got this idea and you've got this idea, and let's have a debate about our ideas." They don't want a debate. Those ideas won't produce outcomes that any rational person would want under any circumstances. Those are manifestations of some larger force acting upon us.[27]

The strangeness of this life, the events that happen to us, and the forces we see at work in the world lead us inexorably to something greater than us. Tucker was submitting himself to that greater force.

And because Tucker had made a commitment to tell the truth, in things big and small, he began to see the lies that are so prevalent in our society. The left doesn't want a debate with the right over our differing ideas. They want us expunged from the public discourse, which is why deplatforming and shadow-banning are their new civil rights.

Tucker ended his talk by asserting his own inadequacy to speak with any authority about religious matters but urged the audience members to pray for their country for at least ten minutes a day.

It may have been the single greatest declaration of the presence of God in American life by any public figure since Lincoln urged us to be guided by "the better angels of our nature."[28]

* * *

You probably wouldn't expect Alex Jones to praise the accuracy of an article from *Vanity Fair*. But from what I know, their article on Tucker Carlson and the effect his speech at the Heritage Foundation had on Fox owner Rupert Murdoch was extremely accurate. Good job, *Vanity Fair*! Here's how the article opened:

> Twenty-four hours after Fox News ousted its highest-rated host, the network has yet to explain one of the most shocking defenestrations in cable news history. "I'm not going beyond the release," a Fox News spokeswoman texted yesterday when I asked her for comment. In this information void, multiple theories about why Fox fired Carlson circulated in the media. It was fallout from the $787.5 Dominion settlement; punishment for vulgar text messages published in Dominion court filings; or a consequence of former Fox producer Abby Grossberg's lawsuit, which alleged Carlson oversaw a hostile work environment.[29]

In the mainstream media, the ouster of Tucker Carlson was a mystery. Was it because he criticized the pharma advertisers of Fox, allowing well-known vaccine skeptic and now presidential candidate Robert F. Kennedy

Jr. to appear on his show? Was it because he had allowed discussions about election interference in the 2020 election? Was it because of the Dominion lawsuit, as well as other claims currently in litigation? Or was it because Tucker had found God? The well-known cartoonist and political commentator Scott Adams is fond of noting that decisions are rarely made for one specific reason. There are usually a host of contributing factors.

The article continued with the speculation, noting that several of the suggested reasons didn't make sense. Others, like Maria Bartiromo at Fox, had covered the election claims in greater depth. And the Fox management was on record as saying the lawsuits against Tucker were going to be "vigorously" defended.[30]

Then the article came to its main claim: Murdoch had removed Carlson because he didn't approve of Carlson's religious awakening.

> A new theory has emerged. According to the source, Fox Corp. chair Rupert Murdoch removed Carlson over remarks Carlson made during a speech at the Heritage Foundation's 50th Anniversary Gala on Friday night. Carlson laced his speech with religious overtones that even Murdoch found too extreme, the source, who was briefed on Murdoch's decision-making, said. Carlson told the Heritage audience that national politics has become a Manichean battle between "good" and "evil." Carlson said that people advocating for transgender rights and DEI programs want to destroy America and they could not be persuaded with facts. "We should say that and stop engaging in these totally fraudulent debates . . . I've tried. That doesn't work," he said. The answer, Carlson suggested, is prayer. "I have concluded it might be worth taking just 10 minutes out of your busy schedule to say a prayer for the future, and I hope you will," he said. "That stuff freaks Rupert out. He doesn't like all the spiritual talk," the source said.[31]

Could it be that Tucker was taken off the air because he gave a speech in which he asked people to pray for ten minutes a day for their country? If you read a historical account of some dictator who threw somebody in prison for suggesting a prayer, you'd say to yourself, *Yeah, that sounds like what a dictator would do.* But is that much different than silencing a person's voice? Media reports have been suggesting that Murdoch wants to keep Tucker silenced through the 2024 election.[32]

News flash to Fox News. That ain't gonna happen.

Tucker Carlson is going to be bigger without Fox News than he ever was with Fox News.

And you can't say that Tucker didn't try to play the game. Luckily, I've never had bosses I've had to please, but I understand that's not the experience of most people. For most people, they try to, if not ingratiate themselves to the boss, at least make it so they're understood.

The *Vanity Fair* article contained a fascinating story about Tucker being placed in a difficult position at a dinner with Murdoch and his then-fiancé, Ann Lesley Smith, who had very different opinions about religion.

> Rupert Murdoch was perhaps unnerved by Carlson's messianism because it echoes the end-times worldview of Murdoch's ex-fiancé Ann Lesley Smith, the source said. In my May cover story, I reported that Murdoch and Smith called off their two-week engagement because Smith had told people Carlson was a "messenger from God." Murdoch had seen Carlson and Smith discuss religion firsthand. In late March, Carlson had dinner at Murdoch's Bel Air vineyard with Murdoch and Smith, according to the source. During dinner, Smith pulled out a bible and started reading passages from the Book of Exodus, the source said. A few days after the dinner, Murdoch and Smith called off the wedding. By taking Carlson off the air, Murdoch was also taking away his ex's favorite show.[33]

There are so many things in this single paragraph that show how great the gulf is between the atheistic media and the devout public. When a religious person calls somebody "a messenger from God," we mean they are doing God's work. It's a compliment. When the atheists see anybody doing what the rest of us call "God's work," what the leftists see is some David Koresh-like, crazed, "messianic" cult leader.

The media also seems horrified that people having dinner at a fancy vineyard might pull out a bible and read some passages. In the eyes of the left, this is almost akin to the imposition of Sharia law.

And are we to believe that the real reason Murdoch took Tucker off the air was because he wanted to punish his ex-fiancé?

Where does all of this go?

It might go to some very interesting places, such as the January 6, 2020 protest at the US Capitol, when supporters of President Donald Trump asked Congress for additional time to inspect what seemed like election irregularities. Yes, this has been a controversial topic, but it may be Tucker who finally breaks this issue open, as he told a curious story to podcaster Russell Brand on July 7, 2023. This is part of what Tucker said:

> These are people who thought the election was stolen from them, there's some evidence they were right. We could debate that, but that's what they thought. That's a meaningful thing. If you've got a big population in your country that doesn't believe your elections are on the level, you need to figure out a way to convince them that the elections are on the level, or you can't have a democracy, because it's a faith-based system. So that was the first thing I noticed. There was no effort at all to convince people. "Actually, electronic voting machines are secure!" Which they are not. By the way, that's a lie, and any country that has electronic voting machines is by definition at risk of having its election stolen. By definition, no country that cared about democracy would have electronic voting machines, okay? And by the way, many Democrats have made that point. Not now, but ten years ago.
>
> There was no effort to reassure anybody. They immediately used it as a cudgel to make their political opponents shut up. And in a lot of cases, to send them to jail. So, I noticed this. I'm like, "Wait a second, nobody here in good faith at all." They're just immediately lying with maximum aggression. . . . They immediately recoiled when you

> asked any questions about January 6, and that was a tip off to me. I mean, I had no thought in my head as I watched this happen on television, and in the subsequent weeks, that US law enforcement or military agents had anything to do with it.
>
> I never thought it was a false flag or anything like that. I'm not a conspiracist by temperament. I never thought that. And then I interviewed the chief of the Capitol Police, Steven Sund, in an interview that was never aired on Fox, by the way. I was fired before it could air. I'm going to interview him again.
>
> But Steven Sund was totally non-political, worked for Nancy Pelosi, I mean, this is not some right-wing activist. He was the chief of the Capitol Police on January 6. And he said, "Oh, yeah, yeah, that crowd was filled with federal agents." What? Yes. Well, he would know, of course, because he was in charge of security at the site. So the more time has passed, now it's been two and a half years, it becomes really obvious that core claims they made about January 6 were lies.[34]

Any person who genuinely investigates the January 6 event at the US Capitol will come away with more questions than answers. In 2023, the conspiracy theorists have more credibility than any government agency or mainstream news media organization.

Take your pick of conspiracies. You might not like vaccines: you'll find lots of information to make you even more worried. The same thing will happen if you investigate the World Economic Forum, the influence of Communist China on our political system, the monetary system, the dangers of AI, the surveillance state, or the actions of our intelligence agencies, at home and abroad.

I understand it's easy to feel overwhelmed by the number of ways in which we've been deceived.

But I consider it to be good news, because you have to see the problem clearly before you can solve it.

* * *

The early evidence is that Rupert Murdoch's firing of Tucker Carlson may be a mistake of Biblical proportions.

Here is an excerpt from a May 10, 2023 article from *The Hill* with the headline "Tucker Carlson Tweet Announcing New Twitter Show Tops 100 Million Views":

> Carlson's tweet captioned "We're back" amassed 100 million views in less than 24 hours, and the three-minute video included netted 21 million watches in the same time frame.
>
> During his short message, Carlson did not address his ouster from Fox, but he offered a critique of the news media more generally, saying "amazingly that as of tonight, there aren't many platforms left that allow free speech," and lauding Twitter as a place "where our national conversation has long incubated and developed."
>
> The former prime-time host did not provide any further details on the new venture he was planning.
>
> A similar video message from Carlson, released just days after his ouster from the network racked up 57 million views in less than 24 hours.[35]

When Tucker tweets something important, he can count on somewhere between fifty to a hundred million people reading his remarks, and somewhere around twenty million taking the time to listen to his full remarks.

Consider the anemic ratings that Fox News has in comparison to what Tucker pulled off with broadcasting on Twitter. This is from the *Hollywood Reporter:*

> After the surprise of Fox News and Tucker Carlson "agree[ing] to part ways" on Monday, the network's 8 p.m. hour had a significantly smaller audience Monday night. The debut of *Fox News Tonight*, hosted by Brian Kilmeade (the first in a series of rotating hosts), pulled in just under 2.6 million viewers—about 21 percent below the average for *Tucker Carlson Tonight* (3.3 million views) over the past eight Mondays.

> *Fox News Tonight* also took a hit in the key news demographic of adults 25-54: It's 0.24 rating was 37 percent lower than the 0.38 Carlson averaged over the prior eight Monday shows.[36]

The collapse of globalist mainstream media is happening on an accelerated time frame, thanks to the courage of people like Tucker Carlson. When people ask whether I genuinely believe we're going to win, I look at the numbers.

An anemic 2.6 million watch the desiccated corpse of *Fox News Tonight,* and more than 100 million take the time to read what Tucker Carlson posts on X.

That looks like winning to me.

* * *

I believe that God gives all of us the choice between being a villain or a hero. And I believe we are given this choice up to the end of our lives. Whichever path we choose, God will use it for the good.

Consider Roger Ailes. He was unquestionably a talented man, and in many ways, as demonstrated by his genuine concern for a young Robert F. Kennedy Jr., a good man.

But as Ailes grew in power, he was given a choice. He could use the power to be a hero or a villain. It seems in many instances he chose the path of evil, and we should never forget it.

One of the ways he became a villain was to use his increasing power to harass and seduce female journalists who'd previously done a good job and were looking for a promotion. In the documentary *Divide and Conquer: The Story of Roger Ailes,* his creepy behavior was on display. There was one woman who said the line Ailes used on her was: "If you want to play with the big boys, you need to lay with the big boys."[37]

Ailes became a villain as he rose in power by choosing to prey on vulnerable women. Another way he became a villain is that he refused to put Robert F. Kennedy Jr. on one of his television shows to highlight the risk of vaccines and allow the parents of vaccine-injured children to tell their stories.

Ailes betrayed the man who was almost like a son to him, in addition to the parents of vaccine-injured children, in order to keep his Big Pharma advertisers happy.

Roger chose to value the advertising dollars of his Big Pharma sponsors over injured children, and his longtime friend, Robert F. Kennedy Jr. During those years, I had Dr. Andrew Wakefield on *InfoWars* several times, discussing his findings of a link between the MMR shot and the development of the devastating condition of autism, as well as several other doctors making similar claims. We also had the parents of these children on to tell their stories.

Let Roger Ailes be forever condemned by the judgment of history for valuing advertising dollars over the lives of children.

But I believe God used the evil choice made by Roger Ailes to His own advantage.

Robert F. Kennedy Jr. has told the story often of what Roger Ailes said to him about not mentioning vaccines, and Tucker Carlson, a good man, heard it.

Tucker was given a choice.

Kennedy had announced he was running for president, the "Warp-Speed" COVID-19 vaccine program had opened the eyes of many to problems with vaccines in general, and Tucker decided it was time to have Kennedy on and proclaim his full-throated support of the questions about vaccines Kennedy had raised.

God offered Tucker Carlson the opportunity to be a hero in the eyes of many long-suffering families with vaccine-injured children, to have their concerns validated, and Tucker chose the path of righteousness.

The left would have you believe that the richer and more successful one becomes, the less one has a need for God. Or that God might not be able to reach out to you in spite of your distance from Him. However, I believe God offered a choice to even ninety-two-year-old Rupert Murdoch to become a hero.

What other explanation is there for the fact that at the age of ninety-two Murdoch apparently fell in love and was planning to marry a woman of deep religious faith? God was giving Rupert Murdoch the chance to become a hero.

But all of us have free will, even Rupert Murdoch. That is another gift from God. He can show you the way, but you have to choose it. God will never force your choice.

However, there will be consequences.

Rupert Murdoch turned away from God and became a villain.

Tucker chose to proclaim his faith, even at the cost of losing his position as the most popular news figure on television.

But God doesn't require us to suffer when we make the choice to follow Him. In fact, we will ultimately be rewarded for it. I predict that Tucker will be one of the great, indispensable figures of our time.

And Robert F. Kennedy Jr. just might end up as president of the United States.

And for those who have waited for decades, everybody will know the truth of what happened to millions of vaccine-injured children. "Thou shalt not bear false witness against thy neighbor" is the ninth of God's Ten Commandments given to Moses. This commandment is as critical today as it was thousands of years ago.

Roger Ailes and Rupert Murdoch tried to prevent that truth from coming to light.

But God can frustrate the plans of even Big Pharma and media-mogul billionaires.

We will get the truth and God will be restored to His rightful place at the center of our existence.

The biggest choice of our lives is whether, when God calls us, we choose to be the villain . . . or the hero.

Chapter Nine

Jeffrey Epstein—Renfield to the Globalist Draculas (but Even Worse, Because They Prey on Their Own Children)

I believe that understanding the Jeffrey Epstein story is like unlocking the Rosetta Stone to comprehend the way our world really works.

I could begin by telling you exactly what I think happened in this story.

But I don't think you're ready for it.

Instead, I'm going to tell you the story as the mainstream media told it, then pick apart the inconsistencies, until you understand how their account makes absolutely no sense, and you'll be more likely to consider my version.

* * *

Where should we begin the Jeffrey Epstein story?

Should we begin it with the resignation of Trump's Labor secretary, Alex Acosta, in 2019, for failing to properly prosecute Jeffrey Epstein in 2008? This is how it was described in the pages of the *New York Times*:

> President Trump's embattled labor secretary, R. Alexander Acosta, announced his resignation on Friday amid continuing questions about the handling of a sex crimes case involving the financier Jeffrey Epstein when Mr. Acosta was a federal prosecutor in Florida.

> Mr. Trump, who announced the resignation, said Mr. Acosta had called him on Friday morning to tell the president he planned to step down. Mr. Acosta's decision came only two days after he held a news conference to defend his handling of the 2008 sex crimes prosecution of Mr. Epstein while trying to quell a chorus of Democratic calls for his resignation and convincing Mr. Trump he was strong enough to survive.[1]

If that's all you read about the story, you'd probably just shrug your shoulders and say to yourself, *It seems like something weird was going on, but I'm sure happy that prosecutor who didn't do his job in 2008 finally suffered some consequences.*

Then you move on to the next fake news story.

But we shouldn't be so quick to abandon the story of Alex Acosta. One of the few investigative journalists who aggressively pursued the Jeffrey Epstein story over the years was Julie K. Brown, an award-winning investigative reporter for the *Miami Herald*. The Epstein case was initially investigated by Detective Joe Recarey, who would quickly find himself embroiled in the most unusual case of his career. As Brown detailed the early maneuverings of the Epstein case, it seemed that a formidable army was being assembled to defend the wealthy pedophile.

> Epstein hired the flamboyant Harvard lawyer Alan Dershowitz, who met with Barry Krischer, the Palm Beach state attorney responsible for prosecuting the case. Soon, criminal prosecutors were no longer scrutinizing Epstein; they were excoriating his underage victims.
>
> Over the course of a year, everything Recarey believed about justice was shaken to its core. Krischer, seemingly dazzled by Dershowitz's fame, would turn his back on the victims and the police working the case; Epstein and the private investigators hired by his lawyers stalked and threatened the girls and their families, tearing their lives apart. Ultimately, the FBI would take over the investigation. The man who would oversee the case was a young, rising star in the Republican Party who had ambitions to become a U.S. Supreme

> Court Justice. Rene Alexander Acosta, thirty-seven, was sworn in as U.S. Attorney in Miami in October 2006, just as the FBI began to suspect that Epstein's crimes went well beyond South Florida.[2]

Let's consider the initial moves in this drama. Evidence is assembled by an honest Florida detective, and charges are brought against Epstein. Now the machinery of Epstein's defense swings into action. Epstein is able to get famed Harvard lawyer Alan Dershowitz on his side. Dershowitz apparently "dazzles" the Palm Beach state attorney and gets him to turn his investigative team on the underage victims, rather than Epstein.

I applaud Brown's work, but there's something with which I take serious exception.

Brown claims the Palm Beach state attorney was likely "dazzled" by Dershowitz, and that explains his action.

Can Brown provide me any proof for that claim? Or is that what one says when they don't have any evidence for why a law enforcement official would take the side of an alleged pedophile?

And while Brown is definitely staying in the shallow end of the investigative pool, she suggests that whatever nefarious methods were at work on the democratic side of the aisle, they were equally at work on the republican side.

> Epstein had given liberally to Democratic candidates and causes, but he knew that if he wanted the Republicans then in the White House in his corner, he needed someone with clout in Washington. His legal dream team included Kenneth Starr, the former independent counsel who had employed his skills of moral outrage and prosecutorial skill to make the case for President Bill Clinton's 1998 impeachment.
>
> Citing a "solemn intent to ensure fairness and integrity in the administration of justice," Starr asked the Justice Department to essentially quash the federal case the prosecutors in Miami were mounting against Epstein.[3]

When the media goes after me for my "conspiracy theories," I just want to stop them and say, "People, don't you have even a shred of skepticism in your souls? Have you spent years among the lying political class and you still swallow the latest bit of garbage as if it's a filet mignon?"

Does Kenneth Starr want us to believe that he spent four years investigating Clinton, only coming up with blowjobs by Monica Lewinsky, an adult intern at the White House, and yet Jeffrey Epstein, having sex with underage girls, was a model of moral rectitude that should be freed?

You might be surprised to hear me say this, but I'm inclined to give thirty-seven-year-old Alex Acosta, the newly sworn-in US attorney in Miami, a break. From my experience of how public officials are corrupted, it's usually only when they've reached a high level that the curtain is pulled back and they see how the show is really run. My suspicion is that the Epstein case was when the curtain was first pulled back a little for Acosta. That explains this allegation, which appeared in *Newsweek* and didn't get much traction at the time, but which starts to put the pieces together for me.

> New allegations from the *Daily Beast* and journalist Vicky Ward reported that Acosta told the Trump Administration during the screening process for his current role that he was asked to cut a deal with Epstein because he was told the financier "belonged to intelligence," and that the issue was "above his pay grade."[4]

That explanation makes a great deal of sense to me and is consistent with what I have been told about the operations of the Deep State. There was thirty-seven-year-old Alex Acosta, the newly minted US attorney in Miami, and suddenly he's facing off against Alan Dershowitz, Kenneth Starr, and these nameless officials telling him this is an intelligence matter that is above his pay grade.

What do you do if you're interested in continuing your ascent to become a US Supreme Court justice? You back off when the spooky man tells you to back off. What do you know about intelligence matters? You're a new US attorney, ignorant of such matters, and you get what I'm assuming were top intelligence officials telling you to drop the case. You probably do exactly what they tell you to do.

Despite Acosta doing what he was told in the Epstein case, I get the impression he wasn't really favored by the intelligence community for recruitment. He seemed to be loyal to Trump in his job, and when the Epstein story got hot, he got scapegoated and sacrificed.

That's not generally how the intelligence community treats its own.

* * *

Or should the story start in 2007, when Jeffrey Epstein was first charged with sex-trafficking crimes in Florida, and his attorney, Alan Dershowitz, claimed to the court that Epstein was part of the original brain trust for the Clinton Global Initiative, writing:

> "Mr. Epstein was part of the original group that conceived the Clinton Global Initiative, which is described as a project 'bringing together a community of global leaders to devise and implement innovative solutions to some of the world's most pressing challenges," attorney Alan Dershowitz and Gerald Lefcourt wrote in the letter, which was first reported by *Fox News* in 2016 and resurfaced Monday by the *Daily Caller*.[5]

Was the plan to say to the judge, "Yes, your honor, we know he's a pedophile, but look at all this good work he's doing for the world?"

Or should we start with the cameras, allegedly in his properties in Manhattan, Little Saint James Island in the Caribbean, and Zorro Ranch in New Mexico?

> Jeffrey Epstein had surveillance cameras filming every room in his Manhattan mansion and Little St. James estate, and a dedicated employee who monitored the feeds at all times.
>
> The homebase for his operations in New York City was actually described by former sex slave Virginia Roberts in a memoir she

> submitted as evidence during her defamation case against Ghislaine Maxwell.[6]

The claim of surveillance cameras and other odd accessories at an Epstein property was corroborated by Eddy Aragon, a local New Mexico radio station owner who interviewed Epstein's architect and a former IT contractor who worked on Epstein's internet systems between 1999 and 2007.

> The *Sun* reported that the underground floor measures 8,000 square feet (743 square meters) and has rooms for working out, getting a massage, as well as a jacuzzi area that later made way for a pool. The plan also shows three "mechanical rooms." Ms. Farmer, 51, said these areas were where Epstein and Maxwell's computers and video gear were stored . . .
>
> "All of that in the basement feels more like a dungeon with the nebulous mechanical rooms," he said. A six-foot-by-six-foot oversized portrait of Ghislaine Maxwell, with her legs fully spread, completely naked, and a golden dagger in her right hand, was dead center in the elevator hall of the basement."
>
> "I think that was used to intimidate the young women, who were there alone and isolated," he added. "The contractor who supplied the photographs stated that he can't ever get the image out of his mind, and it is one of the most bizarre things that he's ever seen."[7]

There are so many unbelievable parts to the Jeffrey Epstein story that it can be difficult to hold all of the competing pieces in your mind. Many books have been written about Epstein, and I don't know that any has fully captured what I believe about the man and his evil network.

I will do my best to present what I believe was going on with Jeffrey Epstein, but until all of his files, pictures, and videos are released, every one of us is guessing.

* * *

One might be tempted, as several former Dalton School alumni have, to joke that the school had an "Epstein-Barr problem."[8]

The joke may not make sense to you unless you understand that Jeffrey Epstein first entered New York society due to being hired as a math teacher by Dalton School headmaster, Donald Barr. And Epstein exited that same society under the auspices of his son, William Barr, who as attorney general under Trump, declared that Epstein's death while in detention at a secure federal prison in New York City was a suicide.[9]

In an article on his time at the Dalton School, the *New York Times* wrote:

> Dalton has long been known for its rigorous academics, repeatedly ranking among the nation's best private schools while drawing the sons and daughters of New York titans of finance, media, and art. Among the alumni are the CNN journalist Anderson Cooper, the actress Claire Danes and the comedian Chevy Chase.
>
> Mr. Epstein's time at Dalton was brief, and an administrator said it ended in a dismissal. While Mr. Epstein later developed a reputation in the world of finance as a man of brilliance—"He was a Brooklyn guy with a motor for a brain," *New York* magazine wrote about him in a 2002 profile—the administrator told *The Times* that he had dismissed Mr. Epstein for poor performance.
>
> But the accounts offer a window into Mr. Epstein's early adulthood, before he developed extensive private wealth that allowed him to acquire a $56 million mansion just a mile south of the Dalton School. It was there, prosecutors said this week, that Mr. Epstein and his employees paid "numerous" underage girls to engage in sex acts with him.[10]

If you'll allow me, I need to add some context to this article so that you can better understand what I believe is happening. If you understand the history of the Office of Strategic Services, which later became the Central Intelligence Agency, you'll know that the intelligence agencies were basically a creation of Ivy League graduates from the East Coast, who used their alumni networks to recruit those whom they believed would share their worldview. I also have to add to the picture that, among the elite, there's often a healthy appreciation for the eccentrics or visionaries, who see the world in a slightly different light. Most innovation is driven by unusual and eccentric people, or as George Bernard Shaw might say, the "unreasonable man" who will not conform himself to the ways of the world but seeks to change the world to fit his perceptions.

That's why at a surface level the eccentric or the visionary might believe their true home is among these elites. The culture is quite welcoming to those who feel ill at ease in the rest of the world. The intelligence operatives hiding among the elites want you to fly your "freak flag."

But it's a trap, just the way a farm is a trap to the well-fed and cared-for turkey, not realizing that Thanksgiving is just around the corner. Consider this description of Donald Barr from the *New York Times*:

> In a school known for creativity, administrators prohibited denim jeans and "bizarre and eccentric costumes." If Mr. Barr caught students using marijuana, he would often send them to therapy as a condition of staying in school. He himself described his leadership style as "by *ukase,*" using the Imperial Russian term for an edict from the czar.
>
> Staff members would sometimes turn students away from their morning classes; girls for skirts that were too short, and boys for hair that was too long.
>
> Some students balked at the constraints. Still, the school continued to draw families of fame. Around the years of Mr. Epstein's tenure, records show the student roster included Prudence Murdoch, the daughter of the media mogul Rupert Murdoch; the fashion designer Jill Stuart; and several future actresses, including Jennifer Grey, Tracy Pollan and Maggie Wheeler.
>
> While Mr. Barr was strict on the school culture, he made it a point to hire teachers from unconventional backgrounds, recalled Susan Semel, a social studies teacher at Dalton from the 1960s to the 1980s who later wrote a book on the history of the school.

> "Barr didn't care about credentials as long as you were interesting and knew your stuff," Mrs. Semel said.[11]

It's remarkable how much Donald Barr fits the profile of a competent administrator, or an intelligence recruiter. He'd be well-placed to identify the most promising new members of the elite, as well as their biggest potential enemies.

Does it seem as if I'm being too hard on dear Donald Barr, father to William Barr? One needs to read the dispatches of the enemy, as they often let slip important pieces of information, as did this obituary in the *New York Times* from February 2004, for the elder Barr: "Donald Barr, who was born in Manhattan on August 2, 1921, majored in mathematics and anthropology at Columbia, graduating in 1941. He went into the Army and served with the Office of Strategic Services in Washington and Europe."[12]

There's really no other way to state it than to say Donald Barr was CIA, even before the CIA came into existence. In her book on Jeffrey Epstein, author Julie K. Brown painted this picture of Barr:

> In 1974, Epstein was hired as a mathematics teacher at the Dalton School, one of the most prestigious prep schools in New York, catering to children of the wealthy. Though he had no college degree, he was nevertheless hired by headmaster Donald Barr, the father of William Barr, who would become U.S. Attorney General under presidents George H.W. Bush and Donald Trump . . .
>
> Former teachers at the school said Barr was an eccentric but strict taskmaster who liked hiring people, such as Epstein, who were unconventional choices. Barr himself didn't exactly fit the mold of headmaster of a top private school. In 1973, he published a science fiction novel, *Space Relations*, about a planet of wealthy aliens who kidnap humans and force them into sex slavery.[13]

God forgive me, but I found the idea of William Barr's father writing a science fiction novel about humans kidnapped into having sex with aliens (maybe you write about what you know?) to be so outlandishly absurd that I spent $112.81 on Amazon to get an old mass market paperback version of the book, as well as $49.99 for a paperback copy of his second science fiction masterpiece *A Planet in Arms*.

Are you as immature as I am and dying to read a few passages from Barr's books?

Okay, because you asked me, here's what you'd read on the back cover of his first book *Space Relations*, focused on sex between decadent wealthy alien slavers and their human captives:

> **On a distant planet in the distant future**—When all the galaxies are colonized, John Craig, a young space diplomat, is captured by interplanetary pirates and sold into slavery.
>
> On Kossar, where boredom and absolute power have driven the rulers to a special kind of madness, Craig is auctioned off to the exquisite Lady Morgan Sidney, a beautiful, sensual woman. He soon makes his way from the hellish slave mines into her bed, in the tower of her castle. And it is here, under the strange castle, that he finds the secret that may bring about the end of man in the galaxy.[14]

Almost sounds like a classic story, doesn't it? A young man, kidnapped by pirates and sold as a slave to work in the mines, but who finds his way to the bed of a "beautiful, sensual woman." Here's an excerpt from *Space Relations* when John Craig and Lady Morgan Sidney first become lovers:

> The door opened and her ladyship strode in, alone. She still wore the holster-belt over the scarlet tunic; her face still smudged, was now in repose; she jammed her hands into the side pockets of the tunic and swung around the room.
>
> "So, this was the fellow's boudoir," she said softly. "Not a nice man."
>
> Dr. Khoory: "A squeed room."
>
> The Lady: "No wonder he wouldn't show it to us when we came yesterday. Distinctly a squeed room."

There was an unhealthy brilliance to the colors, and something else . . .

Dr. Khoory: "Before the sorting out. The erection of Narcissus."

The Lady went to the night table and twitched open the drawer. "Yes." She took out a small carved bottle with a tiny golden chalice. "Here." She held the bottle out to the Doctor. Her eyes were hard. "Is that a toilet in there? Get rid of this. Every molecule. Can you use my blast-pistol on the bottle without setting the place on fire?"

Dr. Khoory: "I think so." He took the bottle and the weapon and disappeared.

Craig started struggling to his feet.

The Lady said sharply: "Stay there."

Craig: "May I know what your ladyship intends to do with me?"

She ignored the question. The Doctor returned and held out the weapon for her. She dropped it into the holster.

Dr. Khoory: "With your permission, I shall go over to headquarters and see whether my influence extends to some kitchen somewhere. Will your ladyship join me?"

The Lady: "As you know, I like the salt of hunger."

Dr. Khoory: "Until whenever, then." He bowed and rolled out. Her ladyship locked the door.

Craig: "May I not know what your ladyship intends to do with me?"

She looked down at him with eyes the color of smoke.; slid the harness of her tunic and the tunic off her arms, letting the gear fall to the floor; and stood, scratched, muddy and glowing through the rents in her thin black suit. Then she suddenly clapped her hands and laughed happily. "I just realized," she said, "I forgot all about those lieutenants in the safe. And there can't be much air left in there. Well, never mind them. It'll save trouble." She was poised above him. Her face took on a fiercer amusement. The pale gold hair cascaded over it. Her whisper fell on his skin. "As to your insolent question, slave, the answer is 'Four things.'"[15]

Can we talk about extreme creepiness? This is a woman who laughs at leaving people to die and delights in having sex with a helpless slave. And she's supposed to be one of the two heroes of the book.

What went on in the twisted mind of the man who hired Jeffrey Epstein and fathered Bill Barr?

Or how about this sensuous coupling of the young lovers as depicted by Donald Barr? How much does it turn your stomach?

> The Lady: "You look so ridiculous, gasping and sputtering like that."
>
> Craig: "If your ladyship succeeds in drowning me, I won't be much further use."
>
> The Lady: "That's true. Women *are* at a disadvantage when it comes to necrophilia. But I was getting tired of you anyway. You cloy. You do have talent, though. What I might do is put out your eyes and let you replace Blind Will in the PPC; he's getting old. We'd see how long your tenderness lasts."
>
> Craig thought of the tan-skinned young slaves he had seen and Black Weeden in the PPC "doing" ten women a day. "PPC?"
>
> The Lady: "Planned Parenthood Center. It's in the Clinic over by the wall."
>
> Craig: "I think I understand, Except, why put out Will's eyes, your ladyship?"
>
> The Lady: "Oh, we didn't put out his eyes. He blew them out repairing a machine or something. We had—lost the slave who was there before, and this seemed like a job a blind man could do. But it would help to be blind, I should think: most of the slave women are homely . . . you close your eyes when you're kissing anything, anyway; you're so romantic. Meanwhile, get up there on that rock."
>
> Craig obeyed.
>
> The Lady: "Lie back. Close your eyes."
>
> Craig obeyed. He heard the quick sough as her body left the water to join him. His bright lids were shadowed. He waited for her descent. She seemed to pause above him. He opened one eye. Her

> face was just above his. She was frowning down at him like a child trying to read a grownup's book.
>
> "Close your eyes," she snapped.
>
> He closed his eye. A few drops of cool water were falling from her mane onto his face. But one drop was warm. It fell on his upper lip. Unbelievingly, he stretched up the tip of his tongue and tasted it. It was salt, the salt of the Earth, not the bitumen of the Kossar sea. He felt a swift, feathery kiss on each eyelid.
>
> Then: "Damn your eyes!" and she was her usual self.[16]

Now, I can't say that this provides any evidence that Donald Barr was ever involved in any alien or human sex slavery.

But what can be said is that he did seem to have an unhealthy fascination with it.

The great secret beneath the castle was kept from destroying the universe, Earth and Kossar decided to sign a treaty, abolish slavery, and form something of a league of planets (although it seems Kossar will be a colony of Earth. Nothing like a little Western space imperialism, right?) As one of the main Kossarian characters explained:

> "I am fond of empires. A nation is to an empire as a word is to a sentence. You may use that in your own oratory. I shall not need it again.
>
> "We shall do well as a Terran colony. Several of the conditions that normally disturb the working relations between a mother-country and a colony are absent. To take one instance: empires like to place the most annoying restrictions on the brutality of colonists towards indigenous populations. If we had autochthones on Kossar, we should, of course, be very brutal towards them; but we have not got any, and our imported substitutes have prudently been taken away from us in advance. We are of use to Earth, moreover, not for economic, but for military reasons, and history shows that such colonies are generally the best treated . . . It is in vain that the Earth Ambassador has been pursing his lips deprecatingly and the

> Honorable Delegates arranging their features in grimaces of surprise. Such is the tendency of our situation.
>
> "I conclude. An empire is a good thing, when wisely used. But how to acquire wisdom I have not the time to tell you. We must go to the second and final agenda of this joint session."[17]

For those who can't wait for their copy of *Space Relations* to arrive in the mail, the "second and final agenda" was a romantic signing of the Contract of Matrimony—Form B—Monogamous Relations between John Craig and Lady Morgan Sidney.[18]

Doesn't every man want to subdue a former planet and then marry his former torturer?

Because if you can't fall in love with your former sex slave master, who can you fall in love with?

It's like the Jeffrey Epstein story, but with a happy ending. He and Ghislaine Maxwell get married and live on the French Riviera.

* * *

This is how Donald Barr's second book, *A Planet in Arms,* was described on its back cover:

> A bloody star war had left the tiny planet of Rohan seething with chaos. People swarmed in violent mobs and the government rocked with turmoil. And one man, Carl ap Rys, would stop at nothing to use the confusion to seize power for himself.
>
> Only two people could stop him. Citizen S. Wells, the woman they called "the little bitch." And her trusted agent, Conrader, the brute of a man who loved her.
>
> Then, on the violent penal colony of Laing's Land, the revolution began. A terrifying, murderous civil war that could bring the battered planet to ultimate peace—or devastating ruin. . .[19]

Does this sound as unbearably bad to you as it does to me, almost like a B-grade misogynistic *Star Wars*? The book itself is all about power, which is interesting to me given Barr's occupation as an educator.

Shouldn't an educator be concerned with truth, rather than power?

The book was published in 1981, and the cover, with a green, cra-ter-pocked moon and a Luke Skywalker–type character with a beautiful woman hanging onto his shoulder as well as a distant image of a black clad figure around a half circle shaped table with his military leaders, evokes a definite *Star Wars* vibe. Let's see if Barr's prose had gotten any better in the eight years since his alien and human sex slavery book.

> General Holcott R. McGifford had been coopted from the staff to act as Minister of Armies and Marine. He did not like his colleagues in the Cabinet, did not trust them, and intended to have very little more to do with them, but meanwhile had been instructed to report on the heavy rate of desertions from the armed forces and he was getting up the facts. He had sent for a mathematician to analyze the data, and he had gotten this gnome. It was all very trying.
>
> The gnome, whose name was Professor Smeal, had put together a presentation, which comprised an inordinate number of tables and equations. To make matters worse, the general had spent some time in confusion, until he realized that when Professor Smeal referred to "the model" he meant the real world, which he appeared to regard as one of a number of surprising examples of what he called "the relation axioms."
>
> "Let me see if I understand you correctly," said the general. "The farther any military unit gets from New Nome, the more men desert from it?"
>
> Professor Smeal: "In the model you are concerned with, yes, that would obtain."
>
> General McGifford: "Obtain? Oh, yes, I see. Obtain. Now, you're sure things get worse and worse as units get farther and far-ther from the capital, *not* as units get closer and closer to the enemy?"

> Professor Smeal: "Enemy? Ah, yes-yes-yes. What we have called the gimel space. It is not a Kraushofer space, you know. Quite different. Quite-quite-quite."[20]

Nope. It doesn't look like Barr's writing got any better in the eight years between his alien-human sex book and his how-to-rule-a-planet book.

One can't help but notice that there are some strange preoccupations of the elder Barr.

And what effect did this have on the younger Barr? This is from a *Vanity Fair* profile of William Barr from October 2019:

> At one point, the young Barr even declared to his Horace Mann adviser that when he grew up, he wanted to become head of the CIA . . .
>
> Soon after graduation, Barr joined the CIA as a China analyst while attending George Washington University law at night and married Christine Moynihan, a librarian . . .
>
> According to James Zirin, the legal commentator and former federal prosecutor, "Barr is from the school of *L'etat, c'est moi*—I am the state."[21]

A man, in the end, not unlike his father.

I have to warn you to sort out the wheat from the chaff. The merchants of deceit want to terrify the liberals about the big, bad, conservative bogeyman, Bill Barr, but it's all a ruse.

Barr is on the same side as the globalists, just in a different disguise.

But we'll return to Bill Barr a little later.

Let's look now at the improbable rise of Jeffrey Epstein.

* * *

Again, let's go to the "paper of record," the *New York Times*, which is often forced to provide just enough information to raise more questions than they ever choose to answer.

> He turned up in the gossip columns but lived "a life full of question marks," as New York magazine put it in 2002. More than one writer likened Mr. Epstein to Jay Gatsby, the enduringly impenetrable F. Scott Fitzgerald character. He was said to look a little like the designer Ralph Lauren, who was born in the Bronx.
>
> But Mr. Epstein came from Brooklyn. His father was a city parks employee. Mr. Epstein took classes in physics at The Cooper Union in the mid-1970s and later attended New York University, but did not receive a degree from either school, New York magazine reported.
>
> He began his career as a math teacher at the Dalton School, an elite private school in Manhattan whose alumni include the cable-news anchor Anderson Cooper, the comedian Chevy Chase and the actress Claire Danes.
>
> "By most accounts, he was something of a Robin Williams in "Dead Poets Society" type of figure, wowing his high school classes with passionate mathematical riffs," according to the New York magazine article.[22]

I'm warning my readers. You need to be careful about such seductive prose. If you're a literary type, they expect you to swoon over the comparison to Jay Gatsby, maybe remembering Robert Redford or Leonardo DiCaprio in the title role of the two movie versions of the book. If you're a fashionista, you have an image of the older looking, rugged Ralph Lauren in your mind. If you're an educator or academic, you probably list Robin Williams's performance in *Dead Poets Society* as one of your inspirations for being in the teaching profession.

They want to make Epstein the blank screen upon which you project your own personal fantasy of a mysterious New York financier. And if you're a money guy, this is how they make you want to fall in love with Epstein.

> From there [Dalton] he took his math skills to Bear Stearns, then a powerful Wall Street investment bank.

> Both New York Magazine and Vanity Fair magazine reported that he made connections at Dalton that led him to Alan C. Greenberg, then the dauntless chief executive of the Wall Street firm Bear Stearns. Known as "Ace," Mr. Greenberg was later the firm's chairman and the chairman of its executive committee.
>
> Under Mr. Greenberg and another top executive, James Cayne, Mr. Epstein "did well enough to become a limited partner—a rung beneath full partner," Vanity Fair reported.
>
> He left in the early 1980s, forming a consulting firm called International Assets Group that he ran out of his apartment, according to Vanity Fair. Later he set up a money management firm called J. Epstein & Co. It eventually became the Financial Trust Company, based in the Virgin Islands.[23]

This is where I have to start calling bullshit on the *New York Times*. Does it seem like Epstein just happens to walk between the raindrops and not get wet? Who in the 1980s would set up a consulting firm in their apartment and expect to become successful?

Nobody would do that.

There's one explanation that makes the most sense to me.

Everything about Epstein's rise through the ranks smells of being recruited by an intelligence agency.

* * *

Who makes the accusation that Jeffrey Epstein was an intelligence asset, aside from Alex Acosta, the former secretary of Labor in the Trump Administration?

Epstein's former business partner, Steven Hoffenberg.

The accusation was published in a *Rolling Stone* article by Vicky Ward, published on July 15, 2021. At the time Ward met Hoffenberg, he was serving time in federal prison. She set the scene:

> We sat in a little room near a recreation area, Hoffenberg dressed in the requisite orange jumpsuit, while I, several months pregnant with twins, was dressed per prison requirements: as shapelessly as possible.
>
> It was an absolutely intriguing meeting.
>
> Hoffenberg was serving 18 years in prison for committing a $450 million Ponzi scheme. In the 1980s, he'd been running Towers Financial, a debt collection and reinsurance business, and had worked alongside Epstein, who was a paid consultant. Hoffenberg told me that Epstein had plans to turn Towers into a global colossus—through illegal means.[24]

Let's start putting the pieces together. Do spies like to hang out with good, law-abiding citizens? No, they like to hang out among the criminals, those who operate in the grey world, able to move between corridors of power and the criminal underworld. Hoffenberg was a perfect mark for Epstein.

And do we listen to the criminal, especially after they've been caught?

In most cases, we don't.

But we should, and Hoffenberg is a prime example of why we should listen. If we want to avoid being fooled again, let the criminal in jail tell you how the world really works.

> Hoffenberg said that Epstein had a term for the perfect execution of the grift. He called it "playing the box," which meant that he ensured that even if his crime was uncovered, the victim would be unable to do anything about it, either because of social embarrassment or because the money was tucked away in a place where they couldn't either find it or get it.
>
> (What Hoffenberg had failed to realize, he told me, is that Epstein would con *him*. Epstein would take $100 million of Towers money, move it offshore, and meanwhile cooperate with U.S. prosecutors against Hoffenberg, who was unable to do anything about this because he'd pled guilty, which meant there was no trial—and therefore no discovery.)[25]

We're getting a little more information about how Epstein worked his dark magic. And yet, it's an incomplete picture. It's not bad as an operating system for a criminal, but there's a piece missing.

How do you deal with the authorities?

The idea that a criminal may seek out vulnerable victims, reluctant to go to the police, isn't an idea that Epstein came up with. Many crooks have pursued a similar strategy, and law enforcement officers have also come up with their countermeasures in such situations.

I refuse to accept a view of the world that relies on the main actors to be dumb. Both the cops and criminals are wise to the ways of their enemies.

The mafia was able to flourish in America for so long because they had a code of silence, but they were also often paying off the police, the judges, and the politicians. And, as we all know, the US government partnered with the mafia during World War II to help with the invasion of Sicily, as well as in the 1960s to go after Cuba.

Getting all, or a portion of, the authorities on your side is a really good play for a criminal. Epstein seems to have done just that, according to the *Rolling Stone* article: "Hoffenberg also knew something else Epstein wanted hidden, according to Hoffenberg: He claimed that Epstein moved in intelligence circles . . ."[26]

The story told in the *Rolling Stone* article begins with a British defense contractor, Douglas Leese, who was suspected of being an arms dealer.

> I remember distinctly that in our first meeting Hoffenberg told me that Leese was pivotal in understanding Jeffrey's MO, because Leese had introduced him not only to aristocratic Europeans (who Epstein subsequently fleeced) but to all sorts of people in the arms business—including the late Turkish-born businessman Adnan Kashoggi—and, allegedly, the late media mogul Robert Maxwell. [Author's note – Father of Ghislaine Maxwell.][27]

When the reporter brought up the names Douglas Leese and Robert Maxwell to Jeffrey Epstein, Epstein denied ever knowing them. But that wasn't the story Hoffenberg related:

> Hoffenberg told me that Epstein had said he'd worked on several projects with Robert Maxwell, including solving Maxwell's "debt" issues. (Maxwell died in 1991, under very strange circumstances, apparently having fallen off his yacht, the *Lady Ghislaine*, in the middle of the night and it was discovered in the aftermath that he'd stolen 100s of millions of dollars from the pensions of his employees.)
>
> Epstein had also told Hoffenberg that via Maxwell and Lees he was involved in something that Hoffenberg described as "national security issues," which he says involved "blackmail, influence trading, trading information at a level that is very serious and dangerous."[28]

Was this when Epstein was first introduced to Ghislaine Maxwell, his long-time lover and procurer of young women for him, who is now currently serving a prison term for these crimes? Do you find it odd that Ghislaine is spending time in jail for procuring young women to have sex with powerful men, but no man has been charged with being one of the customers?

This is how the encounters with Jeffrey Epstein and Ghislaine Maxwell were described by underage Virginia Giuffre, in Julie Brown's book, *Perversion of Justice*, shortly after the first "massage," which had involved sexual activity.

> The massage was the same as the day before, with both Epstein and Maxwell orchestrating the session. Virginia followed their orders like a soldier. She and Maxwell caressed each other, and the three of them began having sex.
>
> Virginia soon realized that Epstein had an insatiable sickness that no one person, not even Maxwell, could fulfill.

> "Jeffrey treated us girls like a piece of clothing he could try on for the day and get rid of the next," she would later write in her manuscript.[29]

I'm including this material about the sexual depravity of Jeffrey Epstein to let you know how much of a monster he was, but also so you understand that was only part of what he was doing. Epstein was much more than a rich guy using his money to satisfy his sexual desires.

> It was clear to Virginia that Maxwell was in love with Epstein. But Epstein and Maxwell rarely slept together or shared intimate moments, like holding hands or kissing. Virginia said this was because Maxwell was never able to satisfy Epstein's insatiable appetite for girls. Maxwell came to accept his obsession as long as those encounters remained purely sexual.
>
> The two shared a kind of hedonism, Virginia said.
>
> "It was an arrangement whereby she would bring him the girls, and he would give Ghislaine the kind of self-indulgent life that she was accustomed to growing up."[30]

It's clear that Ghislaine was something of a slave to Jeffrey Epstein. But was Epstein working solely for himself, or was he working for somebody else?

In order to answer that question, we must understand the twisted path of Ghislaine Maxell, the youngest daughter of media mogul Robert Maxwell.

* * *

Sometime on the night of November 4, 1991, while his yacht was sailing to the end of Tenerife in the Canary Islands, Robert Maxwell went missing.

His waterlogged body was soon discovered, and the original autopsy report ruled he'd "died of natural causes, of heart and lung failure."[31]

Although his family doubted the findings and ordered an additional autopsy, a large funeral was held, and the guest list was quite intriguing.

> Six current and former heads of Israeli intelligence services attended Maxwell's funeral. Israeli prime minister Yitzak Shamir eulogized him, describing Maxwell as "a person who was greatly interested in the Israeli economy, invested money in Israel, and offered to put his wide contacts on the international arena at Israel's service."
>
> Indeed, Maxwell had vast financial dealings in Israel, including a majority share in the Israeli daily newspaper *Maariv*.
>
> He was hailed for opening factories that provided jobs and for having helped pave the way for Israel's interests around the world, by cultivating powerful people in politics and business from Moscow to London. He was personal friends with both former U.S. Secretary of State Henry Kissinger and former Russian president Mikhail Gorbachev.[32]

But even from the time of his death, there were rumors that he'd been killed by the Israeli Mossad, because he had become a liability to them.

> In their 2003 book, *The Assassination of Robert Maxwell*, authors Gordon Thomas and Martin Dillion laid out evidence that for two decades Maxwell was a spy for the Mossad, who profited from disseminating Israeli intelligence-gathering computer software to Russia, the U.S., Britain, and other countries. The software was rigged with a mechanism to allow the Mossad to secretly tap into classified information gathered by the world's top intelligence agencies. The authors theorized that Maxwell was murdered because the publishing baron was so desperate to save his fortune that he blackmailed the Mossad, threatening to expose their spy activities if the agency's leaders didn't bail him out of financial ruin.[33]

I think I've demonstrated clearly how there are multiple lines of contact that create evidence suggesting that Epstein was an intelligence asset for somebody. Maxwell is a perfect example of big money, media influence, and intelligence connections.

Who gets six current and former heads of the Israeli Mossad to show up at their funeral?

One might view their appearance as both honoring Maxwell's previous service to the Mossad, and also serving as a warning of what might happen to any who would betray them.

According to investigative reporter Julie K. Brown, after Maxwell's death, the family was in financial trouble, but a benefactor appeared, described by Elisabeth, Maxwell's widow, as a "friend" and "white knight."[34] Although she declined to identify this person, many claim the signs were clear.

> But less than two weeks after her husband's death, the YIVO Institute for Jewish Research paid tribute to Robert Maxwell, an event that was planned prior to his death, to honor both him and his wife for their charitable work.
>
> Elisabeth decided to go ahead with attending the event, held at New York's Plaza Hotel on November 24.
>
> Seated next to Elisabeth and Ghislaine at the event was a pudgy man with curly hair who was unknown at the time.
>
> His name was Jeffrey Epstein.[35]

We have completed the neat little circle of Robert Maxwell, Jeffrey Epstein, and Ghislaine Maxwell. The suspicion of many is that Robert Maxwell was a long-time Mossad agent (witness six former and current Mossad chiefs at his funeral, in addition to the prime minister giving the eulogy), the mysterious death that may or may not have been at the hand of Mossad agents, the financial struggle of the family, and then the sudden appearance of a "white knight" (a.k.a. Jeffrey Epstein).

What happens from here? What is the picture we develop of the mysterious Jeffrey Epstein, one part Robin Williams in *Dead Poets Society*, one part Ralph Lauren, one part sexual Svengali, and one part Jay Gatsby? Let's try to put a little more flesh onto the bones of this enigmatic figure as depicted in bestselling author James Patterson's book on Epstein, *Filthy Rich*, as seen through the eyes of journalist, Vicky Ward:

> "Epstein is charming, but he doesn't let the charm slip into his eyes," she wrote. "They are steely and calculating, giving some hint at the steady whir of machinery running behind them. 'Let's play chess,' he said to me, after refusing to give an interview for this article. 'You be white. You get the first move.' It was an appropriate metaphor for a man who seems to feel he can win no matter what the advantage of the other side. *His* advantage is that no one really seems to know him or his history completely or what his arsenal really consists of. He has carefully engineered it so that he remains one of the few truly baffling mysteries among New York's moneyed world. People know snippets, but few know the whole."
>
> . . . One powerful investment manager wondered about Epstein's conspicuous absence from New York's trading floors. "The trading decks don't seem to know him," he says. "It's unusual for animals *that* big not to leave footprints in the snow."[36]

To complete the picture of Epstein, we see him as some sort of predator, and yet, nobody genuinely understands the ecosystem in which he operates. The game seems to be bigger than money or sex, and yet it's difficult to see behind the disguise.

To get a complete picture of what was happening, I think it's important to realize that multiple parts of the government were in conflict with each other. There were the genuinely good parts of the law enforcement community that were trying to get a wealthy sexual predator off the streets, while in another part of the government there were likely intelligence assets who wanted to protect one of their own. The prosecution of Epstein seemed at odds with common sense because it made no sense. There were elements of the government that wanted him in jail, and elements that wanted him out of jail. But since Epstein had obtained a certain level of public visibility, the Deep State couldn't simply let him walk.

That would make it far too obvious for the public to swallow.

But how to make it seem to the public that he was being punished, without letting him be punished? This is how Epstein's time in prison was described in the book *Dead Men Tell No Tales*.

> In truth, Epstein's time behind bars would be more of a retreat than retribution. To start, he was not sent to federal prison like most sex offenders in the state. Instead, he was given a private wing at the Palm Beach County Stockade Facility, where he enjoyed the care of his own personal security guards.
>
> Even then, remarkably, he spent little time within the confines of the jail. Just over three months into his sentence, Epstein was granted work release, allowing him to leave the premises for up to seven days a week, up to sixteen hours at a time. That period included up to two hours at his Palm Beach sex den . . .
>
> According to records obtained by these authors, one of his nonprofit organizations paid $128,000 to the Palm Beach County Sheriff's Department to cover the cost of his personal detail. They were even known to refer to him as "the client" instead of as "the perp."
>
> Ultimately, Epstein—one of the sickest sex fiends to ever walk the planet—only served thirteen months before he was released on "good behavior."[37]

It's important to have a consistent narrative in your head because, more than anything else, the mainstream media wants you to be confused by the Epstein case. I'm here to make the case as clear as possible.

You're supposed to believe that wealth and power in America allows you to buy your way to innocence, even if you're guilty.

But Epstein pled guilty.

Even if you understand the corruption of our justice system prior to sentencing, you look at the result and see that there was a guilty verdict. All the lawyers in the world couldn't keep Epstein from pleading guilty to something.

The justice system then takes over, right? We don't imagine that you can buy your way out of prison, right? That would take more than money. But somehow, Epstein spent a very pleasant thirteen months attended by his own security detail, free to go where he pleased during the day, and having the sheriff's department treat him like a "client" rather than a "perp."

It sounds as if some very powerful people in the shadows were making things tolerable for the convicted pedophile.

With that suspicion, let's take a quick detour into a troubling accusation about William Barr, the two-time attorney general of the United States, under President George H. W. Bush and Donald Trump.

* * *

In 1994, a highly controversial book, *Compromised: Clinton, Bush and the CIA*, was published by Terry Reed and John Cummings.

Terry Reed claimed to be a former intelligence operative for the Air Force, who later worked for the FBI and CIA on the arms and drug running operation out of Mena, Arkansas, which was unearthed as part of the Iran-Contra investigation. The Iran-Contra investigation began in December 1986 and concluded with a final report on August 4, 1993. John Cummings was a former prize-winning investigator at *N.Y. Newsday*, who had made a long study of intelligence-gathering, money laundering, and drug trafficking.

The book is enormous, a 556-page leviathan, with tiny print, making it a challenging read. I've found that first-time authors often produce such large books because they are so concerned that people believe them that they include everything. I'd like to tell them it doesn't matter. If it attacks the official narrative, the gatekeepers of truth will do everything they can to minimize it. It's much better to write a shorter, more readable book, than go the long route.

For much of the book, the authors use the code names of various individuals given at the time, only letting you know later who they are. I'll just give it to you straight. John Cathey is Oliver North and Robert

Johnson is Bill Barr. Remember, this is a book that was published in 1994, so considering what happened after with Barr, this was either the luckiest guess in the history of lucky guesses, or Bill Barr isn't anything close to how he presents himself to the public.

The scene presented is alleged to be a conversation in March 1986, between Oliver North, William Barr, and Bill Clinton about the Contra supply effort, set up by William Casey, the CIA head under President Reagan.

> Then, Johnson [Bill Barr] rose to speak. He was the only person attending the meeting that Terry did not recognize. Up until now, he had only been a voice on the telephone. He was taken aback with how the young bespectacled, cherubic-looking man appeared. From the sound of his voice, Terry had expected an older man. His boyish and over-serious look reminded Terry of fast-track junior officers he'd seen in his Air Force days. But his aloof, yuppie demeanor made Terry think of him as akin to the "bond daddies" he associated with in Little Rock and as someone who would only be a message-carrier back to men with real power back in Washington. Even his impending introduction did not convince Terry he was truly the man entrusted with decision-making authority for this very serious project.
>
> Johnson [Bill Barr], Cathey [Oliver North] said, was the personal representative of CIA Director William Casey and had been sent to chair the meeting. Casey was too important to show his face, Terry assumed. But he felt honored, and yet surprised to find he'd been dealing with someone so clearly connected to the Director of Central Intelligence, the top of the intelligence pyramid.[38]

Might this be a connection that people have been missing? Bill Barr at the center of the Iran-Contra scandal? We know that William Casey worked for the Office of Strategic Services (forerunner to the CIA) in World War II, as did Donald Barr, Bill Bar's father and the man who hired Jeffrey Epstein to work at the Dalton School.

We have it from no less an authority than *Vanity Fair* that as a young man, Bill Barr aspired to be head of the CIA, and that one of his first jobs was working as a legal analyst for the CIA. Did he just keep putting himself up for "off the books" jobs for the CIA after he left them? Since George H. W. Bush's greatest liability was probably fallout from the Iran-Contra affair, it would make sense to appoint Bill Barr as attorney general, to make sure certain information stays hidden. (It's also important to note that George H. W. Bush had also been head of the CIA.)

It's difficult to shake the suspicion that over the years Bill Barr has been a "fixer" for the intelligence community. The account of the meeting continued:

> "Thank you," Johnson [Bill Barr] said. "As Mr. Cathey [Oliver North] mentioned, I am the emissary of Mr. Casey, who for obvious security reasons could not attend. We are at a major junction of our Central American support program. And I am here to tie up a few loose ends. As you are well aware, the severity of the charges that could be brought against us if this operation becomes public . . . well, I don't need to remind you of what Benjamin Franklin said as he and our founding fathers framed the Declaration of Independence.
>
> Cathey [Oliver North] interrupted. "Yeah, but hanging is a much more humane way of doing things than what Congress will put us through if any of this leaks out." This marked the only time during the briefing that laughter was heard.
>
> "This is true," Johnson [Bill Barr] replied. "And therefore Governor Clinton, I'm going to find it necessary to divide the meeting into groups so that we don't unnecessarily expose classified data to those who don't have an absolute need to know. We can first discuss any old business that concerns either 'Centaur Rose' or 'Jade Bridge,' and I think that you will agree that afterwards you and Mr. Nash [Clinton's aide] will have to excuse yourselves . . ."[39]

The picture painted is of Barr being able to hold the attention of people, much the same way he did when Trump appointed him attorney general after the resignation of his first attorney general, the hapless Jeff Sessions.

There's no doubt that Barr is a smart guy, but is he a good guy?

My bet is that he's as bad as they come.

When I hear Bill Barr talking, I hear the calm and soothing voice of Big Brother and the Deep State, telling me to go to sleep, that the country is in the safe and secure hands of genuine patriots. Don't believe it for a second.

It's somewhat humorous in this account to read how then-Governor Bill Clinton reacted to being told to simply play along like a good little boy.

> Clinton was visibly indignant, giving the angry appearance of someone not accustomed to being treated in such a condescending manner.
>
> "It seems someone in Washington has made decisions without much consulting with either myself or my aide here, Mr. Nash. And I'd like to express my concern about the possible exposure my state has as you guys skedaddle out of here to Mexico. I feel somewhat naked and *compromised*. You're right, there are definitely some loose ends!"
>
> Based upon his comments about Mexico, Clinton already knew of the Agency's plans to withdraw from Arkansas. And he was not happy about being left out of the decision-making loop.[40]

While I can't vouch for the accuracy of this account, it reads as consistent with what I've heard about how these operations go down. You hear inside accounts of these intelligence operations and you're expecting to find some sophisticated, James Bond type at the center of it, but it's usually like a scene out of *The Three Stooges*.

But Barr stood apart. He was an excellent operator. Barr and Clinton argued for several minutes, each pointing out screw-ups on the other side, until it was clear that Clinton had made a significant number of critical mistakes.

The CIA was closing out the Mena, Arkansas drug and gun-running operation begun by Barry Seal (who had recently been killed, allegedly by hit men for Pablo Escobar, but anybody with half a brain suspected the CIA) and moving the program to Mexico, if possible.

> Johnson [Bill Barr] had applied the balm and now the massage began, "Bill, you are Mr. Casey's fair-haired boy. But you do have competition for the job you seek. We would never put all our eggs in one basket. You and your state have been our greatest asset. The beauty of this, as you know, is that you're a Democrat, and with our ability to influence both parties, this country can get beyond partisan gridlock. Mr. Casey wanted me to pass on to you that unless you fuck up and do something stupid, you're No. 1 on the short list for a shot at the job you've always wanted.
>
> "That's pretty heady stuff, Bill. So why don't you help us keep a lid on this and we'll all be promoted together. You, and guys like us, *are* the fathers of the new government. Hell, we're the new covenant."
>
> Clinton, having been stroked, seemed satisfied that the cover-up was expanding to, at least, protect the bond business. Like Lyndon Johnson, Clinton had learned that politics is the "art of the possible." He had not gotten everything he wanted, but he was at least walking away whole.
>
> It appeared to Terry that Johnson [Bill Barr] had won the debate. Clinton and his administration had no grounds to complain about the Agency terminating its operation. Too many errors had been made. The young governor seemed to recognize he had lost, for now, and didn't want to continue the argument in front of the others.[41]

This is the variation I've heard so many times from prominent people of the devil's dance that they undergo with the intelligence agencies. They figure out how to compromise you. I have had attempts made to "honey-pot" me by individuals I later found out were connected to intelligence agencies (the FBI), and many other prominent people who are openly skeptical of government proclamations have told me similar stories.

This really isn't too hard to figure out.

Power likes to keep its power. That's why one of its functions will be to identify potential threats to their power and then move preemptively to neutralize them. The power structure doesn't believe in democracy. How many times have you heard from the mainstream media about the need for "stability"?

That's a code word for taking out the opposition, and they will do anything they need to do to keep their power.

Can I tell you for a fact that Bill Barr is an intelligence asset? No, I can't. But when you see that his father was one of the founding members of our current intelligence structure, that as a young man he wanted to be head of the CIA, and that his first significant job was working for the CIA, you should at least entertain the possibility.

How did Barr end up as Trump's attorney general? He was probably told by some people he made the mistake of trusting, that Barr was a good guy. But when one sees what Barr did, from not investigating Hunter Biden's laptop prior to the 2020 election, to his current gig running across the country telling all the mainstream media outlets that Trump should be under house arrest, you should at least ask whether he is an honest officer of the court, or something else.

* * *

After Epstein's 2008 plea to two states' charges of procuring a prostitute under the age of eighteen and his thirteen months of "hard time," he set out to conquer a new field, science. This is how Epstein's romance of the scientists was described in *Dead Men Tell No Tales*:

> For Epstein, it was becoming clear that his time rubbing shoulders with lawmakers and royals was over. Luckily, there was an entirely new class of movers and shakers for him to exploit: brilliant scientists

> and tech gurus who were building the future—and could make his wildest dreams of ultimate power come true.
>
> Epstein had already shown an interest in cultivating such circles.
>
> In 2006, he hosted a conference at the Ritz-Carlton on St. Thomas, which attracted the likes of Stephen Hawking. During the night of the conference, guests were shuttled over to Little St. James for a barbecue and submarine tour. According to reports, the sub was custom fitted for Hawking's wheelchair. A photo of the event shows him being personally attended to by a young blonde with her hair in a ponytail.[42]

What was Epstein's interest in scientists? In order to understand this influence scheme, you have to appreciate how the globalists worship science as their god. Therefore, in order to capture science and force it do their bidding, they have to capture the leading scientists. And who in the early years of the twenty-first century captured the imagination of the public as much as physicist Stephen Hawking? Epstein was much more than a collector of interesting people; he used them as one might use chess pieces or armies in the popular strategy board game *Risk*, in which one tries to take over the world.

Science and scientists also had an advantage over celebrities and politicians, as they usually avoided the public glare of the press. It's one of the dirty little secrets of science, but scientists are usually so strapped for cash that they'll accept unsavory money, as long as they believe it's moving their career forward.

Epstein saw this vulnerability and moved to exploit it. By 2011, he was making enormous progress. One might think of him as Santa Claus and the mythical Mr. Roarke from the TV show *Fantasy Island*, as he showered his wealth and attention on the scientists. This is from the book *Perversion of Justice* by Julie K. Brown:

> In December 2011, Jeffrey Epstein brought together some of the most brilliant scientific minds in the nation on his remote island, known to his friends as "Little St. Jeff's" The purpose of this event belied the

> lavish, pristine surroundings and the extravagant food laid out in front of the guests who flew in from around the country. In the aftermath of the earthquake and tsunami in Tohoku, Japan, the meeting was called "Coping with Future Catastrophes."
>
> It was essentially a Global Doomsday Conference.
>
> The attendees were instructed to identify some of the greatest threats to the earth, contemplating such phenomena as bioterrorism, nuclear warfare, nuclear catastrophes, overpopulation, asteroid and meteor collisions, super volcanoes, rogue machines and computers—and what a press release called "high-energy-chain-reactions that could disrupt the fabric of space itself."[43]

It's funny how these rich people can't stop thinking about global catastrophes, isn't it? I wonder if they sit around in their mansions asking themselves, "What do the common folk hate more than rich people like me? Plagues? Nuclear war? Asteroids? Super-volcanoes? A robot apocalypse?"

Even though they've got more money than they know what to do with, it must be sobering for the global elites to realize they're only slightly more popular than hemorrhoids.

Jeffrey Epstein must have been so concerned about his public image, saying things to himself like, "I only confessed to two counts of hiring a prostitute under the age of eighteen. Give a guy a break! How much money do I have to spend to make you like me?"

The answer is: apparently a lot.

> Among other things, Epstein established a fellowship at the International Peace Institute, an international nonprofit that promotes peace around the world; pledged to build the largest school in earthquake-ravaged Haiti; announced funding for charter schools in inner city neighborhoods; supported music therapy research for premature babies; helped develop computer coding for toddlers; and launched an online learning program about brain science called *Neuro TV*.

> There were press releases about Epstein's endeavors nearly every day, announcing gifts from "Science philanthropist Jeffrey Epstein," "Education activist Jeffrey Epstein," "Evolutionist Jeffrey Epstein," "Science patron Jeffrey Epstein" and "Maverick hedge funder Jeffrey Epstein."
>
> There were gifts to fund research at universities, research institutions, and nonprofits in the search for cures for melanoma, ovarian cancer, multiple sclerosis, Alzheimer's disease, Crohn's disease and colitis, Parkinson's disease, diabetes, breast cancer, and AIDS.[44]

There's one thing I have to note, which may have escaped your attention: it would seem that Epstein was only concerned about how to give away money.

Didn't he spend any part of his day trying to make money?

I mean, he was already settling a number of cases brought by women who claimed he'd abused them (and they didn't seem to total the billion and a half in damages I have against me). Shouldn't that have created some amount of financial concern? Besides getting his "massages" and handjobs from underage teenage girls and meeting with rich people and celebrities, how much of his day was he devoting to making money? It seems as if he simply had some magic money-making machine in his basement, which relieved him of all such concerns.

One would normally have a great deal of respect for these institutions and efforts, but when one sees how easily Epstein was able to worm his way in and earn their approval, it's genuinely sickening.

But was it simply because he wanted to rehabilitate his reputation? Or did he have a deeper, more sinister motive? How wide was he casting his net for his plans? One need only ask the size of Epstein's ambitions to know how much he wanted to bring under his influence.

Would you believe me if I told you that Epstein had purchased influence at both Harvard University and the Massachusetts Institute of Technology, even after his 2008 conviction? This is from a May 1, 2020 article which appeared in the *New York Times*:

> He had no official Harvard affiliation, yet Jeffrey Epstein had his own office, key card and Harvard phone line. He would often swing by on weekends to host dinners with academics he wanted to meet.
>
> According to a university report released on Friday, Mr. Epstein, the disgraced financier who killed himself in jail last year, visited Harvard more than 40 times after he was convicted of sex charges involving a minor.[45]

The thing they want you to say is, "Rich people! They get away with everything!" But that doesn't fully explain it, especially since, in 2008, the president of Harvard, Drew Faust, explicitly forbade Epstein from donating to the school, even though he had previously donated $9.1 million from 1998 to 2008.[46] I'm sure that the leadership of Harvard figured Epstein would just slink away in shame.

But that didn't happen, and people at Harvard actively assisted him in staying. Here's a little more about Epstein and Harvard:

> Epstein frequently visited Office 610, which was known as "Jeffrey's Office," and met with scholars to hear about their work, the review found. He brought his own rug and hung his own photos on the wall. Nowak argued that the office was Epstein's in name only, the report says, but others in the building said it was commonly known to be reserved for the financier . . .
>
> Some professors beyond Nowak appear to have enjoyed close ties with Epstein, the review found. The report says "a number" of faculty members visited Epstein at his homes in New York, Florida, New Mexico, and the Virgin Islands. Some said they visited him in jail or took trips on his planes. The visits were done in a personal capacity, the report said, and do not appear to violate Harvard rules . . .
>
> Although his gifts were blocked after 2008, the report found that Harvard accepted $736,000 between his arrest and conviction. Most went to Harvard's medical school, while $150,000 went to its Faculty of Arts and Sciences.[47]

It seems like the Harvard scientists wanted to hang around Epstein like a bunch of teenage groupies flock around a rock band singer. They were so devoted to him that they even visited him in jail. What all of this seems to say to me is that the Harvard scientists were convinced they'd face no repercussions for hanging around with a generous pedophile.

The most likely explanation to me is that somebody important at Harvard must have known Epstein had intelligence connections and assured the others it was safe to associate with the financier and convicted pedophile.

Ronan Farrow, the Pulitzer Prize-winning journalist who brought down creepy Hollywood mogul Harvey Weinstein (once referred to by Meryl Streep as "god"),[48] would take aim at Epstein's relationship with MIT. This is the opening of his September 2019 article on Epstein and MIT for the *New Yorker*:

> The M.I.T. Media Lab, which has been embroiled in a scandal over accepting donations from the financier and convicted sex offender Jeffrey Epstein, had a deeper fund-raising relationship with Epstein than it has previously acknowledged, and it attempted to conceal the existence of its contacts with him. Dozens of pages of e-mails and other documents obtained by *The New Yorker* reveal that, although Epstein was listed as "disqualified" in M.I.T.'s official donor database, the Media Lab continued to accept gifts from him, consulted him about the use of the funds, and, by marking his contributions as anonymous, avoided disclosing their full extent, both publicly and within the university. Perhaps most notably, Epstein served as an intermediary between the lab and other wealthy donors, soliciting millions of dollars in donations from individuals and organizations, including the technologist and philanthropist Bill Gates and the investor Leon Black. According to the records obtained by *The New Yorker* and accounts from current and former faculty and staff of the media lab, Epstein was credited with securing at least $7.5 million in donations for the lab, including two million from Gates and $5.5 million from Black, gifts the e-mails described as "directed" by

> Epstein or made at his behest. The effort to conceal the lab's contact with Epstein was so widely known that some staff in the office of the lab's director, Joi Ito, referred to Epstein as Voldemort, or "he who must not be named."[49]

How many things are wrong in that single paragraph? Let's see if we can count all of them.

First, there was a directive from MIT that Epstein was "disqualified" to be a donor, because of his pedophilia convictions.

Second, there was an attempt by the staff and director of the MIT Media Lab to conceal the source of those donations, either by marking them as anonymous or attributing them to Leon Black.

Third, despite Epstein's conviction as a pedophile, Bill Gates, and many other wealthy people were more than happy to associate with him.

Fourth, in private emails among the staff at the MIT Media Lab, they wanted it known that Epstein had "directed" the donations or that they'd been made at his behest.

Fifth, the staff was aware that what they were doing was wrong, as evidenced by referring to Epstein as "Voldemort" or "he who must not be named."

And it isn't as if there weren't faculty members making objections to this course of action, specifically associate professor Ethan Zuckerman, who pulled the lab's director, Joi Ito, aside at one point and said, "I heard you're meeting with Epstein. I don't think that's a good idea."[50]

The reported response of the lab director was, "You know, he's really fascinating. Would you like to meet him?"[51]

One has to ask the question, are these academics just a bunch of money-grubbers?

Does one believe that people in general lack a genuine moral compass and will do anything that they believe they can get away with?

Or was there another force, almost like a black hole that you can't see, exerting its influence, keeping Epstein aloft in polite society, when other mere mortals would crash to Earth?

Does the lust for money explain everything? Many might take that position, and I understand the cynical world view of these people. And yet for me, there's something deeper, almost like the famous Sherlock Holmes case of the dog that didn't bark. Like *Alice in Wonderland*, I want to go down the rabbit hole and see how deep it goes. Farrow's account of Epstein's relationship with MIT continued:

> In the summer of 2015, as the Media Lab determined how to spend the funds it had received with Epstein's help, Cohen informed lab staff that Epstein would be coming for a visit. The financier would meet with faculty members, apparently to allow him to give input on projects and to entice him to contribute further. Swenson, the former development associate and alumni coordinator, recalled saying, referring to Epstein, "I don't think he should be on campus." She told me, "At that point it hit me: this pedophile is going to be in our office." According to Swenson, Cohen agreed that Epstein was "unsavory" but said "we're planning to do it anyway—this was Joi's project." Staffers entered the meeting into Ito's calendar without including Epstein's name. "There was definitely an explicit conversation about keeping it off the books, because Joi's calendar is visible to everyone," Swenson said. "It was just marked as a V.I.P. visit."[52]

People often say to me, "Alex, if things are truly as corrupt as you say they are, certainly many people would be reporting it. They can't all be evil globalists."

My response is usually, yes, most people are good, but the vast majority don't want to do things that will cause trouble at their job. It isn't that they want to do the wrong thing; it's that they understand they may be punished for doing the right thing, like keeping a pedophile off school grounds.

Why did Epstein act as if he was invulnerable? Maybe because he knew who was genuinely in charge, and it wasn't President Donald Trump.

> A controversial new book from the journalist Michael Wolff claims that the pedophile Jeffrey Epstein bragged that Bill Barr was the man in charge during Trump's time in office and that the president "lets someone else be in charge, until other people realize that someone, other than him, is in charge. When that happens, you're no longer in charge."[53]

Bill Barr? The man who, as a sophomore at Horace Mann, told his guidance counselor that he wanted to be the head of the CIA, but ended up twice as attorney general, once to help the elder Bush to keep clear of the Iran-Contra affair, and once in the Trump Administration, keeping the Russia collusion story going, as well as other hoaxes?

The book *Too Famous: The Rich, the Powerful, the Wishful, the Notorious and the Damned* has a section in which the former Israeli prime minister, Ehud Barak, asks Epstein who was really in charge in the Trump White House.

> Wolff claims that Epstein interrupted the former politico and called Trump—his former playboy party pal—a "moron," then confided, "At the moment, Bill Barr is in charge." The pedophile financier continued: "It's Donald's pattern . . . he lets someone else be in charge, until other people realize that someone, other than him, is in charge. When that happens, you're no longer in charge."
>
> Barak allegedly pressed, "But let me ask you, why do you think Barr took this job, knowing all this?"
>
> "The motivation was simple: money," Epstein replied. "Barr believes he'll get a big payday out of this . . . If he keeps Donald in office, manages to hold the Justice Department together, and help the Republican Party survive Donald, he thinks this is worth big money to him. I speak from direct knowledge. Extremely direct. Trust me."[54]

How is it that these people are so supremely confident that they will never be genuinely prosecuted for their crimes? One might say that claims by people like me of some vast conspiracy are the rantings of a far-right figure, but what should one believe when this article comes from the left wing *Daily Beast*?

> Wolff says Barak was part of "a revolving door of friends, acquaintances, experts, visiting international dignitaries and despots, petitioners for contributions and investments, lawyers, and other holders of vast fortunes—a network of worldly influence and interest arguably as great as any in New York—who sat at Epstein's dining-conference table, engaged in something that was part seminar, part gossip-fest, part coffee klatch, part elite conspiracy."
>
> Elsewhere, Wolff claims Barak joked that, "We have nothing to worry about. The secrets are safe."[55]

Many of us genuinely try to keep from saying things like the elite are involved in a secret conspiracy that they don't want to tell us about, but we keep running across articles like this from people like Michael Wolff, who the mainstream media has told us in other instances that we should believe. I mean, this article is from the *Daily Beast*, which is supposed to be the vanguard of the left.

And what are the "secrets" that they might need to conceal?

For the answer to that question, we probably need to go to New Mexico.

* * *

We know about Epstein's island and his New York and Florida homes, but little has been written about his New Mexico property, known as Zorro Ranch.

On July 31, 2019, after Epstein had been charged a second time with sex trafficking, this time by the federal authorities, the *New York Times* published what must surely be one of the strangest stories ever written about a public figure. And yet, I believe it only scratches the surface of

Epstein's unholy ambitions. In the art world, they often talk of "negative space," the parts of the painting where nothing seems to be happening.

> Jeffrey E. Epstein, the wealthy financier who is accused of sex trafficking had an unusual dream: He hoped to seed the human race with his DNA by impregnating women at his vast New Mexico ranch.
>
> Mr. Epstein over the years confided to scientists and others about his scheme, according to four people familiar with his thinking, although there is no evidence that it ever came to fruition.
>
> Mr. Epstein's vision reflected his longstanding fascination with what has become known as transhumanism; the science of improving the human population through technologies like genetic engineering and artificial intelligence. Critics have likened transhumanism to a modern-day version of eugenics, the discredited field of improving the human race through controlled breeding.[56]

As strange as this information was, and the fact I believed some of it was accurate, did it mean I suddenly started trusting the *New York Times*?

Not in the slightest.

What I do believe is that when the intelligence agencies want to lie to the public, they'll choose a lie that is close to the truth and might pass the "fact-checking" that has become ubiquitous these days.

There will be some truths mixed in. But they want you to follow the shiny object away from what they're trying to hide in the shadows. For those familiar with the workings of intelligence, this kind of partial admission is often called a "limited hangout."

This is what I believe, based on the *New York Times* article.

Epstein did want to impregnate many women with his DNA. (But not for the purpose of having children.)

Epstein talked about his plans to many people over the years, who never thought to make it part of the public conversation.

Epstein was a transhumanist, who wanted to use genetic engineering, artificial intelligence, and controlled breeding to bring about his perfect society.

The *New York Times* article continued to spin their tale of Epstein:

> Mr. Epstein attracted a glittering array of prominent scientists. They included the Nobel Prize-winning physicist Murray Gell-Mann, who discovered the quark; the theoretical physicist and best-selling author Stephen Hawking; the paleontologist and evolutionary biologist Stephen Jay Gould; Oliver Sacks, the neurologist and best-selling author; George M. Church, a molecular engineer who has worked to identify genes that could be altered to create superior humans; and the M.I.T. theoretical physicist Frank Wilczek, a Nobel laureate.
>
> The lure for some of the scientists was Mr. Epstein's money. He dangled financing for their pet projects. Some of the scientists said that the prospect of financing blinded them to the seriousness of his sexual transgressions, and even led them to give credence to some of Mr. Epstein's half-baked scientific musings.
>
> Scientists gathered at dinner parties at Mr. Epstein's Manhattan mansion, where Dom Perignon and expensive wines flowed freely, even though Mr. Epstein did not drink. He hosted buffet lunches at Harvard's Program for Evolutionary Dynamics, which he had helped start with a $6.5 million donation.[57]

This is where it starts to become ludicrous, and it becomes clear that the *New York Time*s wants to throw you off the scent. Let's consider some of these lies. They want you to believe that two Nobel laureates, Murray Gell-Mann and Frank Wilczek, were so blinded by the prospect of getting money from Epstein that they didn't think about the fact he was a convicted pedophile. For those who know much about science, two of the other names, Oliver Sacks and Stephen Jay Gould, were both giants in their respective fields of neurology and paleontology. And George Church? He is in charge of the Harvard University team that wants to bring back the Woolly Mammoth.

Epstein was a freak, and anybody with an ounce of common sense could see it. As I've said before, there was just some X factor with Epstein, and I think it was his role as an intelligence asset that allowed him to live this high-flying existence.

> Once, at a dinner at Mr. Epstein's mansion on Manhattan's Upper East Side, Mr. Lanier said he talked to a scientist who told him that Mr. Epstein's goal was to have 20 women at a time impregnated at his 33,000 square-foot Zorro Ranch in a tiny town outside Santa Fe. Mr. Lanier said the scientist identified herself as working at NASA, but he did not remember her name.
>
> According to Mr. Lanier, the NASA scientist said Mr. Epstein had based his idea for a baby ranch on accounts of the Repository for Germinal Choice, which was to be stocked with the sperm of Nobel laureates who wanted to strengthen the human gene pool. (Only one Nobel Prize winner has acknowledged contributing sperm to it. The repository discontinued operation in 1999.)
>
> Mr. Lanier, the virtual-reality creator and author, said he had the impression that Mr. Epstein was using the dinner parties—where some guests were attractive women with impressive academic credentials—to screen candidates to bear Mr. Epstein's children.[58]

Twenty women at a time? Does that sound like he wants to be daddy to a new and improved human race? Does Jeffrey Epstein strike you as somebody who was dying to become a father?

I can accept that he wanted to impregnate twenty women at a time, but it wasn't because he wanted children.

I think it's probably true that Epstein was looking at some of the women at his dinner parties for the possibility of impregnating them, but as for the next stage, well, that's a little more complicated.

This last section I'll quote from the *New York Times* article provides a clue in my mind as to Epstein's true intentions.

> One adherent of transhumanism said that he and Epstein discussed the financier's interest in cryonics, an unproven science in which people's bodies are frozen to be brought back to life in the future. Mr. Epstein told this person that he wanted his head and penis to be frozen.
>
> Southern Trust Company, Mr. Epstein's Virgin Island-incorporated business, disclosed in a local filing that it was engaged in DNA analysis. Calls to Southern Trust, which sponsored a science and math fair for school children in the Virgin Islands in 2014, were not returned.
>
> In 2011, a charity established by Mr. Epstein gave $20,000 to the World Transhumanist Association, which now operates under the name Humanity Plus. The group's website says that its goal is "to deeply influence a new generation of thinkers who dare to envision humanity's next steps."[59]

So, Jeffrey Epstein was a transhumanist? Where have I heard that expression before? Oh, that's right, from Yuval Noah Harari and the whole World Economic Forum crowd led by Klaus Schwab.

Whenever people talk about transhumanism, this belief that man has finally attained Godlike powers, I can only shake my head at the hubris of such people. It makes me think of the quote from the French philosopher, Blaise Pascal, often misquoted as, "There is a God-shaped vacuum in the heart of every person, and it can never be filled by any created thing." The full and accurate quote is much deeper, as it speaks to so much of the vain physical and emotional seeking we often do in this world, when we should be looking elsewhere to fulfill our spiritual needs.

> What else does this craving, and this helplessness proclaim but that there was once in man a true happiness, of which all that now remains is the empty print and trace?
>
> This he tries in vain to fill with everything around him, seeking in things that are not there the help he cannot find in those that are,

> though none can help, since this infinite abyss can only be filled with an infinite and immovable object; in other words by God himself.[60]

If you do not believe in God, in an afterlife, that there is an abundant universe in which you are meant to prosper, maybe it makes sense to think about having your head and penis cryogenically frozen to be thawed out at a later date.

But in a world where God exists, considering such things makes you a freak and a demon of the highest order.

Aside from having his head and penis frozen, what other steps was Jeffrey Epstein taking to make sure he lived as long as possible in what he believed was the only world he would ever know?

* * *

To answer this question, I think we need to go north, to Canada, and the story of the man many regarded as the Canadian Jeffrey Epstein, Peter Nygard, the fashion mogul worth an estimated $700 million, who was arrested in December 2020 on sex-trafficking charges. This is how the *New York Times* covered his arrest.

> Peter Nygard, the Canadian fashion executive, has been charged with sex trafficking, racketeering conspiracy and other crimes that involved dozens of women and teenage girls as victims in the United States, the Bahamas and Canada, federal prosecutors in Manhattan said on Tuesday.
>
> Mr. Nygard, 79, used his company's influence, its money and its employees to recruit adult and "minor-aged female victims" over a 25-year period for the sexual gratification of himself and his associates, according to a nine-count indictment. He was arrested in Winnipeg, Manitoba, on Monday at the request of the United States under an extradition treaty, the U.S. Attorney's Office in Manhattan said. He is now being held in a Manitoba jail.

> The indictment accused Mr. Nygard of targeting victims from disadvantaged economic backgrounds and, in some cases, with a history of abuse. Mr. Nygard sexually assaulted some, it said, while his associates assaulted or drugged others "to ensure their compliance with Mr. Nygard's sexual demands."[61]

I can genuinely understand how good people, living their lives and going to a job, hear my complaints about the elites and conspiracies, and shake their head, thinking I'm too suspicious. My response is it might be helpful if you read more to better understand that what you see at your job and among your friends is not how it is everywhere. Much of history is a list of atrocities perpetrated by truly evil people and the weak people who agree to do their dirty work. There are some genuinely bad people out there.

And what's more terrifying is that people like Nygard and Epstein can engage in these behaviors for decades, getting their employees to assault or drug their victims for them. They are not lone wolf criminals; they are more like the alpha males of a troop of demons. With the next passage from the *New York Times* article, we move a little closer to the ultimate goal of these devils.

> Federal authorities previously investigated Mr. Nygard on allegations of sex trafficking between 2015 and 2017 without filing any charges. The FBI conducted two brief inquiries, while the Department of Homeland Security investigated him for nine months.
>
> For decades, Mr. Nygard portrayed himself as a playboy, describing the young women and teenage girls he surrounded himself with as "the source of youth," according to a video he produced about his attempts to fight aging. He dated celebrities like Anna Nicole Smith and fathered at least 10 children with eight women. Born in Finland, he grew up in Canada, launching his multinational fashion company, Nygard International, in Winnipeg more than 50 years ago.
>
> He divided his time between Canada, the United States and the Bahamas, where he built a sprawling Mayan-themed compound,

> with sculptures of animal predators and naked women, that he described as the "Eighth Wonder of the World."[62]

This story closely resembles the Epstein story, down to the Caribbean island lair. But I found the previous paragraph to be the most illuminating. I always like to look at the words a person uses to understand their underlying state of mind.

He talks about the "young women and teenage girls" as "the source of youth."

That's an interesting combination of words.

What might he mean?

A book published in 2020, *Predator King: Peter Nygard's Dark Life of Rape, Drugs, and Blackmail*, by Melissa Cronin contains what I believe to be the answer to the question I raised as the beginning of this chapter, as to the true motivation of the hedonistic and atheistic Jeffrey Epstein. The answer seems to be stem cells, but not quite the type you often hear about in the news. According to the book, Nygard was attempting to make the Caribbean the world center for stem cell treatments, but with methods that would have appalled Dr. Frankenstein.

> In St. Kitts, local papers christened the debacle "The Stem Cell Scandal," and breathlessly reported on the mystery of what Nygard had been doing behind closed doors. The "In St. Kitts Nevis" news website, which calls itself "the premier information portal for St. Kitts and Nevis" even suggested that Nygard was using the placenta of new mothers at the hospital for his treatments—without their knowledge.
>
> They weren't the only ones to make that outrageous claim. Nygard's former house manager, Richette Ross, said in an interview recorded for this book that Nygard "told me himself about his stem cell harvesting."[63]

Nygard was suspected of stealing the placenta of women who had just given birth. One might think that was the extent of Nygard's crimes, but his former housekeeper said Nygard went to an even darker place. Nygard reportedly started with umbilical cord stem cells, but then worked to perfect something he thought far superior.

> According to Ross, Nygard claimed he had found a way to improve even farther on that material: She alleged that he said he harvested umbilical cords from babies he had fathered. After getting a girlfriend pregnant, she said, "He told me he takes the girls to . . . abort the fetuses." (Umbilical cords form at just five weeks into pregnancy.) Ross said Nygard claimed that since his own DNA was in the cord blood, it was a better "match."
>
> One girl, Ross claimed, was even sent to China to have them harvest stem cells through her fetus. She claimed to have heard similar stories from other girls, too. "After they aborted," she said, "they told me they had just gotten back."[64]

The mind boggles at the accusation. Getting a woman pregnant for the sole purpose of generating a fetus that one plans to abort for the purpose of harvesting its stem cells must surely rank as one of the most heinous crimes against nature. This strikes me as nothing more than the inevitable end point of abandoning a belief in God, or at least the idea that there must be some greater purpose in the universe.

Without a belief in some greater purpose, all we're left with is our own survival. If one is solely concerned with themselves, then any and all things are permissible, including creating children so you can destroy them for your own benefit.

This accusation against Nygard didn't come just from his housekeeper, but was verified by a former girlfriend, Suelyn Medieros, a supermodel (of course!) Here is her account:

> Suelyn Medeiros claims that she almost became Nygard's stem cell donor. In her 2014 memoir, she spins a bizarre and terrifying story. It all began out of the blue during a trip to Kiev, Ukraine. [Why does Ukraine, prior to the Russian invasion, seem to have been the

> center of so much globalist mischief?] Nygard was having stem cell research done, and Medeiros was interested in biotechnology because her mother suffered from lupus.
>
> "When he was finished, he said he had to talk to me about something," she writes. "He took me into a board meeting-type room with a large table surrounded by about 30 chairs. After we sat down, he asked, 'Suelyn, do you know what the best stem cells are?'"
>
> She did: Embryos.
>
> "Correct!" she says Nygard responded excitedly. "And you know what? If you got pregnant and had an abortion, we could use those embryonic cells and have a life's supply for all of us: you, your mother, and me. A lot of people are doing it."[65]

Bingo! Are the pieces starting to fall into place for you? *InfoWars* obtained video of Peter Nygard talking with his business partner and some black women who appear to be in their twenties, sitting around a table, bidding for the eggs of these women so they could perform these atrocities. This is a partial transcript of that disturbing video:

> **STEVE POWERS:** The stem cell technology that Peter and I are investing in is called SCNT, which takes the eggs of a young, perfect woman specimen, takes the egg, and takes out the nucleus and puts our DNA into the nucleus. They just go in and take it out.
> **WOMAN #1:** Do they pay for it?
> **STEVE POWERS:** Yeah.
> **WOMAN #2:** Jesus Christ.
> **STEVE POWERS:** And this is part of the genetic greatness that we don't see in any other race on the planet. These curvy, sexy Black women from Africa. You girls have a kind of monopoly on this genetic perfection. And we want some of that. So, girls, for $100, we will pay you for your eggs.
> **WOMAN #1:** Are you serious?
> **WOMAN #2:** A hundred dollars? You got to pay a lot more than that.

> **STEVE POWERS:** Well, how much do you want for it? Let's bid.
> **WOMAN #2:** No, it's not-
> **STEVE POWERS:** I bid $500.
> **PETER NYGARD:** I'm prepared to go higher.
> **STEVE POWERS:** Whatever I bid, he's going to outbid me.
> **PETER NYGARD:** I'm prepared to bid $60,000 for the eggs. If you have an abortion, that's very valuable. The umbilical cord, you know, the placenta, even your period blood is so rich with stem cells. We regard it as waste and it shouldn't be. It should be captured and recycled. It shouldn't go to waste. It's life for somebody else. It's life for mankind. The best eggs are 16 through 18 years old. Those are the best eggs. As you get older, your eggs get weaker and weaker. So you may not be our top target.[66]

Sometimes to understand what one rich person is doing, you have to go to another rich person, understanding that many of them work in tandem. The ultra-rich are a small club, and most of them know each other.

The cover story the mainstream media put together about Epstein's Zorro Ranch was that he wanted to create a "master race" based on his own genetic code. They expect you to read that, shake your head, think he's a creep, and then try to wipe that from your mind.

What they don't want you thinking is that he wanted to "impregnate up to 20 women at a time" because he wanted to abort these children and harvest their stem cells to extend his own life and those of his good friends.

That would be the story of the century.

* * *

Let's look at Epstein's mysterious death in federal custody, how it was covered, and the part Trump's attorney general, Bill Barr, played in essentially giving the country his version of the Warren Commission.

Was it a coincidence that Barr's final pronouncement on the death of Jeffrey Epstein was reported in the *New York Times* on November 22,

2019, the fifty-sixth anniversary of the assassination of President John F. Kennedy? Or was the Deep State giving a sick wink to fellow members of the Cabal, or warning off those who might be inclined to delve more deeply into the story? Here's how the Deep State wanted to set the stage, letting all the great unwashed, the suspicious, and the conspiracy theorists know that, yes, there was some reason for concern, but Big Daddy Bill Barr has investigated things, and you can all rest easy now. It was just incompetence, not anything evil.

> Mr. Epstein's death in August at a federal detention center in Manhattan set off a rash of unfounded conspiracy theories on social media that were picked up and repeated by high-profile figures, including Mayor Bill de Blasio and former mayor Rudolph W. Giuliani. No matter their ideology, the refrain of the theories was the same: Something did not add up.
>
> Even after New York City's chief medical examiner ruled the death a suicide by hanging, conspiracy theories continued to percolate onto the internet after lawyers for Mr. Epstein challenged that finding. Then Mr. Epstein's family hired a forensic pathologist who claimed that the broken bones and cartilage in Mr. Epstein's neck "points to homicide."
>
> Mr. Barr said that he, too, was initially suspicious. How could someone who had been on suicide watch kill himself in one of the most secure jails in America?[67]

I wish I could have more respect for the members of the Deep State Cabal, you know, being the "focus of evil" in the modern world and all. But they just don't strike me as that bright. The writer of this *New York Times* article can't even keep a single narrative going for three paragraphs without contradicting herself. Like Dr. Evil often laments in the *Austin Powers* movies, it can be so difficult to get good, evil henchmen (and women).

In the first paragraph we're told that the initial report of Epstein's death set off a "rash of unfounded conspiracy theories."

Okay, I understand the standard.

Don't jump to conclusions until all the evidence is in.

I don't agree with it (given how Epstein was able to avoid prosecution for years, and the US attorney who did prosecute him said he was told to go easy because he was connected to "intelligence"), but I understand that's the standard the *New York Times* is saying is responsible.

But two paragraphs later they tell us Bill Bar was "initially suspicious" when he heard the news. Is Bill Barr a purveyor of "unfounded conspiracy theories" or is he simply attempting to convince the public he's just a "regular guy" like the rest of us?

However, they want you to overlook such inconsistencies and focus on how the "initially suspicious" Bill Barr came to see that Epstein's death raised no suspicions of foul play.

> Attorney General William P. Barr said in an interview published on Friday that the death of Jeffrey Epstein, the financier accused of sex trafficking, in a secure federal prison resulted from a "perfect storm of screwups," rather than any nefarious act.
>
> Mr. Barr's statement refuted suggestions from members of Epstein's family that he may have been murdered. His remarks came the same week that two prison guards were criminally charged, accused in an indictment of failing to check on Mr. Epstein every half-hour as they were required to do and then lying about it on prison logs.
>
> "I can understand people who immediately—whose minds went to sort of the worst-case scenario, because it was a perfect storm of screwups," Mr. Barr said in an interview with The Associated Press as he flew to Montana on Thursday night.[68]

Notice how easily the lies slip off the tongue, with phrases like "perfect storm of screwups," which are designed to lodge in your brain like some marketing slogan and explain away all inconsistencies.

You may disagree with me, but I am done with having incompetence cover as an explanation for evil.

That just doesn't fly with me.

And Bill Barr's meddling doesn't begin and end with Epstein. As Trump's attorney general, he kept the phony Russia investigation going, and out of office he's shown his true colors by his attacks on Trump, showing he is doing the bidding of our intelligence agencies.

> Former US Attorney General Bill Barr thinks former president Donald Trump "has shown he has neither the temperament nor persuasive powers" of a leader, according to excerpts of his forthcoming book obtained by The Washington Post.
>
> "We need leaders not only capable of fighting and 'punching,' but also persuading and attracting—leaders who can frame, and advocate for an uplifting vision of what it means to share in American citizenship," Barr, who served as Trump's second attorney general, wrote in the book, "One Damn Thing After Another," according to the Post . . .
>
> According to the Post, Barr says in the book that the prospect of Trump running for president again was "dismaying."[69]

It is not the normal job of a former attorney general of the United States to disparage the president he served. Given the intelligence connections of his father, his own boyhood desire to become head of the CIA, his early work at the CIA, and the allegations of him working for the CIA during the Reagan administration to cover up the Iran-Contra affair, it is strange that more questions have not been asked of Barr about his true allegiances.

Jeffrey Epstein was the most high-profile prisoner in the Metropolitan Corrections Center, if not the entire country, and he wasn't watched? As Tucker Carlson has pointed out, we still don't know the names of the other prisoners housed with Epstein. Many have said that the approximately sixteen prisoners could interact with each other, so while it may be possible that nobody entered that area during the time in question, what about the other prisoners?

It seems to me that Bill Barr is nothing less than the clean-up man for the intelligence agencies, getting rid of the "Epstein-Barr" problem which started at the Dalton School, under the reign of his father, Donald Barr, as well as any other tasks they assign him.

* * *

In Bram Stoker's classic horror novel *Dracula*, there's a minor character called Renfield, who serves as the vampire's human helper, keeping his master safe during the day, as well as helping Dracula find his victims at night.

The mainstream media would have you believe Jeffrey Epstein was the monster. The truth is that Epstein severed the monsters, who remain hidden even today.

What's the narrative I believe is closest to the truth?

Donald Barr, in his role as the headmaster of the Dalton School, was an intelligence recruiter, who was identifying potential recruits, when he met Jeffrey Epstein.

After hiring Epstein and identifying his proclivities, it was determined they would push him into the financial world, thereby giving him the explanation for the large amount of wealth he would acquire.

When Robert Maxwell was assassinated by the Israeli Mossad, Epstein was chosen as the means to reestablish contact with the family, through Ghislaine Maxwell, and continue Maxwell's blackmail and information-gathering network.

Before we continue, I need to flesh out my view of the intelligence agencies.

Disinformation would have you believe that western intelligence agencies operate independently of each other. For example, some have asked, was Epstein Israeli intelligence, American, or British? There are facts you could point to that would support any of these three claims. But this reveals a fundamental misunderstanding of how closely western intelligence agencies work together. At the very top, American, British, and Israeli intelligence are all one agency, working together. Now, there may be fights and disagreements at times, but they function as one entity.

Sometimes this information leaks out, as demonstrated by this article from the *New York Post*:

> The list of Jeffrey Epstein's possible connections now includes America's spy chief, a college president, and a former Obama White House Counsel, according to a collection of previously unreported documents that included the sex offender's schedule.
>
> The trove of papers, obtained by the *Wall Street Journal*, shows meetings between Epstein and several prominent people, including three with William Burns, the director of the Central Intelligence Agency, when he was the deputy secretary of state in 2014.[70]

Do you see the evidence I do for the involvement of not just the intelligence agencies, but the State Department, as well as attorneys like the former Obama White House counsel, who seem to be suspiciously close to the intelligence agencies, like Bill Barr? It all fits together. The intelligence agencies are not walled off from the rest of the government. The intelligence agencies are in control of the government. That is what they do not want you to understand.

But people like Joe Rogan, as well as others, are starting to notice and comment.

> Joe Rogan thinks that convicted pedophile Jeffrey Epstein may have been an agent of either the CIA or Israel's Mossad who was part of a plot to collect sensitive information about the rich and powerful . . .
>
> "Well, he definitely donated some money to science," Rogan said. "You know, but I had a conversation with a scientist who didn't buy into that Epstein stuff and wouldn't go to meetings and stuff like that. And he said he was really shocked at how little money he actually donated.
>
> "He goes, 'It wasn't that much money.' He goes, it was really like, 'he was more than that,'" Rogan said. "He was bringing them to parties. Like it was an intelligence operation," Rogan said. "Whoever was running it, whether it was the Mossad or whether it was the

> CIA, or whether it was a combination of both—it was an intelligence operation. They were bringing people in and compromising them."[71]

My perspective is that those who went to Jeffrey Epstein's parties and were compromised weren't surprised by what happened. They knew the setup. Is this the reason Bill Gates met so many times with Epstein, something he now says he regrets?[72] Could it also explain why Gates seems, like Epstein, to be so interested in "supporting" scientists?[73] Bill Gates may have been more than happy to pay that price.

In return for having sex with underage girls, powerful people understand the intelligence agencies have blackmail on them.

Perhaps that's the price of admission to the corridors of power.

That's why when people like Jeffrey Epstein's former pilot named some of the well-known passengers on Epstein's plane, such as Hollywood stars Kevin Spacey or Chris Tucker, or British royal Prince Andrew,[74] I don't see them as victims.

They made the decision to join the club.

Raping an underage girl was worth gaining access to power. Rogan went even further, suggesting that Epstein was also controlling former President Clinton on behalf of the intelligence agencies.

> You may have heard of or seen the picture that Epstein had in his Manhattan townhouse of Clinton in a blue dress.
>
> But Rogan made a point about why it was featured so prominently in Epstein's home. It was to demonstrate that he knew things about Clinton, Rogan said.
>
> "That painting is like: 'I got you, bitch,'" Rogan said, adding, "You know he knows about it."
>
> "Imagine if I knew some horrible dark secrets about you and you came over to my house and I have a giant painting of you. Right when you walk into the front door of you in a dress and I'm like, 'Hey buddy.'"

> Guest comedian Duncan Trussell, who initially chalked the painting up to Epstein's poor taste in art, quickly agreed that it was displayed as a power move.[75]

And just so we're being even-handed, who can forget that another piece of artwork in Epstein's Manhattan townhouse depicted former President George W. Bush sitting on the floor of the Oval Office like an adolescent schoolboy, a paper airplane in one hand, and two demolished towers in front of him?[76]

On the question of Epstein's alleged Mossad ties, Dylan Howard, who wrote a book about Epstein, *Dead Men Tell No Tales*, had this to say about Epstein in an interview with an Australian news program.

> "One would ask, why would you have cameras in every single room? Well, as part of our investigation, we've established that Epstein had another room next to where all those cameras fed into, and there were industrial-sized Xerox machines.
>
> "So whatever was taking place inside the four walls of his homes, he was recording it, and printing it out, and keeping DVDs. . .
>
> "As part of our investigation, we spoke to Ari Ben-Menashe, who is a former Israeli spy," Howard said. "He said on the record, unequivocally, that Jeffrey Epstein was working for Israeli intelligence operations, the Mossad, and running a classic honey trap operation: that is, lure people inside, record their activities, and use it to blackmail them.
>
> "This person was also the handler of Jeffrey Epstein's best friend and ex-girlfriend, Ghislaine Maxwell."[77]

As I've said, I think the Mossad connection is only part of the story. Is anybody foolish enough to think our intelligence services would allow such an operation to exist in plain sight on American soil without benefitting from the arrangement in some manner?

I find myself in agreement with the Twitter/X comment of Jim Ferguson from the United Kingdom, made on July 24, 2023, which, in a single day, was viewed more than three million times:

> Ghislaine Maxwell was found guilty of sex trafficking children. The judge refuses to release the list of who she sold them to. Up until the list is released, we have only one conclusion: all of them are in on it. Every last billionaire, prince, and politician. Every media mogul, banker and person of interest.[78]

The evidence is strong that Jeffrey Epstein and Ghislaine Maxwell began working together on creating an intelligence and blackmail network, and also establishing a close, personal relationship.

The problem with Epstein, from the viewpoint of the American/British/Israeli intelligence network, seemed to be that Epstein wanted to be famous.

He didn't want to be the "mysterious man in the shadows." Epstein wanted us to see him, in all his perverted glory, and realize we were powerless to stop him.

This is the flaw of all secret societies that seek to gain ultimate power. Human beings, even the devils among us, will refuse to be slaves.

Epstein's sexual proclivities were used for two purposes; the first being to recruit young, underage women who could compromise celebrities and politicians, and the second was to create a stable of women who would be impregnated by the elite, so that the resulting abortions would be used to create a steady flow of stem cell treatments to keep these rich atheists alive as long as possible.

The intelligence agencies tried to clip Epstein's wings in 2008, with the slap on the wrist of the Acosta plea and joke of a prison sentence, but Epstein kept wanting to be famous. Whistleblowers among the scientific community and academia put additional attention on Epstein, and a few honest journalists kept pursuing the story.

Yet he continued to be a liability to the Deep State.

Epstein was arrested and put into jail, where the intelligence agencies killed him.

Ghislaine Maxwell was arrested, tried, and put in jail for procuring young, underage women for prostitution.

As of this date, no men who had sex with the underage girls lured into prostitution by Ghislaine Maxwell have been convicted, or even charged, and no pictures or videos from the hundreds of cameras Epstein had placed throughout his residences have been released.

That doesn't sound like a "perfect storm of screwups" to me.

It sounds like the Deep State is frantically trying to keep the lid from blowing off this story.

I know there are good people who have access to all or part of the truth about Jeffrey Epstein and his masters and can get this information out to the public.

If you are one of the good people who know the names of those behind the veil, I ask you to search your conscience and do the right thing by naming the monsters and handing us the evidence of their crimes.

Bring these monsters into the light so that we can see them as God sees them.

Even in the heart of these demons, they know that God rules the universe, and they long to be brought to judgment.

Give them what they want.

Chapter Ten

The COVID-19 Lies and Deception

For many people the COVID-19 crisis was a wake-up call, the red pill, which began for them the process of asking more questions, especially when they saw how those who raised them were shouted down by the mainstream media, or simply removed from tech platforms like YouTube, Facebook, or Instagram.

But the COVID-19 playbook was something I'd learned about in 2009, from Dr. Rima Laibow. I was so impressed by her background, and what she told me, that I encouraged former Minnesota Governor Jesse Ventura to interview her for his show *Conspiracy Theory*. This is from that broadcast, with me talking to Ventura at a private airfield, just before Dr. Laibow flew in for their interview.

> **JESSE VENTURA:** Alex, you sounded urgent.
>
> **ALEX JONES:** There's an entire agenda afoot to force the population to undergo different types of medical treatments, namely vaccines. We're seeing a medical tyranny being set up, not just in the United States, but worldwide, under the UN and the World Health Organization.
>
> **JESSE VENTURA:** Who's behind all this?
>
> **ALEX JONES:** The Bilderberg group. They want a planetary dictatorship so they can carry out their depopulation agenda. And they want to do it through the medical system. And that's why vaccines are so important. We know that many of these vaccines turn out to have serious adverse reactions and this is being done by design. They kill you slowly over time. That's why they're called soft kill.[1]

Remember, this was a broadcast from 2009, and the pandemic started in 2020. Some of Dr. Laibow's specific comments about how the pandemic would unfold were not correct, but the thrust of what she related was startlingly accurate and prophetic.

> **DR. RIMA LAIBOW:** They will induce a pandemic using the nasal mist vaccine, which is a live attenuated virus. This means that if I take it, I can infect you. You're going to get the flu, everybody around us is going to get the flu.
>
> Then, the United States government, based on their statements that they've already made will say, "Oh, my, we have a pandemic. Oh, my goodness, we don't have enough doses. So, we'll add squalene at the 90,000 injection stations that the Department of Health announced that they will ship the vaccines to . . . What that means is a holocaust, a genocidal holocaust. Men and women will sicken and die. And those who survive will be infertile . . .
>
> In 2003, I had a patient in my drug-free medical practice who was a head of state. And one day, she said, "You know, it's almost time for the great culling to begin."
>
> **JESSE VENTURA:** The what?
>
> **DR. RIMA LAIBOW:** That's what I said, "The what?" She said, "The great culling." When you thin the herd. I said, "What are you talking about?" She said, "It's almost time for the useless eaters to be culled." And she said, "Those are people who are consuming our non-renewable natural resources." I said, "Who are the people who make this decision?"
>
> **JESSE VENTURA:** The chosen few?
>
> **DR. RIMA LEIBOW:** She said, "We, the aristocrats."[2]

The globalists had eleven years to modify their plans, which is exactly what I think they did. At the time, Dr. Laibow thought the threat was likely to come from a swine flu epidemic, but maybe the globalists couldn't make that scenario work. Dr. Laibow also thought there was likely to be more of a public uprising against the shots than there ultimately turned out to be. But I think it's because they took the extra time to plan their psychological war games against the public.

I believe Dr. Laibow was one of the most prophetic voices of the vaccine hysteria of COVID-19, as well as the soft-kill scenario that has been deployed against many of our population. We must use all our brains and intellect now to help those who have taken the poison shots and save as many as we can.

But first, let's review what happened during the COVID-19 crisis, the lies they told us, and how many fell for them, believing that if their fellow citizens merely gave up their liberty and skepticism, Big Brother would keep them safe.

We must understand our recent past, so they will not fool us again.

* * *

We are now three years beyond the start of the COVID-19 lockdowns in March 2020[3] and while many may have believed the false claims put forth during the "fog of war," it is certainly time to review decisions and claims made, so that we may dispassionately determine what was true and what was false.

The first question that needs to be answered is where did SARS-CoV-2, the virus that causes COVID-19, come from?

I believe the best piece of evidence on this question was revealed by *Project Veritas*, when it was led by the incomparable and incorruptible James O'Keefe. As they reported on January 10, 2022:

> Project Veritas has obtained startling never-before-seen documents regarding the origin of COVID-19, gain of function research, vaccines, potential treatments which have been suppressed, and the government's efforts to conceal all of this.
>
> The documents in question stem from a report at the Defense Advanced Research Projects Agency, better known as DARPA, which were hidden in a top-secret shared drive.

> DARPA is an agency under the U.S. Department of Defense in charge of facilitating research in technology with potential military actions.[4]

For those of you unfamiliar with DARPA, they are the mad monk squad of scientists working on behalf of our military-intelligence complex, who have been responsible for some amazing advances but also for some schemes that can only be described as bat-shit crazy.

This is from a 2004 *Mother Jones* article on the founding of DARPA:

> When, in October 1957, the USSR launched the first manmade satellite, the basketball-sized Sputnik, it caught the United States off guard and sent the government into fits. Not only had the Soviets exploded an atomic bomb years before the Americans had predicted they would, but now they were leading the "space race."
>
> In response, the Defense Department approved funding for a new U.S. satellite project, headed by former Nazi SS Officer Wernher von Braun, and created, in 1958, the Defense Advanced Research Projects Agency (DARPA) to make certain that the United States forever maintained "a lead in applying state-of-the-art technology for military capabilities and to prevent technological surprise from her adversaries."[5]

Let's just agree that, as a historical fact, DARPA's first leader was a former Nazi SS officer. Now, you may say, well, he wasn't really a bad Nazi SS officer; he was more of a scientist who simply got recruited.

But here's an excerpt from a *Smithsonian* magazine interview with Michael Neufeld, who chaired the Space History Division at our National Air and Space Museum, who had written a well-regarded book, *Von Braun, Dreamer of Space, Engineer of War*, on the question of Braun's Nazi past.

> **Neufeld:** That's been the traditional kind of defense: that he was trapped, that he couldn't do anything. The problem with that is that it makes him look like someone who really didn't want to be in the

> Third Reich—someone who didn't like the Nazis. But all the evidence I have is that he was quite comfortable with the Nazis and the Third Reich until late in the war. And it was only in the very last year or two—through a combination of his last encounter with Hitler, witnessing concentration camp labor, but above all, his own arrest by the Gestapo—that he became disillusioned about this regime that he was working for. Up to that time, although not enthused about joining the party and the SS, he'd been a fairly loyal member of the Third Reich and in some sense or other, a Nazi, if not an ideological one or one who cared about the race theory very much.[6]

Neufeld makes the argument that Braun essentially sleep-walked into a Faustian bargain with Hitler and the Nazis, so it's probably most accurate to characterize him as a man of "flexible morals" willing to work with any odious characters, as long as they leave him alone to conduct his experiments. I contend that Braun is typical of most scientists: willing to do anything their paymasters ask them to do.

In other words, most scientists don't get any training in moral courage.

Which is why the response of DARPA to the proposal by EcoHealth Alliance, led by Dr. Peter Daszak, is so remarkable. For all the criticism one might give DARPA for parts of its history, in this instance they appeared to have displayed an extraordinary amount of common sense and skepticism that Daszak could safely conduct his proposed experiments.

On March 24, 2018, Daszak sent a letter from EcoHealth Alliance to the DARPA program called, "Preventing Emerging Pathogenic Threats" (PREEMPT) detailing what he wanted for the $14,209,245 he was requesting from them. This is from the Executive Summary prepared by Daszak:

> <u>Technical Approach</u>: Our goal is to defuse the potential for spillover of novel bat-origin high-zoonotic risk SARS-related coronaviruses in Asia. In TA1 we will intensively sample bats at our field sites where we have identified high spillover risk SARSr-CoVs. We will sequence their spike proteins, reverse engineer them to conduct binding assays, and insert them into bat SARs-CoV (WIV1, SCHO14) backbones

> (these use bat-SASr-CoV backbones, not SARS-CoV, and are exempt from dual-use and gain of function concerns) to infect humanized mice and assess capacity to capacity to cause SARS-like disease.
>
> Our modeling team will use these data to build **machine-learning genotype-phenotype models** of viral evolution and spillover risk. We will uniquely validate these with serology from previously collected human samples via LIP assays that assess which spike proteins allow spillover into people.
>
> We will build **host-pathogen spatial models** to predict the bat species composition of caves across Southeast Asia, parameterized with a full inventory of host-virus distribution at our field test sites, three caves in Yunan Province, China, and a series of unique global datasets on bat-host-viral relationships. By the end of Y1, we will create a prototype app for the warfighter that identifies the likelihood of bats harboring dangerous viral pathogens at any site across Asia.[7]

The most charitable frame that could be put on this research is that they wanted to determine whether bat coronaviruses might cross over into the human species. They intended to mess around with the viruses they'd collected from three caves in Yunan Province, sequencing "their spike proteins, reverse engineer them to conduct binding assays, and insert them into bat (WIV1, SHC014) SASr backbones." In other words, this was gain of function research, which was prohibited in the United States at that time.

They'd use "machine-learning" to figure out possible directions this viral evolution might take, and all of this was to create a "prototype app for the warfighter," which would identify what bat viruses they might encounter if they were deployed in Asia. It's somewhat odd that Americans were working with Chinese scientists from the Wuhan Institute of Virology on viruses our troops might encounter if they were deployed somewhere in Asia, like say, China? Would we be happy to have Chinese scientists investigate viruses endemic to the American Southwest, like maybe Arizona, New Mexico, or Texas? The executive summary continued:

> In TA2, we will evaluate two approaches to reduce SARSr-CoV shedding in cave bats: (1) Broadscale immune boosting, in which we will inoculate bats with immune modulators to upregulate their innate immune response and downregulate viral replication; (2) Targeted immune boosting, in which we will inoculate bats with novel chimeric polyvalent recombinant spike proteins plus the immune modulator to enhance innate immunity against specific high-risk viruses.
>
> We will trial inoculum delivery methods on captive bats, including a novel automated aerosolization system, transdermal nanoparticle application and edible adhesive gels. We will use stochastic simulation modeling information informed by field and experimental data to characterize viral dynamics in our cave test sites, maximize timing, inoculation protocol, delivery method and efficacy of viral suppression. The most effective biologicals will be trialed in our test cave sites in Yunan Province, with reduction in viral shedding as proof-of-concept.[8]

I think it's important to realize that DARPA thought this plan was unworthy of supporting because of the potential danger. They were going to boost the immune system of the bats, and they were going to use "novel chimeric polyvalent recombinant spike proteins" in addition to the "immune modulator" to suppress any virus. Let's just call a "novel chimeric polyvalent recombinant spike protein" what it is: a stitched-together virus that is more like Frankenstein's monster than anything you might find in nature.

They wanted to create real monsters to defend against potential monsters they believed might evolve in the future.

This might be called bringing into existence the very thing you fear the most.

Even worse was their "Management Approach," which used the Wuhan Institute of Virology, which had poor safety controls, as documented by our own State Department.[9]

> Management Approach: Members of our collaborative group have worked together on bats and their viruses for over 15 years. The lead

> organization, EcoHealth Alliance, will oversee all work. EHA staff will develop models to the probability of specific SARS-related CoV spillover, and identify the most effective strategy for delivery of both immune boosting and immune targeting inocula. Specific work will be subcontracted to the following organizations:
>
> - Prof. Baric, Univ. N. Carolina, will lead targeted immune boosting work, building on his two-decade track record of reverse-engineering CoV and other virus spike proteins.
> - Prof. Wang, Duke-Natl. Univ. Singapore, will lead work on broadscale immune boosting, building on his group's pioneering work on bat immunity.
> - Dr. Shi, Wuhan Institute of Virology will conduct viral testing on all collected samples, binding assays and some humanized mouse work.
> - Dr. Rocke, USGS National Wildlife Health Center will optimize delivery of immune modulating biologicals, building on her vaccine delivery work in wildlife, including bats.
> - Dr. Unidad, Palo Alto Research Center will lead development of novel delivery automated aerosolization mechanism for immune boosting molecules.[10]

When one reads this document released by *Project Veritas*, which, to my knowledge, nobody has claimed is false as of yet, the global scope of this catastrophe becomes clear.

Can I blame the Chinese Communist Party for the actual release of the virus?

Yes, I can.

But it's a little like blaming the getaway driver of a bank heist for running over a little old lady in the street. Technically, it's true, but there are so many levels to this problem.

Here's what the *Washington Post* reported in April 2020 about US concerns about the safety of the Wuhan Institute of Virology:

> Two years before the novel coronavirus pandemic upended the world, U.S. Embassy officials visited a Chinese research facility in the city of Wuhan several times and sent two official warnings back to Washington about inadequate safety at the lab, which was conducting risky studies on coronaviruses from bats. The cables have fueled discussions inside the U.S. government about whether this or another Wuhan lab was the source of the virus—even though conclusive proof has yet to emerge.[11]

It doesn't get much plainer than that. Two years before the pandemic, our own government was worried about safety at the lab. In fact, one might even say these cables from the US Embassy in Beijing predicted the COVID-19 outbreak as detailed by the *Washington Post*.

> What the U.S. officials learned during their visits concerned them so much that they dispatched two diplomatic cables categorized as Sensitive But Unclassified back to Washington. The cables warned about safety and management weaknesses at the WIV lab and proposed more attention and help. The first cable, which I obtained, also warns that the lab's work on bat coronaviruses and their potential human transmission represented a risk of a new SARS-like pandemic.
>
> "During interactions with scientists at the WIV [Wuhan Institute of Virology] laboratory, they noted the new lab has a serious shortage of appropriately trained technicians and investigators needed to safely operate this high-containment laboratory," states the Jan. 19, 2018, cable, which was drafted by two officials from the embassy's environment, science, and health section who met with WIV scientists. (The State Department declined to comment on this and other details of this story.)[12]

One of the ideas I believe is important for people to keep in mind is that the government, and even the intelligence agencies, which we justly criticize, are not monoliths. Enormous evil can be done by relatively few people in charge, leaving the rest of the organization in the dark as to what's happening behind the scenes.

If we accept as true that our own embassy officials in China were warning the United States about the safety problems at the Wuhan Institute of Virology, then we must ask: why wasn't appropriate action taken?

I think it's important to go back to the genesis of where this problem started, with Peter Daszak and EcoHealth Alliance. In 2022, Dr. Andrew Huff, the former vice-president and senior scientist of EcoHealth Alliance, published his blockbuster book, *The Truth About Wuhan: How I Uncovered the Biggest Lie in History*, which made some startling allegations about who was funding EcoHealth Alliance. This is what Dr. Huff claims:

> Dr. Peter Daszak approached me in late 2015 and stated that somebody from the Central Intelligence Agency (CIA) approached him and stated that they were interested in the places we were working, the people we were working with, and the data we were collecting. Peter then proceeded to ask me for my advice, and specifically whether we should work with them. I was shocked that Peter asked me this and was excited for the opportunity. I stated to Peter that "It never hurts to talk to them. There could be money in it." Peter then later confirmed over the next two months, between our weekly meetings, that the relationship with them was proceeding.[13]

I think it's important to view the machinations of the globalists as consisting of equal parts evil and stupidity. They want to control the world, but they're also exceptionally bad at trying to accomplish this goal. They're always making mistakes, and we must not be shy about pointing them out.

All of us are in the dark as to the origins of SARS-CoV-2, but that doesn't mean we shouldn't listen to experts in the field like Dr. Huff. In many ways, he is just as puzzled as the rest of us. In attempting to explain what happened, Huff wrote:

> The cover-up of SARS-CoV-2 began with the Chinese in September 2019, and this fact should not be surprising.

> If communist superpowers exist, then the people that live and work in those systems will be incentivized to protect the party at all costs. The emergence of SARS-CoV-2 is the second time in history [the first time being the Soviet disaster at Chernobyl] where a massive cover-up operation was deployed to conceal the true nature and extent of a disaster.
>
> The US cover-up of SARS-CoV-2, which was also likely supported by some of its closest allies, likely began in October 2019, as this was the same time DARPA attempted to blindly recruit me for a position that I was not vaguely interested in at the time.
>
> I am guessing that the intelligence community and DoD were hoping that the disease would burn out, which often happens with emerging infectious diseases, and they were probably not aware of the extent to which SARS-CoV-2 had already spread globally.[14]

Most of the time, I don't see a confederacy of evil in the world but a confederacy of dunces. (Although personally, I think the devil finds it much easier to influence stupid people than smart people with a conscience.) So, you've got your pick, evil or stupid.

It doesn't really matter in my mind because, in both instances, you're likely to end up just as dead. Let's list just a few of the possible lies at the heart of the COVID-19 crisis.

The CIA was running EcoHealth Alliance.

The Wuhan Institute of Virology had poor safety protocols.

Both the Americans and the Chinese involved in working on bat coronaviruses understood how the work might escape from the lab and cause a pandemic.

Despite the fact that the Chinese and American scientists were working together, they were also lying to each other about certain key facts.

They say when you tell that first lie, you just have to keep telling more lies, and the web of deception has to grow, as Huff explains:

> In January 2020, Dr. Kristen Anderson of the Scripps Research Institute had been examining the genetic characteristics of

> SARS-CoV-2. While I worked at EcoHealth, Dr. Andersen and I had been looking for ways to collaborate. In an email exchange with Anthony Fauci and Jeremy Farrar (Wellcome Trust), Anderson stated:
>
> > *The problem is that our phylogenetic analyses aren't able to answer whether the sequences are unusual at individual residues, except if they are completely off. The unusual features of the virus make up a really small part of the genome (<0.1%) so one has to look really closely at all the sequences to see that some of the features (potentially) look engineered . . . all find the genome inconsistent with expectations from evolutionary theory . . . there are still further analyses to be done, so those opinions could change.*
>
> Just four days later, Andersen gave feedback in advance of a National Academies of Sciences, Engineering, and Medicine letter that was referenced in the prestigious *The Lancet* medical journal to argue against the idea that the virus had been engineered and brand it a conspiracy theory.[15]

Huff doesn't seem to think Andersen was a bad guy (as he previously wanted to work with him), but that's what happens when there's a money race for science and that money buys a person's conscience. I believe that's why you need to have God or a Higher Power at the center of your life, or you might easily be tempted to whore yourself out to the highest bidder. You have no soul to sell. Huff continued his examination of Andersen's actions:

> Dr. Andersen called the idea that the virus was engineered "crackpot theories," stating that "engineering can mean many things and could be done for basic research or nefarious reasons, but the data conclusively show that neither was done."
>
> So I decided to examine all of Dr. Andersen's funding from NIH, and you will never guess what I found.

> Dr. Andersen's funding from NIH and NIAID dramatically increased after he reversed his position that SARS-CoV-2 had all the signatures of being engineered.
>
> In fact, his funding in 2020 increased at a rate that I have never heard of or seen in the field of emerging infectious disease research. His "continuing funding," a statistic used by government agencies that fund research, more than triples from $7,141,011 to $23,724,681.[16]

We might have finally found the value of Dr. Kristen Andersen's soul: $16,583,670.

* * *

Although the Chinese government claims that the first patient with COVID-19 became sick on December 1, 2019,[17] other credible sources have suggested a much earlier exposure, namely the October 2019 World Military Games, which were held in Wuhan, China.

An article in the *Washington Post* from June 2021, discussed the claim:

> In October 2019, more than 9,000 international athletes from more than 100 countries traveled to Wuhan, China—and many of them later got sick with Covid-19-like symptoms. But there has never been a real investigation into whether the virus that causes Covid-19 was already spreading at the Wuhan Military World Games. Now, multiple U.S. lawmakers are demanding the U.S. government begin one.
>
> The Military World Games, which are held every four years, are like the Olympics for military athletes. The games in Wuhan were the largest in the event's history, and the Chinese government went all out. The U.S. delegation came with 280 athletes and staff representing 17 sports, ranging from wrestling to golf. (Team USA brought home the bronze in the later competition.) During the two-week event, however, many of the international athletes noticed that something was amiss in the city of Wuhan. Some later described it as a "ghost town."[18]

Are we looking at some unfortunate coincidence, that the cream of the world's military forces were in Wuhan just when a deadly, engineered virus escaped from a lab? If I was suspiciously minded, it's easy to construct the following plausible scenario.

If the Chinese knew that the healthier a person, the less likely they were to be seriously affected or die from the virus, it might make the perfect vehicle for a sneak attack.

The military athletes would be the perfect carriers, first spreading the virus through their country's military forces and then to the general population of that country. The *Washington Post* article continued:

> As the Covid-19 pandemic took hold worldwide in early 2020, athletes from several countries—including France, Germany, Italy and Luxembourg—claimed publicly they had contracted what they believed to be Covid-19 at the games in Wuhan, based on their symptoms and how their illnesses spread to their loved ones. In Washington, military leaders either dismissed the idea out of hand or weren't aware of it. Meanwhile, nobody performed any antibody testing or disease tracing on these thousands of athletes. No one even attempted to find out whether the games in Wuhan was, in fact, the first international pandemic superspreader event.
>
> If more evidence was discovered, it would add to the growing body of evidence that the virus was circulating in Wuhan as early as October 2019, months before the Chinese government acknowledged it to the rest of the world. U.S. intelligence reports have said that researchers at the Wuhan Institute of Virology were hospitalized with covid-like symptoms in November 2019. But U.S. officials have said they have other information suggesting that the outbreak began even earlier.[19]

Let me ask the obvious question: Why does it appear that our military and intelligence agencies seem curiously uninterested in whether China staged a bioweapon attack/or suspiciously timed "lab leak" on the entire world?

We pay them to protect us in the United States, so shouldn't getting to the bottom of this question be their first priority?

One of the most well-respected books to come out about COVID-19 is *What Really Happened in Wuhan* by two-time Walkley Award-winning journalist Sherri Markson. A good deal of her book focuses on the allegations of Wei Jingsheng, a high-level Chinese defector who had come to the United States in 1999, but still maintained contacts with disaffected Chinese nationals.

On the question of whether COVID-19 was an intentional release, Wei seems conflicted, not having any specific evidence, but is suspicious because of his own understanding of the Chinese leaders, whom he long served, and their methods. Markson began this section of the book by writing:

> No one currently in government or intelligence I interviewed for this book holds the view coronavirus was a deliberate release. Not one person. Wei's personal view, however, is that it would be within the realm of CCP conduct to release the virus, although he has no evidence to support his theory.
>
> Wei says that before the Covid-19 outbreak there were rumors that a biological attack would be committed by terrorists against China and there needed to be training exercises for it. "In September 2019, the Chinese government held a large-scale 'anti-coronavirus exercise' in the airport and hospitals in Wuhan, which was equivalent to a military exercise," he says. "The reason is that the upcoming 2019 Military World Games may bring in the SARS and MERS like epidemic. Such a large scale exercise was far beyond the norm and aroused my vigilance . . . According to the custom of the Chinese Communist Party, this was in preparation of public opinion for a certain action—planning in advance is their traditional method."[20]

Given the closed nature of China's society, and what I've already explained about the nature of China's Communist Party, it's clear that they do not value human life in the same way most in the West do. This is circumstantial evidence, at best. "Because they could" is not evidence that they did. But it's not accurate to say there's no evidence. There is some evidence, but it is far from complete. Markson continues with Wei's speculations:

> There is no evidence that China was planning an attack or that Covid-19 was a deliberate release and no experts support this theory. It is true, however, that on September 18, 2019, there was a coronavirus drill at the Wuhan airport. The Wuhan Military Games executive committee held an emergency exercise where it simulated the responses to a new coronavirus infection found at the airport and a case of nuclear radiation discovered in luggage. "The exercise included epidemiological investigation, medical investigation, and temporary quarantine. There are multiple links such as regional setting, quarantine, case transfer, and sanitation treatment," a Chinese-language article on the Xinhua news site about the drill states. It's quite a bizarre coincidence that in September 2019, right before the coronavirus outbreak in Wuhan occurred, there was a test-drill for this exact situation at the airport.[21]

I think it's fair to say there is some smoke, but maybe we can't yet identify a fire. This could all be explained as a colossal series of missteps and a resulting attempt to cover up those mistakes. I understand why that might be the most logical explanation in the minds of many people.

However, when the best defense is that the most powerful leaders in a country are stupid and incompetent, I have trouble accepting that premise. I grant my enemies some measure of intelligence and planning, if not necessarily a conscience. Let's give Wei the last word:

> I put to Wei specifically that no one I have interviewed thinks the virus was an intentional release. What makes him think this is a possibility? "The kindness of Western scientists is worthy of respect. Therefore, they cannot understand the evil way of thinking and cannot understand the extent to which Chinese scientists exaggerate their achievements," he said. "In the past several decades, the

> CCP's capacity to seal information is hard to be understood by you Westerners. There are things that are knowledge to everyone in a small circle, that the outside world would not know even decades later. That is because anyone who releases information to the outside, even just out of that small circle, would soon be severely punished."[22]

Sometimes the things you don't see are the things you can't see. That isn't to say you're blind, but the pieces just don't add up to a recognizable picture. Many have made the claim that, after the Japanese attack on Pearl Harbor, it was clear what the Japanese were doing. But that means you have to have the imagination to believe the Japanese were about to do something that had never been done before in history: sneak a fleet thousands of miles from their home base and launch an air attack on warships anchored in a shallow bay. It was bold and daring, especially since nobody had ever done something like that before.

It was a failure of imagination, more than anything else.

Perhaps we are not suspicious enough of the Chinese, or our own government.

Maybe the evil hides in plain sight, in the laps of both sides.

* * *

How can I be so confident that the risks of manipulated bat coronaviruses were understood by the scientific community prior to the COVID-19 crisis?

Because they said so in their publications.

You see, I do this very dangerous thing called "doing my own research," or, as it used to be called when I was a kid, "reading." (I don't turn my brain over to some corporate "fact-checker.")

This is from the journal *Nature Medicine*, on November 12, 2015, five years before the world ever heard of COVID-19.

> An experiment that created a hybrid version of a bat coronavirus—one related to the virus that causes SARS (severe acute respiratory

> system)—had triggered renewed debate over whether engineering lab variants of viruses with possible pandemic potential is worth the risks.
>
> In an article published in Nature Medicine on 9 November, scientists investigated a virus called SHC014, which is found in horseshoe bats in China. The researchers created a chimaeric virus, made up of a surface protein of SHC014 and the backbone of a SARS virus that had been adapted to grow in mice and to mimic human disease. The chimaera infected human airway cells—proving that the surface protein of SHC014 has the necessary structure to bind to a key receptor on the cells and to infect them. It also caused disease in mice, but did not kill them.[23]

The following paragraphs talked about how this surface protein had been found in at least one other bat population in the wild, which raised the justifiable question of whether this bat-to-human transmission had happened in the past. I probably need to spend a little bit of time explaining what a "spike protein" is, because unless I do you're likely to miss its importance. As has been explained to me by scientists like Dr. Judy Mikovits, the spike protein is probably best thought of like the grappling hook a pirate might throw on a ship he wants to plunder, allowing his murderous crewmates to get on board.

And Judy has also informed me that the spike protein can cause a lot of trouble to the cell itself and also cause disease. In the example of a grappling hook used by a pirate, the grappling hook is simply a tool. It doesn't harm the ship itself. But the spike protein may, in some instances, be the most dangerous part of the virus.

The next three paragraphs of the *Nature Medicine* article made my blood run cold:

> But other virologists question whether the information gleaned from the experiment justifies the potential risk. Although the extent of any risk is difficult to assess, Simon Wain-Hobson, a virologist at the Pasteur Institute in Paris, points out that the researchers have created

> a novel virus that "grows remarkably well" in human cells. "If this virus escaped, nobody could project the trajectory," he says.
>
> The argument is essentially a rerun of the debate over whether to allow lab research that increases the virulence, ease of spread or host range of dangerous pathogens —what is known as 'gain of function' research. In October 2014, the US government imposed a moratorium on federal funding of such research on the viruses that cause SARS, influenza and MERS (Middle Eastern respiratory syndrome, a deadly disease caused by a virus that sporadically jumps from camels to people.)
>
> The latest study was already under way before the US moratorium began, and the US National Institutes of Health (NIH) allowed it to proceed while it was under review by the agency, says Ralph Baric, an infectious disease researcher at the University of North Carolina at Chapel Hill, a co-author of the study. The NIH eventually concluded that the work was not so risky as to fall under the moratorium, he says.[24]

This story writes itself without any effort on my part. They engineered a bat virus that infected humans remarkably well, and even the brightest people in the field were saying in effect, "Holy bat guano! If this gets out of the lab, it could be bad news for the human race."

They want us to feel safe, right? These are smart people debating big and important issues. Of course, they'll choose the right course.

But in December 2017, the National Institutes of Health (the Francis Collins/Anthony Fauci cabal) rescinded the order prohibiting "gain of function" research[25] and a new government apparatus was put in place, the "Framework for Guiding Funding Decisions about Proposed Research Involving Enhanced Potential Pandemic Pathogens."

That doesn't sound terrifying at all: "Enhanced Potential Pandemic Pathogens." This is how the Framework opened:

> **Section I. Purpose and Principles**
> Research involving potential pandemic pathogens (PPPs) is essential to protecting global health and security. However, there are biosafety and biosecurity risks associated with undertaking such research that must be adequately considered and appropriately mitigated in order to help safely realize the potential benefits. The HHS Framework for Guiding Funding Decisions about Proposed Research Involving Enhanced Potential Pandemic Pathogens (HHS P3CO Framework) is intended to guide HHS funding decisions on individual proposed research that is reasonably anticipated to create, transfer, or use enhanced PPPs.
>
> The HHS P3CO Framework is responsive to and in accordance with the recommended Policy Guidance for Departmental Development of review Mechanisms for Potential Pandemic pathogen Care and Oversight issued by OSTP on January 9, 2017 and supersedes the previous Framework for Guiding Department of Health and Human Services Funding Decisions about Research Proposals with the Potential for Generating Highly Pathogenic Avian Influenza H5N1 Viruses that are Transmissible Among Mammals by Respiratory Droplets 2.
>
> The HHS P3CO Framework ensures a multi-disciplinary, department-level prefunding review and evaluation of proposed research meeting the scope outlined herein to help inform funding agency decisions. In so doing, the HHS P3CO Framework seeks to preserve the benefits of life sciences research involving enhanced PPPs while minimizing potential biosafety and biosecurity risks.[26]

This is not science fiction; it's science terror brought to you in boring bureaucratic language. They're admitting, "Hey, we might be creating new bird flu viruses that can spread to humans by "respiratory droplets (known as "sneezing or coughing" to us regular folks in flyover country)!"

And if you find yourself saying, "Alex, why are you getting so worked up about a 'Potential Pandemic Pathogen?' I know it sounds a little scary, but I'm sure if you do a little more research, it won't seem so terrifying."

In section II, they're helpful enough to give a definition of a "Potential Pandemic Pathogen":

> **Section II. Scope and Definitions**
> For the purposes of this HHS P3CO Framework:
> A. A potential pandemic pathogen (PPP) is a pathogen that satisfies both of the following:
>
> 1. It is likely highly transmissible and likely capable of wide and uncontrollable spread in human populations; and
> 2. It is likely highly virulent and likely to cause significant morbidity and/or mortality in humans.
>
> B. An enhanced PPP is defined as a PPP resulting from the enhancement of the transmissibility and/or virulence of a pathogen. Enhanced PPPs do not include naturally occurring pathogens that are circulating in or have been recovered from nature, regardless of their pandemic potential.[27]

I know sometimes you may feel you need to be a lawyer to read that kind of language, but I've kept it fairly short. The key points are that, to be a "potential pandemic pathogen," it has to be "highly transmissible," capable of "wide and uncontrollable spread in human populations," virulent, and likely resulting in "significant morbidity and/or mortality in humans." In other words, a "potential pandemic pathogen" is like a biological atom bomb.

Taking that "potential pandemic pathogen" and enhancing it is like turning that atom bomb into a hydrogen bomb, or perhaps the mythical "cobalt bomb" (proposed by nuclear physicist Leo Szilard) I worried about as a kid, which was supposedly so powerful it could destroy the entire world. They might just enhance the transmissibility of the virus, or its ability to kill you, and shockingly, they might do both! Isn't science great?

Here's what I think is clear.

Scientists created an enhanced bat coronavirus, which was capable of affecting humans, particularly their respiratory tract. The lab mice they tested it on showed evidence of infection, but they were probably healthier on average than the typical American. That is, the mice weren't significantly overweight, on the American average of four prescription medications, or elderly.

I think we probably said to China, "Here, why don't you take this virus and do your own experiments on it?"

China may have had some nefarious plans of their own (my opinion) or their lab may simply have had bad containment, and it just happened to escape during the Military World Games, or sometime after.

The government of China had information on us that we didn't want to come out, and vice-versa, so there was a mutual interest in both sides saying, "Hey, we don't know where it came from! Maybe a pangolin and a bat were star-crossed lovers and one of them ended up in a Chinese soup."

Then the news media in both countries, as well as the scientists, piled on like Dr. Fauci and Dr. Collins did in saying the idea of a lab leak was nothing but a crazy conspiracy theory dreamed up by somebody like Alex Jones.

* * *

Did you think I'd forgotten about the mad monk squad of DARPA, who received this original crazy proposal?

> **Reasons for Rejection**
>
> The Biological Technologies Office of DARPA reviewed the EcoHealth Alliance DEFUSE proposal and the Evaluation Reports and decided it was "**selectable.**" In doing so, two out of three reviewers considered the aim of preempting "zoonotic spillover through reduction of viral shedding in the bat caves" as of interest to DARPA. These reviewers assessed the EHA and Collaborators team and concluded that:
>
> - They have plenty of prior experience.
> - They have access to Yunnan caves where bats are infected with SARSr viruses.
> - They have carried out past surveillance work.

- They have developed geo-based risk maps of zoonotic hotspots.
- Their proposed experimental work is logical and can validate molecular and evolutionary models.
- Their proposed preemption approaches can rapidly be validated using bat and "batenized" mouse models.

However, the Biological Technologies Office did not recommend it be funded **at that time** because significant weaknesses were identified:

1. The proposal is considered to potentially involve GoF/DURC research because they propose to synthesize spike glycoproteins which bind to human cell receptors and insert them into SARSr-CoV backbones to assess whether they can cause SARS-like disease.
2. However, the proposal does not mention or assess potential risks of Gain of Function (GoF) research.
3. Nor does the proposal mention or assess Dual Use Research of Concern (DURC) issues, and this fails to present a DURC risk mitigation plan.
4. The proposal hardly addresses or discusses ethical, legal, and social issues (ELSI).
5. The proposal fails to discuss problems with the proposed vaccine delivery systems caused by the known issues of variability in vaccine dosage.
6. The proposal did not provide sufficient information about how EHA would use any data obtained and how they would model development or perform any necessary statistical analysis.
7. The proposal did not explain clearly how EHA will take advantage of their previous work, nor how that previous work could be extended.
8. The proposal failed to clearly assess how it would deploy and validate the "TA2 preemption methods" in the wild. This refers to carrying out experiments with effective immune boosting molecules and delivery techniques via FEA aerosolization mechanism at one test and two control bat cave sites in Yunnan, China (PARC, EHA, WIV).

9. The proposal does not address concerns about these vaccines not being able to protect against the wide variety of coronaviruses in bat caves which are constantly evolving, due to insufficient epitope coverage.

DRASTIC independently assesses that the tone of the proposal (see for instance the 'our cave complex') and the deep suggested involvement of some of the WIV parties (Shi Zhengli employed half-time for 3 years—paid via the grant—and invited to DARPA headquarters at Arlington), may not have helped either—especially in the absence of any DURC risk mitigation program.

It is clear that the proposed DEFUSE project led by Peter Daszak could have put local communities at risk by failing to consider the following issues:

- Gain of Function
- Dual Use Research of Concern
- Vaccine epitope coverage
- Regulatory requirements
- ELSI (ethical, legal, and social issues)
- Data usage

END[28]

It's difficult to imagine a more devastating rejection letter from a military/intelligence research agency known for taking risks. But that is exactly what was given by DARPA to Peter Daszak's proposal from EcoHealth Alliance.

Let's see if we can put all of this into perspective.

We know from Dr. Andrew Huff, the former vice president and senior scientist at EcoHealth Alliance, that one of the "alliances" they likely had was with the CIA.

We see from the DARPA rejection that they were terrified by the proposal to "synthesize spike glycoproteins which bind to human cell receptors and insert them into SARSr-CoV backbones to assess whether they can cause SARS-like disease" and did not think Daszak had properly considered the risk of "gain of function," the possible deadly results from these experiments, or "Dual Use Risk of Concern." He also had not provided any risk mitigation plan.

DARPA did not believe problems with the vaccine delivery system had been addressed.

DARPA could not understand how the data would be used.

DARPA was skeptical that the proposed mitigation programs at the caves would work.

Perhaps the most serious of the criticisms leveled by DARPA relates to the potentially compromised loyalty and judgment of Peter Daszak. They were troubled by the fact that he referred to the Yunnan caves in China as "our cave complex," as well as the fact that DARPA was being asked to pay half the salary of a Chinese virologist (Shi Zhengli) and that she had been invited to DARPA headquarters in Arlington, Virginia.

It is likely that DARPA leadership was unaware that EcoHealth Alliance may have had an alliance with the CIA, and that Daszak probably believed this gave him *carte blanche* to show this Chinese researcher all around the DARPA facilities.

It can be difficult to understand Daszak's game plan, whether it was executed with the full understanding of our intelligence agencies or whether this was something he cooked up on his own and got people to agree to without a full understanding of the dangers of his scheme.

But in any event, Peter Daszak, more than any person on the planet, likely bears the greatest responsibility for the more than six million people who lost their lives in the COVID-19 pandemic.

* * *

We need to spend some time with Chinese scientist Shi Zhengli, often referred to as "bat woman" for her work with bat coronaviruses.[29]

This is how the *New York Times* described the increasingly embattled position in which she found herself in June 2021, as questions continued to be raised about whether SARS-CoV-2 escaped from the Wuhan Institute of Virology.

> To a growing chorus of American politicians and scientists, she is the key to whether the world will ever learn if the virus behind the devastating Covid-19 pandemic escaped from a Chinese lab. To the Chinese government and public, she is a hero of the country's success in curbing the epidemic and a victim of malicious conspiracy theories.
>
> Shi Zhengli, a top Chinese virologist, is once again at the center of clashing narratives about her research on coronaviruses at a state lab in Wuhan, the city where the pandemic first emerged.
>
> The idea that the virus may have escaped from a lab has been widely dismissed by scientists as implausible and shunned by others for its connection with former President Donald J. Trump. But fresh scrutiny from the Biden administration and calls for greater candor from prominent scientists have brought the theory back to the fore.[30]

Remember when I said that it's fine to read mainstream news media, like the *New York Times* or the *Washington Post*, if you understand that while they may not tell the truth initially, if you read and pay attention long enough, they might eventually tell the truth? This article is a prime example of that view: If you read it with a critical eye, it contains many startling admissions. In other words, if Dr. Shi Zhengli gave these same answers in a court of law, she'd likely be found guilty by a jury in a few hours and be sent to jail for a long time.

But first, the *New York Times* had to give the defense to Dr. Shi, courtesy of Dr. Robert Gallo, who was famously forced to leave government service for trying to steal credit for the discovery of the HIV virus from French researcher Dr. Luc Montagnier, who was eventually awarded the Nobel Prize for this research in 2008.[31]

> In less polarized times, Dr. Shi was a symbol of China's scientific progress, at the forefront of research into emerging viruses.
>
> She led expeditions into caves to collect samples from bats and guano, to learn how viruses jump from animals to humans. In 2019,

> she was among 109 scientists elected to the American Academy of Microbiology for her contributions to the field.
>
> "She's a stellar scientist—extremely careful, with a rigorous work ethic," said Dr. Robert C. Gallo, director of the Institute of Human Virology at the University of Maryland School of Medicine.[32]

The *New York Times* reporters covering this story gave us the positive information about Dr. Shi, but then like good attorneys, they listened and provided their readers with the answers from Dr. Shi that showed that the claims leveled against her were likely to be true.

> But some of her most notable findings have since drawn the greatest scrutiny. In recent years, Dr. Shi began experimenting on bat coronaviruses by genetically modifying them to see how they behave.
>
> In 2017, she and her colleagues at the Wuhan Lab published a paper about an experiment in which they created new hybrid bat coronaviruses by mixing and matching parts of several existing ones—including at least one that was nearly transmissible to humans—in order to study their ability to infect and replicate in human cells.
>
> Proponents of this type of research say it helps society prepare for future outbreaks. Critics say the risks of creating dangerous new pathogens may outweigh potential benefits.[33]

How crazy does all this sound? They are admitting out in the open that they're creating potentially dangerous new pathogens and that these pathogens may devastate human society. But it's all presented in a relatively bloodless, "Well, on one hand . . . and yet on the other," type of justification. But the price of getting it wrong is unleashing a deadly global pathogen.

Now, here's where the article gets really nuts, and I wonder how much of a fight went on between the reporters (who generally seemed interested in getting to the bottom of this very important question) and the editors of the *New York Times*.

> The picture has been complicated by new questions about whether American government funding that went to Dr. Shi's work supported controversial gain-of-function research. The Wuhan Institute received around $600,000 in grant money from the United States government, through an American nonprofit called EcoHealth Alliance. The National Institutes of Health said it had not approved funding for the nonprofit to conduct gain-of-function research on coronaviruses that would have made them more infectious or lethal.
>
> Dr. Shi, in an emailed response to questions, argued that her experiments differed from gain-of-function work because she did not set out to make a virus more dangerous, but to understand how it might jump between species.
>
> "My lab has never conducted or cooperated in conducting GOF experiments that enhance the virulence of viruses," she said.[34]

In any other situation, this would have been an acknowledgment that, "Hell, yeah, we were doing gain of function research." How else is one supposed to interpret the claim that "her experiments differed from gain-of-function work because she did not set out to make a virus more dangerous, but to understand how it might jump between species." It sounds to me that she was performing whatever procedures necessary to make the virus transmissible to humans, but she was doing this to see how it could happen, not to make the virus more deadly. What is left unsaid, though, is that she might very well have made the virus more deadly, even though that wasn't her intention. (Kind of like your teenagers choosing to throw a football around inside the house, and then when they break a lamp or window, they escape punishment by saying, "I didn't mean to do that!") Sometimes, the very act of performing a dangerous act is enough to place blame when an accident happens.

On the question of how much money the United States government, and Anthony Fauci's National Institute of Allergy and Infectious Diseases, paid to the Wuhan Institute of Virology, I present this article from *Newsweek*, from April 2020.

> But just last year, the National Institute of Allergy and Infectious Diseases, the organization led by Dr. Fauci, funded scientists at the Wuhan Institute of Virology and other institutions for work on gain-of-function research on bat coronaviruses.
>
> In 2019, with the backing of NIAID, the National Institutes of Health committed $3.7 million over six years for research that included some gain-of-function work. The program followed another $3.7 million, 5-year project for collecting and studying bat coronaviruses, which ended in 2019, bringing the total to $7.4 million.[35]

This is the kind of information that should be at the front of every article about coronavirus deaths around the world. All it would need to be is a single paragraph, maybe like the community notes that Elon Musk now has on X/Twitter.

It would read something like, "Although not proven, any person who is not an idiot suspects that the bat coronavirus research approved by Anthony Fauci's National Institute of Allergy and Infectious Diseases and gain of function research performed at the Wuhan Institute of Virology in China are responsible for the global outbreak." The *Newsweek* article was exceptionally clear in describing this research.

> The NIH research consisted of two parts. The first part began in 2014 and involved surveillance of bat coronaviruses and had a budget of $3.7 million. The program funded Shi Zhengli, a virologist at the Wuhan Lab, and other researchers to investigate and catalogue bat coronaviruses in the wild. This part of the project was completed in 2019.
>
> A second phase of the project, beginning that year, included additional surveillance work but also gain of function research for the purpose of understanding how bat coronaviruses could mutate to attack humans. The project was run by EcoHealth Alliance, a non-profit research group, under the direction of President Peter Daszak, an expert on disease ecology. NIH canceled the project just this

> past Friday, April 24, *Politico* reported. Daszak did not immediately respond to *Newsweek* requests for comment.
>
> The project proposal states: "We will use S protein data sequence, infectious clone technology, in vitro and in vivo infection experiments and analysis of receptor binding to test the hypothesis that % divergence thresholds in S protein sequences predict spillover potential."[36]

The article went on to note that spillover potential "refers to the ability of a virus to jump from animals to humans," and that SARS-CoV-2 was "adept at binding to the ACE2 receptor in human lungs and other organs."[37]

Does this begin to give a flavor of the relationship between the Wuhan Institute of Virology and the US health establishment, with Anthony Fauci's National Institute of Allergy and Infectious Diseases right in the middle of it?

Think of somebody you've worked with for six years.

Chances are it's a pretty close relationship, especially if you had to go to the other side of the world to make it work.

Maybe it's understandable why Fauci didn't want the country asking too many questions about his long-term relationship with the Chinese scientists, even if they may have also been keeping secrets from him.

* * *

How did President Trump handle the COVID-19 pandemic?

Really bad.

His instincts were good, but he didn't follow them. In the end, he listened to the Deep State establishment, people like Fauci; Alex Azar, head of Health and Human Services; and Scott Gottlieb, head of the Food and Drug Administration (both former lobbyists for Big Pharma).

Early in the crisis, Trump was skeptical of the information he was receiving from the COVID-19 Task Force, which was why in April 2020 a call was placed to Dr. Paul Alexander, who at the time was advising the World Health Organization and the Pan American Health Organization as an evidence synthesizer for the COVID pandemic, as well as working for the Infectious Diseases Society of America.

As Paul recalls in his book, *Presidential Takedown: How Anthony Fauci, the CDC, NIH, and the WHO Conspired to Overthrow President Trump*, coauthored with my coauthor on this book, Kent Heckenlively:

> After saying hello to the caller, my wife was quiet for a few minutes. I wondered if it was some solicitor with a really good pitch, because she usually hangs up rather quickly with one of those calls, but she didn't.
>
> Instead, in a rather quiet voice she said, "Paul, it's someone saying they are talking from or on behalf of the White House and US government and they want to talk to you."
>
> I took the phone from her and said, "This is Dr. Paul Alexander," not quite believing her.
>
> The person speaking on behalf of the White House, sounding credible enough, identified himself and the nature of his call, and then said, "We know of some things you've said publicly and read some of the recent papers you've published on different issues. And that's gotten the attention of persons in the Oval Office. And they wanted to know if you'd be interested in joining the administration and having a seat at the table."
>
> "Are you guys joking?" I asked, still not believing this was real.
>
> The man on the other end of the line replied, "Well, no. We want to know if you want to have a seat at the table. We've done our study of you. And we realized you could be an asset to the administration. You're somebody who can be trusted, and we like your technical competence. And we want you to join us."
>
> I think it's important for the reader to understand what I say next because it best explains my frame of mind as I began my work.
>
> "Are you saying the task force can't be trusted?" I asked. I tend to be very blunt and brutally honest, especially in these types of situations.

> There was a pause on the other end of the line. "The president wants to expand the table with people he trusts and who are optimally competent."
>
> "So he doesn't trust them?" I asked, pressing the question again.
>
> "I wouldn't put it that way," he replied. "He doesn't feel he's being fully, properly, and optimally served by the present members of the task force. We want other people in those meetings, giving their insight. If we're all in agreement, we're good. If not, well, we have to figure out the next steps. Will you join us?"[38]

This passage fills me with many mixed emotions. On the one hand, it highlights the things I loved about Trump, like his willingness to have different thinkers in the room—sometimes a veritable rogue's gallery of outcasts, the same kind of patriots who made this country.

And on the other, this is the man who agreed to "Fifteen Days to Slow the Spread," which turned into years of lockdowns, harming children, and devastating small businesses, as well as sanctioning an insane "Warp Speed" COVID vaccine development and doing nothing when his public health establishment went after therapeutics, killing hundreds of thousands of Americans and millions around the world. He had the pirates and the renegades at the table, and he sided with the establishment.

That's the way I see it.

Is it an excuse to say he's simply one of those people of a certain age who thinks of vaccines as some kind of a "miracle-moon shot" and as much as he's listened to stories of vaccine damage, he couldn't quite pull the trigger and investigate what they're doing to people?

I know people who are supporting Trump, despite this glaring flaw, and those who say his failure during COVID-19 means they could never support him again.

I understand both positions, and I don't judge.

I am genuinely uncertain how I will vote in 2024.

What I am certain of is that I will keep telling you the truth as I see it. This is what Dr. Alexander wrote about the viper's nest Trump found himself in:

> They—Dr. Fauci, Dr. Birx, and the Deep State technocrats at CDC, NIH, FDA, etc.—lied to him about the lockdowns, they lied to him about therapeutics, and they lied to him about the vaccines. They collectively lied to him daily and conspired to make the United States ungovernable, unmanageable, chaotic, distraught, and a disaster. This was told to me bluntly by officials in government who I would say are part of the Deep State bureaucracy. They, Dr. Fauci and Dr. Birx and others, ensured the lockdowns were long, hardened, painful, and destructive so that President Trump would be blamed. The accrued harms and death from the lockdown policies rests at their feet.
>
> I tried to tell the task force about the poor safety testing of the vaccines, so that there would be a permanent record of what had been done.
>
> Nobody listened.[39]

Everything about that passage makes sense and rings true to me. Trump was in a tough position, perhaps the toughest position any president ever found himself in.

And as for those who still defend Trump as acting as best as he could during the crisis, let me provide this piece of information about the near-absolute control people like Anthony Fauci and Francis Collins had over the scientific establishment.

> NIH received $41.6 billion in FY [Fiscal Year] 2020. Of this amount, $30.8 billion was awarded to 56 [&] 169 new and renewed meritorious extramural grants (excludes research and development contracts.) This investment was up $1.3 billion from FY 2019 (4.4 percent increase), with 1,157 more grants funded (2.1 percent increase). These awards were made to 2,650 academic universities, hospitals, and other organizations throughout the U.S. and internationally.[40]

Dr. Francis Collins, head of the NIH, and Dr. Anthony Fauci, head of the National Institute of Allergy and Infectious Diseases (and the highest paid individual in the US government), had more than $30 billion a year to hand out to their friends in science.

That buys a lot of influence in science.

By comparison, in the 2020 election, both political parties spent only a combined $5.7 billion dollars to elect a US president.[41]

Collins and Fauci had an essential slush fund to buy influence in science that, on a yearly basis, was more than five times greater than the amount we spend to elect a president of the United States every four years.

And can we say that Dr. Francis Collins and Dr. Anthony Fauci acted honorably during the COVID-19 crisis, promoting reasonable scientific debate, especially when it came to dissenting voices?

We cannot.

Probably the most vivid example of their iron-fisted control over science was the attack Collins and Fauci launched on three researchers—Martin Kulldorff from Harvard University, Sunetra Gupta from Oxford University, and Jay Bhattacharya from Stanford University. These three had created something called the Great Barrington Declaration, which argued that the evidence favored "focused protection" of high-risk populations, such as the elderly, those with chronic health conditions, and the obese, but that the rest of the population, the healthy working class and professionals, as well as children, should continue with their regular lives.

This is what the editors of the *Wall Street Journal* wrote in a December 2021 opinion piece when it was revealed that Collins and Fauci had colluded in a scheme to sideline these experts.

> In public, Anthony Fauci and Francis Collins urged Americans to "follow the science." In private, the two sainted public-health officials schemed to quash dissenting views from top scientists. That's the troubling, but fair conclusion from emails obtained recently via the Freedom of Information Act by the American Institute for Economic Research.
>
> The tale unfolded in October 2020 after the launch of the Great Barrington Declaration, a statement by Harvard's Martin Kulldorff, Oxford's Sunetra Gupta, and Stanford's Jay Bhattacharya against

> blanket pandemic lockdowns. They favored a policy of what they called "focused protection" of high-risk populations such as the elderly or those with medical conditions. Thousands of scientists signed the declaration—if they were able to learn about it. We tried to give it some election in these pages.[42]

In any other instance, this attack on fellow scientists would have resulted in Fauci and Collins being driven from science and having their names forever listed among the greatest traitors to our nation, like Revolutionary War turncoat Benedict Arnold.

But $30 billion a year buys one a lot of friends in science.

The editorial board of the *Wall Street Journal* continued its condemnation of Fauci and Collins.

> Focused protection of nursing homes and other high-risk populations remains the policy road not taken during the pandemic. Perhaps this strategy wouldn't have prevailed if a debate had been allowed. But it isn't enough to repeat, as Dr. Collins did on Fox News Sunday, that advocates are "fringe epidemiologists who really did not have the credentials," and that "hundreds of thousands would have died if we followed that strategy."
>
> More than 800,000 Americans have died as much of the country followed the strategy of Drs. Collins and Fauci, and that's not counting the cost in lost livelihoods, shuttered businesses, untreated illnesses, mental illness from isolation, and the incalculable anguish of seeing loved ones die alone without the chance for a family to say goodbye.
>
> Rather than try to manipulate public opinion, the job of health officials is to offer their best scientific advice. They shouldn't act like politicians or censors, and when they do, they squander the public's trust.[43]

I believe all of this is true.

Trump was like a lion surrounded by a pack of wolves.

And yet, he sold himself to us as the meanest SOB on the block, able to see through the lies and do the right thing.

COVID-19 was the hill a worthy president should have fought and died upon.

* * *

What was the result of our lockdown policy?

It hurt our children. This is from a September 2022 article by the *New York Times* on the effect of the lockdown on American students.

> This year, for the first time since the National Assessment of Educational Progress tests began tracking student achievement in the 1970s, 9-year-olds lost ground in math, and scores in reading fell by the largest margin in more than 30 years.
>
> The declines spanned almost all races and income levels and were markedly worse for the lowest performing students. While top performers in the 90th percentile showed a modest drop—three points in math—students in the bottom 10th percentile dropped by 12 points in math, four times the impact.
>
> "I was taken aback by the scope and magnitude of the decline," said Peggy G. Carr, Commissioner of the National Center for Education Statistics, the federal agency that administered the exam earlier this year. The tests were given to a national sample of 14,800 9-year-olds and were compared with the results of tests taken by the same age group in early 2020, just before the pandemic took hold in the United States.[44]

All of this was unnecessary. A paper in the *Journal of the American Medical Association* from June 2020 detailed not only the relatively few children who had come down with the virus, but also a possible explanation as to why this was true.

> Children account for less than 2% of identified cases of coronavirus disease 2019 (COVID-19). It is hypothesized that the lower risk among children is due to differential expression of angiotensin-converting enzyme (ACE2), the receptor that severe acute respiratory syndrome coronavirus 2 (SARS-CoV-2) uses for host entry. We investigated ACE2 gene expression in nasal epithelium of children and adults.[45]

It's probably best to imagine the ACE2 receptor on a cell as a flower that needs to be open so a bee can land on it to collect nectar. If the flower hasn't bloomed, then it doesn't make any sense for the bee to land on it since it can't collect any nectar.

Imagine the SARS-CoV-2 virus as a bee buzzing around your body, but instead of looking for a flower, it's looking for a cell with an ACE2 receptor active and open, so it can gain access to the cell. In children, for the most part, the ACE2 receptor is not open. It's why children by and large avoided the infection, and when they did become sick, their symptoms were generally mild.

> The results from this study show age-dependent expression of ACE2 in nasal epithelium, the first point of contact for SARS-CoV-2 and the human body. Corviate-adjusted models showed that the positive association between ACE2 gene expression was independent of sex and asthma. Lower ACE2 expression in children relative to adults may help explain who COVID-19 is less prevalent in children.[46]

The simplest way to understand this research is to realize that children, by and large, cannot get severely sick with COVID-19 because the virus cannot get into significant numbers of the cells and replicate. Low viral numbers in the body mean that the innate immune system will deal with the virus fairly quickly, usually in a few days.

How much did the failure to implement early treatment affect the hospitalization and death rate from COVID-19? This is an article from the Brownstone Institute written by Dr. Paul Alexander, Trump's former senior pandemic advisor, which sought to answer that question.

> The evidence accumulated very early on in the pandemic that the use of sequenced multi-drug therapeutics (SDMT) under physician guidance was beneficial and that some medications were safe and effective. We refer to repurposed therapeutics that have been regulatory approved and have been used in some instances for decades for other illnesses.
>
> We have extensively written and published treatment algorithms and protocols as well as evidence of the benefit of early outpatient (ambulatory) treatment of SARS-CoV-2 virus and the consequent disease COVID-19. With highly targeted and SMDT regimens that include early application of antiviral drugs, combined with corticosteroids and anti-platelet/anti-thrombotic/anti-clotting therapeutics, the risk of hospitalization is significantly reduced by as much as 85 to 95%, and the risk of death is eliminated for high-risk patients and younger individuals presenting with severe symptoms.
>
> COVID-19 presents as either a mild flu-like condition (asymptomatic or mild symptoms) or more serious illness in those at high risk. A small fraction of persons infected with COVID virus progress to more serious illness (typically elderly with underlying medical conditions, obese or younger with underlying medical conditions/risk factors). The complex and multidimensional pathophysiology of life-threatening COVID-19 illness including viral mediated organ damage, cytokine storm, and thrombosis warrants early interventions to address all components of the illness.[47]

According to the World Health Organization, as of June 7, 2023, there have been 6,941,095 deaths from COVID-19, with the worldwide case total being 767,750,853.[48] While Dr. Alexander claims that early intervention would have essentially eliminated deaths, let's take the most conservative number he gave for the benefits of early intervention, which was an 85 percent reduction in hospitalizations, and use that as a proxy for reductions in death.

That means early intervention would likely have saved at least 5,899,930 lives, with a reduced global death toll of 1,041,164 deaths.

What has been the result of the COVID-19 vaccines?

Many have raised the question of whether these vaccines are causing an increase in excess deaths, as suggested by this January 10, 2023 article from the BBC with the title, "Excess Deaths in 2022 Among Worst in 50 Years."

> More than 650,000 deaths were registered in the UK in 2022—9% more than in 2019.
>
> This represents one of the largest excess death levels outside the pandemic in 50 years.
>
> Though far below peak pandemic levels, it has prompted questions about why more people are dying than normal . . .
>
> Covid is still killing people, but is involved in fewer deaths now than at the start of the pandemic. Roughly 38,000 deaths involved Covid in 2022 compared with more than 95,000 in 2020.
>
> We are still seeing more deaths overall than would be expected based on recent history.[49]

Of course, the BBC article went on to speculate that the excess deaths were due to people missing medical appointments (and there may be some contribution from that), but as for me, I suspect the vaccine is harming a large number of people we are not currently counting.

I am particularly intrigued by the investigation of the Pfizer documents currently being spearheaded by Dr. Naomi Wolf. Dr. Wolf is the author of seven national bestsellers, has associated with the "third wave" of the feminist movement, and advised President Bill Clinton in 1996, as well as Vice President Al Gore during the 2000 election. In the years since 2000, she has made an interesting political evolution, coming to side with conservatives on many issues, while still retaining her strong feminist beliefs. You can find her excellent writing on Substack: "Outspoken with

Dr. Naomi Wolf." This is what she said at a recent event, as reported by the *Daily Clout*:

> "One thing people have been able to do for thousands of years is to have sex and have babies without any intervention or help from anyone else. It's a tremendous way that the human race is self-reliant—that it can survive catastrophe. Well the Tech Bros. and probably China want to take that away from us. This is clear in the Pfizer documents."
>
> "There's a section of the Pfizer documents in which Pfizer breaks down the adverse events and concludes that women sustain 72% of them," she continued. "And of those—and these are Pfizer's words—16% are quote-unquote 'reproductive disorders' compared to 0.49% for men. So they're very focused on reproduction, female reproduction."
>
> "It's my belief that they were trying to disrupt especially female reproduction," Dr. Wolf determined. "And the question is, how do I know that? And the answer is from the structure of what they looked at. Again, I'm a literary critic, but this is a mystery novel in which the question is, how do we stop women from having healthy babies? That's the story of the Pfizer documents . . ."
>
> Dr. Wolf detailed "super-strange things" with the Pfizer documents, such as "ten-year-old girls menstruating on first being injected" and "long-post menopausal women in their 80s and 90s bleeding again after being injected."[50]

While some may dispute her assertions that the pattern of what they looked at suggests what they wanted to do, I find myself in agreement with her that this seems to be part of a depopulation agenda. Further in the article she says:

> "So now it's 2023," mourned Dr. Wolf, as those fertility problems have come to fruition. "Igor Chudov compared databases in countries around the world. There are a million missing babies in Europe.

> They never got born. [There are] double the number of miscarriages and spontaneous abortions in Scotland [and a] 13% to 20% drop in live births around the world. [There are] two or three times the number of spontaneous abortions and miscarriages in Tel Aviv as before. And so on around the world. And now we know why. Now we know the mechanism."
>
> "It's not just an attack on us. It's not just a mass murder, which is the language that Ofcom obejected to, but it's an existential attack. And think about it chronologically. I'm very worried that a source in Britain said they wanted to embargo this information for 20 years. Because I'm like, what do they expect to have happened in 20 years?"
>
> "I think this is the tip of the iceberg," she continued. "We've [DailyClout/War Room Volunteers] got a report on turbo cancers, we've got a report on strokes, we've got a report on liver damage, kidney damage."
>
> "I don't want to depress you, but all around you are people who are suffering from illnesses," mourned Dr. Wolf. "None of their doctors are telling them that these illnesses are in the Pfizer documents as side effects and now we understand the mechanisms of them."[51]

Did I ever think I'd be on the same side about the global depopulation agenda as a former Clinton and Gore adviser?

I did not, but I am happy to have Dr. Wolf in the fight.

* * *

Am I going to be forced to say something nice about the alien robot boy, Mark Zuckerberg?

I'd encouraged you to be alert to any possible movement away from darkness among our enemies, so I guess I have to be consistent, right?

On June 9, 2023, in an interview on the *Lex Fridman Podcast*, Mark Zuckerberg (CEO of Facebook, now Meta) lamented the censorship decisions he made during the COVID-19 lockdown. In some ways it made me want to scream even louder, but maybe that's not the most positive reaction. I'll let you decide.

> The Facebook CEO said that the medical establishment "often waffled" on COVID claims, and requested the removal of material that ended up being debatable or true.
>
> "Just take some of the stuff around COVID earlier in the pandemic where there were real health implications, but there hadn't been time to fully vet a bunch of the scientific assumptions," said Zuckerberg.
>
> "Unfortunately, I think a lot of the kind of establishment on that kind of stuff waffled on a bunch of facts and asked for a bunch of things to be censored that, in retrospect, ended up being more debatable or true. That stuff is really tough, right? It really undermines trust."[52]

On the one hand, I guess I should be happy that Zuckerberg has come to the realization that the medical establishment lied to him or put forth dubious assertions, which only served to strengthen their financial interests. But the point I've made time and again in this book is that *nobody* should have the power to censor public debate.

There has never been a time in human history when the censors have been the good guys.

The challenge in any society is not how to restrain the people, but how to restrain the government or powerful interests.

God made man in His own image, not corporations, governments, or activist groups.

Nobody has been a more eloquent voice in this debate than Robert Kennedy Jr., as shown in the November 2021 speech he gave at the Ron Paul Institute and their conference on "Pandemic and the Road to Totalitarianism."

> Kennedy described a recent simulation, Event 201, a pandemic "tabletop exercise" that simulated a global pandemic nearly identical to

COVID. The event took place in October 2019 at the Johns Hopkins Center for Health Security.

Dr. Tom Ingelsby, director of the Center for Health Security, facilitated the simulation. Bill Gates of the Bill and Melinda Gates Foundation, global health officers and people from social media groups, large pharmaceutical companies and global corporation attended or sent representatives.

Kennedy said:

"What were they simulating? They were simulating a pandemic, but they weren't simulating a medical response to that pandemic. They were simulating a militarized response. How do you use that pandemic to, particularly in that Event 201, to impose censorship globally? And that's what they were modeling."

Describing CIA operations and organized mind control programs at top universities, conducted on "expendable" subjects such as the military and incarcerated, Kennedy said the same techniques are used in today's lockdowns:

"The most potent technique, incidentally, that they learned again and again, and again—more potent than physical torture—was isolation . . . And they did this in sensory deprivation tanks . . . and also just locking people in solitary confinement.

"You can get [people] to do almost anything you want after a certain period of time. It will drive them mad, because we're social animals, we're social beings. And when you tear the social fabric, it makes people desperate, fearful, and obedient to do anything."[53]

We are meant to live in community with each other, sharing our thoughts and feelings. When tyrants seek to control society, they do it by separating people, sowing division amongst us, and hoping we will choose to self-isolate.

But don't succumb to their drug of division.

Every person should make a declaration that they will listen to different opinions with an open heart and mind, point out any errors of fact or interpretation they see, and be without fear in deciding whether a good argument has been made.

The only remedy for speech with which you do not agree is to make a better argument.

* * *

More than three years after COVID-19 caused the lockdown of our country, we started to get information we should have had in the first three days, such as the names of the first three people infected and what they shared, such as maybe a fondness for "bat soup."

That was not what they shared; it was, instead, a similar place of employment, the Wuhan Institute of Virology. From the *New York Post* on June 13, 2023.

> Scientists conducting research on novel coronaviruses at the Wuhan Institute of Virology were the first humans to contract COVID-19, according to a new report.
>
> "Patients zero" included Ben Hu, Ping Yu and Yan Zhu—scientists researching SARS-like viruses at the institute, according to an investigation by journalists Michael Shellenberger and Matt Taibi published on the Substack newsletter Public.
>
> The three scientists were researching "gain of function" experiments with the virus—which increases the infectiousness and makes pathogens stronger in order to better understand their dangers—when they became sick in the fall of 2019, multiple US government officials reportedly told the journalists.[54]

What would have been the effect of this information coming to light in March or April 2020? It would have rightly informed the world of the origin of the virus, shone a spotlight on dangerous scientific practices, and probably kept Trump in the White House. Everybody in America would have been calling it the "China virus" because it would have been accurate.

And do you know who would not have led the COVID response?

Not Anthony Fauci, who approved this dangerous research.

Anybody associated with Fauci would have had a bad smell, and we might have had an effective response to the virus, including the use of easily administered therapeutics like hydroxychloroquine and ivermectin, dramatically reducing the death rate.

Was all of this a "cover your ass" move, or does it suggest something much more nefarious?

Is there a "I was just trying to keep some things secret" defense to mass murder?

I'll consult with my lawyers on that question, but I'll go out on a limb and say there isn't.

The facts get even worse, as detailed in the article:

> In 2019, two of the allegedly infected scientists, Hu and Yu, coauthored a paper about the genetic lineage of SARS-related coronavirus in bats across China that they had studied.
>
> Hu studied under virologist Shi Zhengli who is known as "the bat woman of China" for her research on SARS-like coronaviruses of bat origin. Zhengli has come under intense scrutiny since the outbreak of COVID-19 was traced back to Wuhan.
>
> "Ben Hu is essentially the next Shi Zhengli," Alina Chen, a molecular biologist at the Broad Institute of MIT and Harvard, told Public. "He was her star pupil. He had been making chimeric SARS-like viruses and testing these in humanized mice. If I had to guess who would be doing this risky virus research and most at risk of getting accidentally infected, it would be him."[55]

It's like the scene in the classic film *Casablanca*, where Rick says, "Of all the gin joints in all the world and she had to walk into mine."

Coincidence?

Of all the people in the world to first come down with COVID-19, the first three were scientists at the Wuhan Institute of Virology, including the "star pupil" of the "bat woman of China." And what does Shi have to say of this amazing coincidence?

> Dr. Shi has repeatedly denied the allegations that her or her students' research caused the devastating pandemic due to a lab leak.
>
> She has called the allegations that multiple of her colleagues had gotten ill with similar symptoms to COVID-19 before the outbreak emerged baseless and said that her lab did not hold any source of the strain that caused the pandemic in a June 2021 interview with the New York Times.
>
> "I don't know how the world has come to this, constantly pouring filth on an innocent scientist," she said over text.[56]

Deflecting blame onto others may work in communist China, but in the more skeptical West, we have some additional questions. We don't believe her denials, just as we don't believe the denials of our own public health agencies, about the origin of the virus, the lockdown and masking protocols, or the safety of the vaccines they have pushed as a result.

Are we looking at powerful individuals who are evil or stupid, or possibly both? In an environment where so much is hidden from the view of the public, what are we to make of what is genuinely happening behind the scenes? Is this a depopulation agenda?

I suggest that in the absence of evidence, one must assume the very worst about these powerful forces.

However, at the very least, these scientists seem to resemble children playing with matches and gasoline on a global scale, and hoping they don't burn down the planet.

* * *

What does this all mean to us and our future?

I believe we have been through nothing less than a great war, and although there have been high casualties, there have also been victories. I point to a Pew Research Center poll from 2022 as evidence for this position.

> Overall, 29% of U.S. adults say they have a great deal of confidence in medical scientists to act in the best interests of the public, down from 40% who said this in November 2020. Similarly, the share with a great deal of confidence in scientists to act in the public's best interests is down by 10 percentage points (from 39% to 29%), according to a new Pew research Center survey . . .
>
> Scientists and medical scientists are not the only groups and institutions to see their confidence ratings decline in the last year. The share of Americans who say they have a great deal of confidence in the military to act in the public's best interests has fallen from 39% in November 2020 to 25% in the current survey. And the share of Americans with a great deal of confidence in K-12 public school principals and police officers have also decreased (by 7 and 6 points respectively) . . .
>
> The public continues to express lower levels of confidence in journalists, business leaders, and elected officials, though even for these groups, public confidence is tilting more negative. Four-in-ten say they have a great deal or a fair amount of confidence in journalists and business leaders to act in the public's best interests; six-in-ten now say they have not too much or no confidence at all in these groups. Ratings for elected officials are especially negative: 24% say they have a great deal or fair amount of confidence in elected officials, compared with 76% who say they have not too much or no confidence in them.[57]

Let's frame these findings correctly. The people who are paying attention (from 60–76 percent) don't trust scientists, medical scientists, the military, school principals, journalists, business leaders, or elected officials.

In any election, that's called a landslide.

The only people with any trust in these groups are either terminally stupid (probably as a result of their Ivy League education, or long-time addiction to the *New York Times*, CNN, or the *Washington Post*), or they've been living under a rock for the past decade.

We are in the majority.

When Trump was elected in 2016, I'd say about a third of the time I was out in public, about a third of the people who'd come up to talk to me had some criticism or negative comment to make about supporting Trump, or some other observation I'd made about the election.

In the past nine months, even though I still go out in public often, I don't think I've had a single negative comment made to me. The people who come up to me are black, white, Asian, gay, straight, etc., with crew-cuts, long hair, tattoos, pink or blue hair, and universally they'll tell me how much they appreciate me, or how they once thought I was crazy, but now they've seen the light.

There is no doubt we have suffered great losses in the COVID war, but these losses have opened the eyes of so many.

Don't let them convince you that we're losing.

This has been a marathon war, and though we have lost some battles, we have won many more.

And as we go forward, I believe we will never let ourselves be slaves again.

Too many of us are awake.

* * *

As this book was being finished on July 27, 2023, the following article about a secret Chinese lab in Fresno County, California was published by NBC News.

> Local and federal authorities spent months investigating a warehouse in Fresno County, California, that they suspect was home to an illegal, unlicensed laboratory full of lab mice, medical waste and hazardous materials . . .
>
> Hundreds of mice at the warehouse were kept in inhumane conditions, court documents said. The city took possession of the animals in April, euthanizing 773 of them; more than 175 were found dead.

> The Centers for Disease Control and Prevention tested the substances and detected at least 20 potentially infectious agents, including coronavirus, HIV, hepatitis and herpes, according to a Health and Human Services letter dated June 6 . . .
>
> "The other addresses provided for identified authorized agents were either empty offices or addresses in China that could not be verified," court documents said.[58]

And you thought you simply needed to worry about secret bio labs in China, or possibly in Ukraine. There might be a bio lab in your town, or in the next county, run by the Chinese, or possibly even our own intelligence services, and you would have no information about it until something goes wrong.

The mad scientist cabal needs to be broken up and reconstituted into a force that serves humanity, rather than planning for its destruction.

Chapter Eleven

Selling Your Soul to Hollywood (and Probably the CIA)

This might be the most disturbing chapter of the entire book.

I understand if people want to skip this chapter because there are some dark places you don't want your mind to go.

But as a Christian man, a truth teller to the best of my ability, I would be remiss if I didn't write this chapter.

I started off innocent, like everybody else, making my way in the media business and trying to get noticed, and when that happened, took meetings with people who were higher up on the food chain than me.

One of the people I met early on was film director Richard Linklater, a fellow Texan, probably best known for putting a young Matthew McConaughey in his feature, *Dazed and Confused*, about high school stoner culture. Rick is a great guy, not a part of Hollywood, and he put me in two of his films, *Waking Life* (2001) and *A Scanner Darkly* (2007), with Keanu Reeves, Robert Downey Jr., Woody Harrelson, and Winona Ryder. If you want to understand how little I've changed over the years, here's my speech from *Waking Life* in 2001, just as the George W. Bush presidency was beginning.

> "You can't fight city hall." "Death and taxes." "Don't talk about politics or religion." This is all the equivalent of enemy propaganda, rolling across the picket line. "Lay down, GI! Lay down, GI!" We saw it all through the twentieth century. And now in the twenty-first century, it's time to stand up and realize that we should NOT allow

> ourselves to be crammed into this rat maze. We should not SUBMIT to this dehumanization. I don't know about you, but I'm concerned with what's happening in this world.
>
> I'm concerned with the structure. I'm concerned with the systems of control. Those that control my life and those that seek to control it EVEN MORE. I want FREEDOM! That's what I want, and that's what YOU should want.
>
> It's up to each and every one of us to break loose of just some of the greed, the hatred, the envy, and yes, the insecurities. Because that is the central mode of control. Make us feel pathetic, small, so we'll willingly give up our sovereignty, our liberty, our destiny. We have GOT to realize we're being conditioned on a mass scale.
>
> Start challenging this corporate slave state. The twenty-first century's gonna be a new century. Not the century of slavery, not the century of lies and issues of no significance, and all the rest of the modes of control. It's gonna be the age of humankind, standing up for something PURE and RIGHT! What a bunch of garbage, liberal, Democratic, conservative, Republican, it's all there to control you, two sides of the same coin. Two management teams, bidding for control of the CEO job of Slavery Incorporated!
>
> The truth is out there in front of you, but they lay out the buffet of LIES. I'm SICK of it and I'm NOT GONNA TAKE A BITE OUT OF IT! DO YA GOT ME?? Resistance is NOT futile! We're gonna win this thing. Humankind is too good. WE'RE NOT A BUNCH OF UNDERACHIEVERS, WE'RE GONNA STAND UP, AND WE'RE GONNA BE HUMAN BEINGS!
>
> WE'RE GONNA GET FIRED UP ABOUT THE REAL THINGS! THE THINGS THAT MATTER—CREATIVITY AND THE DYNAMIC HUMAN SPIRIT THAT REFUSES TO SUBMIT! Well, that's all I've got to say. It's in your court now.[1]

It doesn't really seem like I've changed much over the years, does it? This is when the left really loved me.

A Scanner Darkly, released in 2007 after 9/11 and the massive civil liberty violations of the Patriot Act, was based on a Phillip K. Dick novel about a near-future dystopia of drugs, paranoia, and surveillance. The plot centered on a suit an individual could wear to make them invisible to governmental surveillance. In the story, a quarter of the population were addicts, and this provided an excuse for the government to crack down on its citizens.

That gave me something of a foothold in Hollywood, as many considered my work to be an indictment of George W. Bush's Patriot Act and the Global War on Terror, which it was. In 2005, I was seen as being allied with the left, and one of my anti-war documentaries, *Martial Law 9/11: Rise of the Police State*, was brought to the attention of the actor Emilio Estevez. He brought it to the attention of his brother, Charlie Sheen, and their father, Martin Sheen. Charlie Sheen called and told me, "I'd like you to fly out to California," and I accepted. What they were most interested in was my publicly challenging various aspects of the 9/11 story, particularly the fall of Building 7.[2] That video was attracting hundreds of millions of views. I'd tangled with George W. Bush when he was governor of Texas. And when Bush was president, I'd raised questions about 9/11, the War on Terror, and the plans of the neo-cons to invade countries all across the Middle East under the sponsorship of Vice President Dick Cheney, whom I considered to be one of the most villainous men to ever occupy high office in this country.

I arrived at Martin Sheen's house in Malibu and was greeted warmly by him and his wife. Martin put on my anti-war documentary so we could watch it together, and, in the first few minutes, he told me how much he appreciated my work. I'm as vulnerable to flattery as the next guy, and here I'm being praised by the lead actor of one of my favorite films, *Apocalypse Now*, who also did a great job playing the fictional president of the United States, Josiah Bartlett, in the Emmy-award winning series *The West Wing*. It was pretty heady stuff.

After maybe a half hour, the actor Anthony Hopkins arrived, as well as Sheen's two sons, Charlie and Emilio Estevez. They all sat down to watch the documentary, and I was praised by these people like I was the belle of the ball.

For some reason, Charlie Sheen seemed to really like me, offering to fly me out again to California so I could stay at his house. At that time, Charlie was dating actress Denise Richards and wasn't on drugs, but he was a chain-smoker.

Hollywood really is its own private little club, but with the approval of the Sheen family I was granted access to it. Later Charlie flew me out to California and had me stay at his house. While I was there, he said to me, "Hey, Alex, I want some Taco Bell. Take the Porsche down the hill and get me some things." I took the Porsche, but the damned thing was so powerful it scared me, and halfway down the hill I turned back around. He looked confused when I came back so quickly, so I said, "Let me take another car. I can't drive that. It'll kill me."

Charlie would later appear on my show and cause some controversy for himself.[3] Charlie was always good to me and over the years I've tried to counsel him (not very successfully) on some of his issues.

Because I was new to Hollywood (fresh meat), I got taken behind the curtain by several people to tell me the way things genuinely worked, but not the Sheens. At that point, I already knew many iconic people in Hollywood, and I was catapulted into having access to some of the A-list of Hollywood actors. I didn't like what I found. It was worse than the rumors I'd heard.

I went to dinner with Buzz Aldrin, the second man to walk on the moon, and he told me all about aliens on our nearest celestial body, our secret bases, and obelisks that hadn't yet been revealed to the public. Another thing that struck me as odd at the time was Aldrin's claim that we knew there was water on the moon, but we were going to let the Indians discover it. Yet, in 2009, that's exactly what happened, as reported by *The Guardian*:

> An Indian space mission claims to have found water on the moon, raising hopes that a manned base could be established there within the next two decades.

> It had been widely believed that the moon was dry, but data from India's Chandrayaan-1 mission allegedly found clear evidence of water there, apparently concentrated at the poles and possibly formed by the solar wind.
>
> What's more, water still appears to be forming, advancing the possibility that human life could be sustained there. Scientists hope that astronauts could one day not only drink the water but extract oxygen from it to breathe and hydrogen to use as fuel.[4]

I remember being in an airport in 2009 when I saw the headline on a newspaper about water on the moon, picked it up, and read through it. I thought to myself, *This is absolute bullshit. According to Aldrin, we've already got bases up there.* I'm not much of an alien guy (that's more Joe Rogan's territory than mine), but I've got a pretty good bullshit detector in me.

And when I have had alien investigators on my show, like Dr. Steven Greer, they've always impressed me with their thoroughness and care in distinguishing between what they know and what they suspect. If you woke me up in the middle of the night and asked if I was scared of aliens, I'd tell you I'm far more scared of human monsters than aliens and then turn over and go back to sleep.

I was getting to know all these other Hollywood people, going on TV shows, and doing some reality TV shows about conspiracies. (One pattern I've noticed is that whatever side feels out of power is much more willing to consider conspiracy/corruption theories. The left *loved* what I was saying about the Patriot Act and the War on Terror when Bush was in office. (But not so much when Barack Obama took office.) And some of these new people I was getting to know started to tell me about the real shape of power in Hollywood.

They told me, "You think Hollywood is cool? There are three groups here. First, there are the people who come here to make money and try to live outside the system. Second, there are the scientologists. And third, there are the occult CIA devil worshippers. There are these cults, but they all feed into the larger CIA group. Some of them even brand the women on their bellies." (This was long before anybody had heard of the NXVIM sex cult founded by Keith Raniere in 1998.[5]) I was also told that there were these islands where they'd take politicians and scientists, where they'd have sex with underage girls and try to compromise them. And these islands were run by our CIA, the British intelligence agency, MI-6, and the Israeli Mossad. I heard this story from many entertainers and well-known musicians, as well as others, and it's why a lot of them left the business.

But sex was just the entry door.

What these powerful entities were genuinely after was to get high-profile individuals to pledge themselves to the devil.

My good friend, Mark Dice, has spoken publicly about an incident where he was asked to make such a pledge. Dice was doing well in Hollywood—he's a funny guy—and he'd been offered a major show by the largest reality television group. The head of the company brought Mark into an office and said, "Mark, we want you to pledge yourself to Lucifer."

Mark replied, "But I'm a Christian."

The company head made a dismissive gesture. "We know you say you are. But let's just get this out of the way."

"Is this a joke?" Mark asked.

"No. I'm deadly serious," replied the company head.

Mark walked out of the room.

I have not been asked to pledge myself to the devil, but there have been offers that I believe were setting me up to eventually be asked that question.

One time, a top official of the Kissinger Group out from New York had a meeting with me and my producer, John Harmon. He said, "We want you to come and work for us. We want you to come to New York next week. We've only got a few thousand people in our super class, but we want you to join them. You'll basically lead the populist liberty movement. You'll get to have a seat at the table, but you'll have to do what we tell you. You'll be able to have some input. So, your two choices are you can be on your own crusade, and we'll make sure you fail, or you can join us."

All of this was out in the open. You see, this is always the dangle. You'll have more power than you ever believed, but you'll have to be under our control. It doesn't take much of a working brain to understand you're being asked to take the devil's deal.

Another time I had this major executive offer me ten million dollars a year for a show and multiple books a year. He said, "You just come in and do the show. But we'll control what you do."

During the pitch, his wife walks into the executive's swanky office, and she's super beautiful, which I'm sure was the point. The executive looks at his wife, then at me and says, "I hear you like to have fun. You want to have sex with my wife? She thinks you're hot. What do I need to do? Sex with my wife before or after you sign the contract? Do I need to get down on my knees and beg you to sign this contract?"

I must note that this approach, getting down on their knees and begging you, is a common tactic among these people. Once, I had a famous CIA guy making a similar pitch to me (without his wife), and he offered to get down on his knees and beg me to sign the contract he was offering. I guess the idea is, if somebody is down on their knees begging you, it's supposed to make you feel powerful. But you quickly realize it's just a ploy to get the harness around your neck, like you're a plow horse. You're like that rare baseball card they want to buy and put in their collection. When they see you're on your way up, that's when they make the offer, so they have you when you become popular.

You might not believe Alex Jones when I tell you about the CIA in Hollywood, but how about the same story from Oscar-winning director and actor Ben Affleck?

In 2012, he directed and starred in a movie called *Argo*, which told the true story of a 1980 CIA operation to rescue some of our hostages from Iran by smuggling them out as part of a fake Hollywood movie crew. (My sources also told me that the CIA regularly puts a few agency members into film crews on location in countries that are of interest to our intelligence agencies.) This is from a BBC News article about the film and the true story behind it:

> Ben Affleck's film *Argo* tells the bizarre story of how in 1980 the CIA—with Canadian help—sprang a group of Americans from Iran after they escaped a US embassy overrun by protestors.
>
> The film, which has received seven Oscar nominations including one for best picture, is based on real-life events. But how much of it is fiction?
>
> When Mark Lijek took Tehran as his first posting in the US foreign service, he wasn't opting for an easy life.
>
> "I was asked to volunteer in October 1978 and things in Iran were already pretty bad," he explains.[6]

The movie makes it abundantly clear that the CIA maintains fictional front companies in Hollywood as part of its regular operations. While the movie did take some dramatic license, specifically in heightening the suspense as to whether the Iranian authorities would discover the plan, the movie stuck pretty close to the actual story.

> The central element of the story sounds incredible but is in fact true. The CIA cooked up a plan to spirit the six out of the country on a scheduled flight from Tehran's Mehrabad airport, masquerading as Canadians working on a non-existent science fiction film.
>
> Mark Lijek recalls that of the group, he was the most immediately enthusiastic. "I thought it had the right amount of pizazz. Who else but filmmakers would be crazy enough to come to Tehran in the middle of a revolution? I had no problem pretending to be in the movie industry."[7]

I think it's important to understand that if our intelligence agencies are never sanctioned in any way for their actions, they will do whatever they want. The CIA is specifically forbidden from operating in the United States, but *Argo* openly broadcasts that this is a lie.

As to what is currently happening in Hollywood, this is from an interview Ben Affleck gave to *The Guardian* shortly after the movie came out.

> **BEN AFFLECK:** One of the themes of *Argo* is about storytelling and how powerful it is. From political theater to the way we communicate with our children to the way we inspire people. And it's interesting that Hollywood and the clandestine services both spend most of their time convincing people of something that's not true . . . Hollywood has developed this way of telling stories and oftentimes uses that for philanthropic and political causes which people may or may not think are good. But there are really positive offshoots. Mostly, I think, self-serving and designed to be that way. But I think some good things do also happen. This is an exceptional example of a good thing happening . . .
>
> **INTERVIEWER:** Are there many actors in Hollywood, who also moonlight as agents, do you think?
>
> **BEN AFFLECK:** I think there are probably quite a few. Yeah. I think Hollywood is probably full of CIA agents, and we just don't know it. And I wouldn't be surprised at all to discover that it's extremely common.[8]

While *Argo* depicted a CIA operation with goals most people would applaud, do you genuinely believe this is the bulk of what the CIA does with its Hollywood and other domestic operations? Most of the time they're engaged in much more nefarious operations, which they hope will never be depicted in a Hollywood movie. Although the 1980 operation to extract our personnel from Tehran was a noble endeavor with a successful outcome, the agency still didn't publicly acknowledge the operation until 1997.[9]

If you want a more current example of "offers" being made to powerful individuals by shady characters to change their behavior, you need look no further than the example of Kari Lake. I count myself among those who believe Lake won the governorship of Arizona and that she has been one of the most effective critics of corrupt practices in our election system.

In other words, she is an enemy of the Deep State.

And how might the Deep State respond to Lake's challenge? This is from a July 1, 2023 *Breitbart* article about her book, *Unafraid: Just Getting Started*, and possible plans to run for the US Senate:

> Breitbart News Washington Bureau Chief Matthew Boyle asked Lake, last year's Republican gubernatorial nominee in Arizona, if she was considering another bid for office in the Grand Canyon State. Lake, who had the backing of the MAGA coalition and is challenging her razor-thin election loss, said she is thinking of another run, though she emphasized she has not given up on her legal battle.
>
> "Politics is gross. It's a slimy business, but I think we need real people to be in it. And so I am contemplating running for office again," Lake said. "I want everyone out there to know we have filed a notice of appeal on our case. We're not giving up on securing our elections and reforming our elections, and we're going to work through the court system."
>
> "I may run for Senate, I'm considering that," she said.[10]

Kari Lake is a fighter, and we need more people like her in politics. While the *Breitbart* article focused mostly on her upcoming book and possible Senate run, there was a section of the interview that drew my attention, as it confirmed much of what I believe is genuinely hidden from the public.

> Lake, a former Fox 10 Phoenix anchor who left the world of news because of left-wing political bias, asserted she had been approached by a "high-profile person" attempting to "bribe" her to stay out of politics. The interaction happened when she was writing *Unafraid* after the election.
>
> "Originally, I was going to name the book, I was going to title it *Unafraid*, and then I had a pretty high-profile person come to my door and offer me money to put my movement on hold and my political career on hold—offered me a cushy job, nice paycheck, position on a board, and I said 'Are you kidding me? I left a cushy job . . . I'm not motivated by money,'" Lake recounted. "And then the

> conversation turned, 'Well, what would it take for you not to run for office again, at least until after 2024?' And I thought, 'Oh my gosh, this is the kind of stuff of movies.'"
>
> "If these people, the political elite, want me out of politics so badly that they're willing to bribe me, that tells me I need to stay in. So that's when I decided to add the subtitle, *Just Getting Started* just to give them a little bit of fear because I'm just getting started," she laughed.[11]

I've heard so many variations of this story from different people with no connection to each other that I simply consider it part of the operating system of the Deep State, just like a criminal profiler will eventually understand the habits of a serial killer and predict his next move.

One needs to have a strong moral compass and, I believe, a deep faith in God to overcome the obstacles these demons will place in front of good and honest people.

I was told other things by people who live in this world.

Once I was flown by a pilot on a private jet, who'd been the pilot for the head of a major entertainment company, and he had a story he wanted to tell me. He said he was told to simply fly to a specific set of coordinates.

"There's nothing there," the pilot said. "It's just ocean."

"No, just fly there," the pilot was told. "It's a private island. It's seven stars. No homeless, just billionaires." That's the level of control these people have. This wasn't Epstein's island. It's another one that they don't want you to know about.

I guarantee you that every famous person you've heard about has had this kind of approach made to them. Joe Rogan hasn't told me directly that these speeches have been made to him. But he's come close enough when we've had dinner and I've broached the subject. He said something like, "screw them," and it appeared to me that he's heard the same speeches I have.

I remember when I was in Hollywood that I had some people warn me, "You think Hollywood is cool, Alex? What are you going to do when you're at some party, and they bring in some sixteen-year-old girl and start having sex with her? That's why you shouldn't go to that party tonight. This place is dangerous, and you need to watch out."

That's the kind of stuff I've had prominent people in Hollywood tell me about. There were many who avoided it, like the Sheen family. They were good, strong Catholics, and although Charlie has had his share of troubles, he is *not* part of that Hollywood.

I grew up Christian and believe in God, but frankly, claims of devil worship and secret ceremonies sounded like something from the Middle Ages. When as a teenager I saw rock and roll groups emulating satanic themes, I imagined it was just something they were doing to shock the public and drive record sales.

However, as I began to learn more, I saw that Hollywood, and possibly other groups of powerful individuals, was setting up what could only be considered an alternative belief system to Christianity.

I can't prove to you there is a devil, but these people believe it, and they want to dedicate themselves to this false god.

* * *

I saw this alternative belief system when I infiltrated the Bohemian Grove in California in 2000, as reported by the *Washington Post* in a 2023 article.

> Bohemian Grove has all the hallmarks of an eyebrow-raiser: The men's-only retreat in Sonoma County has a massive owl statue, a reported history of public urination, mysterious ceremonies and a top-secret guest list that has included presidents, wealthy businessmen, international power players and other newsmakers . . .
>
> The cremation event in particular has drawn scrutiny, especially since Infowars founder Alex Jones snuck into the encampment and filmed the ceremony in 2000. Mainstream journalists are also fans of trying to pierce the veil: A Washington Post reporter was escorted back to his car after trying to get in. A writer for Spy Magazine snuck in for several days in the 1980s. And a Vanity Fair contributing editor was arrested for trespassing.

> Perhaps appropriate for a campground that has been called "exclusive," "mysterious," and "the very definition of the old boys' club," Bohemian Grove has been a magnet for conspiracy theorists on the right and protestors on the left, though the demonstrations have shriveled in recent years.[12]

In Hollywood in the mid-2000s, I was a hero to the left for having infiltrated the secretive summer gatherings at the Bohemian Grove. But during my time in Hollywood, I was being told that the entertainment industry was similarly compromised by powerful forces.

And in 2005, in the wake of the recent presidential election between George W. Bush and John Kerry, people were interested in my investigations of the Skull and Bones society at Yale University, which both men had attended. This is from the opening of an article about Yale's most secretive society:

> Legend has it that in 1918, under the cover of darkness, Yale student Prescott S. Bush, dug up the grave of Geronimo.
>
> Bush, along with several co-conspirators took the skull and two bones of the famed Apache leader back to Yale University in New Haven, Connecticut, where they've been on display at the headquarters of one of America's most mysterious secret societies.
>
> Prescott Bush, the father of President George H.W. Bush and grandfather of George W., is a Bonesman. He, along with his cohorts, was a member of an elite club at Yale University known as the Skull and Bones Society.
>
> Throughout history, some of the most prominent American figures have been Bonesmen, handpicked members of Yale's undergraduate class selected to join the ranks of elite students. In addition to the Bush's—both H.W. and W. followed in Prescott's footsteps during their time at the university—members have included hundreds of government officials, such as former Secretary of State John Kerry, as well as members of the entertainment industry, such as actor Paul Giamatti.[13]

It doesn't take much sleuthing to find connections between some of the most powerful members of our country and these secret societies. I'm not even opening the can of worms regarding US Senator Prescott Bush and how he may have been one of the main architects of handing our government over to the intelligence agencies during the Eisenhower Administration, which was the very thing Eisenhower tried to warn us against in his farewell "Military-Industrial Complex" speech.

Does your head start to spin when you fully understand how certain families have been close to the center of our governmental power for decades? The article continued:

> The initiation process of the society has long been shrouded in secrecy, driving many to believe that it involves occult practices, black magic, and even animal sacrifices.
>
> Like all societies at the university (of which there are seven), the Skull and Bones society have a headquarters. Known colloquially as the Tomb, the Skull and Bones Hall is a gothic, windowless building on High Street, just off campus, where the members can gather for meetings and events.
>
> It is also the rumored resting place of the bones of Geronimo, after being stolen by Prescott Bush, as well as the skulls of former president Martin Van Buren and Mexican revolutionary Pancho Villa.[14]

I read widely and then compare what I read with what I understand from other sources. I like things to add up and have some sort of narrative logic. However, I also understand that just because something makes sense, doesn't make it true. But I do believe that things that are true make sense, and we can understand it if we have all the facts. Consider this passage from the same article.

> Some claim that the group was behind the Kennedy assassination, that they were responsible for creating the nuclear bomb, that they

> are sponsored and influenced by the Illuminati, and even that they control the entire Central Intelligence Agency.
>
> However, the theories, as off-kilter as some of them may sound, aren't really that off-base when considering the members.
>
> At different points throughout history, Bonesmen have had control over the fortunes of the Rockefellers, the Carnegies, and the Fords. They've also had members rise through the ranks and obtain high offices in the Council on Foreign Relations, powerful media corporations such as TIME, and of course, three Presidents of the United States (William Howard Taft, in addition to the Bushs).
>
> In fact, during the 2004 Presidential Election, both the Republican and Democratic nominees, George W. Bush and John Kerry, were Skull and Bones members.[15]

I'm not in a position to tell you what's true about that passage, but when I compare that with what I've heard from other sources, I tend to believe in the general thrust of the article.

Skull and Bones is not just some social club.

It's the collegiate farm league for those who want to run the world.

I'm comfortable admitting I may have some of the details wrong. When the powerful hide what they're doing from us, is it our fault if we make a few mistakes?

But do you understand why I use a similar analytical framework, whether I'm looking at groups like the World Economic Forum, the Tri-Lateral Commission, the Club of Rome, the Bilderberg Group, or the World Health Organization?

Anytime I see the combination of power and secrecy, I get nervous.

But the answer isn't to be frightened and hide from the facts.

We just need to draw these villains out into the light, where the rest of us can see them clearly for the devils they are.

Chapter Twelve

Combat Tactics for Victory

The globalists have already planned your future.

They want your future to be one of sickness from their toxic chemicals, pharmaceutical drugs, and vaccines. They imagine a dystopian world of censorship, social credit scores, and digital currencies that they can hang over you like a sword of Damocles, tiny homes, overcrowding, meatless meals, plugging the "useless eaters" into virtual reality, and giving you hallucinogenics so that you never complain about your political masters.

The globalists are trying to bring down our modern world, because our ideas of freedom, the innate value of every human being, and the ladder of opportunity that has lifted billions out of poverty, have been so remarkably successful and durable. The globalists seek to blow up that ladder of opportunity, knowing, if they can implement their ideas of scarcity, poverty, and governmental control, you will forget there ever was such a thing as freedom and opportunity. The globalists seek nothing less than to capture the entire world.

This is a big deal.

A scientific and managerial elite has sought to take control over the top levels of corporate and governmental systems (and has mostly succeeded), and now they seek to take control over our individual lives, our information systems that allow us to have informed and respectful debates, and even our bodies through "health care." All sorts of alternative technologies and medicines have been suppressed, and they're trying to get rid of the marketplace of ideas by plugging you into video games all day and giving you drugs.

Surely you can see glimpses of what they're doing to us? The evidence has been mounting for years.

This is just the tip of the iceberg.

However, our responses must balance both challenging and opposing their authoritarian ideas with promoting our own ideas of freedom. If we do this, it can result in unprecedented human progress and happiness. I am not seeking to create a false utopia, but a healthy political ecosystem in which the furnace of vigorous debate ensures that the best ideas rise to the top. I encourage you to push these authoritarians to explain why they don't believe that vigorous debate will lead to the best ideas being promoted. The thing they can't say out loud is that they think you're stupid. They hijack the intelligence, massage it, and believe you'll swallow their lies.

We know that the answer to the globalist model of censorship and control is the free and open society that was envisioned by the great minds of the Enlightenment and the Renaissance. These ideas found full flower in the eventual creation of the United States and were fueled by the wisdom about human nature that was discerned by our Founding Fathers.

We must also not be terrified by our current situation. We must understand there are cycles of history, just as there are cycles to the seasons, and that democracies will always descend into a period of decadence, corruption, tyranny, and collapse. But on the other side, if we stand up, we will witness a rebirth of freedom.

The globalists have set up the Great Reset, but we have our own plans, the Great Renaissance.

I recently heard an expression about the times in which we find ourselves, with which I strongly agree. It goes something along the lines of, "Bad times create strong men. Strong men create good times. Good times create weak men. Weak men create bad times." And the circle goes round. Now, I'd have to add that women should be part of that equation, but I think we're in the "bad times" period of our great republic. However, our current bad times are creating incredibly strong men and women, and we know what they have always done.

As you may have realized in this book, I have strong opinions. However, the last thing I want you to do is unequivocally accept my opinions. More than anything, I believe in individual thought, not groupthink. Competition, free from corporate or governmental meddling, will always bring about the best result. And it lies in the collective power of fair debate.

I believe it's also important to reclaim our personal relationships. The fabulous documentary by Mikki Willis, *The Great Awakening*, opened with talking about how the COVID response from the government seemed to take a page from Mao's Cultural Revolution by isolating people from their friends and families, which will make people much more likely to turn to the government as their protector.

When I pair what Mikki Willis covered about the strategies used by Mao in the Cultural Revolution in *The Great Awakening* with what I learned in the mouse utopia experiments, all I see is an attempt by the globalists to collapse our society. How else can one interpret the move by the globalists to herd us into high-density housing, to exhaust us by too much interaction with others (due to high-density housing in cities), and to thus turn us into sexless hermits? We need human contact, but we also need the rejuvenating properties of nature, religion, and prayer so that we maintain our connection to the spiritual realm and the divine source of all life.

For myself, I know that I couldn't do what I do without God. It is contemplation of the infinite that gives you discernment into the greatness of creation, and that it's all real, the angels and the devils. It's a bit like the song by Bob Dylan, "You've Got to Serve Somebody." I agree with rock and roll legend Bob Dylan that, no matter who you are, you're going to serve somebody, God or the devil. There really isn't any other choice. You may think you're just going to serve humanity, but eventually you're going to come up against your own mortality. And if you're looking at oblivion, the wiping away of all that you are, the decisions of wealthy individuals, like Peter Nygard, to destroy the fetuses of his unborn children to harvest their stem cells for the purpose of prolonging his life and vitality make a twisted sort of sense.

If nothing ultimately matters, then everything is permitted, as long as it might benefit the individual.

I have friends, good people, who seem to acknowledge this dilemma, and they'll say things like, "I don't believe in God. But I respect and admire the principles of Christianity. I also observe that Christian principles appear to have a positive effect on society, as well as in the lives of those who follow them."

To me, that's like saying, "I live my life as if gravity matters, but I don't believe in the law of gravity." Everything one observes about a genuinely Christian life suggests that there is a benevolent order to the universe, which demands our acknowledgment of it.

In order to move in a Godly direction, we have to acknowledge there is a God.

It's like at your traditional Thanksgiving table when there's the kid table and the adult table. The globalists sit around and write books, have their conferences, and plan all of this terrible stuff for us. They're at the adult table. But so many adults in our society are content to sit at the kid table, where they're just talking about what's on Netflix, their favorite sports team, or the latest pop culture shiny object.

We need to move to the adult table and talk about these things.

Just the other day I was reading one of the United Nations' own reports where they said we need to cut energy consumption worldwide by at least 45 percent by 2030, and even more in the years beyond.[1] If you cut energy consumption by 20 percent, it's going to kill at least a hundred million people. If you cut it 50 percent, you're going to have a death toll in the billions.

The point is realizing we're already in a crisis. Part of the Great Awakening is realizing that you can have an impact and make the world a better place. This isn't about liberals wanting more of your tax dollars to create a more generous social safety net, or conservatives wanting fewer taxes to unleash human creativity.

This is about the globalists wanting to blow up our entire system and force us into the designs of their highly restrictive system.

What I'm trying to tell people is that the decision has already been made that you're obsolete. It's not a question of whether you are a "useless eater." In their eyes, you are. That's why during the COVID lockdowns they declared some people to be "non-essential." They want to get you used to that programming.

But I am telling people that they are essential, despite what the globalists are trying to convince you. I am a human supremacist because I believe humans can collectively make the earth better and that we all have value. The social engineers want you to believe we're inherently, irredeemably evil and can't be improved. They want us to turn off our divine life force and roll over and die.

The Great Awakening is about saying "No" to these lies and declaring we were built by an amazing Creator. Humans can create beautiful architecture, music, culture, and scientific wonders. When we seek to create in accordance with the divine, we create things that renew that sense of awe and reverence in us and reflect a grandeur in spirit like the great cathedrals of Europe do in stone.

It is in going back to that source that we're going to find the empowerment and enlightenment that will lead us out of our current Dark Age.

The globalists have decided we're fallen, ugly, and doomed as a species and that lies and corruption are the way to go. Yes, they will try to organize their evil and lies into an empire of wickedness. We must reject their empire and realize that every great city in which they take control collapses. Every country in which they come into power begins to fall apart. In their wake come only human trafficking, wars, poison chemicals, GMO abominations, and a tyranny of mad scientists' intent on changing the very source code of life.

We must emancipate ourselves, spiritually, physically, and financially from their systems of control. These globalist technocrats have projected their own self-hatred onto us, and we must reject it. We must say we understand we are imperfect and fallen creatures, but through God, we can individually and collectively be made whole. We are definitely not going to be made better and sanctified and purified by their new state religion of climate change and authoritarianism and their leftist new world order garbage. They have abandoned God, and, as Bob Dylan says so well, that only leaves one other powerful entity to serve, the devil.

I care about the individual countries of the world and the different cultures because I understand they're all part of the rich tapestry God has created for our delight and enjoyment. However, in what I see of the final equation, we're being taught that transhumanism is already here, we're a failed species, and only the scientists can save us.

I pray we come together in solidarity, a new union of individuals of every race, color, and creed that share the values of a pro-human future, and celebrate what we are and what it means to be a human being.

They want us turned around, scrambled in our thinking, and confused. They want us to accept the human and animal cloning and the babies with the DNA of three people, as part of their mad scientist revolution. They want to take control, steal the future, and proclaim the end of history. They're trying to cut us off from the vigor and vibrancy of free and open societies because they understand their system of governmental and corporate tyranny just can't compete. They want a total tyranny over your speech, your movement, even your body: a nightmare dystopia wrapped in a modern woke liberal ideology, and we must reject it with every part of our soul.

There are many who have fallen victim to this scientific death cult, and we must do our best to wake them up. We need better leaders in our political movements—the strong, smart, and pure—that can attract even those who have fallen into darkness and create a new golden age.

I hope more and more people say "No" to their scientific death cult. Humanity has not come to its end. Our glorious history remains to be written. There can be a rebirth of wonderment, exploration, rugged individualism, and creativity. As Thomas Jefferson wrote about in his time, I say in our own, that this will be the animating contest of liberty. We can break out of this decadent cycle of collapse and tyranny and replace it with the golden age of all golden ages.

As an example of things starting to go our way, I must thank GOP presidential candidate Vivek Ramaswamy for calling on Elon Musk in late July 2023, to unban me from X/Twitter.[2] It seems to me the globalists have exhausted all their ammunition, and the only thing left to do is retreat from our brave army of patriots.

I believe we are on the verge of an incredible renaissance, in which we will spread out into the stars and become a civilization worthy of the name. How exciting it is to live in such times. Humanity has been like a caterpillar, entering its cocoon, not able to imagine the next stage of its evolution, and then, when all around constricts and seems lost, it bursts forth from that cocoon as a beautiful butterfly. We may be dazed at first, trying to let our wings fully dry, but we will have the power to launch ourselves into the greatest adventure of human history.

I hope we can join together in this journey.

Chapter Thirteen

The Final Battle

There are two genuinely terrifying thoughts that every truth-seeking person must eventually confront.

The first is that we're all alone and there is no God. It's all just a random mix of atoms, molecules, and luck that we're alive and have consciousness.

The second is that we're not alone and there is a God. The universe is so vast, diverse, well-organized, and optimized for life that it seems beyond belief that it all came about by chance.

It's been my experience that, with these dueling ideas, atheism is the first response of the rebellious and the interesting. It seems fun, defiant, and a clear break from the more traditional example of many of our elders.

I tried that for a while as well, but there was something I began to notice. As much as you can fill your life with people, activities, and possessions, the inevitable reality is that there are times you will be alone. And it's having God in your life that makes you comfortable to be in your own skin.

Because when you have God in your heart, and in your mind, you're never truly alone.

And I noticed that those friends of mine that had embraced atheism in their youth, and maintained that belief, seemed to become more and more unhappy. Their lives didn't work out the way they'd planned, their kids were often in trouble, and life just seemed to be one tribulation after another. Over time, it seemed many of them didn't handle those obstacles well.

However, I also noticed that those who'd given up their atheism, who had embraced God, exhibited a lightness and joy that I didn't find among the atheists, even when the believers had similar problems.

I cannot empirically tell you that God is real, but I can tell you that religious people seem to have more happiness, better social relations, and have a better, more grounded purpose in life, which tends to sustain them through difficult times.

Even Stanford University seems to believe this is true, as demonstrated by this November 2020 article published in their newspaper about a book titled *How God Becomes Real: Kindling the Presence of Invisible Others* by anthropologist Tanya Lurhmann:

> In her book, Lurhmann explains how her scholarship is inspired by two straightforward, but often overlooked, features of religion. "First, religion is a practice in which people go to effort to make contact with an invisible other. Second, people who are religious want change. They want to feel differently than they do," she writes. "Yet instead of exploring these features, most theories of religion begin by treating belief in an invisible other both as taken for granted and as a cognitive mistake."
>
> Luhrmann argues that individuals of faith often have to work hard to make supernatural beings real and that those who are able to do so experience helpful changes. "If they're lucky, they're able to attend differently to their thoughts, feel calmer and more beloved," she said. And these positive outcomes reinforce religious practices, encouraging sustained commitment to ritual and observance.[1]

I understand what she says at a visceral level. I do not reach God through my rational mind. I reach God through my creative mind. When I pray, I try not to present God with a list of problems but simply to clear my mind, so that I might more clearly understand His will.

The only point on which I may differ with this Stanford anthropologist is that when I clear my mind, I believe this gives me the ability to see reality more clearly than when I am simply consumed by the physical world.

However, there were other points with which I agreed.

Research has repeatedly shown that people of faith report feeling better and healthier.

> One of the most striking findings in social epidemiology, Luhrmann notes, is that religious involvement with God is better for your body in terms of immune functions and reducing loneliness. One explanation for this, Luhrmann writes, is that for those with an intense faith, God becomes a social relationship. MRI results indicate that in terms of brain function, talking to God resembles conversing with a friend.
>
> But the nature of that relationship is also key in terms of health. The more that God is seen as judgmental and negative, the more mental health symptoms are reported. In contrast, people who represent their relationship with God as being loving and satisfying pray more and report fewer mental health symptoms. "The data suggest that when it's a good relationship, it's better for the body," Luhrmann said.[2]

I don't find anything to object to in what Luhrmann reported. It's true in the physical world. Good relationships make us healthier. Of that there can be no doubt.

And yet, when I made my commitment to believe in God, it was a complete, not a partial, one. Even though I cannot see God, I accept He is a physical reality.

I am a Christian and fully accept the teachings of the Bible, though I am very comfortable in also saying that with my limited human understanding I may not understand, or even be aware of, every aspect.

And because I have lived my life as a person of faith, seeking to discern God's purpose in the world, I have come to my own conclusions. Just as there is ultimate good in the world in the form of God, there is also ultimate evil, otherwise known as Satan, the father of lies, or the devil.

God has given us the gift of free will and would never take that from us. The angels who remained with God watch over us, and when we get into the proper frame of mind, we can feel their presence and even see the results of their influence.

By contrast, the devil seeks to ensnare us in his lies, and one of the ways he seeks to lead us astray is by convincing people to be humanists. In other words, you can be a good person without God. I believe that the attempt to be a good person without a need for God will always eventually lead to failure, although it may take years, or even a lifetime, to become visible.

The unseen works upon us in very visible ways, so whenever I see things that strike me as evil, I am always aware of a dark presence.

When I see good works, I am aware of the presence of God. This used to be the common understanding of Western civilization. Amidst our own Civil War, Lincoln called upon his countrymen to listen to the "better angels of our nature." Everybody understood that life was a battle between good and evil, in society and within each person.

When I review the atrocities of the Nazis, Stalin's Russia, and Mao's China, I see the devil in those places. Those regimes sought to either crush religion or bring the churches under the control of the State, just as many governments tried to do with the COVID-19 crisis.

The attempt to control a population always starts with an assault on God. Maybe it's a direct attack, or maybe it's an attempt to just get people to stop talking about Him, like when they banned prayer in public schools. They want you to lose faith in God and lose faith in each other, so you will turn to the State as your savior.

It's exactly the strategy Chairman Mao used in China during the Cultural Revolution.

I often ask my guests where they believe we are in this fight against evil. It's time I answer the question I so often pose to others. I believe our moment in history most closely resembles the Biblical story of Exodus, as Moses found himself and his followers pursued by Pharaoh's army and facing the Red Sea. Here is that story:

> Pharaoh was already near when the Israelites looked up and saw that the Egyptians were on the march in pursuit of them. In great fright they cried out to the LORD. And they complained to Moses, "Were there no burial places in Egypt that you had to bring us out here to die in the desert. Why did you do this to us? Why did you bring us out of Egypt? Did we not tell you this in Egypt, when we said, 'Leave us alone. Let us serve the Egyptians'? Far better for us to be slaves of the Egyptians than to die in the desert."
>
> But Moses answered the people, "Fear not! Stand your ground, and you will see the victory the LORD will win for you today. These Egyptians whom you see today you will never see again. The LORD himself will fight for you; you only have to keep still."
>
> Then the LORD said to Moses, "Why are you crying out to me? Tell the Israelites to go forward. And you, lift up your staff and, with hand outstretched over the sea, split the sea in two, that the Israelites may pass through it on dry land. But I will make the Egyptians so obstinate that they will go in after them. Then I will receive glory through Pharaoh and all his army, his chariots and charioteers. The Egyptians shall know that I am the LORD, when I receive glory through Pharaoh and his chariots and charioteers."[3]

And we know what happened next. The Israelites were able to pass safely through the waters, and when the Egyptians sought to pursue, the waters closed on Pharaoh's army, leaving not even a single survivor.

I believe God has made our enemies so obstinate that they are actively pursuing us like Pharaoh's army to their own destruction.

The stories of the Bible give us a template to use today.

For me, as the story of Exodus teaches us, turning the tide always begins with an acknowledgment of God and humbling ourselves before His mighty throne.

I believe we stand at a crossroads, with one future filled with wonders and morality and another filled with terror and wickedness. When people ask me what will turn the tide, I always say the same thing.

It is us and our devotion to God and the life of abundance He wants us to have.

Evil wants us to act against our nature, embracing fear and anger rather than confidence and calm, and hate and chaos rather than love and understanding. We will not beat the Deep State because we know every single fact about them. We will defeat our enemies because they will see the goodness of our souls and if they heed God's warning, they will have a chance to turn away from the darkness.

If not, they will face destruction, as surely as Pharaoh's army.

We may feel like the Israelites did, looking behind us to see Pharaoh's terrifying army and, in front of us, the deep waters of the ocean. We may even wonder for a moment about the wisdom of our fight against these dark forces. But even though we have been terrified of the strength of the enemy, we have taken many courageous steps against them.

And just as in the time of Moses, if we stand strong and whisper to ourselves, "Be still and know God," He will open a glorious path for our liberation.

You do not need to worry about or figure out a fix for every wicked act in the world. Just be the person God intended you to be, in the part of the world where you have influence. Only worry about the fight that comes to you. Rest assured, there will be enough fights to go around, and you'll have your chance to make a stand with God.

Rather than turning our gaze outward to the many problems of the world, we should turn inward and ask God for the strength to deal with what lies in front of us. We're all in this fight together, and, with no individual more important than another, our power lies in God's collective humanity.

Don't worry about who they are.

Worry about who you are, and which master you serve.

I want to leave you with the Beatitudes from the Book of Matthew:

> And seeing the multitudes, He went up into a mountain; and when He was set, His disciples came until Him:
>
> And He opened His mouth, and taught them, saying,

> Blessed are the poor in spirit: for theirs is the kingdom of heaven.
>
> Blessed are they that mourn: for they shall be comforted.
>
> Blessed are the meek: for they shall inherit the earth.
>
> Blessed are they which do hunger and thirst after righteousness: for they shall be filled.
>
> Blessed are the merciful: for they shall obtain mercy.
>
> Blessed are the pure in heart: for they shall see God.
>
> Blessed are the peacemakers: for they shall be called the children of God.
>
> Blessed are they which are persecuted for righteousness' sake: for theirs is the kingdom of heaven.
>
> Blessed are ye, when men shall revile you, and persecute you, and shall say all manner of evil against you falsely, for my sake.
>
> Rejoice, and be exceeding glad: for great is your reward in heaven: for so persecuted they the prophets which were before you.[4]

We are, as we have always been, Children of God, assaulted on all sides by agents of the devil who wish to steal our joy.

But the God who led the Israelites out of Egypt, who gave us His only begotten Son so that we would not know death, is still in charge.

Conclusion

How You Know You're Winning

Finding the truth is difficult.

The quest for truth has bedeviled generations of journalists, writers, lawyers, scientists, researchers, and people of faith. We all want the truth, but what is the best way to pursue it?

For the better part of five hundred years, Western civilization has had an answer. The answer was to have an open conversation: letting every person speak until they're finished, discussing the quality of the information presented, and then drawing a conclusion. However, because we also understand that any conclusions we make likely rest on shaky ground, we're happy to revise it if additional information is received.

In this system that has endured for more than five hundred years, from the time Europeans crossed the Atlantic until we landed on the moon to having sent probes to the farthest parts of our solar system while billions have been lifted out of poverty and suffering, we have celebrated the individual seeker of truth. Built into the very spiritual DNA of this Renaissance is the understanding that all of us are presumed to be equal in our desire to find the truth and live according to its guidance.

But that has changed, and I'd have to mark the beginning of that change as the fight over childhood vaccines, starting in the early 2000s, with the assault on Dr. Andrew Wakefield, whom I have interviewed several times on my show.

Consider the magnitude of the possible harm we have allowed to be inflicted upon our children. If increasing numbers of vaccines given to children during the earliest stages of life are causing harm, we have failed at one of our most basic tasks as a species.

Which is why, when Robert F. Kennedy Jr. appeared on Joe Rogan's podcast for a three-hour discussion on June 16, 2023, sparks were likely to fly. Joe asked Kennedy the question millions of people were wondering themselves. Namely, why not have a debate to settle this question between Robert F. Kennedy Jr. and Dr. Peter Hotez, so that we might have some sort of clarity on this issue? After all, Stephen Douglas and Abraham Lincoln debated slavery in the years before the Civil War. When Charles Darwin rushed his theory of natural selection into print because another scientist, Alfred Russel Wallace, had begun speculating in that same area, representatives of the two men held a debate at the Linnaean Society in London, England in 1858 to settle the question.

Are we incapable in 2023 of asking similarly difficult questions?

According to most in the mainstream media, we are, like this article from *Fortune* magazine seems to claim.

> Put a well-known vaccine scientist, a controversial podcast host, an anti-vaccine candidate, and a couple of billionaires in the room—a.k.a. a Twitter thread—what could possibly go wrong?
>
> Over the weekend, Dr. Peter Hotez, the co-director of the Texas Children's Center for Vaccine Development (CVD) and author of the forthcoming book *Preventing the Next Pandemic: Vaccine Diplomacy in a Time of Anti-Science*, tweeted a *Vice* article titled, "Spotify Has Stopped Even Sort of Trying to Stem Joe Rogan's Vaccine Misinformation." It came after the podcast host Joe Rogan brought presidential candidate Robert F. Kennedy Jr. on his show to vocalize his anti-vaccine stance.
>
> Hotez called the podcast interview "nonsense" and shared that he received attacks on Twitter as a result.
>
> The conversation brewed a storm, to say the least. After Hotez denied an immediate offer from Rogan of $100,000 to the charity of his choice [it later swelled to more than $1.5 million from others who wanted to hear the debate], to debate RFK Jr. in real time on his show, Twitter CEO Elon Musk tweeted, "He's afraid of a public debate, because he knows he's wrong."[1]

Notice how the *Fortune* article seeks to frame the narrative, not as a search for truth by Joe Rogan, Robert F. Kennedy Jr., or Elon Musk, but as an attempt to stem "misinformation." Was Galileo guilty of presenting "misinformation" when he said his observations led him to conclude that the Earth revolved around the Sun? Was Rachel Carson guilty of promoting "misinformation" when she suggested that the pesticide DDT was causing a catastrophic collapse of bird populations in the United States, and its use should be banned?

Although I am hopeful that long-suppressed ideas are making their way into the public consciousness, I am fearful that dark forces may yet try to silence them. I worry that if the legal assaults on former President Trump do not have the intended effect of tarnishing him in the public's mind that the intelligence agencies will try to kill him, possibly by sabotaging his plane. I am concerned that Robert F. Kennedy Jr. may be attacked and killed by somebody posing as a "pro-vaxxer" angry about his call for greater oversight of the pharmaceutical industry.

Could two prominent political figures be taken out in a single political season without outraging the public? In 1968, both Martin Luther King Jr. and US Senator Robert F. Kennedy were killed, paving the way for President Richard Nixon to be elected.

Let us hope that is not what God has planned for us. Maybe there are patriots in the Deep State that are willing to let us try and fulfill the possibility of being a constitutional republic.

Consider this remarkable article from *Vox* titled "Joe Rogan Wants a 'Debate' on Vaccine Science, Don't Give it to Him." The article essentially argues against the principles of the Enlightenment, the Renaissance, and more than five hundred years of remarkable progress for our species.

> Debates are a less-than-ideal forum for having conversations about contentious issues—especially when they're issues whose understanding is clouded with misinformation.
>
> There are several reasons for that. For starters, a debate about a scientific issue implies that there is scientific disagreement about that issue, said Rupali Limaye, a social scientist at Johns Hopkins

> University's public health school who studies vaccine communication. You're "giving individuals a platform to really promote something that goes against scientific consensus," she said.[2]

I am struck by several horrendous ideas put forth by this article. The first is that "debate" is not well-suited for "conversations about contentious issues." What is the purpose of "debate" then? How about the contentious idea that a person may be guilty of murder? That's why in a criminal case the state *and* the defendant are both allowed to present their very best case. [Although in my civil case, I was *not allowed* to put on a defense. Starting to see a pattern?] In an election, the public likes to see both candidates debate each other, so they can make a comparison. But, of course, Joe Biden doesn't want any debates on the democratic side,[3] and if Trump is the republican nominee, probably won't want that debate, either.

I'm stunned by the idea I see being put forth in most mainstream articles about science, that the public should be concerned about this idea of "consensus." From the real scientists I've talked to over the years, they understand the only genuine measurement is "validation" or "confirmation" of a scientist's findings.

What somebody "thinks" does not matter in the slightest if there is information that strongly disproves that idea.

But this anti-human agenda put forth by the elites seeks to strip away the skeptical nature of the Enlightenment, which demands proof of claims made by the powerful. In the barrage of mainstream articles that accompanied the Joe Rogan, Robert F. Kennedy Jr., Peter Hotez, and Elon Musk controversy, probably none better expressed the view of the pharma-controlled media than this one from the *Houston Chronicle* titled, "Why Hotez is Right Not to Debate RFK Jr." You might find yourself amazed, as I was, by the remarkable mental gymnastics of this opinion writer, who is essentially arguing against differing opinions being expressed in public forums.

> Hotez, who has faced the wrath of the anti-vaccine movement since he began calling it out a couple decades ago, knows better. He knows

> that a debate with someone as unserious as RFK Jr. could have very serious consequences. Hotez has gone on Rogan's show before, and offered to go on again to discuss the COVID vaccine—particularly, the hundreds of thousands of deaths attributable to vaccine misinformation—but refused "to turn it into the Jerry Springer show" by appearing alongside RFK Jr.
>
> Critics, unsurprisingly, called him chicken. Several accused him of being a shill for Big Pharma. Never mind that Hotez has worked tirelessly to bypass Big Pharma, even earning a Nobel Peace Prize nomination for the low-cost patent-free COVID vaccines he and Maria Elena Bottazi developed that have reached millions of impoverished people during the pandemic.[4]

Let me provide my take on what's being done here. Hotez is being set up as some type of Mother Theresa, immune from criticism.

Are we to believe that a debate with Robert F. Kennedy Jr., with his articulate and fact-heavy presentations, is likely to resemble some Jerry Springer episode of women fighting over the question of "Who's your baby daddy?" complete with punches and thrown chairs?

Both sides would be expected to bring their "A" game. But, given Hotez's reticence to engage in such a debate, one suspects that Hotez has no "A" game.

But this is a bigger question than simply whether Peter Hotez should debate Robert F. Kennedy Jr. The question is whether our science can be questioned by the justice system, or whether unchecked science will be allowed to obtain ultimate control over our society.

If a doctor harms a single patient in the course of treatment, he or she can expect to face a lawyer in a courtroom asking difficult questions. But a vaccine scientist, whose product might harm hundreds of thousands, or even millions of people, knows he *will never* face an attorney asking questions, because of the 1986 National Childhood Vaccine Injury Act and the subsequent expansion of Big Pharma immunity of vaccines to include adult vaccines as decided by the Supreme Court in the case of *Bruesewitz v. Wyeth Laboratories*, decided in 2011.[5]

The vaccine injured in our country have been "patient zero" of the cancer inflicting our body politic, having metastasized into comments like this by Larry Fink, of the massive fund BlackRock, that "You have to force behaviors, and, at BlackRock, we're forcing behaviors," in discussing how the fund was trying to force compliance to Environmental and Social Goals (ESG).[6]

There is a war for the world, but people are fighting back, like German member of Parliament Christine Anderson, who said recently of the World Health Organization and its plan to control the nations of the world through pandemic fear:

> "An unelected body, like the WHO, controlled and run by multi-billionaires, should never be allowed to act in place of a democratically elected government . . . It is you [WHO] that is the small, fringe minority . . . You are the ones who do not have the right to dictate to the people what they want and what they don't want. So, take it from me . . . take it from the millions and millions of people around the world. We will bring you down. And we will not tire until we have done just that. So, brace yourselves. We are here, and the fight is on. So, let's have that fight."[7]

How else does one explain the fury with which Congresswoman Debbie Wasserman Shultz tried to shut down Robert F. Kennedy Jr. when he testified before the Weaponization of Government committee?

> **CONGRESSWOMAN DEBBIE WASSERMAN SCHULTZ:** Point of order pursuant to House Rule 11, Clause 2, which Mr. Kennedy has violated above. I move that we move into executive session because Mr. Kennedy has repeatedly made despicable anti-Semitic and anti-Asian comments, as recently as last week.
>
> Rule 11, clause two says, "whenever it is asserted by a member of the committee that the evidence or testimony at a hearing may tend to defame, degrade, or incriminate any person, or it is asserted by a witness that the evidence or testimony that the witness would give at

> a hearing may tend to defame, degrade or incriminate the witness," and it goes on.
>
> Mr. Kennedy, among many other things, has said, "I know a lot now about bioweapons. We put out hundreds of millions of dollars into ethnically targeted microbes. The Chinese have done the same thing. In fact, COVID-19, there was an argument that it is ethnically targeted. COVID-19 attacked certain races disproportionately. The races that are most immune to COVID-19 are—"[8]

But when brave individuals like Robert F. Kennedy Jr. stand up to bullies like Congresswoman Debbie Wasserman Schultz, people start to take notice. Here is Kennedy pushing back against the smears of the Democrats on that committee.

> **ROBERT F. KENNEDY JR.:** Again, there was an effort to suppress information. In fact, if you read the Twitter files and the email correspondence between Facebook and the White House, there was an acknowledgement that they were being asked and they were complying with censoring information that everybody knew to be true or highly likely to be true. In fact, the term misinformation did not denote falsehood or veracity. Rather it was a euphemism for any information that departed from government orthodoxies. It is very dangerous.
>
> The congressman a minute ago said a million people have died because of misinformation about vaccines in this country, but in fact our country had one of the highest vaccination rates in the world and the worst health outcomes. We have 4.2 percent of the global population. We have 16 percent of the COVID deaths. Blacks in Haiti with a 1 percent vaccination rate were dying at a rate of 15 per million population and same in Nigeria. They had a 1.3 vaccination rate. They were dying at one in 14 per million population. In our country, Blacks were dying at 3,000 per million population, 200 times death rates in other countries.

> This holds throughout the world. We needed information. We should have all been sharing information openly and talking to the 15 million doctors through the internet who were treating patients on the frontline all over the world and channeling the best therapies, the most successful treatments so that we could all figure it out. This is not a time in a pandemic to—I'll just say this one thing. Trusting the experts is not a function of science. It's not a function of democracy. It's a function of religion and totalitarianism and it does not make for a healthier population.[9]

And we are left with what I believe is the essential question of our time.

Will we allow the censoring of debate, putting an end to the Enlightenment and centuries of progress, or will we stand up and say that all of us have a right to speak? It seems that the defenders of freedom are just getting started, as a recent decision from a federal court on July 4, 2023 as reported by ABC News seems to suggest:

> A judge on Tuesday prohibited several federal agencies and officials of the Biden Administration from working with social media companies about "protected speech," a decision called "a blow to censorship" by one of the Republican officials whose lawsuit prompted the ruling.
>
> U.S. District Judge Terry Doughty of Louisiana granted the injunction in response to a 2022 lawsuit brought by the attorneys general in Louisiana and Missouri. Their lawsuit alleged that the federal government overstepped in its efforts to convince social media companies to address postings that could result in vaccine hesitancy during the COVID-19 pandemic or affect elections.
>
> Doughty cited "substantial evidence" of a far-reaching censorship campaign. He wrote that the "evidence produced thus far depicts an almost dystopian scenario. During the COVID-19 pandemic, a period best characterized by widespread doubt and uncertainty, the United States government seems to have assumed a role similar to an Orwellian 'Ministry of Truth.'"[10]

To me, the building evidence is clear.

When your opponents refuse to debate you, when they try to censor you, that's proof you have what it takes to defeat them.

There have been tremendous attempts to silence me with lawfare to drive me into bankruptcy. But due to the fact that so much of what I predicted and reported on has turned out to be accurate, there has been a major resurgence of support across the political system. It hasn't been my goal to be partisan, left or right, but to bring people together to discuss the important questions of the day. For those of you who haven't seen me because I've been banned from the large social media platforms, I want you to understand you can still find me at www.infowars.com/show or at www.banned.video. We are rebuilding the broadcast, and in many ways making it stronger than ever. In addition to this book, I hope you'll read my first book, *The Great Reset: And the War for the World*, with which Kent Heckenlively also ably assisted me with some of the writing and shaping of that work.

I am going to be in this fight as long as it takes. The only thing that will stop me is my death, which I hope and pray is many decades in the future. These past years have put me under enormous stress, but it has also been my honor to be the tip of the spear in the animating fight for liberty. The censorship is increasing, but we are also opening the eyes of many of our fellow citizens. As George Orwell once said, "During times of universal deceit, telling the truth becomes a revolutionary act." It is important for humanity to beat the censors, and I am confident we will.

The new human renaissance appears bright if we take action and have faith. We will fight by using our pocketbooks, our voices, our faith in God, and what we watch and read, because the enemy takes note of all these indicators. I encourage you to watch my show, as well as those of the other truth tellers. We need to let the voices of the people be heard. Together, we can defeat this current darkness.

A Golden Age of humanity awaits us, if only we have the courage to seize it.

Author's Note

Writing for Alex Jones

I grew up in what I continue to believe to this day is the single most beautiful spot on the face of the Earth. We lived just off the fourteenth hole at Round Hill Country Club in Alamo, California, about thirty-five miles east of San Francisco.

The fourteenth hole is a long par five, dogleg right, with a duck pond and an overhanging oak tree about a hundred and thirty yards from the green. In about thirty steps, I could walk from my backyard and be standing on the banks of the pond with some bread to feed the ducks.

Round Hill was just a few years old when we moved there in 1965, and it had the energy and brashness of new money, populated by creative thinkers who'd figured out how to grab an outsized share of the American Dream. Directly across from my house on the other side of the fourteenth hole, they built a twelve-thousand-square-foot mansion, at the time the largest house in the county. The owner had a popular restaurant, The Elegant Farmer, on the waterfront at Jack London Square in Oakland. I often played at that house, always pausing when I entered their front door to look at the enormous eight-foot-tall stuffed polar bear just inside the entrance.

I understand that in many ways I did not have a typical American childhood.

At various times in my life, I could've been talking at a party with baseball legend Joe DiMaggio or star basketball player for the Golden State Warriors and one-time NBA record-holder for best career free throw percentage, Rick Barry, being wished happy birthday on the radio by the Bay Area's most popular AM disc jockey, Dr. Don Rose, throwing a football around with various members of the Oakland Raiders, playing a few holes with professional golfers like Johnny Jacobs or Ron Cummins, or blowing off fireworks on the Fourth of July with Marvin Starr, who wrote the definitive textbook on California real estate law. If my parents had died when I was young, I would've been taken care of by Angelo Sangiacomo, at the time the largest landowner in San Francisco.

I got to see a lot of famous and controversial people up close when I was young, and they fascinated me as much as the books I constantly devoured.

My parents had a similar curiosity about the people who populated our neighborhood, as well as the greater world. My parents met at the 1956 Republican Convention in San Francisco, and although we were Republican, my father was always open to different ideas. I have vivid memories of people talking with him about social icons or political figures and my father saying, "I don't know much about him/her. What do you like about them?"

He'd listen to what they had to say, usually thanking them for providing their point of view. Once, after the person left, I said, "You hate the guy he was describing. Why did you listen to him go on and on about that guy?"

My father shrugged and said, "Maybe I'll learn something. What does it cost me to listen?"

Which is why, when one of my father's friends suggested he donate to Democratic US Senator Barbara Boxer's campaign as a way to go to some great parties, he jumped at the chance. My father, mother, and I went to several of these parties, where I got to meet then Senator Boxer, Senator Dianne Feinstein, Congresswoman Nancy Pelosi, and I'm assuming the current Vice President Kamala Harris, who was also there.

Around that time, I'd been working as a summer intern for Republican US Senator Pete Wilson. Wilson and Feinstein had been working closely together on some California issues and there was a great mutual respect and fondness between the two.

I remember having a nice conversation of a few minutes with Senator Feinstein at one of these events and saying to her, "You should be the first woman president of our country. Why don't you run?" I may have been a Republican, but I also recognized accomplishment. She'd done a great job taking over as mayor of San Francisco after the assassination of Mayor George Moscone, and had been a reasonable Democrat in the Senate, committed to working across the aisle when she could.

She thanked me for my words but didn't really give me an answer.

After that I remember going up to my parents, as well as Angelo Sangiacomo, my de facto godfather, and saying, "I don't know why Senator Feinstein doesn't run for president."

"She's got a China problem," said Angelo. "Her husband's made a lot of money with the communists. That wouldn't fly in a national election." (When her husband Richard Blum died in 2022, their estate was valued at $1 billion.[1] The two had been married since 1980.)

I tell you this story to let you know that when I saw something positive about a politician from the other side of the aisle, I would admit it. However, I also tell this story as a warning that you may not know critical facts about a public figure.

Be friendly and open to the good, but also retain some skepticism.

A 1997 article from the *Los Angeles Times* detailed this potential conflict of Feinstein arguing for better US-China relations, while her husband was doing deals with the rising communist superpower.

> On Capitol Hill, Sen. Dianne Feinstein (D-Calif) has emerged as one of the staunchest proponents of closer U.S. relations with China, fighting for permanent most-favored-nation trading status for Beijing.
>
> At the same time, far from the spotlight, Feinstein's husband, Richard C. Blum, has expanded his private business interests in China—to the point that his firm is now a prominent investor inside the communist nation.[2]

To this day I remain confused as to why more investigation was not made of this potential conflict of interest.

In 2018, it was revealed by CBS News that Senator Feinstein had employed a Chinese spy in her Senate office for twenty years.

> New details emerged Wednesday about how a mole for the government of communist China managed to stay by Senator Dianne Feinstein's side for nearly 20 years . . .
>
> The column revealed that the Chinese spy was Feinstein's driver who also served as a gofer in her Bay Area office and was a liaison to the Asian-American community.
>
> He even attended Chinese consulate functions for the senator.
>
> Feinstein—who was Chair of the Senate Intelligence Committee at the time—was reportedly mortified when the FBI told her she'd been infiltrated.[3]

When the story broke in the news, I recalled what I'd heard from Angelo in the early 1990s. Might there be any connection between Feinstein's husband doing deals with the communist Chinese and the placement of a Chinese spy in Feinstein's office?

That remains a mystery to me for which I have no answer.

But I have my suspicions.

When I was young, I wanted to be a criminal prosecutor, a crusader, almost like Elliot Ness in Chicago taking on Al Capone, or Rudy Giuliani, who'd been so effective at dismantling the New York mafia.

But I was also fascinated by the criminal defense attorneys, people like F. Lee Bailey, William Kunstler, Alan Dershowitz, and Gerry Spence. They seemed to be the single individual standing up to an entire system, and although I thought they were often wrong, I admired their courage. What must it feel like to confront the awesome power of the state and disapproval of the public, using only your intelligence and powers of persuasion? I loved the example of Atticus Finch, as portrayed by Gregory Peck in the classic movie *To Kill a Mockingbird*, as an example of standing up for principle against prejudice.

In law school I was fortunate enough to take several classes with the famed criminal defense attorney Bernie Segal, who had defended Jeffrey

McDonald, the so-called "Green Beret killer," an army surgeon who was charged and (according to Bernie) unfairly convicted of murdering his wife and family. (McDonald always maintained the murders had been committed by a group of hippies, including a woman named Helena Stoeckley, a local drug addict, who repeatedly confessed to, and later recanted, her participation in the murders.)

For two summers while in law school I worked for the US Attorney's Office in San Francisco, one summer assembling wiretap evidence against Oakland drug kingpin Rudy Henderson,[4] and the second summer bringing misdemeanor cases in federal court. I recall my younger self, the very model of a country club conservative, hanging out with my fellow legal eagles in training at the cafeteria when in walked our greatest nemesis, Tony Serra, the famed criminal defense attorney on the other side of the government's war on drugs.[5]

Serra was a remarkable specimen to be walking around the federal courthouse in the late 1980s: tall, broad-shouldered like a linebacker, maybe in his early fifties, with long white hair cascading well past his shoulders, as if he'd kept his 1960s hairstyle as a protest against the conservative times. We'd heard lurid stories about Serra's exploits: he thought pot should be legal, hung out with drug dealers, and often had parties late into the night at his law firm with his criminal clients, with loud music, wild dancing, and, of course, lots of drugs. One of Tony Serra's cases was portrayed in a bad 1980s movie called *True Believer*, in which he was played by the actor James Woods. When the movie came out and Tony was asked if the movie was an accurate portrayal of him, he said something along the lines of, "I smoke a joint in the opening scene of the movie, and that's the only thing they got right about me."

Tony Serra was a wild man to us, and yet on that day, he had his daughter with him, who appeared to be all of nine or ten years old. I watched how tender he was with his young daughter, helping her with her food tray, listening to her, talking and laughing, and found myself thinking, *Is he really the bad guy? Maybe we're the bad guys, the people sitting with me, shooting dirty looks at him, and muttering insults under our breath.*

I have a daughter now, vaccine-injured, who requires daily cannabis to keep her from having devastating seizures.

And I can't help but think to myself, how many things have I been wrong about?

I was certainly wrong about marijuana, although I'm still so much of a straight-arrow that I've never smoked pot. (Old habits die hard.) However, by the same token, I've never been drunk, even though I'm part-owner of a prestigious vineyard in the Napa Valley. (And I don't disagree with people who say alcohol has caused more problems in the world than pot ever has.)

At the time I was in law school, one of the big issues Professor Bernie Segal talked about was the government having the power to seize the assets of alleged drug dealers. He believed this to be an unconstitutional power grab by the federal government, designed to prevent suspects from being able to pay their lawyers.

I disagreed with him at the time, but now realize I was wrong. One can never countenance injustice against any group of people, regardless of how much you may dislike them. Eventually the government will seek to do the same to others.

After the 9/11 attacks, I supported the Patriot Act. The revelations of Edward Snowden and Julian Assange made me change my mind, and I consider the continuing legal assault on them to be a sign that, in many ways, our country has become dictatorial.

I considered the Iraq War to be a good thing in 2003. After all, Saddam Hussein was a bad guy. The world would be better off without him. But after seeing the disarray we caused in the Middle East, I came to believe I was wrong.

I thought vaccines were a great scientific advance and that any parent who didn't give them to their child should have their head examined. Now I believe that vaccines and the pharmaceutical companies that make them, free from any financial liability for harm caused by their products, pose an existential risk to humanity.

I've been wrong about a lot of things in my life.

Maybe you feel the same way, and like me, you're trying to do better.

There are many things I've done that I believe I got right and those fill me with pride.

I'm proud of the four books I've coauthored with Dr. Judy Mikovits.

I'm proud of having written the opening narration for the twenty-six-minute *Plandemic* video with Dr. Mikovits and Mikki Willis, the most viewed and banned piece of film in history.

I'm proud of the four books I've coauthored with *Project Veritas* whistleblowers.

I'm proud of the book I wrote on the revelations of senior CDC scientist Dr. William Thompson (based on documents I received from the office of US Congressman William Posey) that reported earlier administration of the MMR vaccine was resulting in high numbers of autism in children, particularly among African American boys. This constitutes, in my opinion, the greatest assault on the Black community since the Tuskegee Syphilis Experiments.

I'm proud of the book I wrote with long-time university professor Dr. Joseph Cummins, *The Case for Interferon*, which detailed the forty-year history of this overlooked immune modulator and cancer treatment that received a special commendation from the prestigious *Kirkus Reviews*. Despite the controversial nature of the twelve books I've published, four have received positive reviews from *Kirkus*.

I'm proud of the two books I've worked on with Alex Jones, the most persecuted man on the planet, with a billion and a half dollars in fines hanging over his head because of views he expressed on his *InfoWars* show. I don't remember the *New York Times* getting punished in a similar manner for promoting the Iraq War or for failing to warn the public of potential health risks from childhood vaccines or the COVID-19 shots.

I wear as a badge of honor that my scheduled April 9, 2015 talk with Dr. Judy Mikovits and Dr. Brian Hooker at the Commonwealth Club, titled "American Whistleblowers: The Promise and Peril of Science,"[6] was canceled because of protests and never rescheduled.

I will forever be proud of being banned from speaking about vaccines in Australia from August 2017 to August 2020,[7] becoming, to the best of my understanding, the only living American writer banned from an entire continent.

I am beyond amused that, on his May 17, 2020 broadcast, Chuck Todd devoted an entire five minutes of his show, *Meet the Press*, to trashing my book with Dr. Mikovits, *Plague of Corruption*, as well as the twenty-six-minute *Plandemic* video, without mentioning the name of the book or the authors.[8] That must be a first in television history.

How can I do anything but laugh at the fact that Amazon de-listed my August 2020 book with Dr. Judy Mikovits, *The Case Against Masks*, which featured a wonderful satirical cartoon cover by renegade cartoonist Ben Garrison of the Statue of Liberty suffocating behind a cloth mask.

When my agent presented this project to me and said I'd be working with Alex Jones, I jumped at the opportunity. What self-respecting writer wouldn't want to take on such a controversial subject and see where it led?

I recalled the criminal defense attorneys I'd been fascinated with as a kid and thought, *Yeah, this is something they would do. They wouldn't be scared off by a billion and a half in fines and the pearl-clutching terror of the mainstream establishment. If anything, they'd eat it up like Joe Biden attacking an ice cream cone.*

There must always be a place in our society for the fearless, even if they're sometimes mistaken.

It's been great working with Alex. He's a wonderful collaborator with a brilliant, almost photographic memory. I've taken to calling myself his "bird dog," the hound who accompanies his master on a hunt and then, when the master fires his shotgun, races off into the tall grass to retrieve what was hit. However, instead of bringing back game, I'm chasing down stories Alex remembers or confirming narratives he's developed over decades in the business. Ninety-five percent of the time I've found his recollections to be dead on. For most of the remaining five percent, the sources I found didn't rise to a level I consider to be credible and thus I didn't include them. I can't recall a single instance when he told me something for which I couldn't find any information.

I've seen Alex when he's angry, happy and jovial, or overcome with strong emotion and close to tears. He's a man who cares deeply about the world, as well as other people. The person you see on the show is pretty much the same person I've seen behind the scenes. Amidst the frenzy of putting out a daily show, he has remarkable social intelligence, pushing his production team to be their best, while also giving very specific praise for their good work. He's a man of enormous personal kindness, which is a trait I greatly admire.

I hope you'll be enlightened by what Alex had envisioned as a "deep dive" into many controversial topics that occupy his mind. More than anything else, Alex wanted this to be an "optimistic" book, giving people hope for a new renaissance of humanity, with God at the center of that glorious future.

It has been my great pleasure to assist Alex in turning that vision into reality. I hope to see you somewhere down that road and have a conversation about one of these topics.

After all, friendly conversation and debate are the American way.

—Kent Heckenlively

Notes

Chapter One

1 Greg Wehner, "Air Force Pushes Back on Claim that Military AI Drone Sim Killed Operator, Says Remarks Taken 'Out of Context,'" *Fox News*, June 1, 2023, www.foxnews.com/tech/us-military-ai-drone-simulation-kills-operator-told-bad-takes-out-control-tower.

2 Ibid.

3 Kate Conger & Lauren Hirsch, "Elon Musk Completes $44 Billion Deal to Own Twitter," *New York Times*, October 22, 2027, https://www.nytimes.com/2022/10/27/technology/elon-musk-twitter-deal-complete.html.

4 "Twitter Ends COVID Misinformation Policy under Musk," *BBC*, November 30, 2022, www.bbc.com/news/technology-63796832.

5 "Elon Musk with Tucker Carlson (FULL INTERVIEW) AI, TruthGPT, Twitter, Banking Crisis, Aliens," YouTube, April 19, 2023, https://www.youtube.com/watch?v=AmaPIiDnRMA.

6 Ed Gent, "Google's AI-Building AI Is a Step Toward Self-Improving AI," *Singularity Hub*, May 31, 2017, www.singularityhub.com/2017/05/31/googles-ai-building-ai-is-a-step-toward-self-improving-ai/.

7 Ibid.

8 Jasper Hamill, "Elon Musk's Fears that Artificial Intelligence Will Destroy Humanity are 'Speciest', said Google Founder Larry Page," *Metro News*, May 2, 2018, www.metro.co.uk/2018/05/02/elon-musks-fears-artificial-intelligence-will-destroy-humanity-speciesist-according-google-founder-larry-page-7515207/.

9 Yale Hanlon, "Elon Musk Reveals US Intel Agencies had 'Full Access" to Private Twitter DMs, Discloses New Encryption Features," Fox News, April 17, 2023, www.foxnews.com/media/elon-musk-us-intel-agencies-full-access-private-twitter-dms-discloses-new-encryption-feature.

10 "What is Speciesism?" PETA website (Accessed July 25, 2023), www.peta.org/features/what-is-speciesism/.

11 "About Me," Peter Singer personal website (Accessed April 21, 2023), www.petersinger.info/about-me-cv.

12 Jasper Hamill, "Elon Musk's Fears that Artificial Intelligence Will Destroy Humanity are 'Speciest', said Google Founder Larry Page."

13 David Marchese, "Yuval Noah Harari Believes This Simple Story Can Save the Planet," *New York Times Magazine,* November 7, 2021, www.nytimes.com/interactive/2021/11/08/magazine/yuval-noah-harari-interview.html.

14 Ibid.

15 Ibid.

16 Wesley J. Smith, "Transhumanist Theorist Calls the AI-Unenhanced 'Useless People,'" *National Review*, April 24, 2022, www.nationalreview.com/corner/transhumanist-theorist-calls-the-ai-unenhanced-useless-people/.

17 Ibid.

18 Ryan Chase, "A Life Unworthy of Life," *Decision* magazine, June 1, 2021, www.decisionmagazine .com/a-life-unworthy-of-life/.

19 "Read Yuval Harari's Blistering Warning to Davos in Full," World Economic Forum, January 20, 2020, www.weforum.org/agenda/2020/01/yuval-hararis-warning-davos-speech-future-predications/.

20 John Hittler, "An Antidote to the Rise of the 'Global Useless Class,'" *Forbes*, October 15, 2018, www.forbes.com/sites/forbescoachescouncil/2018/10/15/an-antidote-to-the-rise-of-the-global -useless-class/.

21 Ibid.

22 Cade Metz, "'The Godfather is A.I.' Leaves Google and Warns of Danger Ahead," *New York Times*, May 1, 2023, https://www.nytimes.com/2023/05/01/technology/ai-google-chatbot -engineer-quits-hinton.html.

23 Ibid.

24 Robby Soave, "Covid-16 is Probably 99% Survivable for Most Age Groups, but Politi-Fact Rated this False," *Reason*, August 9, 2021, www.reason.com/2021/08/09/covid-19-is-probably -99-survivable-for-most-age-groups-but-politifact-rated-this-false/.

25 "NEAS Final Form Ep12: The One with That One Call," YouTube, May 8, 2023, https://www .youtube.com/watch?v=usl7bWUt3tg..

26 Ronald Bailey, "To Save the Planet, Kill 90% of People Off, Says UT Ecologist," *Reason*, April 3, 2006, www.reason.com/2006/04/03/to-save-the-planet-kill-90-per/.

27 John Vidal, "Cut World Population and Redistribute Resources, Expert Urges," *The Guardian*, April 26, 2012, www.theguardian.com/environment/2012/apr/26/world-population-resources-paul -ehrlich.

Chapter Two

1 "Social Darwinism," *Encyclopedia Brittanica* (Accessed June 3, 2023; last updated May 16, 2023), www.britannica.com/topic/social-Darwinism.

2 Joshua A. Kirsch, "When Racism was a Science," *New York Times,* October 13, 2014, www .nytimes.com/2014/10/14/science/haunted-files-the-eugenics-record-office-recreates-a-dark -time-in-a-laboratorys-past.html.

3 Ibid.

4 Ibid.

5 "On the Correct Handling of Contradictions Among the People," Speech at the Eleventh Session of the Supreme State Conference," *Marxists.org*, February 27, 1957, https://www .marxists.org/reference/archive/mao/selected-works/volume-5/mswv5_58.htm.

6 Ibid.

7 Wengi Yang and Fei Yan, "The Annihilation of Femininity in Mao's China: Gender Inequality of Sent-Down Youth during the Cultural Revolution," *Sage Journals*, February 13, 2017, https://journals.sagepub.com/doi/10.1177/0920203X17691743.

8 "Private Dinner Conversation with Dr. Wolf by Kent Heckenlively," May 12, 2023, Camper Restaurant, Menlo Park.

9 Yu Xianghzen, "Confessions of a Red Guard, 50 Years after China's Cultural Revolution," CNN, May 15, 2016, www.cnn.com/2016/05/15/asia/china-cultural-revolution-red-guard -confession/index.html.

10 Ibid.

11 Ibid.

12 Ibid.

13 Valerie Strauss & Daniel Southeri, "How Many Died? New Evidence Suggests Far Higher Numbers for the Victims of Mao Zedong's Era," *Washington Post*, July 17, 1994, https://www.washingtonpost.com/archive/politics/1994/07/17/how-many-died-new-evidence-suggests-far-higher-numbers-for-the-victims-of-mao-zedongs-era/01044df5-03dd-49f4-a453-a033c5287bce/.

14 "On the Correct Handling of Contradictions Among the People."

15 David Rockefeller, "From a China Traveler," *New York Times*, August 10, 1973, www.nytimes.com/1973/08/10/archives/from-a-china-traveler.html.

16 "COINTELPRO," The FBI Records: The Vault (Accessed June 25, 2023), https://vault.fbi.gov/cointel-pro.

17 Maya Rhodan, "FBI Letter to Martin Luther King, Jr. Reveals Ugly Truths from Hoover's Era," *TIME*, November 12, 2014, www.time.com/3582004/fbi-letter-hoover-mlk/.

18 "The Sworn Testimony of Former FBI Senior Agent in Charge Ted Gunderson," *Rense*, November 18, 2018, https://rense.com/general96/the-sworn-testimony-of-former-fbi-senior-special-agent-in-charge-ted-gunderson.php.

19 "The FBI Exposed," Truth Justice, Twitter, August 10, 2023, www.twitter.com/SpartaJustice/status/1689715109583609856.

20 Dave Roos, "How the East India Company Became the World's Most Powerful Monopoly," History Channel, October 23, 2020, www.history.com/news/east-india-company-england-trade.

21 Ibid.

22 Ibid.

23 H. G. Wells, *The New World Order* (Legend Books, 2022), 46.

24 Ibid. at ix.

25 George Orwell, *A Collection of Essays* (San Diego, Harcourt Press, 1918), 237-238.

26 Mike Isaac and Kevin Roose, "Facebook Bans Alex Jones, Louis Farrakhan, and Others From Its Service," *New York Times*, May 2, 2019, www.nytimes.com/2019/05/02/technology/facebook-alex-jones-louis-farrakhan-ban.html.

27 Ibid.

28 Newswroom, "Former KKK Leader Invokes Trump's Name," CNN, August 12, 2017, www.cnn.com/videos/politics/2017/08/12/david-duke-trump-charlottesville-protest-nr.cnn.

29 "Flashback: Remember When Facebook Called for the Murder of Alex Jones & Others? Bombshell Report Reveals How Big Tech Advocates Open Violence, Threats Against Political Targets," *InfoWars*, June 1, 2023, www.infowars.com/posts/flashback-remember-when-facebook-called-for-the-murder-of-alex-jones-others/.

30 Carol D. Leonnig and Aaron C. Davis, "FBI Resisted Opening Probe into Trump's Role in Jan. 6 for More Than a Year," *Washington Post*, June 19, 2023, www.washingtonpost.com/investigations/2023/06/19/fbi-resisted-opening-probe-into-trumps-role-jan-6-more-than-year/.

31 Ibid.

32 Tim Pearce, "'It Should be a No!': Congressman Explodes After Wray Refuses Question on FBI, January 6, 2022," *Daily Wire*, November 15, 2022, www.dailywire.com/news/it-should-be-a-no-congressman-explodes-after-wray-refuses-question-on-fbi-january-6.

33 Helen Pluckrose and James Lindsay, *Cynical Theories: How Activist Scholarship Made Everything about Race, Gender, and Identity—And Why This Harms Everybody* (Durham, North Caroline, Pitchstone Publishing, 2020), 265-266.

Chapter Three

1 Ben Johnson, "Five Ways a Bioethicist Wants to Change Our Bodies to Fight Climate Change," Marketplace, December 15, 2016, www.marketplace.org/2016/12/15/five-ways-bioethicist-wants-change-our-bodies-fight-climate-change/.

2 "Life in Our Image – The Ethics of Altering the Human Genome," World Science Festival, YouTube, December 16, 2016, https://www.youtube.com/watch?v=qP7qL1Hyblk.

3 "Alpha-gal Syndrome," Ticks, CDC (Accessed August 19, 2023), www.cdc.gov/ticks/alpha-gal/index.html.

4 Ibid.

5 Ewen Callaway, "Fearful Memories Passed Down to Mice Descendants," *Scientific American*, December 1, 2013, www.scientificamerican.com/article/fearful-memories-passed-down/.

6 Ibid.

7 Ibid.

8 "Trauma's Epigenetic Fingerprint Observed in Children of Holocaust Survivors," *Science Daily*, September 1, 2016, www.sciencedaily.com/releases/2016/09/160901102207.htm.

9 Oliver Homes, "Netanyahu Touts Pfizer Deal as 20% of Israelis get COVID Jab," *The Guardian*, January 10, 2021, www.theguardian.com/world/2021/jan/10/netanyahu-touts-pfizer-deal-after-20-of-israelis-get-covid-jab.

10 Isabel Kershner, "As Israel Reopens, 'Whoever Does Not Get Vaccinated Will Be Left Behind,'" *New York Times*, February 18, 2021, www.nytimes.com/2021/02/18/world/middleeast/israel-covid-vaccine-reopen.html.

11 Zev Stub, "Netanyahu to Davos: Israel is World's Laboratory for Immunity,'" *Jerusalem Post*, January 27, 2021, www.jpost.com/israel-news/netanyahu-to-davos-israel-is-worlds-laboratory-for-immunity-656901.

12 "Benjamin Netanyahu Admits to Using the Israeli Population as Lab Rats (December 5, 2022)," Bitchute, December 30, 2020, https://www.bitchute.com/video/kvEuQAvuLlEN/.

13 "Amazing Facts About Fleas," One Kind Planet Animal Education and Facts, (Accessed April 22, 2023), www.onekindplanet.org/animal/flea/.

14 Darold Treffert, "Genetic Memory: How We Know Things We Never Learned," *Scientific American*, January 28, 2015, https://blogs.scientificamerican.com/guest-blog/genetic-memory-how-we-know-things-we-never-learned/.

15 Ibid.

16 Ibid.

17 R Melzack, E. Pennick, and A. Beckett, "The Problem of 'Innate Fear' of the Hawk Shape: An Experimental Study with Mallard Ducks," *Journal of Comparative Physiological Psychology*, vol. 52(6), p. 694-698, (1959), www.doi.org/10.1037/h0038532.

18 Sam Kean, "Mouse Heaven or Hell?" *Science History Institute*, May 17, 2022, www.sciencehistory.org/distillations/mouse-heaven-or-mouse-hell.

19 Ibid.

20 Ibid.

21 Ibid.

22 Ibid.

23 Jonathan Vanian, "Meta Lost $13.7 Billion on Reality Labs in 2022 as Zuckerberg's Metaverse Bet Gets Pricier," CNBC, February 1, 2023, www.cnbc.com/2023/02/01/meta-lost-13point7-billion-on-reality-labs-in-2022-after-metaverse-pivot.html.

24 Mike Isaac, "6 Reasons Meta is in Trouble," *New York Times*, February 3, 2022, www.nytimes.com/2022/02/03/technology/facebook-meta-challenges.html.

25 Tristan Bove, "One Week Working in the Metaverse Led to 19% More Anxiety and 16% Less Productivity, New Study Finds," *Yahoo News*, June 21, 2022, https://www.yahoo.com/video/one-week-working-metaverse-led-164453743.html.

26 Elroy Boers, Mohammed H. Afzali, Nicola Newton, et al., "Association of Screen Time and Adolescence," *Journal of American Pediatrics*, vol. 173(9), p. 853-859, 856-857, (July 15, 2019), doi:10.1001/jamapediatrics.2019.1759, www.jamanetwork.com/journals/jamapediatrics/fullarticle/2737909.

27 Ibid.

28 Andrea Peterson & Alex Janin, "One Simple Thing You Can Do to Relax This Summer," *Wall Street Journal*, August 2, 2022, www.wsj.com/articles/stress-relief-walk-nature-science-11659388504.

Chapter Four

1 Grant Suneson, "The Net Worth of Every US President from George Washington to Donald Trump," *USA Today*, February 13, 2019, www.usatoday.com/story/money/2020/11/05/the-net-worth-of-the-american-presidents-washington-to-trump/114599966/.

2 "George Washington's Account of Expenses while Commander in Chief of the Continental Army," Revolution and the New Nation (1754-1820s), National Archives and Records Administration (Accessed April 27, 2023), www.archives.gov/exhibits/american_originals/acctbk.html.

3 Ivana Pino, "57% of American Can't Afford a $1,000 Emergency Expense, Says New Report. A Look at Why Americans are Saving Less and How You Can Boost Your Emergency Fund," *Fortune*, January 25, 2023, www.fortune.com/recommends/banking/57-percent-of-americans-cant-afford-a-1000-emergency-expense/.

4 "Recent Trends in Monetary Policy," Board of Governors of the Federal Reserve System, (Accessed June 15, 2023), www.federalreserve.gov/monetarypolicy/bst_recenttrends.htm.

5 "Federal Reserve Act," Board of Governors of the Federal Reserve System (Accessed June 13, 2023), www.federalreserve.gov/aboutthefed/fract.htm.

6 Gary Richard, "The Federal Reserve's Role During World War 2," Federal Reserve History (Accessed June 13, 2023), www.federalreservehistory.org/essays/feds-role-during-wwii.

7 Sandra Kollen Ghizoni, "Creation of the Bretton Woods System," Federal Reserve History, November 22, 2013, www.federalreservehistory.org/essays/bretton-woods-created.

8 Charles Kolb, "August 15, 1971, *HuffPost*, www.huffpost.com/entry/august-15-1971_b_4284327.

9 Sandra Kollen Ghizoni, "Nixon Ends Convertibility of U.S. Dollars to Gold and Announces Wage/Price Controls," Federal Reserve History, November 22, 2013, www.federalreservehistory.org/essays/gold-convertibility-ends.

10 Alicia Wallace, "America's National Debt Has Now Surpassed $31 Trillion," CNN, October 4, 2022, www.cnn.com/2022/10/04/economy/us-national-debt-31-trillion/index.html.

11 David Blackmon, "A Spate of Recent Deals Raises Chatter of a Fading Petrodollar," *Forbes*, April 22, 2023, www.forbes.com/sites/davidblackmon/2023/04/02/a-spate-of-recent-deals-raises-chatter-of-a-fading-petrodollar/.

12 Tom O'Connor, "Why Saudi Arabia is Following Iran to Join China and Russia's Security Bloc," *Newsweek*, March 29, 2023, https://www.newsweek.com/why-saudi-arabia-following-iran-join-china-russias-security-bloc-1791326

13 Jan Strupczewski, Kate Abnett, David Lawder, & Andrea Shalal, "G7 Coalition Agrees $60 per Barrel Cap for Russian Oil," *Reuters*, December 2, 2022, www.reuters.com/business/energy/holdout-poland-approves-eus-60-russian-oil-price-cap-with-adjustment-mechanism-2022-12-02/.

14 Bradford Betz, "Japan Puts Russian Oil Above $60 a Barrel Cap, Breaking with U.S. Allies: Report," Fox Business News, April 2, 2023, https://www.foxbusiness.com/markets/japan-buys-russian-oil-above-60-barrel-cap-breaking-us-allies-report.

15 Dalibar Rohac, "France's Macron Picks a Needless Fight with the United States," *New York Post,* April 10, 2023, nypost.com/2023/04/10/frances-macron-picks-a-needless-fight-with-the-united-states/.

16 Max Reyes, "The Search for Lessons From Another US Banking Crisis," *Bloomberg*, June 6, 2023, www.bloomberg.com/news/articles/2023-06-06/2023-banking-crisis-key-lessons-from-the-svb-first-republic-collapses.

17 Jesse O'Neill, "Biden Insists US Economy is 'Strong as Hell' as He Munches an Ice Cream Cone," *New York Post*, October 16, 2022, www.nypost.com/2022/10/16/joe-biden-insists-us-economy-is-strong-as-hell-as-he-munches-an-ice-cream-cone/.

18 Katherine Fung, "Banks Have Begun Freezing Accounts Linked to Trucker Protest," *Newsweek*, February 18, 2022, www.newsweek.com/banks-have-begun-freezing-accounts-linked-trucker-protest-1680649.

19 Oliver JJ Lane, "Debanking Has Arrived: Farage Left Without Bank Account," *Breitbart*, June 30, 2023, www.breitbart.com/europe/2023/06/30/debanking-has-arrived-farage-pursues-legal-action-as-hes-left-without-bank-account/.

20 Ibid.

21 Pippa Malmgren, World Government Summit, 2022, "Digital Currency is Coming," YouTube, www.youtube.com/watch?v=7-Pj1i1RLm4.

22 Lily Kuo, "China Bans 23M from Buying Travel Tickets as Part of 'Social Credit' System," *The Guardian*, March 1, 2019, www.theguardian.com/world/2019/mar/01/china-bans-23m-discredited-citizens-from-buying-travel-tickets-social-credit-system.

23 Peter Patroll & Bryan Chai, "World Economic Forum Speaker Reveals the True Power Behind Governments' Digital Currencies," *Independent Journal Review*, July 9, 2023, www.ijr.com/world-economic-forum-speaker-reveals-true-power-behind-governments-digital-currencies/.

24 Robert D. Knight, "Joe Rogan Podcast Exposes Central Bank Digital Currency (CBDC) Dystopia," Be in Crypto, February 22, 2022, www.beincrypto.com/joe-rogan-central-bank-digital-currency-cbdc-dystopia/.

25 "Event 201", Johns Hopkins/Bloomberg School of Public Health, October 18, 2019, www.centerforhealthsecurity.org/our-work/tabletop-exercises/event-201-pandemic-tabletop-exercise.

26 Smriti Mallapalty, "COVID-Origins Study Links Racoon Dogs to Wuhan Market: What Scientists Think," *Nature*, March 21, 2023, www.nature.com/articles/d41586-023-00998-y.

Chapter Five

1 Richard Nelsson, "The Molotov-Ribbentrop Pact – Archive – August 1939," *The Guardian*, July 24, 2019, www.theguardian.com/world/from-the-archive-blog/2019/jul/24/molotov-ribbentrop-pact-germany-russia-1939.

2 History.com Editors, "Operation Barbarossa," History Channel, November 24, 2022, www.history.com/topics/world-war-ii/operation-barbarossa.

3 Christopher J. Kshyk, "Did Stalin Plan to Attack Hitler in 1941? The Historiographical Controversy Surrounding the Origins of the Nazi-Soviet War," *Inquiries Journal*, www.inquiriesjournal.com/articles/1278/2/did-stalin-plan-to-attack-hitler-in-1941-the-historiographical-controversy-surrounding-the-origins-of-the-nazi-soviet-war.

4 Ibid.

5 Gianluna Gini, Tiziana Pozzoli, & Marc Hauser, "Bullies Have Enhanced Moral Competence Relative to Victims, But Lack Moral Compassion," *Journal of Personality and Individual Differences*, vol. 50, issue 5, p. 603-608 (April 2011), www.sciencedirect.com/science/article/pii/S0191886910005866.

6 Chi Wang, "How Zbigniew Brzezinski Shaped US-China Relations," *The Diplomat*, July 1, 2017, https://thediplomat.com/2017/07/how-zbigniew-brzezinski-shaped-us-china-relations/.

7 "Dr. Rahul Gupta Releases Statement on CDC's New Overdose Death Data," The White House, January 11, 2023, www.whitehouse.gov/ondcp/briefing-room/2023/01/11/dr-rahul-gupta-releases-statement-on-cdcs-new-overdose-death-data-2/.

8 Jeremy Herb & Natasha Bernard, "US Energy Department Assesses Covid-19 Likely Resulted from Lab leak, Furthering US Intel Divide over Virus Origin," CNN, February 27, 2023, www.cnn.com/2023/02/26/politics/covid-lab-leak-wuhan-china-intelligence/index.html.

9 Illya Somin, "Remembering the Biggest Mass Murder in the History of the World," *Washington Post*, August 3, 2016, www.washingtonpost.com/news/volokh-conspiracy/wp/2016/08/03/giving-historys-greatest-mass-murderer-his-due/.

10 Josh Rogin, "Tulsi Gabbard's Syria Record Shows Why She Can't Be President," *Washington Post*, August 1, 2019, www.washingtonpost.com/opinions/global-opinions/tulsi-gabbards-syria-record-shows-why-she-cant-be-president/2019/08/01/f804c790-b497-11e9-8949-5f36ff92706e_story.html.

11 Lolita C. Baldor, "A Look at the US Military Mission in Syria and Its Dangers," *Associated Press*, March 24, 2023, www.apnews.com/article/syria-us-troops-drone-attack-6194dca97f594e3609914637463c4ce3.

12 Somin, "Remembering the Biggest Mass Murder in the History of the World."

13 William Harris, "Psychopaths are Not Neurally Equipped to Have Concern for Others," University of Chicago News, April 24, 2013, https://news.uchicago.edu/story/psychopaths-are-not-neurally-equipped-have-concern-others.

14 Michael Hirsch, "A Q&A with Zbigniew Brzezinski," *Politico*, November 6, 2014, www.politico.com/magazine/story/2014/11/its-time-for-a-new-opening-to-china-112656/.

15 Ibid.

16 Adense Huld, "US-China Trade in Goods Hits New record in 2022 – What Does it Mean for Bilateral Ties?" China Briefing, February 15, 2023, www.china-briefing.com/news/us-china-trade-in-goods-hits-new-record-in-2022-what-does-it-mean-for-bilateral-ties/

17 "China's Xi Jinping Defends Globalization from the Davos Stage," World Economic Forum, January 17, 2017, www.weforum.org/agenda/2017/01/chinas-xi-jinping-defends-globalization-from-the-davos-stage.

18 Ibid.

19 "Transcript: George Soros Interview," *Financial Times*, October 23, 2009, www.ft.com/content/6e2dfb82-c018-11de-aed2-00144feab49a.

20 Ibid.

21 Ibid.

22 David Scutt, "China Has Picked a Big Fight with George Soros," *Business Insider Australia*, January 28, 2016, www.businessinsider.com/china-picks-big-fight-with-george-soros-2016-1.

23 Ibid.

24 Sam Meredith, "BlackRock Responds to George Soros' Criticism Over China Investments," CNBC, September 8, 2021, www.cnbc.com/2021/09/08/blackrock-responds-to-george-soros-criticism-over-china-investments.html.

25 Ibid.

26 Brooke Singman, "Soros Calls China's Xi Jinping 'the Greatest Threat that Open Societies Face Today,'" Fox News, February 1, 2022, www.foxbusiness.com/politics/soros-china-xi-jinping-greatest-threat-open-societies-face.

27 Ibid.

28 Isabel Vincent, "How George Soros Funded Progressive 'Legal Arsonist' DAs Behind U.S. Crime Surge," *New York Post*, December 16, 2021, www.nypost.com/2021/12/16/how-george-soros-funded-progressive-das-behind-us-crime-surge/.

29 Maureen Down, "2 U.S. Officials Went to Beijing Secretly in July," *New York Times*, December 19, 1989, www.nytimes.com/1989/12/19/world/2-us-officials-went-to-beijing-secretly-in-july.html.

30 Ryan King, "Obama Blames Trump for Emboldened China," *Washington Examiner*, March 28, 2023, www.washingtonexaminer.com/policy/foreign/obama-faults-trump-emboldened-china.

31 Ibid.

Chapter Six

1 "U.S. Defense Spending Compared to Other Countries," Peter G. Peterson Foundation, (Accessed May 8, 2023), www.pgpf.org/blog/2023/04/the-united-states-spends-more-on-defense-than-the-next-10-countries-combined.

2 Ibid.

3 "Countries with the Highest Military Spending Worldwide in 2022," Statista (Accessed June 13, 2023), www.statista.com/statistics/262742/countries-with-the-highest-military-spending/.

4 Ibid.

5 Ibid.

6 Ibid.

7 Ibid.

8 Ibid.

9 Ibid.

10 Ibid.

11 Ibid.

12 Ibid.

13 Ibid.

14 Ashik Siddique, "U.S. Still Spends More on Military Than Next Nine Countries Combined," National Priorities Project, June 22, 2022, www.nationalpriorities.org/blog/2022/06/22/us-still-spends-more-military-next-nine-countries-combined/.

15 Doug Bamdow, "750 Bases in 80 Countries is Too Many for Any Nation: Time for the US to Bring Its Troops Home," Cato Institutes Commentary, October 4, 2021, www.cato.org/commentary/750-bases-80-countries-too-many-any-nation-time-us-bring-its-troops-home#.

16 Ibid.

17 Ibid.

18 Ibid.

19 Stephen Semeler, "Biden is Selling Weapons to the Majority of the World's Autocracies," *The Intercept,* May 11, 2023, www.theintercept.com/2023/05/11/united-states-foreign-weapons-sales/.

20 Ibid.

21 Ibid.

22 Murtaza Hussain, "Over Two Decades, U.S.'s Global War on Terror Has Taken Nearly 1 Million Lives and Cost $8 Trillion," *The Intercept*, September 1, 2021, www.theintercept.com/2021/09/01/war-on-terror-deaths-cost.

23 Ibid.

24 Ibid.

25 William D. Hartung, "What a Waste: $778 Billion for the Pentagon and Still Counting," Quincy Institute for Responsible Statecraft, February 3, 2022, www.quincyinst.org/2022/02/03/what-a-waste-778-billion-for-the-pentagon-and-still-counting/.

26 Ibid.

27 Ibid.

28 William Arkin, "Sunk Cost," *Newsweek*, April 28, 2023.

29 Richard Knowles Morris, "The Story of the Holland Submarine," U.S. Naval Institute, January 1960, www.usni.org/magazines/proceedings/1960/january/story-holland-submarine-pictorial/.

30 Ibid.

31 Ibid.

32 Ibid.

33 "Billion Dollar Watchdog," *TIME,* March 8, 1943, https://content.time.com/time/subscriber/article/0,33009,774390,00.html.

34 Ibid.

35 Ibid.

36 "President Dwight D. Eisenhower's Farewell Address," National Archives (Accessed May 20, 2023), www.archives.gov/milestone-documents/president-dwight-d-eisenhowers-farewell-address.

37 Lewis Pennock, "Supreme Court Justice Gorsuch Issues Excoriating Review of COVID Lockdown Policies Including Business Closures and Vaccine Mandates and Calls Them 'Among the Greatest Intrusions on Civil Liberties in the History of the Nation'," *Daily Mail,* May 20, 2023, www.dailymail.co.uk/news/article-12106351/Supreme-Court-justice-tears-COVID-lockdown-vaccine-policies.html.

38 Jenna Ryu, "'Screw Your Freedom': Arnold Schwarzenegger Calls Anti-Maskers 'Schmucks' in Powerful Rant," *USA Today*, August 12, 2021, www.usatoday.com/story/entertainment/celebrities/2021/08/12/arnold-schwarzenegger-anti-maskers-screw-your-freedom/8106562002/.

39 Pennock, "Supreme Court Justice Gorsuch Issues Excoriating Review of COVID Lockdown Policies Including Business Closures and Vaccine Mandates and Calls Them 'Among the Greatest Intrusions on Civil Liberties in the History of the Nation.'"

40 Ibid.

Chapter Seven

1 Tim Haines, "RFK, Jr.: My Father Believed the CIA and Allen Dulles Killed My Uncle JFK, 'There's Been a 60 Year Coverup,'" *Real Clear Politics*, May 9, 2023, www.realclearpolitics.com/video/2023/05/09/rfk_jr_my_father_believed_the_cia_killed_my_uncle_jfk_60_year_coverup.html.

2 Peter Feuerherd, "How the Bay of Pigs Invasion Changed JFK," *JSTOR Daily*, April 11, 2019, https://daily.jstor.org/how-the-bay-of-pigs-invasion-changed-jfk/.

3 Ibid.

4 Robert F. Kennedy Jr., "John F. Kennedy's Vision of Peace," *Rolling Stone*, November 20, 2013, www.rollingstone.com/politics/politics-news/john-f-kennedys-vision-of-peace-109020/.

5 Lieutenant Commander Pat Paterson, "The Truth About Tonkin," *Naval History Magazine*, February 2008, Vol. 22, Number 1, www.usni.org/magazines/naval-history-magazine/2008/february/truth-about-tonkin.

6 Ibid.

7 Ibid.

8 Ibid.

9 Ibid.

10 Ibid.

11 Ibid.

12 Ibid.

13 Ibid.

14 Ibid.

15 Ibid.

16 Ibid.

17 "Robert S. McNamara," The World Bank – Explore History (Accessed June 14, 2023), www.worldbank.org/en/archive/history/past-presidents/robert-strange-mcnamara.

18 "A Timeline of the Iraq War," *PBS Newshour*, March 7, 2023, www.pbs.org/newshour/world/a-timeline-of-the-iraq-war.

19 Glenn Kessler, "The Iraq War and WMDs: An Intelligence Failure or White House Spin?" *Washington Post*, March 22, 2019, www.washingtonpost.com/politics/2019/03/22/iraq-war-wmds-an-intelligence-failure-or-white-house-spin/.

20 Ibid.

21 Noreen Malone, "What the Iraq Invasion Revealed About How America Works," *Slate*, April 22, 2021, www.slate.com/news-and-politics/2021/04/iraq-invasion-slow-burn-intro.html.

22 Anna Fifield, "Contractors Reap $138B from Iraq War," CNN, March 19, 2013, www.cnn.com/2013/03/19/business/iraq-war-contractors/index.html.

23 Ishaan Tharoor, "The Death Toll in Ukraine is Huge. It may Still be Far Behind Tigray," *Washington Post*, May 3, 2023, www.washingtonpost.com/world/2023/05/03/tigray-ethiopia-casualty-death-ukraine-russia/.

24 "Kennedy Speaks About Ukraine Losses," Azerbaycan 24, April 21, 2023, www.azerbaycan24.com/en/kennedy-speaks-about-ukraine-losses/.

25 Daniel L. Davis, "What is the US Getting in Ukraine for $100 Billion?" *Business Insider*, January 10, 2023, www.businessinsider.com/congress-explain-how-ukraine-military-aid-advances-us-interests-2023-1.

26 Jeffrey D. Sachs, "The War in Ukraine was Provoked – And Why That Matters to Achieve Peace," *Common Dreams,* May 23, 2023, www.commondreams.org/opinion/the-war-in-ukraine-was-provoked-and-why-that-matters-if-we-want-peace.

27 Ibid.

28 Ibid.

29 Miranda Devine, "Hunter Biden's Ukraine Salary Was Cut Two Months After Joe Biden Left Office," *New York Post*, May 26, 2021, www.nypost.com/2021/05/26/hunter-bidens-ukraine-salary-was-cut-after-joe-biden-left-office/.

30 Ibid.

31 Ibid.

32 Hersch, "How America Took Out the Nord Stream Pipeline."

33 Ibid.

34 "Nord Stream Rupture May Mark Biggest Single Methane Release Ever Recorded, U.N. Says," *Reuters*, September 30, 2022, www.reuters.com/world/europe/nord-stream-rupture-may-mark-biggest-single-methane-release-ever-recorded-un-2022-09-30/.

35 Seymour Hersch, "How America Took Out the Nord Stream Pipeline," Substack, February 8, 2023, https://seymourhersh.substack.com/p/how-america-took-out-the-nord-stream.

36 David Ruppe, "U.S. Military Wanted to Provoke War with Cuba," *ABC News*, May 1, 2001, https://abcnews.go.com/US/story?id=92662&page=1.

37 Hersch, "How America Took Out the Nord Stream Pipeline."

38 "Leaked Video: Retired Four Star General McChrystal Claims US Behind Nord Stream Pipeline Bombing," *Newswars*, July 22, 2023, www.newswars.com/leaked-video-retired-four-star-general-mcchrystal-claims-us-behind-nord-stream-pipeline-bombing/.

39 Chris Menahan, "WSJ: The West Knew Ukraine Wasn't Prepared for Counter-Offensive, Hoped their 'Courage and Resourcefulness Would Carry the Day,'" *InfoWars*, July 26, 2023, www.infowars.com/posts/wsj-the-west-knew-ukraine-wasnt-prepared-for-counter-offensive-hoped-their-courage-and-resourcefulness-would-carry-the-day/.

Chapter Eight

1 Israel Salas-Rodriguez & Tereza Shkurtaj, "Who Are Tucker Carlson's Parents?" *U.S. Sun*, April 24, 2023, www.the-sun.com/news/2486984/get-to-know-fox-host-tucker-carlsons-parents/.

2 "Malcolm X. Quotes," GoodReads (Accessed July 24, 2023), www.goodreads.com/quotes/74430-the-media-s-the-most-powerful-entity-on-earth-they-have.

3 "Larry Silverstein WTC7 'Pull It' Statement," YouTube, November 6, 2007, www.youtube.com/watch?v=p34XrI2Fm6I.

4 "Alex Jones Predicted Tucker Would Get Fired Last Month," *Salty Cracker*, April 24, 2023, www.saltmustflow.com/aoc-wants-tucker-banned-from-tv-copy/.

5 "Tucker Carlson on Twitter," May 23, 2023, www.twitter.com/TuckerCarlson/status/1656037032538390530?lang=en.

6 Nick Gilbertson, "Report: Fox Lost to CNN, MSNBC in Key Demo During Tucker Carlson's Old Slot," *Breitbart*, May 9, 2023, www.breitbart.com/the-media/2023/05/09/fox-loses-cnn-msnbc-key-demo-tucker-carlson-old-slot/.

7 Cheryl Teh, "Paul Ryan Didn't Hesitate to Blame Tucker When Asked About 'Toxic Sludge' and 'Misinformation' on Fox News," *Business Insider*, March 1, 2023, www.businessinsider.com/paul-ryan-tucker-carlson-fox-news-toxic-sludge-disinformation-2023-3.

8 Nicholas von Hoffman, "Journalism and the CIA," *Washington Post*, October 5, 1977, https://www.washingtonpost.com/archive/lifestyle/1977/10/05/journalism-and-the-cia/de80094a-6b88-4e7a-94ef-3da744351fba/.

9 *Tucker Carlson Tonight*, YouTube, April 20, 2023, www.youtube.com/watch?v=t9eN19qkZRk.

10 Ibid.

11 Ibid.

12 Jeff Bercovi, "Eight Things You Didn't Know About Fox News' Roger Ailes," *Forbes*, March 19, 2013, www.forbes.com/sites/jeffbercovici/2013/03/19/eight-things-you-didnt-know-about-fox-news-chief-roger-ailes/.

13 "Straight Ahead with Roger Ailes," YouTube, May, 1995. www.youtube.com/watch?v=EU32wrSptwE.

14 Ibid.

15 Ibid.

16 Ibid.

17 Ibid.

18 Liz Smith, "Kennedy and Ailes Pitch a Tent," *Newser*, January 6, 2006, www.adweek.com/tvnewser/kennedy-ailes-pitch-a-tent/.

19 "Episode 127: Presidential Candidate Robert F. Kennedy, Jr. in Conversations with the Besties," *All-In Podcast*, May 5, 2023, https://podcasts.apple.com/us/podcast/e127-presidential-candidate-robert-f-kennedy-jr-in/id1502871393?i=1000611941938.

20 "Tucker Carlson Address at the Heritage Foundation," YouTube, April 22, 2023, www.youtube.com/watch?v=ebG2POkoHgU.

21 Ibid.

22 Ibid.

23 Ibid.

24 Ibid.

25 Ibid.

26 "Robert F. Kennedy Quotes," GoodReads (Accessed June 14, 223), www.goodreads.com/quotes/8215370-moral-courage-is-a-rarer-commodity-than-bravery-in-battle.

27 "Tucker Carlson Address at the Heritage Foundation."

28 Ronald C. White Jr., "Honest Abe Reminds Us of the Power of Words," *NPR*, March 4, 2011, www.npr.org/2011/03/04/134162178/150-years-later-lincolns-words-still-resonate.

29 Gabriel Sherman, "Tucker Carlson's Prayer Talk May Have Led to Fox News Ouster: 'That Stuff Freaks Rupert Out'," *Vanity Fair*, April 25, 2023, www.vanityfair.com/news/2023/04/tucker-carlson-fox-news-rupert-murdoch.

30 Ibid.

31 Ibid.

32 Mike Redmond, "Tucker Carlson Reportedly Could Be Off the Air Until 2024, if Fox News Has Its Way," *Viral*, April 28, 2023, www.uproxx.com/viral/tucker-carlson-fox-news-contract-2024/.

33 Sherman, "Tucker Carlson's Prayer Talk May Have Led to Fox News Ouster: 'That Stuff Freaks Rupert Out.'"

34 "Tucker Carlson Interview with Russell Brand," *Rumble*, July 7, 2023. www.rumble.com/v2ypa20-russell-brand-interviews-tucker-carlson-full-interview.html.

35 "Dominick Mastrangelo, "Tucker Carlson Tweet Announcing New Twitter Show Tops 100 Million Views," *The Hill*, May 10, 2023, www.thehill.com/homenews/3998093-tucker-carlson-tweet-announcing-new-twitter-show-tops-100-million-views/.

36 Rick Porter, "Fox News Takes Ratings Hit after Tucker Carlson's Exit," *Hollywood Reporter*, April 25, 2023, www.hollywoodreporter.com/tv/tv-news/fox-news-takes-ratings-hit-after-tucker-carlsons-exit-1235400150/.

37 Erik Wemple, "Sexual Harassment Victims Drive Fox News – Roger Ailes Documentary," *Washington Post*, November 15, 2018, www.washingtonpost.com/blogs/erik-wemple/wp/2018/11/15/sexual-harassment-victims-drive-fox-news-roger-ailes-documentary/.

Chapter Nine

1 Anne Karni, Eileen Sullivan, and Noam Scheiber, "Acosta to Resign as Labor Secretary Over Jeffrey Epstein Plea Deal," *New York Times*, July 12, 2019, https://www.nytimes.com/2019/07/12/us/politics/acosta-resigns-trump.html#:~:text=Alexander%20Acosta%2C%20the%20labor%20secretary,say%20it%20to%20the%20press.

2 Julie K. Brown, *Perversion of Justice: The Jeffrey Epstein Story* (Mw York - Dey Street, an Imprint of William Morrow, 2021), xii.

3 Ibid. at xii – xiii.

4 Nicole Goodkid, "'No Regrets is a Very Hard Question,' Alex Acosta Defends Jeffrey Epstein Plea Deal," *Newsweek*, July 10, 2019, www.newsweek.com/alex-acosta-epstein-sex-trafficking-department-labor-1448568.

5 Jack Crowe, "Epstein's Lawyer Claimed the Alleged Pedophile Helped Devise the Clinton Global Initiative," *Yahoo News*, July 8, 2019, www.yahoo.com/now/epstein-lawyer-claimed-alleged-pedophile-223701676.html.

6 Chris Spargo, "Rape, Lies and Videotape: Jeffrey Epstein had Surveillance Cameras in Every Room of His NYC and Little St. James Properties – for Security and to Feed his Depraved Perversions," *Daily Mail*, August 14, 2019, www.dailymail.co.uk/news/article-7357357/Jeffrey-Epstein-surveillance-cameras-room-NYC-Little-St-James-properties.html.

7 Gustaf Kilander, "Epstein Victim Claims He Had Surveillance Rooms and Secret Cameras at New Mexico Ranch," *The Independent*, October 21, 2021, www.independent.co.uk/news/world/americas/crime/jeffrey-epstein-victims-ranch-cameras-b1942944.html.

8 Jerry Lambe, "The 'Epstein-Barr' Problem at New York City's Dalton School," *Law and Crime*, July 13, 2019, www.lawandcrime.com/high-profile/the-epstein-barr-problem-of-new-york-citys-dalton-school/.

9 Katie Benner, "Barr Says Epstein's Suicide Resulted From 'Perfect Storm of Screw-Ups,'" *New York Times,* November 22, 2019, www.nytimes.com/2019/11/22/nyregion/william-barr-jeffrey-epstein-suicide-investigation.html.

10 Mike Baker and Amy Julia Harris, "Jeffrey Epstein Taught at Dalton. His Behavior was Noticed," *New York Times*, July 12, 2019, www.nytimes.com/2019/07/12/nyregion/jeffrey-epstein-dalton-teacher.html.

11 Ibid.

12 Wolfgang Saxon, "Donald Barr, 82, Headmaster and Science Honors Educator," *New York Times*, February 10, 2004, www.nytimes.com/2004/02/10/nyregion/donald-barr-82-headmaster-and-science-honors-educator.html.

13 Brown, *Perversion of Justice*, 47.
14 Donald Barr, *Space Relations* (Fawcett Crest – Connecticut), 1973, back cover.
15 Ibid. at p. 98-99.
16 Ibid. at 116-117.
17 Ibid. at 253-254.
18 Ibid. at 254.
19 Donald Barr, *A Planet in Arms* (New York, Fawcett Crest, 1981), back cover.
20 Ibid. at p. 127.
21 Marie Brenner, "'I Had No Problem Being Politically Different,' Young William Barr Among the Manhattan Liberals," *Vanity Fair*, October 7, 2019, www.vanityfair.com/news/2019/10/the-untold-tale-of-young-william-barr.
22 James Barron, "Who is Jeffrey Epstein? An Opulent Life, Celebrity Friends, and Lurid Accusations," *New York Times*, July 9, 2019, www.nytimes.com/2019/07/09/nyregion/jeffrey-epstein-who-is-he.html.
23 Ibid.
24 Vicky Ward, "Was Jeffrey Epstein a Spy?" *Rolling Stone*, June 15, 2021, www.rollingstone.com/culture/culture-features/jeffrey-epstein-steven-hoffenberg-intelligence-agencies-spy-1197708/.
25 Ibid.
26 Ibid
27 Ibid.
28 Ibid.
29 Brown, *Perversion of Justice*, 211.
30 Ibid.
31 Ibid at 220.
32 Ibid. at 221.
33 Ibid.
34 Ibid. at 223.
35 Ibid. at 224.
36 James Patterson & John Connolly with Tim Malloy, *Filthy Rich* (New York, Little Brown and Company, October 2016), p. 146 -147.
37 Dylan Howard, with Melissa Cronin & James Robertson, *Dead Men Tell No Tales: Spies, Lies, and Blackmail*, (New York - Front Page Detectives, 2019), p. 106-107.
38 Terry Reed & John Cummings, *Compromised: Clinton, Bush, and the CIA*, S.P.I. (New York, S.P. Books, 1994), p. 229.
39 Ibid.
40 Ibid.
41 Ibid. at p. 235.
42 Howard, *Dead Men Tell No Tales*, 127.
43 Brown, *Perversion of Justice*, 369, 370.
44 Ibid. at p. 371.
45 Michael Levenson, "Harvard Kept Ties with Jeffrey Epstein after '08 Conviction, Report Shows," *New York Times*, May 1, 2020, www.nytimes.com/2020/05/01/us/jeffrey-epstein-harvard.html.
46 Ibid.

47 Collin Binkley, "Jeffrey Epstein Frequented Harvard, Had Own Office, Report Finds," *CBS Boston*, May 1, 2020, www.nbcboston.com/news/national-international/epstein-frequented-harvard-had-own-office-report-finds/2117275/.

48 "Meryl Streep, Who Once Called Harvey Weinstein 'God,' Speaks Out Against Him after Sexual Harrassment Allegations," *KTLA LA*, October 9, 2017, www.ktla.com/news/local-news/meryl-streep-who-once-called-harvey-weinstein-god-speaks-out-against-him-after-sexual-harassment-allegations/.

49 Ronan Farrow, "How an Elite University Research Center Concealed Its Relationship with Jeffrey Epstein," *New Yorker*, September 6, 2019, www.newyorker.com/news/news-desk/how-an-elite-university-research-center-concealed-its-relationship-with-jeffrey-epstein.

50 Ibid.

51 Ibid.

52 Ibid.

53 Lachlan Cartwright, "Jeffrey Epstein Bragged Bill Barr was in Charge, Not Trump," *Daily Beast*, October 15, 2021, www.thedailybeast.com/epstein-bragged-barr-was-in-charge-not-trump.

54 Ibid.

55 Ibid.

56 James B, Stewart, Matthew Goldstein, and Jessica Silver-Greenberg, "Jeffrey Epstein Hoped to Seed Human Race with his DNA," *New York Times*, July 31, 2019, www.nytimes.com/2019/07/31/business/jeffrey-epstein-eugenics.html.

57 Ibid.

58 Ibid.

59 Ibid.

60 Nick Nowalk, "Pascal's God-Shaped Hole," *Icthus*, May 2, 2011, https://harvardichthus.org/2011/05/pascal_hole/.

61 Benjamin Weiser, Kim Barker, and Grace Ashford, "Fashion Mogul Peter Nygard Indicted on Sex-Trafficking Charges," *New York Times*, December 15, 2020, www.nytimes.com/2020/12/15/world/canada/peter-nygard-sex-trafficking-charges.html.

62 Ibid.

63 Melissa Cronin, *Predator King: Peter Nygard's Dark Life of Rape, Drugs, and Blackmail*, New York – Hot Books, 2020), p. 71.

64 Ibid.

65 Ibid at. p. 72.

66 "Shock Video: TV Producers Interview Real Vampires," *Newswars*, October 16, 2022, www.newswars.com/shock-video-tv-producers-interview-real-vampires/.

67 Benner, "Barr Says Epstein's Suicide Resulted From 'Perfect Storm of Screw-Ups.'"

68 Ibid.

69 Devan Cole, "Washington Post: Bill Barr Says Trump 'Has Neither the Temperament nor Persuasive Powers' of a Leader," CNN, February 27, 2023, www.cnn.com/2022/02/27/politics/bill-barr-trump-criticism-new-book/index.html.

70 Steve Janoski, "New Jeffrey Epstein Docs reveal Pedophile Met with CIA Chief, Former White House Counsel – After His Child Sex Crime Conviction," *New York Post*, April 30, 2023, www.nypost.com/2023/04/30/epsteins-newly-released-calendar-includes-planned-meets-with-cia-chief-college-head-and-former-white-house-counsel/.

71 Ariel Zilber, "Joe Rogan: Jeffrey Epstein May Have Been CIA or Mossad Spy," *New York Post*, August 1, 2022, www.nypost.com/2022/08/01/joe-rogan-jeffrey-epstein-may-have-been-cia-or-mossad-spy/.

72 Amanda Holpuch, "Bill Gates Says Meetings with Jeffrey Epstein were 'Huge Mistake,'" *The Guardian*, August 5, 2021, www.theguardian.com/us-news/2021/aug/05/bill-gates-jeffrey-epstein-meeting-huge-mistake.

73 Jay Greene, "The Billionaire Who Cried Pandemic," *Washington Post*, May 2, 2020, www.washingtonpost.com/technology/2020/05/02/bill-gates-coronavirus-science/.

74 Jessica Napoli, "Jeffrey Epstein's Pilot Reveals Names of Hollywood Stars who Flew on His Plane," Fox News, December 1, 2021, www.foxnews.com/entertainment/jeffrey-epstein-pilot-names-hollywood-stars-flew-private-plane.

75 Nick Arama, "Joe Rogan Just Dropped Bill Clinton with Comment About Jeffrey Epstein and that Infamous Painting," *Red State*, July 23, 2023, www.redstate.com/nick-arama/2023/07/23/joe-rogan-just-dropped-bill-clinton-with-comment-about-jeffrey-epstein-and-that-infamous-painting-n781017.

76 Kyle McBreen, "Artist Who Painted Bill Clinton in a Dress Also Painted George W. Bush Re-Enacting 9-11," *Newswars*, August 16, 2019, https://www.newswars.com/artist-who-painted-bill-clinton-in-a-dress-also-painted-george-w-bush-re-enacting-9-11/.

77 Hattie Hamilton & Jenny Ki, "Jeffrey Epstein was a Mossad Spy, Says Investigative Journalist Dylan Howard," *The Morning Show*, August 12, 2019, www.7news.com.au/the-morning-show/jeffrey-epstein-was-a-mossad-spy-says-investigative-journalist-dylan-howard-c-595812.

78 Jim Ferguson, Twitter comment, July 24, 2023, https://twitter.com/JimFergusonUK/status/1683388043196088321.

Chapter Ten

1 "Flashback: Alex Jones Predicted Forced Vaccine Tyranny Over 10 Years Ago," *InfoWars*, May 21, 2021, www.newswars.com/flashback-alex-jones-predicted-forced-vaccine-tyranny-over-10-years-ago/.

2 Ibid.

3 "COVID-19 Timeline," David J. Sencer Museum: In Association with the Smithsonian Institution, Centers for Disease Control (Accessed June 7, 2023), www.cdc.gov/museum/timeline/covid19.html.

4 Military Documents About Gain of Function Contradict Fauci Testimony Under Oath," *Project Veritas*, January 10, 2022, www.projectveritas.com/news/military-documents-about-gain-of-function-contradict-fauci-testimony-under/.

5 Nick Turse, "DARPA's Wild Kingdom," *Mother Jones*, March 8, 2004, www.motherjones.com/politics/2004/03/darpas-wild-kingdom.

6 Diane Tedeschi, "How Much Did Wernher von Braun Know, and When Did He Know It?" *Smithsonian Magazine*, January 1, 2008, www.smithsonianmag.com/air-space-magazine/a-amp-s-interview-michael-j-neufeld-23236520/.

7 Peter Daszak, "Project DEFUSE: Defusing the Threat of Bat-Borne Coronaviruses," EcoHealth Alliance, March 24, 2018, www.projectveritas.com/news/military-documents-about-gain-of-function-contradict-fauci-testimony-under/.

8 Ibid.

[9] Josh Rogin, "State Department Cables Warned of Safety Issues at Wuhan Lab Studying Bat Coronaviruses," *Washington Post*, April 14, 2020, www.washingtonpost.com/opinions/2020/04/14/state-department-cables-warned-safety-issues-wuhan-lab-studying-bat-coronaviruses/.

[10] Daszak, "Project DEFUSE...".

[11] Rogin, "State Department Cables Warned of Safety Issues."

[12] Ibid.

[13] Andrew Huff, *The Truth About Wuhan: How I Uncovered the Biggest Lie in History*, (New York, Skyhorse Publishing, 2022), p. 182.

[14] Ibid. at p. 213.

[15] Ibid. at p. 214.

[16] Ibid. at 214-215.

[17] Rogin, "State Department Cables Warned of Safety Issues."

[18] Josh Rogin, "Congress is Investigating Whether the 2019 Military World Games in Wuhan was a Covid-19 Superspreader Event," *Washington Post*, June 23, 2021, www.washingtonpost.com/opinions/2021/06/23/congress-wuhan-military-games-2019-covid/.

[19] Ibid.

[20] Sharri Markson, *What Really Happened in Wuhan* (New York, Harper Collins, 2021), p. 296.

[21] Ibid.

[22] Ibid at 297-298.

[23] Declan Butler, "Engineered Bat Virus Stirs Debate Over Risky Research," *Nature*, November 12, 2015, www.nature.com/articles/nature.2015.18787.

[24] Ibid.

[25] "NIH Lifts Funding Pause on Gain-of-Function Research," National Institutes of Health, December 19, 2017, www.nih.gov/about-nih/who-we-are/nih-director/statements/nih-lifts-funding-pause-gain-function-research.

[26] "Framework for Guiding Funding Decisions about Proposed Research Involving Enhanced Potential Pandemic Pathogens," U.S. Department of Health and Human Services, 2017, p. 1, https://www.phe.gov/s3/dualuse/documents/p3co.pdf.

[27] Ibid. at p. 3.

[28] "Rejection of DEFUSE Project Proposal," *Project Veritas*, January 10, 2022, www.projectveritas.com/news/military-documents-about-gain-of-function-contradict-fauci-testimony-under/.

[29] Jane Qiu, "How China's 'Bat Woman' Hunted Down Viruses from SARS to the New Coronavirus," *Scientific American*, June 1, 2020, www.scientificamerican.com/article/how-chinas-bat-woman-hunted-down-viruses-from-sars-to-the-new-coronavirus1/.

[30] Amy Qin and Chris Buckley, "A Top Virologist in China, at Center of a Pandemic Storm, Speaks Out," *New York Times*, June 14, 2021, Updated August 25, 2021, www.nytimes.com/2021/06/14/world/asia/china-covid-wuhan-lab-leak.html.

[31] "Luc Montagnier Facts," The Nobel Prize (Accessed August 30, 2023), https://www.nobelprize.org/prizes/medicine/2008/montagnier/facts/.

[32] Amy Qin and Chris Buckley, "A Top Virologist in China."

[33] Ibid.

[34] Ibid.

[35] Fred Guterl, "Dr. Fauci Backed Controversial Wuhan Lab with U.S. Dollars for Risky Coronavirus Research," *Newsweek*, April 28, 2020, www.newsweek.com/dr-fauci-backed-controversial-wuhan-lab-millions-us-dollars-risky-coronavirus-research-1500741.

[36] Ibid.

37 Ibid.

38 Dr. Paul Elias Alexander and Kent Heckenlively, JD, *Presidential Takedown: How Anthony Fauci, the CDC, NIH, and the WHO Conspired to Overthrow President Trump* (New York, Skyhorse Publishing, 2022), p. 84-85.

39 Ibid. at 110.

40 Mike Lauer, "FY 2020 by the Numbers: Extramural Investments in Research," National Institutes of Health: Office of Extramural Research, April 21, 2021, https://nexus.od.nih.gov/all/2021/04/21/fy-2020-by-the-numbers-extramural-investments-in-research/.

41 Karl Evers Hilstrom, "Most Expensive Ever: 2020 Election Cost $14.4 Billion," *Open Secrets*, February 11, 2021, www.opensecrets.org/news/2021/02/2020-cycle-cost-14p4-billion-doubling-16/.

42 Editorial Board, "How Fauci and Collins Shut Down COVID Debate," *Wall Street Journal*, December 22, 2021, https://www.wsj.com/articles/fauci-collins-emails-great-barrington-declaration-covid-pandemic-lockdown-11640129116.

43 Ibid.

44 Sarah Mervosh, "The Pandemic Erased Two Decades of Progress in Math and Reading," *New York Times*, September 1, 2022, www.nytimes.com/2022/09/01/us/national-test-scores-math-reading-pandemic.html.

45 Supinda Bunyavanich, Anh Do, and Alfin Vicenio, "Nasal Gene Expression of Angiotensin-Converting Enzyme in Children and Adults," *Journal of the American Medical Association*, June 16, 2020, Vol. 323, Number 23, https://jamanetwork.com/journals/jama/fullarticle/2766524.

46 Ibid.

47 Dr. Paul Elias Alexander, "Early Outpatient Treatment for COVID-19: The Evidence," Brownstone Institute, January 22, 2022, https://brownstone.org/articles/early-outpatient-treatment-for-covid-19-the-evidence/.

48 World Health Organization, "WHO Coronavirus (COVID-19) Dashboard," (Accessed June 10, 2023), https://www.who.int/emergencies/diseases/novel-coronavirus-2019?adgroupsurvey={adgroupsurvey}&gclid=Cj0KCQjw9fqnBhDSARIsAHlcQYSrvJzS2mRyXrF3bmj-znZk1uM5Fj33OnQ4WTWTTxUJQBlZR6xrBK4aAg68EALw_wcB.

49 Robert Cuffe & Rachel Schraer, "Excess Deaths in 2022 Among Worst in 50 Years," BBC, January 10, 2023, www.bbc.com/news/health-64209221.

50 The Vigilant Fox, "Dr. Naomi Wolf Uncovers Pfizer's Depopulation Agenda, as Evidenced by Its Own Documents," *Daily Clout*, June 1, 2023, https://www.globalresearch.ca/dr-naomi-wolf-uncovers-pfizer-depopulation-agenda-evidenced-its-own-documents/5821250.

51 Ibid.

52 Allum Bokhari, "Zuckerberg: Medical Establishment Demanded Facebook Censor Coronavirus Info that was 'Debatable or True,'" *Breitbart News*, June 10, 2023, www.breitbart.com/tech/2023/06/10/zuckerberg-covid-authorities-censor-true-information/.

53 Children's Health Defense Team, "'Our Country is Under Attack,' RFK, Jr. Speaks on CIA and Totalitarianism," The Defender, November 5, 2021, www.childrenshealthdefense.org/defender/rfk-jr-defender-chd-cia-totalitarianism-us-constitution/.

54 Allie Griffin, "Wuhan Lab Scientists Researching Coronavirus Were the First to Contract COVID-19," *New York Post*, June 13, 2023, www.nypost.com/2023/06/13/wuhan-scientists-were-the-first-to-contract-covid-19-report/.

55 Ibid.

56 Ibid.

57 "Americans' Trust in Scientists, Other Groups Declines," Pew Research, 2022, www.pewresearch.org/science/2022/02/15/americans-trust-in-scientists-other-groups-declines/.

58 Doha Madani, "CDC Detects Coronavirus, HIV, Hepatitis, and Herpes at Unlicensed California Lab," *NBC News*, July 27, 2023, https://www.nbcnews.com/news/us-news/officials-believe-fresno-warehouse-was-site-illegal-laboratory-rcna96756.

Chapter Eleven

1 "Alex Jones: Man in Car with P.A.," Independent Movie Database (IMDB), (Accessed August 30, 2023), https://www.imdb.com/title/tt0243017/characters/nm1093953.

2 Joshua Ostroff, "Martin Sheen: 9/11 Questions 'Unanswered,' Building 7 'Very Suspicious,'" *Huffington Post,* November 13, 2012, https://www.huffpost.com/archive/ca/entry/11-questions-unanswered-building-7-very-suspicious_n_2118828.

3 Laura Donovan, "Charlie Sheen's Rambling Radio Interview: 'I'm an F-18, Bro and I Will Destroy You," *Yahoo News*, February 25, 2011, https://news.yahoo.com/charlie-sheen-rambling-radio-interview-m-f-18-20110225-043538-214.html.

4 Helen Pidd, "India's First Lunar Mission Finds Water on the Moon," *The Guardian*, September 23, 2009, www.theguardian.com/world/2009/sep/24/water-moon-space-exploration-india.

5 Carla Correa, "A Timeline of the NXVIM Sex Cult Case," *New York Times*, September 8, 2021, www.nytimes.com/article/nxivm-timeline.html.

6 Vincent Dowd, "Argo: The True Story Behind Ben Affleck's Globe Winning Film," BBC News, January 14, 2013, www.bbc.com/news/entertainment-arts-21003432.

7 Ibid.

8 The Guardian, "Ben Affleck on Argo: Probably Hollywood is Full of CIA Agents," YouTube, November 7, 2012, www.youtube.com/watch?v=LCq97j4VakQ.

9 Dowd, "Argo: The True Story..."

10 Nick Gilbertson, "Arizona Republican Kari Lake Floats Possible U.S. Senate Run," *Breitbart*, July 1, 2023, www.breitbart.com/2024-election/2023/07/01/exclusive-arizona-republican-kari-lake-floats-possible-u-s-senate-run/.

11 Ibid.

12 Hannah Sampson, "What is Bohemian Grove? The Secretive Camp Visited by Clarence Thomas," *Washington Post*, April 6, 2023, www.washingtonpost.com/travel/2023/04/06/clarence-thomas-crow-bohemian-grove/.

13 Katie Serena, "The Secret History of the Skull and Bones Society – And the Powerful Men Behind It," All That's Interesting, October 5, 2021; updated July 8, 2022, www.allthatsinteresting.com/skull-and-bones-society.

14 Ibid.

15 Ibid.

Chapter Twelve

1 "Emissions Gap Report 2022: the Closing Window - Climate Crisis Calls for Rapid Transformation of Societies," United Nations Environment Program, Reliefweb (Accessed July 26, 2023), https://reliefweb.int/report/world/emissions-gap-report-2022-closing-window-climate-crisis-calls-rapid-transformation-societies-enarruzhsw?gclid=Cj0KCQjw9fqnBhDSARIsAHlcQYRFvarzyXmzdfqcGSEP012EzrBf0CkHKUNJ3MGY_Qm7bTllflVo8fEaAj5UEALw_wcB.

2 "Vivek: If Twitter Supports Free Speech, then Unban Alex Jones," Newswars, July 27, 2023, www.newswars.com/vivek-if-twitter-supports-free-speech-then-unban-alex-jones/.

Chapter Thirteen

1 Sandra Feder, "Religious Faith Can Lead to Positive Mental Benefits, Writes Stanford Anthropologist," *Stanford News*, November 13, 2020, https://news.stanford.edu/2020/11/13/deep-faith-beneficial-health/#:~:text=Religious%20faith%20can%20lead%20to,says%20Stanford%20anthropologist%20Tanya%20Luhrmann.

2 Ibid.

3 "The New American Bible – Catholic Edition," Catholic Bible Press – Nashville, Tennessee, 1986, Exodus, Chapter 14, verses 10-18.

4 "The New American Bible – Catholic Edition," Catholic Bible Press – Nashville, Tennessee, 1986, Matthew, Chapter 5, verses 3-11.

Conclusion

1 Alex Mikhail, "After Elon Musk, Joe Rogan Vaccine Twitter Brawl, Scientists Say 'Vile Rhetoric & Misinformation' is Forcing Them Off the Platform," *Fortune*, June 20, 2023, www.fortune.com/well/2023/06/20/elon-musk-joe-rogan-peter-hotez-anti-vaccine-twitter-harassment/.

2 Karen Landman, "Joe Rogan Wants a 'Debate' on Vaccine Science. Don't Give it to Him," *Vox*, June 22, 2023, www.vox.com/2023/6/22/23768539/rogan-rfk-hotez-debate-vaccine-deniers-better.

3 Diana Gelbova, "Biden, DNC Take Criticism From All Sides on Lack of Primary Debates," *Daily Caller*, May 8, 2023, www.dailycaller.com/2023/05/08/biden-dnc-marianne-williamson-rfk-jr-debates-2024-election/.

4 Regina Lankenua, "Why Hotez is Right Not to Debate RFK Jr.," *Houston Chronicle*, June 22, 2023, www.houstonchronicle.com/opinion/outlook/article/peter-hotez-joe-rogan-rfk-jr-vaccine-twitter-musk-18165180.php.

5 *Bruesewitz v. Wyeth, LLC*, Justia U.S. Supreme Court, Decided February 22, 2011, (Accessed July 25, 2023), www.supreme.justia.com/cases/federal/us/562/223/.

6 Aubrey Spady, "BlackRock CEO Slammed for 'Force Behaviors' Comment after 2017 Interview Re-Emerges about DEI Initiatives," Fox Business, June 5, 2023, www.foxbusiness.com/politics/blackrock-ceo-slammed-force-behaviors-dei-initiatives.

7 "'We Will Bring You Down,' German MP Vows to Dismantle WHO's Grip on Government," *Zero Hedge*, July 17, 2023, www.zerohedge.com/geopolitical/we-will-bring-you-down-german-mp-vows-dismantle-whos-grip-governments.

8 "Robert F. Kennedy Jr. Testifies on Social Media and Alleged Censorship," YouTube, July 20, 2023, www.youtube.com/watch?v=OokHd05Tq4E.

9 Ibid.

10 Jim Salter, "Biden admin blocked from working with social media firms on 'protected speech,'" ABC News, July 4, 2023, https://abcnews.go.com/US/wireStory/injunction-blocks-biden-administration-working-social-media-firms-100671515.

Author's Note

1 "Richard Blum, Dianne Feinstein's Husband: 5 Fast Facts You Need to Know," Heavy.com, September 2018; updated February 28, 2023, https://heavy.com/news/2018/09/richard-blum-dianne-feinstein-husband/.

2 Glenn F. Buntling, "Feinstein, Husband Hold Strong China Connections," *Los Angeles Times*, March 28, 1997, www.latimes.com/archives/la-xpm-1997-03-28-mn-43046-story.html/.

3 "Details Surface About Sen. Feinstein and the Chinese Spy Who Worked for Her," CBS News Bay Area, August 1, 2018, www.cbsnews.com/sanfrancisco/news/details-chinese-spy-dianne-feinstein-san-francisco/.

4 Thaai Walker, "Drug Kingpin's Sentencing Ends Bloody Era in Oakland/Decades of Turf Warfare as Citizens Reclaim Their City," *SF Gate*, February 16, 1999, https://www.sfgate.com/bayarea/article/Drug-Kingpin-s-Sentencing-Ends-Bloody-Era-in-2946651.php.

5 "Tony Serra – The Original True Believer – Stanford," *Love Thy Lawyer*, August 10, 2022, www.lovethylawyer.com/tony-serra-the-original-true-believer-stanford/.

6 "American Whistleblowers: The Promise and Peril of Science," Commonwealth Club of California, (Accessed June 17, 2023), www.commonwealthclub.org/events/2015-04-09/american-whistleblowers-peril-and-promise-science.

7 "Anti-Vaccination Advocate Kent Heckenlively Denied Entry to Australia," *SBS News Australia*, August 31, 2017, www.sbs.com.au/news/article/anti-vaccination-advocate-kent-heckenlively-denied-entry-to-australia/hnafua7lm.

8 "Meet the Press Broadcast (FULL) – May 17, 2020/Meet the Press/NBC News," YouTube, May 18, 2020, www.youtube.com/watch?v=p3eQ_JmHB0c.

Acknowledgments

I could not have remained in this fight if not for the unwavering support of my family through the years. From the bottom of my heart, thank you. I love you.

I would like to thank all our predecessors in this timeless struggle for human liberty. We are all indebted to those who came before us, the ancestors, the pioneers who fought and died for freedom, for a dream that we know today as western civilization. We are the blessed inheritors of that dream, but only if we succeed in defending it against the assaults of the modern age.

Thank you to everyone currently involved in the effort to preserve classic western values and a classical liberal system against the insidious influences of technofascism and neo-globalism. We are facing a powerful enemy, almost too powerful to comprehend. The very soul of America as we know it is falling victim to a takeover, a coup d'état. Our beautiful land is captured and polluted by factory farms, our treasured schools poisoned with technocratic ideologies disguised as truths, and our constitutional rights jeopardized by apocalyptic new policies that take aim at the essence of western democracy. The human mind and heart are turned into corporate commodities to be manipulated and used in the pursuit of inconceivable concentrations of power. But worst of all, these are not uniquely American threats. The target of the takeover is the whole world.

Yet we must believe, if we are to continue, in the capacity of the human spirit to transcend even those obstacles that seem insurmountable, and to triumph over even those enemies that seem too determined, too powerful to ever be vanquished. But have no fear. We have seen it in every culture and context; ultimately, the deep-rooted human urge toward freedom will always prevail over the lesser urges of greed on the one hand and fear on the other. This is a long-term struggle to build a better world for our children. Thank you for joining me in these pages, for opening your mind to a terrifying reality, for resisting the myriad forces that seek to control what you think and read, for standing up against the almost endless propaganda and censorship. I hope you will continue to resist; for America and for all of humanity.

Finally, I'd like to thank writer extraordinaire, Kent Heckenlively. I am deeply grateful for his help in condensing and organizing the research presented here and look forward to working with him on future projects.

—Alex Jones

* * *

I'd first like to thank my wonderful partner in life, Linda, and our two children, Jacqueline and Ben, for their constant love and support. You make this life worthwhile. I'd also like to thank my mother, Josephine, and my father, Jack, for teaching me to have courage for the fight and respect for others. I have the best brother in the world, Jay, and am appreciative to his wife, Andrea, and their three kids, Anna, John, and Laura. Family always comes first.

I've been fortunate to have some of the greatest teachers in the world, Paul Rago, Elizabeth White, Ed Balsdon, Brother Richard Orona, Clinton Bond, Robert Haas, Carol Lashoff, David Alvarez, Giancarlo Trevisan, Bernie Segal, James Frey, Donna Levin, and James Dalessandro.

Thanks to the fantastic friends of my life, John Wible, John Henry, Pete Klenow, Chris Sweeney, Suzanne Golibart, Gina Cioffi Loud, Eric Holm, Susanne Brown, Rick Friedling, Max Swafford, Sherilyn Todd, Rick and Robin Kreutzer, Christie and Joaquim Perreira, and Tricia Mangiapane.

My life has been immensely enriched by the brave whistleblowers I've come across in my writing, such as Judy Mikovits, Frank Ruscetti, Nobel Prize winner Luc Montagnier, Zach Vorhies, Ryan Hartwig, Mikki Willis, Michael Mazzola, Henry Marx, Cary Poarch, David Johnson, and of course, James O'Keefe, who provides not only a platform, but support for those with the courage to blow the whistle on corruption.

I wish to acknowledge the wonderful staff at Skyhorse: the fabulous Caroline Russomanno, the amazing Hector Carosso, and my wonderful publisher, Tony Lyons. I am honored to serve with all of you in the fight for freedom.

—Kent Heckenlively